D1596019

The Union of The State

by Corey Stulce

First Edition

Library of Congress Cataloging-in-Publication Data
has been applied for.

ISBN 978-0-9974005-1-9

For Kendall and Katy
I barely deserve you two

Contents

Contents (Continued)

Foreword

Keegan-Michael Key
Co-creator/co-star of "Key and Peele"
with Jordan Peele

I have to tip my cap to "The State" because when I was in graduate school, they were what I watched. They were the thing. I insisted on having a steady diet of these comedians. There was something that they were doing that was really resonating with me.

I never had cable. I was in my mid-twenties. I started watching MTV, and it was the first time I saw sketch. I think about the monster under the bed. Kerri goes under the bed, and she's canoodling with the monster. Kevin is on top of the bed, and he's terrified and confused. "Wait a minute," my ears pricked, "what is this?" And that was the cold open. I was hooked just like that.

"The State" was one of the shows that we were thinking about when Jordan and I talked over what we wanted the tone of our show to feel like. I think some of the sillier, absurd stuff comes from "The State." Like Barry and Levon, putting their butts in pudding; it's clear that this made Michael and Tom laugh. So they just did it.

There were some sketches that were so niche, they were literally just for an MTV audience, and then other sketches were patently absurd, and other sketches were very scatological and low-brow.

"The State" generated this new comedy mafia, in a manner of speaking. You might see somebody of another period who is trained or now teaches at the Upright Citizens Brigade that is also in "Wet Hot American Summer."

I love that they ran the gamut, and they weren't afraid to run the gamut.

October 17, 2015

Introduction

Across the universe, or at least across the suburbs, the seeds for The State were being planted by iconic comics in the '60s and '70s: Monty Python and Steve Martin, Bill Murray and George Carlin, John Belushi and Fozzie Bear. Eleven middle-class kids dreamt of acting for or directing like Scorsese, knowing that they didn't quite belong where they were. Magnetism pulled the future members of The State to New York University, where they nearly instantly found one another.

A desire for camaraderie landed them in a new comedy troupe, one they could twist, mold and make their own. The group was spurred by ego and the desire to impress — or infect with giggles — the person standing to their left.

"You have to believe that the people you're working with are funnier than you are; otherwise, it won't work," said Michael Showalter.

A healthy swagger — not rampant narcissism — edged them into the belief that this group was their destiny and that it was more important than college or individual careers — and that they belonged on television, because everything else on at the time was lesser than.

"The group just seemed very ambitious — people who really wanted to do this work," said Michael Ian Black. "I think it was a commingling of friendship and work and being young, not knowing what else to do with your time and not having any money. So you might as well go make sketches. It just happened to coincide with the perfect time in our lives to do that kind of stuff."

A family friend of David Wain's helped open the door at MTV, which led to two sketch shows, "You Wrote It, You Watch It" and "The State." The latter began life hated and mocked by critics and viewers and almost as quickly became a phenomenon among high school and college students. Three seasons later, The State, perhaps prematurely, left its home at MTV for network television — a brief disaster that edged the group toward a tumultuous split.

It's remarkable that a bunch of college kids performing for beer money could land a TV show. In fact, graduation is the point where most college comedy groups would come to an end. However, the union of The State was too sticky, and the deep desire to continue challenging each other for laughs was not going anywhere. Since the end of The State as a TV show, the eleven members have continued to collaborate on and create some of the best (if not underrated and under-seen) comedy projects of the last two decades: "Wet Hot American Summer," "Reno 911!," "Children's Hospital," Stella, "Role Models," "Drop Dead Gorgeous," "The Ten," "Viva Variety," "Party Down," and the list goes on.

Not too long after The State's breakup, Kerri Kenney-Silver said in 1997, "There's no question in my mind that we always will work together in one form or another. It was bizarre that we ever got together in the first place, but we got together for a reason. I could tell a psychic that, and if they tell me otherwise, I'd tell them to shove it."

Oddly enough, years later, Kerri did visit a psychic (for the first and only time) who not only predicted a lot about her future husband but also told her, "You're about to do something for your work involving your brothers." "And I was like, 'OK, I have one brother, and I'm not going to work with him. OK, lady,'" Kerri said. "[The psychic] said, 'I keep seeing the number eleven. You'll do this work now, and then it will go away, but just know that it will come back, and it will be a very important part of your work.' 'OK, that doesn't mean anything to me.' Years later, I got the notes from that meeting from the psychic, and it kind of blew me away because "Reno 911!" was on Fox Channel 11. That time, we didn't get picked up, and then years later we did get picked up. And [the guys from The State] are my brothers. So I found it very interesting."

This is the story of The New Group which briefly became Medium Head Root which became The State, in the words of its eleven members: Kevin Allison, Michael Ian Black, Robert Ben Garant, Todd Holoubek, Michael Patrick Jann, Kerri Kenney-Silver, Thomas Lennon, Joe Lo Truglio, Ken Marino, Michael Showalter and David Wain.

Also commenting are The State's collaborators and co-stars, including Paul Rudd, Keegan-Michael Key, Janeane Garofalo, Chris Meloni, Rob Corddry, "The Tonight Show with Jimmy Fallon" Head Writer A.D. Miles, President of Viacom Doug Herzog, bestselling children's book author Mo Willems, cast members from "Reno 911!" and "Wet Hot American Summer" and others.

It was amusing to sometimes hear conflicting memories. (They were digging back decades into their noggins.) Some of these inconsistencies have been left in partly because they're funny and partly because they are true to whoever said them at the time. Also, this book is structured somewhat chronologically but more thematically.

The State last reunited during October 2014, performing a reunion show in Los Angeles, in front of thousands of screaming, crazed comedy fans at Jack Black's Festival Supreme. It was the first time in more than five years that all members performed together on the same stage — and here's a big hope that it's not the last.

"I feel like we're always working on things even when it doesn't seem to the outside world like we are. There is always a State reunion in the works on some level, even if it's an up high in the sky kind of thing," Showalter said. "There's always this feeling, even if we're not in that moment working on something, there's always something on the horizon that's likely to bring us back together."

"When the family is functioning, there's no better family," Kenney-Silver added.

Young Kerri Kenney auditions a pair of go-go boys.

CHAPTER 1

The State Kids Discover the Seduction of Comedy

"When I was around eleven or twelve, there was the very first, primitive, gigantic video camera available to mortals. .... I started making little, weird videos and skits with my friends. I just never stopped."

David Wain

The comedy bug bit hard and early. While the eleven members of sketch comedy troupe, The State, were scattered across the United States as youngsters, the same, silly stuff kept getting wedged into their collective consciousness.

Kerri Kenney-Silver: I was a very quiet kid. I wasn't very pretty, and I didn't quite know how to be and what my thing was and how to be noticed. I do remember I was sitting in class, maybe fourth grade, and we had a substitute teacher. Her name was Mrs. Mills, and she wrote her name on the board, and I don't know what came over me, but I stood up when she had gone to the bathroom or something, and I erased the "M" and I put "P," changing it to Mrs. Pills. I remember the whole class laughing, and I felt this power. I suddenly appeared in the room. I hadn't been in the room before. I remember thinking, "Oh, that's what I am; I'm funny." That became a way to be in a group of people. I wasn't the pretty girl. I wasn't the fat girl. I wasn't the smart girl. I wasn't the skinny girl. I was the funny girl. It's powerful.

Larry Kenney (Kerri's father, voiceover artist on "The State" and the voice of The Thundercats' Lion-O): Kerri was a natural-born performer. I remember family reunions back at my house in mid-Illinois, and somebody would say, "Where are all the kids?" We'd find them in the basement, and there are maybe twenty kids, ranging in age from fifteen down to two, and they would all be sitting on the floor, mesmerized by Kerri, who at the time was three [or] four years old putting on a little show for them. It was amazing, this little kid, and all the kids were applauding and cheering. She always loved to do shows. Whenever we went back to visit my folks, she'd get all the cousins together and give them parts, and she'd write all the stuff, and they would put on little plays for us, like "Peter Pan."

Thomas Lennon: As a kid, I had memorized "The Best of Bob Newhart," and Steve Martin's "Wild and Crazy Guy" just blew my mind apart. I also memorized "The Best of Bill Cosby." The biggest thing

for me, on Sunday nights in Chicago on PBS, they would run "Monty Python," "Dave Allen at Large," "Benny Hill," then "Dr. Who." Monty Python ended up being a massive influence on me at the exact right time to sort of get me. I certainly became obsessed and bought all the records.

Todd Holoubek: "Monty Python," I've never been so grateful for anything. You had to wait for PBS to air anything from another country. It seems like the only other country that made television was England. As a kid, you kind of eat it all, definitely the first season of "Saturday Night Live," the really awesome comedies on TV, "All in the Family."

 **Joe Lo Truglio:** I never watched Python; I didn't even know who they were. I think maybe in senior year of high school I started to hear of them, but I never watched their stuff. MAD magazine, Cracked and Crazy were big influences. I was reading a lot of that and collecting them. Crazy had Obnoxio, the Clown; that was one that was a little bit more blue and vulgar than the other two. I remember watching "Carlin at Carnegie" and taping it with my tape recorder and memorizing that. I watched the unexpurgated "Benny Hill Show" because it had boobs in it. I was eight or nine, and it was on HBO; so I watched that. I went for the boobs and came away with the laughs. In high school, I was watching [David] Letterman religiously.

David Wain: We had the first Betamax in 1980, and we taped a couple of the primetime ["Saturday Night Live"] specials. I watched them over and over again, particularly anything that Steve Martin was on. The Steve Martin specials were even more key for

me. They were very similar to The State. I watched those so many times at such a young age, I think those were the things that melted into my subconscious permanently and became part of who I am. I don't think I thought of a thing called "sketch" with that word, but that certainly was something that was in my bones from then on.

 **Michael Showalter:** I grew up loving all of the National Lampoon stuff, in particular "Animal House." I also loved "[National Lampoon's] Vacation." I was really into MAD magazine. I loved Steve Martin's movies, all of his early comedies, "The Jerk," "The Man with Two Brains." I loved Mel Brooks movies. In terms of sketch comedy, Monty Python was definitely on my radar. That wasn't my main thing. My main thing was more "Airplane." I didn't watch a lot of "SNL." I would fall asleep before it was on. I couldn't stay awake. I loved all the movies those "SNL" cast members were in, especially Bill Murray and Chevy Chase. When I think about the things I love the most, they were really silly things. They were so silly and stupid and absurd. I really, really liked that sensibility — and I still do. That's very much my sense of humor. "Airplane" and "Young Frankenstein" to this day are the movies that I would still say are the funniest movies, early Woody Allen movies, too. Lots of sight gags and stupid slapstick, falling-down physical humor, prop gags, puns.

Joe Lo Truglio: When I was really young, I did a cross between comic books and flipbooks. They were very small, maybe the size of your hand. They often would be just re-creations of movies I had seen at the time that I loved. I have one of "Escape from New York." There's one for "Halloween" where Michael Myers and Jason met. This is before they actually met, Freddy and Jason. I think I had a triple play. I think Michael Myers, Freddy Krueger and Jason were all in one of the comics I did. It began at a pretty early age, the illustrating, and carried over.

Kerri Kenney-Silver: I was very influenced by American comedy, because I grew up listening to Tim Conway, Bill Cosby and all these American albums that my dad had. We came from different places but found the same things funny.

Larry Kenney: When Kerri was about ten or twelve, she said, "Dad, I want to get into the business. Can I start going to auditions for plays and commercials and stuff?" I didn't really want her to because I'd worked with a lot of kids in the business and I see what they go through. ... What it can do is just take your childhood away from you, especially if you become successful. A lot of actors will tell you, "I wish I had waited until I was out of school."

Kerri loved my agent, Don Buchwald. We were family friends and went to his house, and he came to our house all the time. I said, "I'll tell you what, I know that you trust Uncle Don. Let's go talk to him, and I promise you I won't brief him, and I won't tell him what I want him to say," and I didn't. We went into his office in Manhattan, and all I told him was, "Don, Kerri would like to talk to you," and I think he knew what it was about. When they came out, she said, "You know, Dad, Uncle Don's got a good idea, I should finish school and do plays in school and have my childhood and then become an actor."

Robert Ben Garant: Growing up, I had two older brothers who made me watch "Monty Python and the Holy Grail." Somehow, we had a videotape of "Holy Grail" in 1977. We had one of those big, old VCRs that weighed like two hundred pounds. My brothers had bootlegged it from somewhere. I must have watched that thing three hundred times. I was one of the first nerdy kids who knew "Holy Grail" really well. I was the first generation of that. I grew up in Tennessee, and on PBS on Sunday nights, there was a block of British comedy, "Benny Hill," "Monty Python's Flying Circus," "Dave Allen at Large," who was this odd sort of British dude, who smoked cigarettes and told dirty jokes, and they would cut to these bizarre one-off sketches. I just loved it. It was this really strange show. I loved all the weird British humor, and in Tennessee, I was clued into something that nobody else knew about, which was a reason why I liked that kind of stuff. I also loved Steve Martin. I was a huge Steve Martin fan. I watched every one of the specials that came out. I had every single one of his albums, "Comedy Isn't Pretty" [and] "Wild and Crazy Guy." When "SNL" started, I stayed up late and watched "SNL."

Ben, center, entertains his two older brothers in his "Hee-Haw" overalls.

Michael Patrick Jann: I would say the same thing as everyone else, Monty Python. I remember being given VHS tapes that a friend of mine in high school had taped off PBS of every "Monty Python" and sitting in my mom's basement watching every one. Having my mind blown. I compare that to when Steve Jobs talked about when he took acid. For me, it was a VHS tape of every episode of "Monty Python." I'm not kidding; it was mind-expanding. "Saturday Night Live," to be honest, is like a regular American variety show with sketches and stuff. Everyone in my age group in the '70s has seen it. It was part of the vocabulary. Python was way out of left field all the time. I've never said this out loud before. It's funny, Monty Python, in a stream of consciousness way, works the way that kids talk. I have a twelve-year-old son, and he was having a birthday party. These ten-to-twelve-year-olds sitting in the living room, playing games, talking. It's so random. A synaptic discharge across the room that would turn into a thing and it would make a joke and move on to another topic and leave that topic hanging. Any topic that didn't have any energy behind it just got dropped, and they moved on. It's totally like a framework of energy as opposed to structure for structure's sake.

Ken Marino: I lived in the Tri-State area [New York, New Jersey, and Pennsylvania], and I watched a lot of afternoon movies, Martin and Lewis, Jerry Lewis movies. When I got a little older, I started getting into "Animal House." "Caddyshack," I think, was the first R-rated movie I saw in the theater. I watched it about two thousand more times. I would sneak in and watch "SNL" at night. Also "Fridays." I specifically remember the pharmacist who was taking all the drugs himself.

Another comedy influence to me when I was younger was "The Muppet Show." I was a huge fan of that. To me, that was sketch. Little vignettes, little sketches that had a little button at the end. It was loose and free and wild, and you didn't know where it was gonna go. I listened to a lot of George Carlin comedy albums and Cheech and Chong's "Big Bambú." It didn't dawn on me until recently that that was a big influence on me, as far as sketch is concerned. That's what all those things were, little sketches — them pretending to be different characters. I would listen to it over and over and over again and recite it verbatim. "Big Bambú" was a huge, huge influence.

David Wain: I was always a ham as a kid. I was the youngest in my family by a lot. I have three much older sisters. So I got a lot of attention as a child. I tended to perform a lot for my family and my friends, just being funny. I was born in 1969. When I was around eleven or twelve, there was the very first, primitive, gigantic video camera available to mortals. ... I started making little, weird videos and skits with my friends. I just never stopped.

Kevin Allison: When I was a little kid, the first movie I saw in the cinema was "Pinocchio in Outer Space." It was a super-cheap German, animated film. I always have disdain when people say, "Oh, a kid will watch anything." No, I think a kid should be shown really great stuff. I knew that "Pinocchio in Outer Space" was not that great a movie, but I was still super-in-awe of the movie experience, staring at this big screen and not knowing if they were doing stuff behind the screen and projecting stuff onto it. What's going on here? I remember when I was seven and saw "The Muppet Movie" and "Star Wars" and "Grease" [and] "Jaws" when I was six. There was something so magical about going to the cinema when I was a kid. There was just nothing quite like it.

Michael Ian Black: "Saturday Night Live" was my entire exposure to sketch, aside from my VHS copy of "Kentucky Fried Movie." That was it. I'd never seen "Monty Python." I didn't know anything about the National Lampoon. I liked "Animal House." That was about it. That's what I knew. I knew "Animal House," "The Muppet Show" and "SNL" and not much else.

Kerri Kenney-Silver: I've always performed. I performed in our local church, singing. I performed in the neighborhood productions, the little plays we would do at the pavilion downtown. I don't remember my first, but I always did it at home with friends, and we would invite neighbors. We did them in the laundry room at family reunions.

Ken Marino: I never wanted to be a comedian or a sketch comedian, even. I liked clowning around in school. I guess that's maybe why I listened to George Carlin's "Class Clown" so much because someone called me a class clown. I took solace in that album. I wanted to be an actor at a very young age. All growing up through junior high and high school, I would take acting classes, whatever kind of acting classes a junior high student could take. I just farted around.

Thomas Lennon: My plan was to be a Broadway stage actor. I grew up in Chicago, which was a very big theater town. My parents are both theater-type people. I was in an experimental theater wing. I didn't consider myself a comedian in any way. I saw myself playing Hamlet and things like that. I took myself as seriously as a sixteen-year-old drama student can, which is very, very serious. I never had any intention of getting into comedy all until I auditioned for The New Group.

Robert Ben Garant: As a kid, I moved at all the wrong times. We moved at fifth grade; at the beginning of junior high I was a new kid, and I moved again in high school. Even if I hadn't chosen to be sort of a weirdo, I would've ended up one anyway. I was trying to be like my older brothers, who were really into Black Sabbath and AC/DC. My brothers were those odd '70s kids with terrible skin, mop hair and heavy metal T-shirts. I sort of copied their style. One of them had "Never Mind the

Bollocks," and I just thought that was so great. And The Cramps came to Knoxville, and I got to see The Cramps. I sort of became a wannabe punk rock kid in the eighth grade. That pretty much sealed my fate.

Kevin Allison: In grade school, I began playing around with friends with a Super 8 camera, and [the movies] were ridiculous. We did what was supposed to be "Jaws," and it's just the rubber shark in a bathtub. We did one that was supposed to be "Friday the 13th" with SpaghettiOs coming out of people's stomachs when they get cut. I was also very into doing audio stuff. I had a Radio Shack tape recorder. I still have a tape called "Allison's Greatest Tape-Recorded Hits, Volume One." It's all phone pranks and songs and sketches. I did a whole half-hour radio drama called "I Was a Teenage Doorknob." It's just an absurd play.

Michael Showalter: I was a cartoonist who drew a lot in middle school and stuff, but then, in high school, I visited my sister at Yale. I saw a pretty well-known college improv group called the Purple Crayon. They are one of the first college improv groups. It was kind of an "aha" moment. It looked so fun to me. What I loved about it was that they were clearly really smart, these guys, and they were clearly cool, but they were acting so silly and stupid. The audience was loving it. They were doing freeze tag. It was very conventional improv stuff. First line, last line, occupation, stuff like that. They were so funny. It felt kind of edgy. It was in a dingy basement. The stage was makeshift. The chairs were folding chairs that had been set up, and everybody was drinking wine out of Dixie cups. They had this kind of forbidden quality to it. It felt somewhat rebellious.

I did improv in high school with some of my friends. We had kind of a joke rap group called The Disposable Rappers. Part of our shtick was we would do improv. We did "shows." Very minimal.

Todd Holoubek: All through high school, I wanted to do comedy. Spending a good portion of your childhood watching these entertainers, you kind of follow that path.

Kevin Allison: In high school, I became known for being the guy who takes all his clothes off at a party. It was in the spirit of, "Let's get this party started!" When you're young, you do crazy things. Why the hell not do this? People always kind of loved that. Now, I'm a kinkster. Now, I go to parties where everyone takes off their clothes. I'm still that nonconformist kind of guy.

David Wain: I liked doing high-school theater. I often would get by on my sense of humor, where my acting chops or anything else was failing. When I was at Shaker Heights High School, we did Shakespeare, musicals, the regular stuff, but we also had a thing called New Stages where they allowed students to write short plays and produce them. They were basically like sketches. I wrote one called "Assorted Cuts of Meat," which was essentially an absurd stream of consciousness, almost avant-garde theater piece. It was a fun starting point of doing weird stuff.

Robert Ben Garant: I think almost everybody in the group secretly was a musical theater kid, except maybe Joe. Everybody else, we were the musical theater fags. I was in "Bye Bye Birdie," and we did "Little Shop of Horrors." I did all that stuff. It was great. I really enjoyed it.

Michael Ian Black: I came to school to be an actor. I knew I was going to be an actor. I knew I was going to study acting. I envisioned myself being a pretty serious dramatic actor. I thought I'd be doing the classics for my career in regional theaters all across the country.

Robert Ben Garant: Tennessee really didn't want anything to do with me. I got really good grades in high school, just because I knew I had to get out. My goal was New York. Later in high school, I discovered "The Young Ones." When I went to New York, I wanted to figure out how to do a show like "The Young Ones," sort of a sitcom, sort of not, and really weird. When I first moved to New York City, if you asked me what I wanted to do, that's probably what I would've said. I just loved them, [The Young Ones].

Michael Showalter: When I went to college, I was looking for a group to join. I was looking for an improv group or a sketch group that I could be a part of, and it was based entirely on seeing this improv group when I visited my sister. It wasn't that I wanted to be a performer per se;

it was that I wanted the experience of being in a troupe like this. I liked the idea that it was in New York City. That was a really big part of it, New York City and everything that New York City represented. Growing up in a suburb in a college town, it felt exciting and risky. That's kind of what it was. NYU at that time was sort of like a city school. For me, it was an opportunity to leave the suburbs and live in the city.

David Wain: My father grew up in Brooklyn and left [there] in 1954. From as early as I can remember, I was always drawn to everything about New York: Woody Allen, The Muppets, "Saturday Night Live." It was the only place I fantasized about being. NYU was really about wanting to be in New York for me more than anything. Applying to NYU film school might not have been something I would've done in another situation, but at NYU it's not the kind of school you just go and, at some point, choose a major. You have to apply to film school; so I did.

Kerri Kenney, Michael Showalter, Todd Holoubek and, in front, Michael Ian Black, became fast friends at New York University.

CHAPTER 2

Assorted Cuts
of Meet

When I first met Tom Lennon,
I thought he was the
snootiest prick in the world."

Joe Lo Truglio

Elder State men, Todd Holoubek, Ken Marino and David Wain, were freshmen at New York University in 1987, while the rest of the troupe was still worrying about SATs, proms and beer busts. But two future State members crossed paths while still in high school.

Thomas Lennon: Kerri and I met when we were about sixteen years old. We both went to the Northwestern University summer camp called Cherubs. We were very, very serious actors back then. We met, then became friends in 1986 or '87. Ever since, we've been stuck together.

Kerri Kenney-Silver: It was very feel-good emotionally. It's the first time when you're an outcast of the school as a young, pimply teenager that you find your people at these theater camps. There's other people like me out there! It was exhilarating. I remember when my dad came to pick me up, I was crying hysterically, and he was really freaked out. "This is some kind of cult. What's happening here?" It is, in a sense.

Larry Kenney: She didn't want to go back [home]. She said, "I'm ready now," and I said, "Do another year of high school just for the hell of it."

Kerri Kenney-Silver: I just fell in love with Tom, with his humor. I just knew that we would be friends for a long time. I remember thinking he was a genius. He had a dry sense of humor. I was drawn to him as an actor and a friend. We all had good intentions, but the other forty people that I said the same thing to, I have never seen since that day. We did that thing of "Let's always work together." Then, he called and said, "I'm going to NYU." I said, "OK, I'm going to NYU, too."

Thomas Lennon: I asked her where she was going to live, because her being from the East Coast. I didn't know anything about New York. We did end up living a couple doors down from each other in Brittany, which is one of the good dorms at NYU.

For some reason, I knew I had to be in New York if I was going to do any of this stuff seriously. I certainly could have stayed in Chicago and try to do the Second City route or something. I applied to Northwestern and did not get in, but luckily NYU let you audition. So my audition got me by even though my grades weren't amazing. I did have a feeling that New York was the place to be. NYU is a great school, and I loved going there. You do, at Tisch [School of the Arts], meet super-motivated people. I sure did.

David Wain has known "State" theme song co-composer, Craig Wedren, since they were toddlers in Shaker Heights, Ohio.

Craig Wedren: [When] David's father first brought a Beta camera and two-track, reel-to-reel tape recorder into the basement, we were like, "OK, thank you. You can go now; we're good," and we've just been doing it ever since. ... If you look at videos of [David] from age eleven, just by himself, alone, in his basement, armed only with this video camera and his mom's old wardrobe from the 1960s, it basically looks like The State — maybe a little less tightly edited.

MTV launched in August 1981; we were eleven. So we just started making music videos. I don't think it necessarily occurred to either of us that you could "score" something. Also, I don't know that we would have known quite how to do that. David did make an insane, very dramatic, semi-narrative video for "Scenes from an Italian Restaurant" by Billy Joel, which is sort of like a proto "Wet Hot," in that it literally is every single one of our friends.

David Wain: [At NYU], I had requested to room with one of my best friends that I grew up with, Craig Wedren, the guy who would be the composer of everything else I've done. He was matched up with a roommate named Ross from Long Island. He was a character. Ross had a friend from high school who was also in the dorm. That was Ken. Ken came down to visit Ross the first day, and within moments it was clear that Craig and I had a lot more in common with Ken than we did with Ross. So we all hung out with Ken a lot. I remember Ken showed up with a milk crate filled with liquor.

Ken Marino: The summer before I went to college, I was a bartender at a yacht club. I stole a lot of bottles of alcohol and put them

17

into milk crates, because they had milk crates back in college. I had two milk crates filled with booze, and I would come down to people's rooms with my milk crate. I went down to see my buddy, Ross, and met David and Craig and wound up hitting it off with them really well. I wound up basically hanging out with them and not hanging out with my friend from high school that much anymore. That was my in. I was the wandering bar.

Craig Wedren: [I] literally met Ken Marino first thing, first day, freshman orientation, and we're still best friends. Our sons are best friends, Ken's and mine and David's. It's kind of freaky, actually — love at first sight. We just met, and we loved each other, and we became — all three of us — best friends, roommates and kind of still are.

[Ken] had a milk crate full of booze, but I had a lot of sweet-ass cassettes; so it was a really symbiotic relationship. He had the booze, and I had Queen's "Greatest Hits." So we were completely ready. One thing about being a precocious, semi-self-aware and totally, idiotically cocky teenager is you're sort of a radar for awesome people. At least our radar for each other was kind of impeccable. It blows my mind, the older I get, how we all found each other and have stayed together.

David Wain: Immediately when I got there, they passed out these purple buttons at orientation. If you were in the film school, they passed out a button that said "Director" to everybody, and the actors got "Actor" buttons. I was like, "Wow, I have a label at eighteen years old." I never really thought about this until right now, but that was sort of the key moment for me. I guess I'm a director. I guess this is what I'm going to be doing.

The way it worked is you start making movies right away at NYU on Super 8 film. They were little, tiny silent-film exercises. I put Ken Marino in all of mine. Pretty much from the moment I got there, I was doing things with people who would eventually be part of The State.

During that first year, David and Todd joined NYU's new sketch comedy troupe, The Sterile Yak. David described the group as having a "Saturday

Night Live" aesthetic, a mix of sketches and comic monologues that attracted a quick and solid following among the students. More on The Sterile Yak in the next chapter. In 1988, Kevin, Tom, Kerri, Ben, Michael Jann, Michael Showalter, Michael Schwartz (not yet Michael Ian Black) and Joe arrived on campus and amazingly started finding each other from the outset.

Kevin Allison: On the first day of school, I'll never forget this, Spike Lee came to talk to us, the freshman class that was coming into Film and TV at NYU. He said something I'll never forget. He said, "You're paying an awful lot to come to the school, but let me tell you something, what you're going to get out of NYU is what's going on in the seats and rows around you. You are here to meet the people around you. Those are people you're likely to be working with for the rest of your careers. As far as the education you'll get here, or the amount that they'll support you in your endeavors, as far as I'm concerned, it's bullshit."

It was so refreshing, and it turned out to be absolutely true. None of us felt that we got a good education at NYU. None of us felt like the school ever really supported us. For example, we had to rent theaters outside of campus by the time we were juniors because the school was so unsupportive of our group. NYU is a real estate company. All they do is buy up real estate in New York. It's so easy to get lost in the bureaucracy. It turns out Spike Lee was absolutely right. It was the other students who ended up being so valuable to us. The State was the ultimate example of it.

Michael Patrick Jann: I remember Spike Lee being incredibly surly, and he seemed to have kind of a chip on his shoulder about NYU in general. NYU generates sort of that "Yeah fuck you" ethos.

Joe Lo Truglio: Mike Showalter was the first person I met at NYU, let alone the first State member, other than my roommate in the dorm. He literally was across the hall. We hit it off immediately. He was the one that got me involved ultimately in The State. At the time, I was always interested in comedy, but I was a much more serious person and in fact went to NYU with the intent to make movies along the line of Scorsese and Coppola and follow Pacino's and DeNiro's careers and do more dramatic things. I had no interest really in comedy. He said, "Listen, there's this sketch comedy group called The Sterile Yak. We should go and check them out." I did it just because I wanted to hang out with Show. I wasn't quite interested in sketch.

Michael Showalter: I would not have known about any of this if I hadn't met Joe, because I was in arts and sciences at NYU. I think I was the only person that was. I think everyone else was at Tisch. The New Group, The Sterile Yak, those are Tisch clubs, so it was almost like a big deal that a guy from arts and sciences would be in this Tisch club. Like I was from an entirely different university.

Joe Lo Truglio: Showalter taught me how to like beer. I never enjoyed beer. In high school, I was pretty straight edge. I got pretty smashed at fourteen, my freshman year, and decided never to drink again. I was doing tae kwon do. I was very much into the honor and integrity of being substance-free. All throughout high school, I was sober, for lack of a better term. When I went to college, I wanted to drink again. I was drinking terrible stuff like melon balls or sweet, girly drinks like wine coolers. Terrible, terrible stuff.

Michael Showalter: The big thing with Joe was Melon Balls. We would drink Corona, and Joe just didn't like the taste of beer. So he would drink Melon Balls — which, if you look up Melon Ball, it's green. It looks like Jell-O. It looks like liquid, green Jell-O, and we used to really make fun of him for his choice of beverage.

Joe Lo Truglio: Showalter, to his credit, was having none of it. He said, "You are going to like beer. We're getting a pack of Rolling Rock, and you and I are just going to drink it. You're not going be ordering Melon Balls with me standing next to you. I won't have it." He was right to put his foot down.

He gave me that, and I gave Showalter a love of U2. He had probably heard some songs but never really listened to the album. I got him hooked on my favorite U2 album, which is "Unforgettable Fire." That was the trade-off that we still joke about it. He gave me beer, and I gave him U2.

Michael Showalter: I never thought being in front of the camera was a career path. I always assumed I would do the more academic route. I would write about it. Joe knew of an audition for a troupe. I didn't have to look for long to find a comedy group because Joe had already found a flier for it.

Michael Patrick Jann: It was one of those things. I guess it was an attracting-light kind of deal. We just met. I met David Wain within four hours of moving into my dorm. I was sitting in my room and wound up several hours later sitting in David's room and playing guitar and doing magic tricks.

Ken Webb (NYU classmate of The State and member of The New Group): Mike Jann might have been the first one I met, and at the time he wasn't in the group, and I feel like I was sort of the conduit for him to become friends with the group. And eventually become a member.

Kevin Allison: I was walking around going from one little orientation event to another in the film school. I saw Joe Lo Truglio. I just thought he was super, super hot. "Oh, my God, that kid is so hot." I just wanted to find out what classes he was taking and what he's up to. It's kind of hilarious that really what got me pursuing the group in the first place was actually my dick. I've got to get to that hot boy.

This must've been in that first week because it's in the first week or two at school when you can do drop-ins. I see that hot guy, and he's waiting to do a drop/add, to drop one class and add another. I've been thinking about doing a drop/add, too. I wondered if I could eavesdrop on his meeting with the counselor and add myself to whatever class he's added himself to. Sure enough, it's not like a hush-hush thing. He adds a class, walks off, and I don't say hello to him or anything. It's kind of like Jimmy Stewart in "Vertigo," lurching and quietly stalking him. I go to the counselor, and I say, I'd like to add Motion, Matter and Meaning. The counselor said, "Oh, that's a popular class today." All of a sudden,

I'm in Joe Lo Truglio's class and so was Mike Jann and so was Ken Webb, who was in the original New Group but didn't end up coming with us to MTV. I'm sitting in class and pining over Joe, and, of course, Joe's movies are all about his heterosexual relationships he's had. I immediately knew I'm barking up the wrong tree here. This is ridiculous.

Joe Lo Truglio: I get a kick out of that. I was flattered. I was completely oblivious to it. He made no blatant overtures to me at all, or if he did, I just had blinders on. I just liked Kevin. Like David, he would be hanging out with the group a lot.

Michael Patrick Jann: That's a big university, and we all found each other, and we all really got each other in one way or another. It was kind of crazy. Here's how Kevin ended up in our production group. I knew Kevin from another class we were taking because he had this crazy-ass laugh. He was the only one dying, laughing hysterically in a room of five hundred freshmen at Jacques Tati's "Mon Oncle." ... The class we were all in was studying it for its innovative use of sound and color, like real academic, and only Kevin Allison was bursting out laughing and actually enjoying it, literally whooping with joy in a totally silent auditorium of his peers. ... Kevin Allison was laughing at it like it was "Holy Grail" or like it was the first time seeing "Animal House" or something. He was the only guy. We took him on based on his laugh. Joe and I and this other guy, [Ken], decided we were going to team up as a production team, and we said, "What about that guy? He seems funny." Flaming red-haired Kevin Allison, he was a guy with a beard at that time.

Joe Lo Truglio: Me, Jann, Kevin and Ken Webb, we were the four-person crew in the film class. We would go out to The Dugout, which was on Third Avenue and 11th or 12th. We'd get these beers that were a dollar a pint or whatever and get so drunk.

Kevin Allison: The Lost Boys of Filmmaking is what we called ourselves.

Joe Lo Truglio: At the time, "American Gladiators" had just come out, and it was the first of those crazy reality game shows. They were so sensationalized and cartoony and new. It was like a Japanese game show almost. We were pretty obsessed with that show. We ended up giving each other Gladiator names. We would challenge the Pink Tornado — I think that was Kevin Allison's name — challenge him to slam some terribly cheap, watery beer out of the mug. I believe I was Prego, which was the name of a spaghetti sauce. Jann's gladiator name was Stilt.

Kevin Allison: I'm still upset that I did not get to be Fuck Bullet. I don't know why, but I said, "I want to be Fuck Bullet," and everyone had already decided that I was Fireball, mostly because of the color of my hair. "NO, I AM FUCK BULLET," and everyone was like, "No, everyone's already calling you Fireball." To this day, I'm like, it should've been Fuck Bullet.

Joe Lo Truglio: We would get drunk, and then Kevin would go on rants, which became a prominent fixture of all of the State characters that were just brilliant. So quick. He would be so funny. I'd never seen anything like this guy. He's a strange cat. He'll just drop his pants and start singing at the drop of a hat and have no problem with it. He embraces his deviant nature with such gusto; it's spellbinding. Let's get him into the group. It was easy to do that because like David and Tom, he was always around the group on a social level well before he was in it. That's how all the members that weren't original members ultimately came into it. We had to know you.

Thomas Lennon: Mike Jann made a lot of heavy student films that I was in, actually co-starring with Kerri. I'm sure I would cringe at the things that we said and did.

Michael Patrick Jann: [Tom and I] just got along the first time we met each other. We both lived in the same dorm, and I remember the first time I met him. I was standing in the student lounge at the Brittany dorm, and he had on this sort of outfit that he was famous for that first year, which was a pair of jeans with big bleach stains on them and white button down shirt, buttoned all the way up, David Lynch-style.

We met each other there and start playing the videogame "Paperboy." That was our thing.

Joe Lo Truglio: When I first met Tom Lennon, I thought he was the snootiest prick in the world. Tom was in the film department and would always dress in a sport coat and white shirt and jeans. He would play tennis in this thing. He would play tennis in jeans.

Joe and Tom

Thomas Lennon: That's probably true. Yeah, I had these acid-washed jeans. I don't know if they mentioned I also wore cowboy boots. I was the lamest dude you ever met. There are a lot of pictures of me from that era that are just positively terrible. Cowboy boots, acid-washed jeans and a blazer or leather jacket.

Joe Lo Truglio: We met at a short-film audition, a short film of a guy named Adam Marcus, who went on to direct one of the "Friday the

13ths," from Connecticut.

Thomas Lennon: For most of my freshman year, I had an eyepatch over my right eye because my second week in New York, I got mugged and beaten almost to death. I could not open my right eye for many, many months. So instead of people asking me about it, I just wore a black eyepatch. So I looked pretty weird.

Joe Lo Truglio: I'm outside in the waiting room, and Tom was there. He's in his outfit, and he's got this eyepatch. At the time, I didn't know he had been mugged and, unfortunately, pummeled in the face. This is like two or three weeks after that mugging. His eye was swollen. No other part of his face showed any kind of marking. I'm in a screening room, looking at this asshole in an eyepatch and realizing we have to go in and read together. We hit it off. That audition couldn't have gone better. We bounced off each other. I just remember clicking with him so quickly. In the middle of the scene, I remember all of that hatred and disdain falling away and thinking this guy is awesome and funny. We became fast, fast friends immediately, and then ended up doing this movie called "So You Like This Girl" that went on to maybe win an award at NYU Festival. That was how I got to know Tom Lennon.

I often cuffed the jeans around my ankle and did no socks and Capezios or boat shoes. It was atrocious. It was literally like Don Johnson coming up to a college, "Listen guys, I know you're New York, but I can flash some style around you Yankees." The "Miami Vice" Florida style that I was just peacocking all over NYU, which included Ocean Pacific shirts, bright neon orange bowling shirts, acid-washed jeans and jacket.

Thank God I went over to Grunge when it was appropriate. Grunge saved me.

Thomas Lennon: I was actually very scared of Ben when I first met him. He seemed like a really strange dude. He had bright green hair like the Joker. He looked like a slightly skinnier Sid Vicious.

Joe Lo Truglio: [Ben] had a safety-pin-lined leather jacket; he had a padlock around his neck, and he carried a switchblade. But he never seemed dangerous to me because he was in the drama department, and who isn't dramatic at that age — including myself? I got the sense he was extremely intelligent from the very beginning.

Robert Ben Garant: I dressed like that back in Tennessee so people hated me. I was really picked on. They sliced my car's tires in the school parking lot four times, all four tires, during the school day.

I had this weird knowledge that I wasn't a freak. There were more of me, just not in Tennessee. So when I got to New York, it was just great. I dressed in kind of Sid Vicious/garage sale look. Anything that would kind of make me look weird.

Our first dorm on 10th and Broadway was one block from the old Ritz, which is now Webster Hall. The shows were ten bucks! The Cramps played there. I saw The Ramones there like five times. It was just great, and it was a block from our dorm, so it was like being thrown into heaven.

Kerri Kenney-Silver: My first day there, I met Michael Black in a creative writing class. He was sort of an outcast like me, and we kind of connected. I felt like we were writing really dark stuff. It wasn't sketch-related at all. I don't know; we just got each other.

Michael Ian Black: Just normal freshman bullshit. Undoubtedly dark poetry. I wasn't thinking of myself as a writer. I felt like I could write OK. I wasn't thinking I'm going to devote any real time or energy to writing, except as required by class. You're not allowed to audition for plays as a freshman, which actually was probably a very good thing for The New Group's history. We couldn't do plays, and had we all been able to do plays, probably some of us would have. My theater school was called Circle in the Square, which went out of business for a while, but I think they might be back in business. There were some sort of financial improprieties and something with The Mob.

Joe Lo Truglio: Black, his outfit I remember was a long trench coat, a skateboard and a backward baseball cap. That's all he wore. He was doing Trench Coat Mafia well before any of that happened. He's got dibs.

Black and Kerri

Mo Willems, top row second from left, formed sketch comedy troupe, The Sterile Yak, at New York University in 1987. It included future State members David Wain, middle row third from left, and Todd Holoubek, far right.

CHAPTER 3

The Sterile Yak

"My vision was that it would be a tight group of writers and performers ... and that they would get a comedy sketch show on MTV and that they would change the face of comedy. That was my dream."

Mo Willems, on The Sterile Yak

In 1987, New York University had its own, official sketch comedy troupe, The Sterile Yak. While the group was also born that year, its members were instantly confident they were the cat's pajamas. Mo Willems was the founder/leader, who would go on to become an award-winning children's television writer and bestselling author of children's books. Willems began doing stand-up comedy in New Orleans clubs while still in high school in 1986, and the day he graduated, Mo hopped on a plane to London and started doing comedy there.

Mo Willems: I came to New York thinking I was a great comic and that I knew this whole new form of comedy, this alternative comedy. I was fairly ignorant of a lot of things. I don't think I'd ever heard of The Groundlings.

Willems ended up in an improv group called Stitches 9, and nearing the end of his freshman year, Mo began forming a sketch troupe.

Mo Willems: My vision was that it would be a tight group of writers and performers, where each writer had their own voice, but somehow it clicked together, and that they would say, "Damn the torpedoes," and that they would get a comedy sketch show on MTV and that they would change the face of comedy. That was my dream.

I just made [the name The Sterile Yak] up. I'm probably a little more old school than all of those guys were. Those guys are much more rock and roll, and they're like, "We're going to call ourselves New Group or The State. It doesn't matter. We're not going to be zany or whatnot; we just have to prove that we're funny." You look at the title sequence for "The State" and contrast that with the title sequence from "Monty Python's Flying Circus," totally different thing. They're just a bunch of guys being cool, and I wanted the Monty Python thing. I wanted the title of the group to be wacky. "Oh, I have an expectation I'm going to see something strange."

The first time we [met], we had something like seventy people show up, and the next time we had like four people show up, and the next week we had like thirty-two people show up. We're never going to put on a show if it's a drop-in sketch comedy group. That's when we had auditions, and because of the auditions that's where the power structure [came in], and that was me which, in retrospect, I regret, but then there were some talented people there, but there were very few driven people. They were all pretty much freshmen, a couple of guys who were a little older, but there weren't any guys who were like, "Ok, I'll make fliers" or "I'll book the gig."

Todd Holoubek: You're the first person to ask me, how did I become part of Sterile Yak. I'm not kidding. Ever. I haven't even asked myself that. How did I get involved with Sterile Yak? It might've been an audition. It's very strange. I don't think I just walked in one day and said, "Hey, I'm involved." Considering how we behaved back then, I wouldn't be surprised.

Mo Willems: [Todd] was pretty much there from the beginning.

David Wain: I went to a show within a month of arriving at NYU as a freshman, which was a group of sophomores putting on a sketch-comedy show. Honestly, there are so many things that happen in the course of the history of The State that are so coincidental. If I didn't happen to walk into that one show that one day; there are so many things like that. Anyway, I saw fliers in the dorm, and I went to see this group called The Sterile Yak. It was a sketch-comedy show pretty much produced and invented by Mo Willems. I just went, "Oh, my God, that looks so fucking fun. I have to be part of this. I have to." I came down and kind of begged them to let me be part of it. I actually did a monologue from that play that I mentioned, "Assorted Cuts of Meat," as my audition. I joined simultaneously that sketch group, and Mo Willems also had an improv group called Stitches 9. So the fall of my freshman year, I was doing both of those groups.

Mo Willems: I would tell you straight up David Wain's audition for The Sterile Yak was the funniest thing I've ever seen in my life. It was so crazy. Later, it must have been [to] Craig [Wedren] or somebody, I said, "David had this great audition." And Craig said, "Did he do the blah blah bit?" I said, "Yeah." He said, "He wrote that when he was twelve." It was a guy running around playing all different characters. He was so talented.

David Wain: Mo was probably just impressed because the piece was very non sequitur and stream of consciousness, and it was a bunch of little things that I had written in journals, some parts that were from a really long time ago. I sort of shaped it into a piece.

Mo Willems: [In Sterile Yak shows], we would do a party format and a news format. The party format was basically "Laugh-In." Everybody's got a joke. We're all milling around at a party, and then two people stand up, and they do their dialogue at the party, and then you get your laugh and you go to something else. That was very frequent.

The group always checked in, in the beginning, like, "How you doing? What'cha doing?" and everybody talked about how they were feeling about a certain bit. I think David was the one who really wanted to [have] everybody in the last bit. We tried to do a Peanuts one, and it never really worked until finally we did one of a kindergarten class that everybody was [in]. I remember it for a couple of reasons, one, because David really wanted this format that everyone is on stage at the same time and, two, because the stage producer [said], "You can't wear shorts in this sketch because your legs are funnier than the sketch."

Robert Ben Garant: I must have really wanted to be a sketch comedian. I gaffed a Sterile Yak show. I volunteered for free. I was like a stagehand, moving their sets and stuff in the blackouts. They had two good jokes. They had one joke with Mo Willems and his partner, Brad [Glenn], and they would say, "Hands across Luxembourg," and the two of them would stand there hand to hand. At the time, I thought that was a really good joke. Brad read this children's book that was this really surreal, acidy children's book. It was about a red bear on a red field and met a little red girl who picked a red flower. Then he would show you the children's book, and it was just a red page. At the time, I thought, that's pretty strange. That's more interesting than anything I've seen before.

Michael Patrick Jann: I remember seeing [a Sterile Yak show]. All I remember is David Wain "reportin' on sportin'." That's literally the only thing I remember from it.

Michael Showalter: It was a good show. It was a funny show. Very straightforward. Just sketches. Lights up, lights down. We actually modeled our show very similar to theirs. David had a character that was very popular, David Wain reportin' on sportin'. It was somewhat a spoof on a sportscast. Even though they had only been there for a year, everyone seemed to know the catchphrase. "I'm David Wain reportin'" and everyone in the audience would say, "On sportin'!" And Todd, I remember him in a sketch as well and remember thinking it was really, really funny, that was he was really, really funny. I can't remember what the sketch was.

David Wain: They had a very blatant "Weekend Update"-type feature. Mo Willems was the anchorman.

Mo Willems: It was stand-up one-liners, not super current. David always criticized me and said [I had] too many jokes about Malcolm McLaren. There was one bit, I think Kate [Devine] was the female newscaster, and I said something disparaging about Ohio, and half of

David Wain and Mo Willems in improv troupe Stitches 9

the cast turned out to be under the news desk, and they pop up from behind and start talking about all of the great presidents who came from Ohio. It becomes this huge song and dance. We were not really locked in the format.

David Wain: I said, "How about, David Wain reportin' on sportin'?" Honestly, I can't remember anything else. I think everyone mentioned that because it was such a stupid thing. I had no knowledge or interest in sports. I guess that was a joke about that.

Robert Ben Garant: What I remember is David would run amok. He would be a newscaster, and he would pull off a ski mask and reveal that he was Richard Dawson, just by saying he was Richard Dawson. I don't understand this guy.

David Wain: I think I brought my sense of humor, which I have to say wasn't so different than it was when I was five or now that I'm forty-four. I brought my thing, and I wrote weird sketches and fun sketches and jumped in with everyone else. The truth is, among The Sterile Yak, I was one of the strongest performers and one of the funniest ones in the group whereas, when I got to The State, I was more toward the bottom, just because those guys for whatever confluence of luck had so much talent.

Michael Ian Black: My sense was that they [The Sterile Yak members] were pretty well respected and maybe even kind of revered, although that may have been they just gave off that vibe. I don't know if they actually were or not. It seemed like they were pretty well established in just the year since they had formed. People knew who they were and liked them and thought they were really funny. Mo certainly projected that. Mo was very self-confident, almost professorial in his demeanor, having returned from London at some point. He had been in London for the summer for something, and I think that's where he learned to roll cigarettes.

David Wain: He was definitely like the guru leader. He had been to London and seen comedy there. So he was sort of the teacher/leader personality of both groups.

Mo Willems: I'm sure my ego was terrible. I'm sure I was a terrible guy. I was not part of that social scene. It's ridiculous. I was a year older. I did not live on campus, and I had a full-time job. Those guys were all in the same dorm. Some of them were roommates. Some of them were sleeping together; some of them weren't. I'm sure there was a lot more going on than I understood or knew.

Thomas Lennon: I saw The Sterile Yak at Hayden Hall. It never occurred to me that I should try out for them or get into one of these groups. I also saw another one, The Normals, I think, which was Mo Willems and a partner. They were also really, really funny. Mo has, of course, gone on to win a ton of Emmys for his TV writing, and he wrote some of the most successful children's books of all time like, "Don't Let the Pigeon Drive the Bus!" and "Knuffle Bunny."

Joe Lo Truglio: I think I saw a couple [Sterile Yak shows]. I don't know if it was the first one that I saw. I remember going up to David Wain, who was swallowing a slice of pizza, just gorging himself. They had an after-show party for the freshmen and the new people. I went up and said, "That was really good, man." He couldn't have blown me off more. He kind of nodded and chewed and said, "Yeah," and sauntered away. I tease him about it all the time because David Wain couldn't be more of a fan of mine. All this stuff after The State he made me a part of. So I tease him about it. I remember how much I thought he was a dick.

Mo Willems: There wasn't so much ego. There was a lot of drama — a lot of drama and a lot of hormones.

Craig Wedren: I still obviously feel bad about this, and I apologized to Mo a few years ago. I remember one time doing something for Mo, and I don't know if it was a Sterile Yak thing or if he was doing a one-man stand-up show. He asked me to sit up in the booth and play certain music and sound effects cues and then to be the voice of the narrator. I just got really drunk because I was nineteen and thought I was above it all and kind of wrecked his show. I think back on that, and I just want to fucking send him a bouquet of flowers.

Joe Lo Truglio: Mo Willems is a terrific animator and children's book author. He was the dominant voice of The Sterile Yak. I saw how that can really kind of color an entire group. Mo is an incredible guy. We saw him again recently at [San Francisco] Sketchfest. We were talking about the old days, and he talked about how he was a complete egomaniac at the time and learned how collaboration is really important. He was very humble and self-aware. It was cool to see. The Sterile Yak, I noticed their arrogance and how they thought they were the shit, which was a little off-putting, but the irony of that, of course, is ultimately what we became. The State and The New Group ended up being exactly that, except we had stronger performers and writers than The Yak did. We had that same swagger, egotistical, we-can-do-no-wrong attitude.

Todd penned this letter on September 13, 1988:

To the members of The Sterile Yak:
Since it is often difficult to clearly express myself concerning Yak business during meetings, I thought I would try to explain some of my thoughts this month concerning the group.
I feel that the idea of forming a new group to fulfill UGSO club requirements is wishful thinking on several levels. How is this group going to function as a club when they approach their second year and they have to admit ten new members? Will we start a new group, then another and another? The only way that The Sterile Yak will achieve any kind of longevity as an NYU club will be if there is always a mix of classes in the group. A healthy club of ten people will graduate a few seniors admit a few new freshmen every year.
We depend on the benefits of the Tisch club setup. We get space, money and support of the UGSO and the Tisch administration. We are not, however willing to assume the responsibilities of a club, which are to change the lineup each year as a new class arrives on campus. There are several reasons why we don't want new people in the group: We want to maintain the ensemble, we don't want an unmanageable amount of people, and we want the right people. All of these are valid concerns in my opinion, but the importance of adding new people

overshadows them. We can achieve these goals and add new members.

We have talked in the past about how we each want different things from the Yak and that we each have different theories of comedy and performance which makes the group interesting. This is true, but if our goals and visions become too divergent, the group will no longer work. It is important that we all understand that The Sterile Yak was the vision of Mo Willems and that the format and theory of the group is Mo's. There is nothing wrong with that. Someone had to lay the foundations for the rest of us to add our creativity and our ideas. It's Mo's foundation but we all shape the direction the group goes in and we move in different paths away from the basic format Mo has set up. As a current member of the Yak, Mo himself challenges and diverges from his own foundation. We must nevertheless acknowledge that as long as The Sterile Yak is The Sterile Yak, we will have that base to work from. I feel a strong commitment to our group. I work hard to make the best show possible and I take pride in that.

My purpose for being in the group, however is not to achieve a career end. Primarily, the Yak for me is an important part of my education and growth as an artist and a human being. I believe that the most important thing is that we can relate to each other professionally and as human beings and we have come a long way in that regard. There seems to be an unhealthy amount of conflict of opinion to the point where I often sacrifice my opinion for the sake of getting some work done.

In talking to other members of the group individually, I have observed that each one of us at one time or another has felt serious discontent with his or her place in the Yak. I have been thinking about a possible solution to some of our problems.

There seems to be a lot of interest in a comedy group from all classes (we will see on Sunday) I wonder if several of us who feel the impetus would like to leave The Sterile Yak and begin a new group with a new format. There are an infinite number of other directions and approaches a comedy group could take. This new group, if done the right way, could strengthen and sharpen both groups.

My personal vision for a comedy group would include a live band, and no electronic or audio visual support (i.e. voice-overs, slides, recorded music, etc.). I would include a bit of improv or some performance arc type work, and possibly some illusion, juggling, etc. I would also choose to avoid of some of the SNL, Monty Python conventions that are built into the Yak. Basically it would have more of a vaudeville flavor while still utilizing a small ensemble.

These are simply thoughts I have today and I feel that maybe we should clarify how we all stand before it's too late on Sunday.

Todd Holoubek: I remember wanting to propose something that wouldn't threaten The Yak. I think it gave us a little breathing room. Naturally, The New Group became everything I said it wouldn't be.

David Wain: I was probably a little bit oblivious to anything going on that didn't specifically involve me, but I remember [Todd] basically was like, "Fine, I'll leave and do the other group," because I don't think he was super-happy.

Mo Willems: [Todd] didn't like the structure of the group. It didn't appeal to him. Also, he didn't like me. I like Todd. I haven't talked to him in years and years. I think he brought the key to it that made [The New Group] great, which was democracy. If I could've brought that to the group that we had — there was talent in that group. Ultimately, I left The Sterile Yak because at a certain point, I felt like these people didn't care enough.

David Wain: I think that the vibe of The Sterile Yak was more probably what it would be or should be when you're freshmen and sophomores in college. You're just doing something that's fun, and everyone's there to have a good time and laugh and do a show. But Mo's mindset, I think, and mine, to some degree maybe, was, "No, this is important. This is serious. We've got to bust our ass."

Mo may have been frustrated. I wasn't at all. I was having a blast. I had come from growing up in Shaker Heights to living in Greenwich Village in Manhattan, and I'm on my own and living with my friends in the dorm and going to film school and going through this really intense freshman year in film school program, and, you know, it would be another year or so before I re-jiggered all of my life priorities to be like ninety percent The State.

Mo Willems: I saw that this was not going to be a group that was going be able to fulfill [me]. I've learned a lot over the years. Never be the smartest guy in the room. If you are the smartest guy in the room, you're in the wrong room. It wasn't that I was better than them or anything, but I wasn't getting anything.

It wasn't feeding me, and I wasn't learning anything. The improv group booked a lot of venues. The [stand-up] duo was booking. I began teaching improv.

Joe and Sho

CHAPTER 4

The New Group Audition

"One of the reasons I wanted to start a group was because (as freshmen) you couldn't do any plays outside of your classes. I thought this was very strange because nobody could do a show. Where was your real-world experience?"

Todd Holoubek

When The State members attended New York University, freshmen in the theater program were not allowed to audition for official university productions; so opportunities to perform on stage were limited. As an official Tisch School of the Arts club, The Sterile Yak was going to be forced to allow more members to join. To get around that, The Sterile Yak proposed a B team, a "new group." Frustrated with the direction of The Sterile Yak, sophomore, Todd Holoubek, jumped at the chance to start what would become The New Group.

Todd Holoubek: It wasn't a satisfactory experience. At the moment in which the university said you had to let more people in, I saw this opportunity to not have to be in [The Sterile Yak] environment. It wasn't feeding me. Maybe I could create something that was of the vision that served more people.

David Wain: [The Sterile Yak was] going to be around for the long haul, way after college. We refused to have new members in, and Todd volunteered to leave the group and start a new group.

Michael Showalter: When I went to college, I was looking for a group to join. I was looking for an improv group or a sketch group that I could be a part of.

Robert Ben Garant: [The Sterile Yak] did a Q&A after their shows. Instead of a curtain call, they would come out and set up chairs and have this "Actor's Studio" Q&A about the show they had just done. Even as a kid, I thought this was very arrogant. It was very pompous and stuffy. David Wain would explain how he came up with the reverend with the lightbulb sleeves character. I was thinking maybe there's another comedy group I could be involved in.

Michael Ian Black: The Sterile Yak put out a flier saying they're going to be doing some sort of informational meeting. I don't know that it was explicitly stated on that flier that they were going to be starting a new group. I think it was implied that they were going to be holding auditions. I knew going into college that I wanted to find whatever improv group there was because I'd seen an improv group at my brother's school, Carnegie Mellon. It looked like something I would enjoy. I was determined to attend.

Kerri Kenney-Silver: [Michael Black said], "I found this flier for a comedy group audition. You want to go? Let's go together." I was really nervous. I said, "OK."

Joe Lo Truglio: I was definitely on the fence. I wanted to do it because I wanted to hang with Showalter. I had just come from Margate, Florida, a smaller town, and I was psyched to be in the city. It was that initial "I've got to find some friends." Sho convinced me to go, and I just thought, "Well, I can always drop out." He was able to get me involved.

Michael Ian Black: They got a room at 721 Broadway, which was the Tisch School of the Arts. It was pretty well attended. They basically spent half an hour talking about how terrific they were and sort of demonstrating some of their characters and talking about the process. Mo Willems was kind of the leader.

David Wain: We were saying, "Here's the deal, how to do sketch comedy." We were very patronizing, very high and mighty, because we already had three months of experience doing it. It was sort of a funny thing. I've been made fun of the way I was that day for twenty-five years since, for being so obnoxious and patronizing.

Michael Showalter: I think as a freshman in college, you're at that time in your life where someone who was a year or two older than you seems way older than you. It was as if they had existed for thirty years the way they talked about themselves. They had all of these incredible backstories as to how they formed and how each member had found space in the group and found their voice. I was totally in awe of it. At the same time, it had an air of popular crowd. "We are popular. We're the cool kids." I have — probably not in a good way — a knee-jerk rejection toward that, even though I'm sure it's because I desperately want to be popular. I sort of felt like, "I'm not cool enough for this."

Joe and I met Michael Black there. They sort of supervised a quick improv session, where we, as prospective members of The Sterile Yak, got the chance to do some quick improv. They made us form two long lines. You would be amazed — two long lines, and you would literally get a chance to say one line of improv. Whoever was at the head of the line stood in front of The Sterile Yak and got a chance to do some quick exchange based on some suggestion. They would throw out a thing, and you would have a chance to quickly be funny. That was it. Pressure was on.

Michael Ian Black: At the end of that informational sort of meeting, they said, "We're going to hold auditions, and we're going to bring two people into the group. We've got a guy in the group who is going to start a new group." Then Todd Holoubek spoke for a little while.

Michael Showalter: Todd's big thing had to do with windows, the idea that everyone in the group would have a window. That window would fit them in some certain way. Everyone's window would be big enough for them. That was part of his pitch. "I want everyone to have a window that's big enough for them," which I thought was very appealing. He had a very inclusive vibe about him. He seemed very democratic. Whereas, The Sterile Yak, they have Mo Willems, and Mo Willems was the leader of the group, and they were kind of all part of his kingdom.

Todd Holoubek: One of the reasons I wanted to start a group was because [as freshmen] you couldn't do any plays outside of your classes. I thought this was very strange because nobody could do a show. Where was your real-world experience?

Michael Ian Black: Todd said he was going to be doing these improvisational workshops, and everyone was welcome to attend to see if they were interested. Todd seemed a lot more chill than everybody else in the room. He was not putting on airs or patting himself on the back for the amazing comedic work he had done. He was like, "I'm looking to start this group, if you want to come by." That was his attitude. It was a lot more accessible to a lot of us than what Mo was doing. Mo was rolling his own cigarettes, and that was scary enough.

Michael Showalter: After the improvisation, Joe and Michael Black and I had a conversation on a street corner, and the gist of the conversation was, "Let's just audition for that new group because we have a better chance of getting in — because there is no group yet." The Sterile Yak was very clear with us; very few people would be accepted. One or two slots. Very competitive. Two hundred people auditioning for two openings kind of thing. I didn't like those odds. I felt very intimidated by The Sterile Yak.

I really liked Todd. I liked his vibe. More than anything, I liked those odds.

Michael Ian Black: I probably would've auditioned for The Sterile Yak if I felt like I could've gotten it because they were the established group, the cool group. I just figured mathematically it made more sense to try to get in the new one.

Michael Showalter: Todd was really proposing something more communal. I can't remember how many, but there would be these weekly or biweekly improv sessions, where we would all meet in a lounge and just play improv games with each other.

I do remember Tom Lennon and Michael Jann both at the impromptu improvisational sessions.

Todd Holoubek: The idea behind that was to let people know what it was going to be like working in the ensemble. I got an idea of who was going to be auditioning. I guess I had two or maybe three of them [improv sessions] that had maybe twenty people come to each one. I got to see everybody in sort of a loose, non-audition environment, which was important.

Robert Ben Garant: We did a bunch of improv, which is really strange, because as soon as the group solidified, we never did improv again. We switched immediately to very rehearsed, very scripted sketches. From those very first improv sessions, almost everybody was there. Kerri Kenney and Michael Black were there from the very beginning. So was Joe. Everybody just sort of responded to these fliers. It's fate or a miracle or something. Everybody I know today I met because they responded to a flier on the wall in 1988. It's really weird.

Joe Lo Truglio: I had another motive for going to all of these things at the beginning. There was the excitement of just meeting new people and new people trying to work together. Many of the people ended up not being in the group, but there was that energy that freshmen have. "We're here. We're independent. We're trying to do something that's cool. We're trying to impress the sophomores."

Robert Ben Garant: One of the improvs I remember specifically was Kerri Kenney and Michael Ian Black acting like little kids running a lemonade stand, going, "Lemonade! Lemonade!" When they would pretend to serve the customer, they would pretend to pee in the lemonade, and they would talk about how much they hated the neighborhood they lived in. I remember thinking those two people are really funny. Somehow Kerri and Mike were light years ahead of the rest of us.

I thought, "I should stick around because something is going to happen because those two are really talented. Wow, they just came up with that off the top of their heads, and it's really funny."

The fliers and improv sessions really did the trick because more than six dozen students arrived to audition for The New Group.

Todd Holoubek: It was crazy. I didn't know what I was getting myself into. That's the only way to do amazing things is you have to step outside of your comfort zone. I was absolutely overwhelmed that there were seventy-seven people. I thought maybe five people would audition, and that would be that. We were in a really small room. It was too small. I think it was in Rubin Dormitory. I'm sure the furniture was from the '20s. There was one wooden chair. I sat there and made notes. Somewhere in a box in a storage space in Brooklyn, there's this whole legal pad of notes on everyone who auditioned.

George Demas (NYU classmate of The State and member of The New Group): My first roommate was Todd Holoubek. ... I had never been interested in sketch comedy, per se, but Todd asked me to come in and help him audition people. ... My point of view was not looking for the best comedian but the people I thought were the most interesting and the best actors. Then Todd asked me to be a part of it, and I was pretty much resistant because I was very much in the head space of the serious-actor thing. That's how I got involved.

Ken Marino: I was friends with Todd, and I remember him saying, "I'm auditioning people." I was like, "Can I just come?" and he said, "Yeah, you don't have to wait in line." "OK, great." So I went in. I don't even think I had to do anything. He's like, "I just want you to meet George..." and whoever else was there. [Todd] was like, "So, you know you're in the group."

At that point, I didn't realize how cool of an experience it was going to be.

Kerri Kenney-Silver: I went in and did my thing. I did at least one or two characters, and God only knows what they were. I'm sure it was horrific. I thank God there's no evidence of that. I'm sure I had a bag of props. That was sure to win them over.

Ken Webb: Someone turned out the lights, and when they came on, I said, "Someone stole my pearl necklace!" It's the one detail that I remember.

Michael Showalter: I remember the main thing was a comedic monologue. I did an Eric Bogosian monologue. I don't recall being very good at all. In fact, I was terrible.

Joe Lo Truglio: The only monologue I think I knew at that time was a monologue that I did in high school for a Florida State Thespian Championship from the play, "Say Goodnight, Gracie." It was a monologue about soup.

George Demas: Not that I was, at age twenty, a great expert in acting. I was just looking at people who had acting ability, and I saw those people as having really strong acting ability. I felt like the writing is something that you can cogitate, you can think it out, and work things out and re-work. The thing that's elusive is that sense of someone who's interesting to watch and thinks quickly, someone who can present themselves not only authentically but beautifully. That is what I was looking for, and those people we chose were interesting in different ways. ... I wasn't looking to be tilting back in my chair laughing. Someone could come in and do a monologue that was not necessarily really funny, but I saw something interesting about the person and their appetite for the stage. That, to me, tipped the scales.

Todd Holoubek: There wasn't anything like you would say a standout talent where chimes went off in my head, and I said, "This kid is gonna be a star!" We were just college kids. We would have a good time and figure out how to put on a show. I didn't have any experience in starting a creative ensemble. I didn't have this knack for finding talent or picking out talent. I kind of followed my gut. If I were to do it again, instead of saying, "You pass the audition. You pass the audition. You pass the audition," I would've had a second round of auditions and try to see what different groups would be like together and see how they worked. That takes time. You're taking a bunch of classes, and you're studying theater. College is busy. I never really did the things I wanted to do like a semester abroad. The moral behind that story is I'm doing it now. Wow, here's my opportunity to finally live in another country, something I've always wanted to do. I couldn't. I had this comedy group that I was trying to start.

Robert Ben Garant: I wasn't going to go to the audition, but my roommate, Bill, who dropped out after like half a semester, he dragged me to the thing because he didn't want to go alone. I showed up because of my roommate. It's really weird; just a simple thing can really change your life.

Michael Showalter: By the time that we auditioned, Michael Black and Joe and I had really become friends. I remember just hoping, hoping, hoping that all three of us got it. And we did, and we were very happy. We were elated.

Todd Holoubek: They just sort of had that energy. I saw who they were and what they were about; I saw something different. I trusted my gut for a lot of those auditions. Not only was I not trained to find the next Steve Martin or George Carlin or Jim Carrey, I was trying to figure it out as I was doing it as well. One of the best ways to do that while you're in college is to just tell yourself you know what you're doing. Tell your brain to shut up. You know what you're doing and just do it. There's no other way when you don't have any instructions.

There was something about each of them, a choice of monologue, a certain energy. We originally had like fourteen. There were fourteen in there. I did that on purpose. I didn't think eleven [who eventually rounded out The State] would stay. The ideal, they say, is five, three men and two women — sort of the Second City formula. Maybe not everyone would perform in every show. I might've been ambitious enough to think multiple shows. If we had fourteen people, and you did a weekly show, then everyone could be in the show every other week. It was going to be more improv and sketch. We rapidly found out we were terrible at improv.

We sucked. We sucked balls.

Joe Lo Truglio: I remember the kind of nurturing and collaborative atmosphere that Todd created, which helped lessen the nervousness of these young freshmen. It created an environment where we really could play and take some risks and not be worried about being judged by upperclassmen. It was a very fine line. When I think about it now, it might've been a little tricky. There was so much politics being in college of who's cooler, who is better. "Are you going to be with us?" Todd very deftly avoided that.

Todd Holoubek: I was looking at it like a multimedia show. Now, that sounds dumb. Back in '88, the words multi and media made you sound like Stephen Hawking. Those early shows, we had video [and] live music. The idea was to be untraditional. We had a big room. We had TVs. We have certain resources; why not use them?

I tried to envision a place where everybody had the ability to do their thing. I made room for music, film, acting. If somebody had a talent, they brought it. You're able to incorporate it into the show.

The possibilities were whittled to the first cast, which included George Demas, Ben Garant, Todd, Kerri Kenney, Scott Leonard, Joe Lo Truglio, Ken Marino, Michael Schwartz, Michael Showalter and Ken Webb. Todd sent acceptance memos to the member of what was soon to become — for lack of a better name — The New Group, which read:

"CONGRATULATIONS! After a long and tiring audition process, we are happy to announce that you are now a part of the new group performance ensemble. (Now that wasn't so hard now was it?) That's right, we're lazy asses — no call backs!!! What the hell, who needs the pressure anyway?

Down to business. I will need your weeklong schedule ASAP so that I can plan our first meeting!!! I'd like to have it sometime this week so that we can get started on our first set of skits and our first show. Just bring it to Brittany, room 903. If you have any questions or queries, please feel free to call me (Todd Holoubek 505-6717).

Welcome! Todd Holoubek,

P.S. It has come to my attention that the new group still doesn't have a name. Let's try to come up with something by the first meeting."

New Group members, Ken Webb,
Michael Showalter and Michael Ian Black

CHAPTER 5

Sketching The New Group

"Kevin Allison always had the best check-ins. ... 'Well, you guys aren't gonna believe why I had to shave off half my beard this morning.' ... It would be hilarious and full of laughter and semen."

Michael Patrick Jann

The New Group didn't get much love from NYU when trying to find rehearsal and performance space. So they huddled together wherever they could, which likely helped them bond over a joint distaste for "the man." Unlike the infrastructure of The Sterile Yak, Todd had no desire to be supreme leader; so The New Group quickly became and mostly remained a democracy where everyone had a vote.

Michael Ian Black: I don't remember anybody really leading the charge. Todd was definitely in charge in the beginning, but he made it very clear that he had no intention of remaining in charge. The group was more or less a democratic institution where there was no leader; we just did what we wanted to do. It was more or less a meritocracy. Nobody was cracking the whip.

Ken Webb: Mo Willems was a little bit of a Gestapo comedy rule guy, and Todd was hippie at heart, which he later fully manifested. But he was a little bit more studious at that time. So he set the tone, that open kind of thing.

Joe Lo Truglio: Rehearsal space at NYU was very tough. I remember being very angry and bitter about it because [of] all the money we were all paying. It was always such a hassle to get space. Sometimes we were rehearsing in the checkout area of the film equipment downstairs in 721 because that was the only space we had. We had to go into a screening room or something. We went anywhere. We would do them in semi-public places. "We're doing this. If we can't find a space, we're going to do it in their lobby." We were real egomaniacs.

Michael Ian Black: There were rooms at NYU that would be empty, and you could reserve them at certain times. Or if they were full, we rehearsed in this little area in the basement where people would check out film equipment. After hours, it was empty, so we would rehearse there. There was this unused, almost like a raw space, that was padlocked, and there were fish painted on the outside, and we called it the fishbowl. I don't know how we had access to it because it seems like nobody would have access to it.

Joe Lo Truglio: I was eating an apple, and I was done with it, and Ken Marino so sweetly and generously was like, "Here, let me get that," and took the apple core and threw it out. That's my earliest memory of Ken Marino, which I think is appropriate since he couldn't be a more generous and sensitive guy.

Ken Marino: We all just sat around in this little black box theater. We sat around and talked about who we are and where we came from, got to know each other a little more. There were certain people I clicked with immediately, like Showalter and Joe, and I knew Todd. Black and Kerri, there were just great people in the group. I want to make these people laugh because they make me laugh.

I don't think anybody ever looked up to the people who were a year older. We were all kids. We all just wanted to make each other laugh.

Michael Showalter: I really looked up to them; they were really funny. I had very funny friends growing up, but this was something else. It was a little bit like finding people who really shared your sort of secret vision of the world. "Oh, you see the world like I do. Wow! You think like I do, and I've never met anyone like you before." The real thing for me was they really made me laugh. These people impressed me comedically. They crack me up.

Joe Lo Truglio: The check-ins were really an exercise in trust and bonding. It began as a theater exercise when we were in college and continued through the TV show. Besides trying to stay open with everyone else, there were also motives of just wanting to vent about stuff and get it off the chest — off each of our chests, as many chests as we could get! To vent before we would jump into a creative day. One of us had a late night and was hungover or something, we could share that. People could be aware of it. There weren't any kind of excuses really; it was just, "This is where I'm at."

Ken Webb: That was all Todd, and I think it was a healthy way to get everyone in a sort of understanding place.

George Demas: It's one thing to deal with someone being pissed off, having a meltdown or being bitchy, and it's another thing to have information about the context in which that is taking place. It's not so much about them being able to vent about what's going on with them; it's so that we know what the hell is going on with each other. That was important, and that was Todd. Todd was critical in the early phase of getting a group together out of the ether and within a university circumstance. Let's face it; university administrators are not known for their courage, and Todd was able to convince them to let us do it and to help us out with some greenbacks and some space (and also something that was a little bit flying in their face as far as what their policy was for performance for freshmen). [Todd] just had that personality that could deal with those people. It shouldn't be understated what value Todd had to the existence of The New Group and ultimately The State.

Kerri Kenney-Silver: I loved [check-ins]. I'm probably the only one who did. That may be the single dividing factor between male and female in the group. I've never thought of this before, honestly. We joke about check-ins to this day if two or more of us are together. Michael Black would come into my dressing room, pop his head in, and the great joke would be, "Hey, let's a do a check-in." It's a recurring joke because it was so ridiculous. If you really sat each of them down, I would suspect that all of them would agree. I loved it though. I lived for check-ins; I was a theater student.

Michael Ian Black: We would literally check in with each other and say what was going on with ourselves. That was very collegiate, I guess. It was like a time to sort of emote, and sometimes people had legitimate things they wanted to get off their chest. It was kind of a safe place to do it. I can't imagine doing that now, being that vulnerable, especially in front of other people.

Joe Lo Truglio: It was more like an open trust exercise. It was a very positive way to let people know about you. If I wanted to befriend people, to kind of put myself out there, I just kind of got used to it. I remember when I broke up with my high school girlfriend in that first year in college. And she broke it off with me, and not only broke up, but I found out she was pregnant by someone else. That was a big check-in. I can't remember if that was helpful or not. I'm sure it was. I was pretty upset about it. It was going to be hard to hide it anyway during that rehearsal. I think that was the most severe story that I told.

Michael Ian Black: I remember other people really pouring their hearts out, but I don't know that I did that really.

Joe Lo Truglio: It was very artsy-fartsy but helpful. It definitely bonded us very well.

Ken Webb: I thought they were healthy.

Kerri Kenney-Silver: I came to the Experimental Theater Wing to express myself and hear other people's expressions of themselves and basically got a degree in how to express myself in other ways and, after class, going to this group of guys that I truly love — my brothers — and getting to hear how they are feeling. As goofy as it was, it also added to the love story of it all. We wanted every part of each other. We couldn't get enough.

Michael Patrick Jann: Kevin Allison always had the best check-ins. He was having what sounded like the time of his life, being this vivacious, antic, Midwestern kid dropping himself into Al Pacino's "Cruising," exploring after-hours gay culture in Manhattan. He would come in every day with some kind of, "Well, you guys aren't gonna believe why I had to shave off half my beard this morning" story, and it would be hilarious and full of laughter and semen. He's such a great storyteller and a cultural adventurer. And funnily enough, he does that professionally now, with his "Risk!" podcast (and live show).

Ken Marino: Check-ins, I think, ultimately were needed and necessary when we first started. They became kind of cliché as we got to know each other. It was a very actor-y thing to do. A lot of us were in acting school, and some of us were in film school. "Let's talk about our feelings for a while." That said, there were more pros to it than cons. At times, it became our little therapy session.

Kerri Kenney-Silver: So much of high school and public school felt like a surface thing, and I was carrying around these deep feelings and emotions and darkness, and everybody else was walking around with matching sweaters, so happy. It was like, why am I so different? And then I come to NYU and meet this group of people and find out they all have the same feelings — or darker. They understand me, and it's not so secret anymore. Then we could turn it around and make it a comedy. Opening up and realizing what someone is capable of doing or thinking or how deep or dark or intense they're willing to go certainly worked its way into sketches. It created stronger, deeper relationships. On the outside looking in, it's a bunch of college students sitting around checking in about their feelings. Oh, Christ.

It was perfect. Nobody got away with shit because you could sit down and go, "OK, we need a check-in. What the fuck is going on with you today?" It's still goofy, and we still joke about it, but I love it. It's nice to have a recurring joke that goes on for twenty-six years.

Michael Ian Black: It was being young and idealistic and earnest in a way that eighteen-year-olds are earnest. It was a really nice thing. I wouldn't even do that with my wife now.

Joe Lo Truglio: Then we would do warm-ups where we would play Zig Zag Zug.

Kerri Kenney-Silver: We had this game one of us learned in one of our acting classes. You would stand in a circle and work on your reflexes. You're being aware of taking and giving and listening to other people and being on your toes. We did it in a circle, and one person would clap their hands, and point to another and say, "Zig," and that person would have to turn to another at say "Zag," and then that person would have to go to another and say, "Zug." "Zig! Zag! Zug! Zig! Zag! Zug!" And then, we would go, "Yay!" It kind of woke us up. It was so stupid.

Joe Lo Truglio: It was more of a reactive exercise to make sure we were bouncing off each other well. There were a couple of other exercises. That was like the first hour before we started doing any type of writing or performance rehearsal. We were very invested. We all wanted to be part of something that was bigger than ourselves.

Michael Ian Black: The reason for the games was to sort of work toward material, but what we learned was that the games weren't generating material.

Thomas Lennon: The biggest thing we did was called Circle of Fear. We would just stand in a circle and stare at each other. If you laughed, you had to get down in a pod on the ground. I don't know why we did it, but it was pretty effective and a lot of fun.

Michael Patrick Jann: I have never lost a game of Circle of Fear. I'm not bragging about it; it's just a fact.

Kevin Allison: In Circle of Death, if you laughed, you were dead, so you'd exit the circle. One day, I did the dying part by submissively crumbling into a pile on the floor like a balled-up hedgehog. From then on, that was the official way to do it. I don't know what the fuck we thought this was establishing, but it did feel like this group game we could do that would at least be funny and would require a little bit of concentration and would have us all looking into each other's eyes. Kerri, Tom and Black were studying acting at NYU. They were pretty familiar with some of these group-mind kind of games. Another one we would do is we would stand in a circle, and you would squeeze hands with the person on your right and then you would exhale. Then, you would squeeze hands with the person on your left and exhale. The squeezing was supposed to move around the circle so that eventually it speeds up and the group is breathing in and breathing out together and squeezing each other's hands. That was another way of trying to feel connected and get in touch with each other and breathe together. We would do that, but, of course, we would make fun of that shit.

Ken Marino: When we realized how ridiculous it was, we continued doing it for another year, and then we put a stop to it.

Kerri Kenney-Silver: Let's all go have a cigarette and come back, and we'll work on that fart sketch.

Michael Showalter: A lot of the improvisation with the group was just the way we interacted with each other. Michael Black and I, to this day, improvise constantly when we're talking to each other, quasi in-character. That's just how we talk, and a lot of us, when we are together, we just start riffing comedically.

Michael Ian Black: I was very much impressed with everybody in the group. I was concerned that they were all better than me. I remember Michael Showalter being very good at improvisation and being very funny and very quick. Joe Lo Truglio, the same. Ken Marino came in, and he was so self-confident. Kerri I admired a lot. Everybody was really strong. I worried that I wasn't good enough. I was sort of desperate to figure out how to write. I didn't really have any concept of how to write a sketch or how to write anything, really. I just wanted to contribute because I felt like if I didn't write, I'd be left behind. If I wanted to keep afloat in The New Group, I had to learn to write.

Robert Ben Garant: Early on, I would write ten sketches and show the group one of them. Showalter really intimidated me writing-wise. I thought Ken Marino was the strongest writer at the beginning, and then, when Showalter began writing, he wrote stuff that nobody could write. It was really interesting and odd. We each tried to pick out a niche of what we would write. We were just pitching to a bunch of other kids, yet we were terrified at what the other people would think of our stuff. I think I respected everybody's opinion more that I respected any teachers or anything.

Joe designed The New Group's logo.

People took real pride. If you took a joke in your sketch that was from anything — the Marx Brothers or an obscure reference to a "Carol Burnett Show" joke — you couldn't use that joke. It was a real nerd Trivial Pursuit kind of contest. People would bring up stuff that nobody had seen, and we wouldn't do the joke just because of that sketch that existed out there on "The Benny Hill" show in 1967. We would not do that joke. People wanted the show to be good, but there was a real competition between us. I think it brought out the best of us. If the sketch was good, nobody would attack it, but if the sketch had any weakness, you are done. We were very, very hard on each other, but I think we were probably harder on ourselves than we were on each other.

Ken Marino: For every one sketch that everybody else would bring, Ben would bring in eight to ten. He liked to crush up NoDoz and eat it or snort it, and then he would walk around the city and write sketches for hours upon hours and hours.

Joe Lo Truglio: Ben always did have a mini-spiral notebook there. It was like a prop. It was like Charlie Chaplin's cane. It never left. He would whip out the pad if we were out and someone thought of an idea. He would bring it out for whoever had the idea, just to get it down. I remember him telling me that, for him, he was able to get it out of his head if he wrote it down. Otherwise, it was floating around there and taking up room. It was almost like purging — he didn't use this word. If he was looking through old notebooks and found something, he could take it from there. I thought it was interesting.

Robert Ben Garant: I think Ken Marino was the first one who would come into The New Group meetings with typed sketches. They were totally absurdist at first. For some reason, we were all really attracted to that because it was black box theater. We were all attracted to sketches that were staged in an interesting way. Ken Marino wrote a sketch about neighbors that lived on top of each other. He would be on one side of the stage yelling up, and Kerri would be on the other side of the stage yelling down. They would hit the floor. The ceiling would boom. Ken came in with a lot of really absurd sketches that we all glommed onto, as I think, the voice of the group.

The New Group ate, drank and celebrated
our nation's independence together, as seen in this photo
with Ken Webb, Sho, Kerri and Joe.

The New Group quickly became inseparable. When members weren't in class, they were writing or rehearsing material. When they weren't doing that, they were bouncing around to hole-in-the-wall bars, drinking nickel pints and talking about the group. Feeding each other's egos filled some time, too.

Michael Showalter: I do know the more we did it, the more often we seemed to want to do it. The only thing we wanted to do was hang out with each other and work on comedy. One thing that's interesting about all of us and our relationships with each other is that we are friends. There is a friendship there that has been there forever, but there has always, always, always been a collaboration component to it. Michael Ian Black is an old, close friend of mine, but that friendship has always been in sort of a work context. The work and the friendship have always been completely connected to each other.

Michael Ian Black: There's no question that all that time together gave us the ability to work together. One of the things that we had going for us was our friendship was strong enough that when material came in and it wasn't working, we would say so. I think a lot of groups don't do that at that age because they don't want to hurt each other's feelings. We were pretty hard on each other from the beginning, and that was helpful. That made us get better. Our friendship developed in concert with our professional lives, but the friendship I would say was more important at the beginning.

Joe Lo Truglio: These rehearsals were four or five hours every night in addition to the school work we had to do. I remember rehearsing sketches over and over and over again.

Michael Ian Black: My entire social life was built around The New Group.

Kerri Kenney-Silver: It was very rare that rehearsal was just rehearsal. We would rehearse, and then we'd go drinking together, and the next day, we would meet in the park. It was a new relationship. We spent all of our time together. Ben Garant was never without a pad of paper in his back pocket. We were always talking about it. Anything that would happen would be written down and would become a sketch or an idea for a character.

Michael Showalter: We were always thinking of bits and jokes and sketches and "Wouldn't that be funny?" and "What if we did this?" It was always connected to material and coming up with material and having experiences that could inform the material.

Ken Marino: We didn't improvise a lot. It was more about rehearsing and getting the music of it down. We probably rehearsed way more than we needed to. Now, when we get together and do that thing, there is a shorthand to it, one-twentieth of the time. We just wanted it to be right. We wanted to get the music of the comedy right. We would work and work and work it, and then work with little, subtle things we could do. Looking back, we probably rehearsed too much. Maybe back then it was just the right amount. We were still figuring it out. That was our comedy college.

Michael Ian Black: I wasn't very confident with improvisation. I had never done it before, and I think I was a little shy about it. Unlike something like Second City or Upright Citizens Brigade or The Groundlings, we would do these improv games, but nobody knew what they were doing. There was no instruction. There was no formulation. We didn't really talk about what makes a good improvisation or what kills an improvisation. We didn't talk about anything. We were just like, "OK, let's do 'This is your supermarket.' Go."

Ken Webb: I never felt super-comfortable writing within the group. I feel like it was a group of eleven or twelve strong personalities and strong performers, and at some point, I feel like the way I presented myself did not command the same attention as others. So I feel like I was present for everything, and I have a sense of humor, and as a director I have a good sense of what works and what doesn't, and I wound up kind of quietly offering my thoughts to other people who then voiced them because if I said it out loud, it wouldn't necessarily be heard, but if I mentioned it quietly to Marino and he said it out loud, it would be heard.

Ken Marino: I've probably calmed myself down a little bit, but I never hesitated with speaking my mind about stuff — and probably to a fault at times. I think mine and Todd's relationship early on was nice because Todd was laid-back and I was a little bit more aggressive and [kept] things on track. I don't remember necessarily doing that with the group, but I probably did, and as we went on I definitely did that more, maybe to the point where I annoyed people. ... I cared about the group very much, and I was definitely passionate about it.

Robert Ben Garant: We would rehearse for an hour and a half of new material, minimum forty times, I would guess. People would submit their material, and we would usually rehearse the show for like three weeks. That's four nights a week for three weeks, four hours each rehearsal. We would do each sketch until we were sick of it and then move onto the next sketch and then do the same thing the next night. We would rehearse a lot. We all took it so seriously from the get-go. It's really strange.

We argued all the time. It seems like all we would do is argue. We had a lot of fun, but we would take it so seriously. It was a lot of politics. There was one sketch, three of the people wanted to do a funny Beastie Boys rap. They were having way too much fun writing it. They would run around, and we heard them singing the lines from it. You felt left out because you're in the same room, but they were running around the corners singing the lyrics of this thing. Literally everybody who wasn't included voted against it because it felt like they were keeping everybody out of the creative process. It was really weird. All the good sketches I think made it through. Anytime anybody had a really good idea, I think it made into a show.

Ken Marino: Ben Garant was our comedy police. He would hear something and would say, "No, no, no, Monty Python did that." Or he would say, "No, that was on SNL." Ben was probably the most educated person as far as comedy was concerned. He knew a lot of it and was aware a lot of it and retained a lot of it. He was always our filter. We would say, "Let's do this," and Ben would say, "No, you can't do that." Of course, for everything that he caught, we probably wrote five other sketches that were very similar to "SNL" or whatever.

Kerri Kenney-Silver: It went dark and weird at times, but I think that is a testament to all the personalities coming together. What was beautiful was someone would write a sketch in their voice and not know how to end it, and someone else would say, "All of a sudden, they just fly out of the scene like birds." I certainly never would've thought of that. You put those two things together, and you've got this new, unique voice.

Ken Marino: I was just trying to ape or mimic something I had seen, something from "SNL," just to figure out structure. The idea back then and what was most interesting about the group was we wanted to honor a format and kind of bend it in some way and come up with a fresh take on it. Nobody in the group was like, "This is how it's done." I think we all wanted to make each other laugh. We all responded to specific comedy, and we had that in common. In order to make the other person laugh, you had to come up with something that was a fresh take. That was the challenge always.

Michael Ian Black: I wasn't thinking about it at all as far as career. I was thinking about it as sketch comedy more or less in terms of it was my social life. It was who I hung out with and what I did when I wasn't in class. I didn't really think of it beyond that. I wouldn't have known how to think of it beyond that. There was no obvious route to even performing outside the confines of NYU. There was no place to go to a show besides Washington Square Park.

Todd Holoubek: This group, sometimes to its detriment, was like a hermetically sealed bubble, in that people in the bubble felt very safe. They could take the kinds of risks that you could not see somebody on their own taking.

Joe Lo Truglio: Todd always was repeating the mantra that everyone has a voice in this group, a creative voice. It was important that not only everybody had a creative voice but that the shows themselves were multimedia. That was always something that we wanted to achieve, that it wasn't just a theater show. Todd is such a terrific artist and thinks outside the box. Having half of us in the film department, it naturally led into an opportunity to do video as well. Todd definitely viewed The New Group shows as multimedia events.

Todd Holoubek: We knew enough about pacing. We knew how a show needed to be built. I am sure I had read some books somewhere or articles about how television shows were made. We would say, "This is a good order of sketches." As theater students, we all probably had been in a compilation show. I remember that being a big deal, the order of things and who did what and when and where. We knew show order was very important. We were also in college. We were being taught how a story is told, beginning, middle and end. Even if our sketches didn't have a beginning, middle and end, we knew there had to be some sort of structure, some sort of arc.

Kerri Kenney-Silver: I've never really enjoyed writing. We decided early on that everybody would write and everybody would perform. Everyone had an equal voice. I feel like when it came to creating a sketch or shooting or coming up with characters or editing or whatever it was, people fell into different roles and ultimately ended up doing what they did best. I think pretty early on people fell into their groove. My love and my strength was always performing.

Todd Holoubek: We didn't really have a director. Part of the idea was to have it really be an ensemble, an experiment in democratic creativity. A lot of things were just by group decision. There was a lot of arguing and debating about words. We argued one time for three days about a word. Just really bizarre.

Kevin Allison: I might be wrong about this. Other people might say Kevin is imagining things, because he was raised Catholic, but I think we even did something like praying before a couple of the first live shows. Praying in the way that a football team goes, "OK, God be with us as we do our very best. We're all here for each other. We love what we're doing. Let's just have fun." That kind of thing.

New Group debut flier by Michael Showalter

CHAPTER 6

The New Group's debut, "I'm Rubber, You're Glue"

"Pretty soon that became the most important thing in all of our lives. I kind of had that feeling, like this is going to last forever, which is a really silly thing to think in your second semester at college, but it's kind of been the case in a way."

Kerri Kenney-Silver

The Sterile Yak was the old guard, the seasoned professionals with a year of shows under their belts. Several dozen audience members, including the cast of The Sterile Yak and amongst them David Wain, paid a buck and crowded into a small room to see what entertainment an offshoot gaggle of freshmen (including George Demas, Ben Garant, Kerri Kenney, Scott Leonard, Joe Lo Truglio, Michael Schwartz, Michael Showalter and Ken Webb) and a couple of sophomores (Todd Holoubek, Ken Marino) could offer on a weekend night. On February 10, 1989, future members of The State were about to perform onstage together for the first time in front of an audience.

Kevin Allison: Joe says, "Hey, the group is doing a show tonight." He gives out some fliers, and it's this group called The New Group. I had never heard of this before. This is going to be the group's very first show. It was called "I'm Rubber, You're Glue." It was going to happen on the seventh floor of 721 Broadway in this tiny black box theater that probably sat about forty or fifty people. I went to that first show.

The lights went out. A finger pressed play on a boom box, and Angus Young's unmistakable guitar riff filled the room.

Ken Marino: We were so obnoxious; we would start every show with [AC/DC's] "Back in Black" playing. The audacity. "These nineteen-year-old, snot-nosed kids think this is funny." We owned it. We would all get pumped up with "Back in Black" playing. It was great, but it was weird. It was not your normal start to a sketch comedy show. I loved it.

David Wain: I went to go see that first show probably a little bit with my arms crossed. "Let's see what these kids are going to do." I do remember very vividly seeing the show, and within moments of it starting being like, "Holy shit, these guys are good."

David actually designed the "I'm Rubber, You're Glue" program on his Mac while Joe drew stick figures of the cast for the interior and back. Joe and Michael Showalter would share drawing duties on The New Group's fliers and programs.

Program art by Joe

Michael Showalter: Joe is much more architectural and methodical in his drawings. He'll take a really long time because he's really constructing something that is really graphic and perfect, and then I'm more of a doodler. I'm more improvisational and sort of, you know, moving the pen around all over the place, and mine is much more of a doodle. And his is much more graphic.

"I'm Rubber, You're Glue" kicked off with a video called Chip and Eddie, played by Michael Showalter and Michael Ian Black, who inform the audience how to enjoy what's about to be presented.

Michael Showalter: One funny thing I remember from it is, we'd say, "If you need to go to the bathroom, politely excuse yourself and go to the bathroom," and we'd demonstrate what that looks like. Then we'd say, "As opposed to," and then Michael Black demonstrates clutching your pants and being like, "I have to go pee!" screaming. It was terrible. It was not funny, and it is edited in camera, too. It was not technically impressive.

Joe Lo Truglio: The first sketch we did for "I'm Rubber, You're

Glue" was called "Child Linguistics," which I wrote with Showalter. If I was writing at all, I was collaborating. I wrote a little bit more when we got to TV. In the early years, it was more collaboration with the writing. I was the artist, illustrator. All the fliers. The logo. I did a couple of short films for the shows. I was more of a visual contributor than writing.

I think Show and I enjoyed scatological humor at the time — and still do. I think we were just kind of talking about insults. [In] "Child Linguistics," the premise is a college professor teaches a very academic, serious lesson about playground talk and insults that are used by elementary kids.

Michael Showalter: It's totally stood the test of time, and it was like the first real thing I ever wrote. It had a classic sketch premise, which is that it's a college professor, and the class that he teaches is sort of a deconstruction of all of the funny things kids say to each other in a playground like, "Nanny nanny doo-doo, stick your head in poo-poo," that kind of thing. He would super-intellectually [say], "What does doo-doo mean?" That kind of thing. It was long, too, like seven pages long, but Joe and I put it together and had a blast and showed it to the group, and the group really liked it, and it was great.

Joe Lo Truglio: I play a guy that is late for class, and we ultimately get into a teacher-student showdown that culminates in a literally standing in front of the class face-to-face-off with Showalter, going back and forth with insults and then doing kind of a weird knick knack paddy whack thing. That was the gist of it.

We had kind of the end of the sketch before we had the sketch. That's how it began. The method, both of us sat over a word processor — that is not a lie — and wrote it together. From what I remember, that's how I ended up collaborating later in The State when we were on TV. I would physically be with them, and we would go back and forth on the computer.

Ken Marino: That one was great. It was the whole group. There was certain music to that pacing. There were certain lines that had to come in at a certain time. If they didn't come in, it would ruin the pacing of the sketch. I remember that one; we rehearsed the shit out of it. That was the definition of a successful group sketch.

The first show featured a couple of videos including one by Ken Webb called "Pound on a Happy Face" about a guy who gets trapped on an elevator with a gaggle of clowns.

Ken Webb: People said it reminded them of Stanley Kubrick because it was super-dramatic and actually a little scary, and I used a Depeche Mode track called "Pimpf" from their "Music for the Masses" album, which really made it, and it was shot on Super 8. It was a cool piece that added a sheen of, "Wow, look at these guys."

George Demas screen shot

Kevin Allison: I think it included a video with the members reflecting on the group as if it had lasted for years and years, even though it was the group's first show. It was so funny when they cut to George Demas because he was just sitting in a red, velour chair, nude, just eating a raw tomato. George is a brilliant actor, kind of an eccentric character. Everyone in the group really admired George. He was more of a serious actor, a thespian. I think that the group was just a little too hyper and silly for him.

George Demas: The idea was that the group was now thirty years old, and it was kind of like the Rolling Stones, that it was this cultural icon. Meanwhile, it was the first show we ever did; that was the joke. We were trying to mimic the cover of the Prince "Lovesexy" album, showing a little thigh and buttock, as I was reminiscing about my early years with the group. Mike Black was pushing heavy for me to have a Dove bar, and I don't know what happened with that, but it ended up being a tomato. ... I remember the feeling of "You cannot imagine how much fun we're having doing this," and I think that was contagious.

Kevin Allison: It was super-clever and had great energy to it.

What I noticed when that first sketch was going on was that in the audience there was just this electric feeling. There was an electric feeling up on stage and in the audience, where everyone in the room seemed to be aware, "Oh, this is actually really special. This is actually very exciting." It was kind of like a déjà vu feeling. I felt like the audience felt like this was something classic that happened to be happening for the first time, but we all felt like it was familiar in some way.

Robert Ben Garant: I think the first thing I wrote was "Eugene Morris Jerome Meets a Bunch of Skinheads," and it was really short. It was making fun of the Matthew Broderick commercials for "Biloxi Blues."

"I'm Rubber, You're Glue" also included a sketch that made its way to the MTV show, "The Waltons," in which Michael Ian Black, Kerri Kenney and Michael Showalter wear variety show-style attire while humming the theme song to "The Waltons" as their mouths start to visibly bleed.

"The Waltons" debuted in the first New Group show and returned years later on MTV, as seen here.

Michael Showalter: Wow! That's one of my favorite sketches of all time. That's my favorite New Group sketch that we've ever done. Every time I'm in that sketch, I laugh, and the reason is because I find it so funny, and I laugh as if I'm watching as an audience member — laughing because I think it's so funny. It's so stupid and such fun to perform it, for me. I think there's something very subversive about it.

David Wain: From the very first sketch, I was like, "Oh, my God." I remember vividly they did a parody of "The Breakfast Club," and Michael Black was the Judd Nelson character, and then Joe Lo Truglio was the Molly

Ringwold character. There was something about it, the energy of it, that was just so unbelievable. I kind of had another vision of what I had when I saw The Sterile Yak, which was I want to do that even more.

Joe Lo Truglio: Actually, I recall Michael Ian Black playing the Molly Ringwold character. That was a sketch called "Tomorrow." I played the Emilio Estevez part. We basically verbatim just did the monologue that Estevez gives about holding down the kid in the locker room and ripping the tape off, and his hair coming off his butt or whatever and being ashamed of that. He just wanted to "win, win, win!"

Robert Ben Garant: We thought it was funny because we all accidentally had the right hair. I think that was why we started doing that sketch. Mike Black had Judd Nelson hair. Joe had

"Tomorrow" screen shot with Kerri, Black, Todd, Joe and Ben as "The Breakfast Club" characters

the jock hair, the Emilio Estevez. I used to have Johnny Rotten-like red, spiky hair, but it had sort of overgrown and faded out. So when I combed it, it looked exactly like Molly Ringwold's haircut. There were really, really big laughs.

Michael Showalter: Todd was Michael Anthony King or whatever.

Joe Lo Truglio: This monologue ends with me saying, "Win, win, win!" I was Estevez. Kerri was, of course, Ally Sheedy. It was a parody, but then it ends with all of us singing "Tomorrow" from "Annie."

We do the parody of "Breakfast Club," and everyone kind of leaves, and Black as the Judd Nelson character is alone on stage, and there's this lull, and he goes, "The sun will come out ... ," and then Ben comes out as Ringwold, "... tomorrow!" Then the other characters come out in the culmination.

The music is going, and we're screaming it, and we're holding hands in a line, and the crowd went ape shit, and we closed the show. Everyone there was music theater freaks; it brought the house down. One of the reasons the show went so well — and we carried it into different shows — you end big and end on a huge laugh. I think we got a standing ovation. That's not to say we were amazing per se, but we knew our audience very well. That was one of the lessons that we took that worked very well later: know your audience.

Michael Patrick Jann: I went to see the first show with my girlfriend at the time. It wasn't like The Sterile Yak. It wasn't like anything else. It was a blast. When I think back, it was probably one of the first things I ever saw by people who were my age that I was like, "That was fucking awesome." I think for a lot of people in the audience it was the first time they'd seen something amazing that spoke to them from their generation. We were only seventeen or eighteen years old. There was this spirit to it that was a whole other level. This is our generation. This is a voice that has not been heard before.

Mo Willems: I remember going to the first New Group show. It's so silly, but some people were like, "I can't believe you're here. They're going to rip you a new one." Really? I do think it was great to have a villain. It was great for everybody. I thought was very funny.

Michael Ian Black: I definitely felt like we had accomplished what we set out to accomplish. Basically, what we set out to accomplish was that we could show The Sterile Yak that we could do it, too. We were just as good as they were. In the beginning, it was as much a rivalry as anything else. The attention was as focused on the other group as it was on the audience. That was a great motivator for us. We get to show these guys that we're not the JV team. We felt like a group the way a band feels like a band, as opposed to a bunch of session players. By the final performance, I think we all felt like, "Oh, fuck, we're good at this." We probably developed as equally an appalling swagger as The Sterile Yak.

Ken Marino: We got high off of it; we were so excited. It was kind of an energy — electricity — that was there that night.

Ken Webb: It was like people responded with one hundred ten percent enthusiasm, and more than a few said this is so much funnier than "SNL." From the beginning, we were all just like, "Well, this is it."

Kerri Kenney-Silver: Absolutely, there was no doubt from that very first show it felt like we really had something. It felt unique. It felt scary in a way. To risk being completely girly, it felt like love. Scary, because you don't ever want this to go away. This is too perfect. The response was enormous, and we felt that. Pretty soon that became the most important thing in all of our lives. I kind of had that feeling, like this is going to last forever, which is a really silly thing to think in your second semester at college, but it's kind of been the case in a way.

After the very first show, we were rock stars and realized that we had something that people liked. In my memory, we would finish a sketch, and it was deafening — the applause and laughter.

Kevin Allison: That first show just blew me away. It was one of those moments where I think all actors and writers feel like a shot to the gut. "Oh, my God, why couldn't I have been a part of that?"

Michael Showalter: It really was like an "Oh, my God" moment. I certainly have never experienced that feeling before, feeling like you did something that was so personal and so our own thing, and then to have it feel like the audience loved it and was really excited about it; it just felt really exciting, and I think we were all like, "Holy shit, that was great!" To have people like David Wain be blown away by it only made it feel that way more. We really cared, deeply, what the people in The Sterile Yak thought. So to know that the members of The Sterile Yak had seen the show and thought it was really good, it was like, "Holy shit, this is good," but, again, most of us were only were eighteen years old. We were still kids.

Joe Lo Truglio: After "I'm Rubber, You're Glue," we had such an overwhelming response. The rehearsals up to that point were rewarding; they really were. I liked everyone. Everyone was funny. The sketches were pretty good for writers at that age. It wasn't until after "I'm Rubber, You're Glue" that I realized the group was special, that something was going on that was certainly bigger than anyone in the group. That sounds pretty lofty. I suppose it is, but it's true.

I remember sitting in a cafeteria with Showalter, and a student came up. She said, "Y'all, I have never seen anything like that ever. That was the funniest thing I've ever seen." Yes, she was from the South. There was this tone of incredulous. That was so weird to be telling to two eighteen-year-old kids. I remember looking at Showalter and having smirks on our faces. "Wow, that was cool." It was after that, I thought, "Wow, this is definitely the place to be. These are definitely people that I could learn from and are nice to be around."

The Sterile Yak's final show was called "Ready for the '80s" and took place on February 24 and 25, 1989, two weeks after The New Group's debut.

David Wain: It was like SNL '79, after Aykroyd and Belushi left. ... It was literally like a lame duck campaign event. It was like playing a football game when you've already been mathematically eliminated from the playoffs.

I'm probably romanticizing just what The New Group was all about at that point, but to me it was like, "Why are we doing this when there's this other group who's killing it so much?" But I do remember doing that show, and Mo was not there, and we just did the sketches, and I think that's when I started to be one of the main guys in The Sterile Yak.

Mo Willems: I wasn't even sure it still existed. There was no legacy or anything to do with me. I didn't feel like, "Oh, I'm the guy. You can't do it without me." None of that. I don't even think I saw their last show.

I didn't live on campus. I wasn't a drama student. I wasn't even a film student. I was an animation student. What animators do is they go in a really dark room, and they don't masturbate. That's it. I had no clue what was going on.

David Wain: I think it was just like apathy. I don't remember any meeting or discussion, but I think that the feeling was, "Should we keep doing this?" "Eh," or maybe somebody quit, and we were just like, "Forget it."

The (inseparable) New Group, includes, from left, Kevin Allison, Mike Schwartz (not yet Black), Tom Lennon, David Wain, Ken Webb, Stephanie Blanchard, and Ben Garant. Yes, The New Group did have other female members aside from Kerri Kenney, and this photo proves it.

CHAPTER 7

The New Group Becomes the Most Important Thing in the World (to The New Group)

"Pretty much for our time at NYU, I don't really remember going to class, but I do remember spending all my time not in class with those guys. ... It was a comedy frat, and it was fantastic."

Michael Ian Black

THE NEW GROUP COMEDY CLUB...

... MAY 5 AND 6, 721 B'WAY, 7TH FL., 7:30

82

The New Group quickly got busy on its next show, to be staged in May 1989, but when Ben Garant got ill, it became "...and Then There Were 10." A "Roll of Remembrance" was included for Ben in the program — as if he were dead.

"Ben was a great actor. I loved his work, but nothing could top when he made doo-doo in my brother's nose," wrote Joe Lo Truglio.

Todd added, "He had his moment in the spotlight. He had his time. Next."

Robert Ben Garant: A bunch of snarky, mean eighteen-year-olds. That was really, really nice.

I got mono. I guess it was just a Southern kid's first winter in New York, and it totally took me out. I thought it was the flu, but it was mono. So I actually had to go home from school early. I was sick as a dog. I think it was from not eating, not taking care of myself.

I thought that was interesting that we all sort of considered ourselves members. I also didn't remember some of those people were even in the group. That was like an early, early incarnation. Some of those names on [the program] I haven't thought of in twenty years.

One of the classic State sketches, "Hormones," made its debut in "... and Then There Were 10." In it, a teenage couple begins to get friendly on a couch, and their hormones are acted out by guys wearing pink and blue sweat suits and bathing caps. The big gag comes when the hormones climax quickly — still congratulating each other — while the female hormones are anxiously awaiting satisfaction.

Robert Ben Garant: Because of Monty Python, we wrote a lot of stuff that was really group stuff. To do that you have to be sort of a commune as we were and not care if you were only a background player. Stuff like "Hormones." People really loved being the background hormones. Not a lot of groups will do that. Not a lot of comedy groups care enough about the ensemble to throw yourself at being a silent character in the background, but we all really did.

Joe Lo Truglio: Ken Marino wrote that sketch, I believe. We were able to rotate roles pretty easily. I wasn't always the lead role. I played one of the hormones a couple times. Depending what sketches were before or after and how much time between, I had to either be the guy or get into a sweat suit with a swim cap on my head. A lot of it was a logistical thing. I liken it to baseball when you have a bunch of different positions you can play.

I feel those sketches where everyone was in it really were the strongest of our State sketches, whether that'd be "Hormones" or "Louie and the Last Supper" or certainly "Porcupine Racetrack." I felt they're the strongest because there's no other sketch group who had that many people doing sketches like that with that many people in it. Naturally, it was unique to The State, but it also happened to work and be funny, which I also thought was special.

Every handful of months, The New Group would create a brand-new show, packing away their tried and true sketches for fresh material. "Isn't This Our Stop?" in November 1989, "34 Stuyvesant Place" in April 1990 and "Enough with the Noise" in October 1991 strengthened the core. Friends/stage crew members of The New Group, Kevin Allison, Thomas Lennon and David Wain, would eventually become full-fledged writers/performers while Michael Patrick Jann offered his filmmaking skills to the multimedia portions of the shows. Other members came and left, and The New Group began thinking beyond black box theaters.

Michael Showalter: You can't plan for going to college and meeting a comedy group and making it your career. So I think all of us were like, "Is this really going to happen?" I think even now we're still fighting it; we're still hedging our bets. There was a lot of, 'I think The New Group is pretty great' or 'I think The State is pretty great, but this isn't really a career. This isn't really going to be the thing that I do.' I think everybody had a bit of one foot in and one foot out, even though we really believed in it and cared about it.

The New Group

Robert Ben Garant: I always sort of directed, but everybody sort of directed. I didn't mind sitting outside of the sketch, sort of helping. By direct, I mean, the rehearsal, the staging and the timing. I always enjoyed that. I think I was pretty good at it. Before I wrote anything, I really very much enjoyed that, stage blocking. After that first show, I really started cranking it out pretty quick. At first it didn't occur to me to actually write material, or maybe I was too nervous to do it.

Everybody wrote, especially during our black box days. People took pride in writing weird stuff. If you could write something really weird and audiences still really enjoyed it, people took pride in that. I think I was really good at that. Ken Marino used to write really weird stuff. I think that's where I made my mark, doing this stuff. I think I also wrote more ensemble stuff than anybody. Other people would write stuff for themselves, David and Joe. They would write these one- or two-person sketches, and I tended to write stuff with everybody in the group. People kind of noticed that, too.

Michael Showalter: Everybody wrote for themselves. We wrote for each other, too, but sketches were currency, and we were all very much trying to be in front and be seen and be featured. The best way to be seen and be featured was to write a sketch for yourself. Being able to write your own sketch was kind of a ticket to being the lead in a sketch which, again, at that point, we all really wanted to be in front. So ninety-nine percent of the time, if I wrote a sketch, I was writing it for myself and other guys in the group or Kerri, but rarely would I be like, "I'm going to write a great sketch for so and so to be in." It was very survival-of-the-fittest kind of attitude.

It was understood that if you wrote the sketch, you could cast it as well. If we felt like one person was being cast in too many things, we might do some recasting and give someone else that role. We tried to keep it relatively even so that everybody was getting parts.

Craig Wedren: There was a really beautiful [sketch] that I loved. It was Showalter and Kerri on swings in a park, and it was about a super-romantic date, like a teenage date thing. I remember there was some good music in that. One of my favorite parts about that bit was these two kids are on a date, and it's really sweet and romantic, and there's all these other characters sort of walking around the park, including Joe Lo Truglio, who is just a park maintenance guy with a pair of Walkman headphones on. He's doing his thing, like bushwhacking in silence, and about every thirty or forty-five seconds, you just hear him sing, "Come On Eileen...!"

Robert Ben Garant: Me and Ken Marino are big Marx Brothers fans. The cadence was so important. We would rehearse stuff so precisely. The handshake would have to come at exactly the right time. We were really well drilled. I didn't know any different. After sophomore year, I saw a couple comedy troupes. I just thought, "Wow, these other people did not rehearse nearly as much as we do!" We would also write stuff that needed to be rehearsed really well. We would write absurdist things. We would pick up Kevin, toss him to somebody else and throw spoons across the room — not Blue Man absurd but Blue Man-type. We were really hard on the precision of the material. People never went off book at all. Nobody veered from the rehearsal. If something is getting a big laugh, people didn't milk it. They didn't make faces at the audience. People were very true to the rehearsal, which I guess is pretty weird. We just started that way.

Precise nonsense is really what we were doing.

David Wain: I very shamelessly went on my hands and knees to The New Group. I had been friends with them by then. (I made the first program for The New Group show on my Macintosh. I was the only guy in college who had a Macintosh computer.) I knew them by then, and I was like, "Hey, can I please, please be in the group?" I think it was like, "OK, leave the room. We'll talk about it." I think they came back and said, "OK."

Mo Willems: People were shocked when David left The Sterile Yak to go to The New Group, which was after my time. My reaction was, "Brilliant! I knew he was smart." Who wouldn't make that decision?

I was jealous of what they did and what they were. I did not think it was any way I could integrate into that group. ... There were a couple guys who never even met me, who really didn't like me. ... It never seemed plausible. As they got more successful and did more shows, I looked at them and said, "They've got their thing. Nobody else could come into that thing."

George Demas: The meetings were tough. The criticism was very open, and while that's great, it can be harsh. That's not so much what I struggled with; what I struggled with was the personal conflict that would arise. I think of that movie "The Kid Stays in the Picture," where Robert Evans says, "Things that are born with no conflict at all usually are lackluster." I think it was good for what the group became, but I had some conflicts ... I was getting very frustrated and making ultimatums, like, "If X doesn't happen, I'm gonna split." If you're willing to do that, you're probably saying, "I'm out of here" anyway.

I remember one of the last things I said was a conflict as to whether to let David Wain and Tom Lennon in the group, because that came up as an issue. ... We knew that there was a lot of not only talent but industriousness and a little bit of swagger, and also we really felt that there was something that was really special about the group and that it could move forward, and that was the dream. I felt letting those two guys in was essential. The opposition to that was the group was getting too big, and I kind of saw where they were coming from, but I also knew that someone like Tom in the group would be extremely dynamic. The amazing thing about this group is the tremendous colors, tremendous talents, tremendous people in the group, but it could be kind of a mess sometimes. I felt that David would be able to take these buckets and gather up this tremendous stuff and be able to make the group make sense to other people.

I think that that was the next step, somehow taking all of these crazy, wonderful people and putting it together in a way that would make sense to someone, so that they could — forgive me for using this economic term — monetize what the group was. I wasn't with the group when this happened, but I think ultimately I was right. I think he did contribute to fusing a sense of industry to the group so it could move forward. I think that Tom's writing was off the charts. I just felt very strongly about them. It was not the conflict, but it was one of the conflicts I had where I started to feel like rather than looking forward to the meetings or finding it challenging, I was like, "Uh, shit, where am I gonna get a drink after this?"

David Wain: This first thing [I] did was this Christmas show, which was a whole story where we're all caught in a cabin. That was how I was introduced to the group. They were like, "Oh, my God, it's David Wain!" We did it in the recreation area of our dorm, Brittany Hall.

Michael Patrick Jann: That Christmas show was also my first appearance with the group. The concept of the show was that the group was in a cabin on Christmas Eve waiting for the man in the red suit to show up. In the end, who shows up is me dressed as Spider-Man. I had two lines, and I was off the charts nervous because I'm not really an actor. I really didn't want to let these guys down, though.

Joe Lo Truglio: In David's first show, the Christmas show at Brittany, Kerri did a monologue about how her father got stuck in the chimney. Then we tell her she's just doing Phoebe Cates' monologue from "Gremlins." She denies it. It goes back and forth until we pull out a TV and VCR and play the entire scene for her. I remember people loving it.

In the fall of 1989, Michael Showalter decided to transfer to Ivy League Brown University. Both of his parents were professors, and the switch seemed like a good fit for his current route of studying academics. At the time, Showalter intended to teach cinema studies.

Michael Showalter: The New Group, we never discussed like "After college, we're going to keep doing this, and we're going to try to make this a career." When I left NYU, it wasn't like, 'I'm leaving my career; I'm switching jobs.' It was just, 'I'm going to another school because I'm in college.' I wanted to leave NYU, and I didn't want to leave The New Group, and The New Group didn't feel like NYU to me. I got teased about it a lot. I was the preppy snob.

I came back to New York very frequently, especially my first year at Brown. I was making money because I'd put my name up on the ride board and say I was going to New York this weekend, and I would charge like fifty bucks to get a ride with me.

David Wain: I left the second half of that year to go to Brown University with Mike Showalter. We would do shows on the weekend. We stayed very committed to it.

I was just feeling like I missed out on regular college life because we were in the middle of Greenwich Village. Also, New Group stuff made it so hard to take any academic classes and take it seriously.

So I decided to take a semester abroad, which frankly I think I was chicken to do. I applied to schools to take a semester as a visiting student. So I was just a visiting student the second half of my junior year at Brown, which is going to be fascinating to somebody.

It took a while to get used to it. I kind of wish I'd gone for a full year. I made some good friends there. That's where I really got to know Michael Showalter.

We would drive back and forth and talk about "Saturday Night Live" trivia. We wrote sketches together at Brown.

Kerri Kenney-Silver: That was a huge deal. All of a sudden someone is taking their education over The New Group. That's a constant joke that I still do with Michael Showalter. "Well, you're going to Brown. So screw you."

Michael Showalter: "We're not smart enough for Mike." Obviously, nothing could be further from the truth.

Kerri Kenney Silver: We were pretty smart characters. Most of us have done well in school and were well read, had gotten into other universities as well. It wasn't a dumb bunch of kids for sure. That helps in comedy. Patton Oswalt is one of the funniest people alive because he is such a genius. I'm not saying we were geniuses. Let me be perfectly clear, we weren't dumb is all I'm giving us.

David Wain: I know there were some people who were upset about it, but I think that it was under the promise that he would be back any weekend we needed him.

Michael Ian Black: [Showalter] wanted to stay involved with the group. It felt to us like he was sort of half-in and half-out. We very much wanted him to be part of the group, but we wanted him to commit to it. I had to have that conversation with him. "You have to step it up. You have to write more. You have to be here more if you want to be in the group," and he did. He definitely upped his game.

Kevin, Michael Jann, Joe and Ken Webb became a filmmaking team and worked together throughout their tenure at NYU.

Ken Webb: After Motion, Matter and Meaning freshman year, there is a film class sophomore year called Sight and Sound that is a very structured class that's been taught the same way for like forty-five years. Groups of four students crew up together at the beginning of the class, and over the course of the class, each student writes, directs and edits five short-film projects. So that means that the four together are working on twenty short-film projects.

Sophomore year we lived in 1101 at the Brittany, and the room was a suite. It was supposed to be three people in one room and two people in the smaller room, and there was a big, walk-in closet. What we did was moved all of the beds into the smaller room and put in two bunk beds. So there were four people living in the smaller room. Ben Garant was living in the closet, of course, and the big room was the hangout space. It wasn't just hanging out after rehearsal; we were in bunk beds for a year with four dudes.

Robert Ben Garant: It was David Wain's closet. He was there the prior semester, and when he left I got in the closet. It was great. All we did was sleep in there anyway; so it was just a mattress on the floor and all my shit. So it was kind of great.

Kerri Kenney-Silver: I didn't socialize much outside of the group. I was in the Experimental Theater Wing, and that was my day job as I think of it — doing lessons and scenes in class. As soon as it's over, I would rush off to the guys to rehearse sketches. Or play. Then when rehearsals were over, we were eating together and drinking together, and many of us were roommates; so it never stopped.

Robert Ben Garant: After the shows, that's where the parties were. We had a little, tiny, shitty TV and a fridge full of beer, and that was the hangout. For New York, it was pretty massive.

The whole group worked there. It was almost big enough for rehearsal but not quite. [During] the parties, you could not move; people would just cram in. Every single person from our audience would go there. People would be making the moves on chicks and smoking dope, and I think that's where I first saw Kerri Kenney on Ecstasy. A lot of really good memories. Somebody had thrown away a dishwasher on the street, and so we snuck it into this room and put a big bow on it and gave [Joe] a broken dishwasher for his birthday. We thought it was the funniest thing any of us had ever heard of; that's one of my memories from that room — presenting him with this big broken dishwasher with a big red bow and all of us thinking that was the funniest joke.

Michael Patrick Jann: I have incredible memories of 1101. We had half a couch that we found in the trash and snuck into our room. I'll always remember Kevin Allison casually coming out to a bunch of us. Watching "Apocalypse Now" on our nineteen-inch TV with George Demas, and both of us having firework epiphanies go off, in the way that only young art students can. Chopping up a damaged 35-milimeter copy of (I think) "Wings of Desire" to make curtains. How fucking lucky were we to have that space to ourselves?

Kerri Kenney Silver: We were always together, always, always together, usually in room 1101. We were always in there, sleeping on the floor. I remember we were such rebels, we wanted to spray paint the walls. You can't spray paint the walls of your dorm room. So like any good rebels, we covered the walls with tracing paper and then spray painted the walls. Totally rebellious! We were always inseparable, through fighting and screaming and throwing chairs, drama and all that great stuff. It was a great, great time.

Robert Ben Garant: It was so funny, like punk rock but practical. We didn't want to get kicked out of school, but we wanted to be punk rock. You walked in, and it looked like "Animal House." There was spray paint all over the walls. Joe drew this Blues Brothers sketch. There was a tribute to Uma Thurman on one wall with magazine cutouts, and at the end of the year, we just ripped the paper down, and it was clean. It was like this weird combination of "Yeah, fuck you, but really we don't want to get kicked out of school." Street smart pussies really wanting to have it both ways.

Ken Webb: We were family.

Thomas Lennon: We were so used to stuff happening to us in the Village all the time. We got jumped; we got beaten up. There's probably no comedy group you've ever met that got beaten up more than us, just because we lived in Greenwich Village in the '80s. The late '80s in Greenwich Village is impossible to describe. Mike Jann got mugged two nights back-to-back. Part of our lives was occasionally getting beat up on the streets of New York, which is probably why we're all still in show business because you just can't kill us.

When we got jumped, it was five of us from The State: me, Todd, Joe got his tooth chipped, Ben and Jann. Who would ever jump five guys?

And the answer is nine guys would do that. It was an intense time. There's literally no way to wrap your head around what New York was like when we moved there in 1988. I mean, there were literally riots, and Tompkins Square was practically on fire all the time. It was just crazy. We would not go at night, certainly, to Avenue A and never to Avenue B or C or D, ever, even in the day time. Now, there's literally the most expensive real estate you could ever imagine and cafes with Wi-Fi. I think there's literally a Gap where Kim's Video East used to be. A Gap.

Michael Ian Black: A lot of us felt like we needed more women. Kerri didn't necessarily feel that way. A lot of different women came and went for whatever reason — some because they left and some because we fired them. It was weird to us that we had nine to ten or eleven guys and just one woman, but Kerri is exceptionally talented, and none of the women that we had could hang with her. They all sort of paled in comparison. They didn't last.

George Demas: Well, I'm a feminist, and so it didn't matter to me the sex of anybody in the group, just who was talented. I didn't believe in adding anybody unless they were talented performers and not only talented performers but the right performers for the group. There were certainly plenty of talented women at Tisch. I didn't think that casting in the group should be based on sex because of my feminism. I didn't think, "Oh, let's find a way to compromise" in terms of somebody who is right for the group but just do it for a sense of political correctness. I didn't want to do that.

[Kerri's] an intellectual. She can find her way into appreciating something goofy, and in the next second can be melting over something highbrow. She has a great range, not only as a performer but as a thinker and someone who appreciates aspects of life.

Kevin Allison: The group had a shit-ton of masculine competitive energy in it. I've always said these are ten guys who grew up being called "theater fags" and had something to prove. ... Even though it's such a gay-seeming group of guys, everyone's always confusing members of the group for being gay when they're not. There was a lot of that competitive male energy in the group. Kerri happened

"34 Stuyvesant Place" interior program art by Michael Showalter

to be able to deal with that like a pro; she could really play with the boys. There were habits of picking on someone for what made them distinct. If people wanted to take me down a peg, it was a fag joke. People wanted to take Marino down a peg, it was a loud, Italian guy joke. David, people would call him a whiny Jew. No one was better at dealing with it than Kerri. More than anything, jokes about women came up because it's a roomful of ten guys. She could always just bat that shit down, have the final joke and knock everyone else down a peg instead.

Kerri Kenney-Silver: I didn't know if I was going to be allowed to stay. Nobody could see the future. There were other women. You just sort of hung on and hoped it was going to continue with you and that your voice was going to be helpful and needed, and I was lucky enough to be one of the ones who did.

Ken Marino: There were three or four more other girls. From what I recall, Kerri ate them; so then there was just Kerri.

David Wain: I hung out with Showalter at Brown, and we wrote some things there, and then I came back and we did the "34 Stuyvesant" show. We just plopped ourselves into a couple sketches there, and that was exciting. I remember doing that show in the Barney building. There was something electric about that show. I felt good about that. Michael and I drove down all the time, and the guys came up sometimes to Brown, not for performances, but I think they came up there for a spring fling, and they came up and partied with us.

"34 Stuyvesant Place," named after the address where the show took place, featured Kevin Allison's first on-stage performance with The New Group, while he was still working sound for the shows.

Robert Ben Garant: "Bob, Sparky and Verbal" was this bizarre sketch of people in weird costumes saying non sequitur sentences. We just loved it because it was so different than "SNL." We loved it because it was weird. Everyone thought, "OK, this is what we do." I think Ken Marino might be responsible for that.

Ken Marino: "Bob, Sparky and Verbal" was a sketch I wrote that was about these three guys. I think it was my attempt at a "Waiting for Godot." I was probably reading "Waiting for Godot" in one of my acting classes. It was something about these two guys waiting for Verbal to come, and then Verbal comes, and it's just Kevin prancing across the stage in his underwear, singing, "Standing in an inch of urine well becomes a sailor man," over and over again. I don't remember anything beyond that. Bob and Sparky were two guys hanging out waiting for Verbal to come. It was stupid and made no sense, and we did it. I think that was one of the wonderful things about The State in the early days; we would write these absurd, ridiculous things that were unlike a normal, straightforward sketch, and sometimes it worked, and sometimes it didn't. I don't remember if that worked or not, but I'm sure it was pretty stupid.

Kevin Allison: This was before I was officially a member. It was literally like a Salvador Dali kind of sketch. Nothing anyone is saying is making any kind of sense. It's just three characters who live in apartment who are just pure bat-shit nuts, and it was a really fun little sketch. At one point, I come out wearing nothing but a leopard skin thong, singing that whaling song. I think I had a parasol that I was twirling. It was just a moment where the audience is dying because a nude guy has run across the stage.

My parents were in town that weekend, and I had been talking to them on the phone every Sunday saying, "Oh, I'm in this group. It's super-talented. We're going places, yada, yada," and they're like, "Oh, my gosh, we'll be in town when this group is doing this show," and then I actually got a role in the show to be naked, more or less. I told them, "This show is the group's worst work. I don't think this is representative of what we do best. So maybe you ought to not see this one."

David Wain wrote a fake article for a pretend publication, Manhattan Arts Review, praising The New Group, which was used to promote the troupe and give them some pretend legitimacy.

OUTRAGEOUS WIT: "New Group" takes comedy to unique heights, By Leslie Brandon, the headline read.

Given the general drought of fresh material coming from the thousands of stand-up comics that have proliferated in the last decade, the New Group comedy troupe from Greenwich Village has a freshness and vitality in their ensemble comedy not seen on these shores since the heyday of the original "Saturday Night Live."

Over the past few years, the New Group's performances — programs of scripted comedy — have shown sparks of originality and sometimes brilliance. Their most recent offering, "34 Stuyvesant Place," (April 19-20, Barney Theater), exploits the New Group's unique ensemble chemistry with glorious results.

The sketches in the show range from the satirical (a dead-on spoof of PBS's "Joy of Painting") to the absurd (three friends who gather each day to watch a man run by in a leopard skin jock strap, singing Irish sea chanties). Much of the appeal seems to come from the combination of innocent humor and an urban savvy that enables them to convey a true funny nature of life to an audience whose funny bone has been desensitized by the formulaic recycled comedy that populates cable televisions and comedy clubs across the nation (save "The Simpsons").

The ten writer/performers that make up the New Group are uniformly strong comedic actors. They are all young, as of yet seem to be untainted by the evils of the world. The writing of the sketches varies in style and subject matter — while rarely exploiting political ground, they seem to have taken on most other aspects of society. Though some of the more risky ideas don't always succeed, it is a pleasure to see a group that is willing to take those chances.

The New Group is currently developing a pilot for a half-hour series — a potentially successful idea, as some of the highlights of their past shows have been short film and video pieces in between sketches.

New York is ripe for the kind of originality that the New Group brings to the stage. The most unique characteristic the New Group has in the post-yuppie Nineties is that they are actually funny. If the New Group is the future of comedy, our funny bones will finally receive that elusive injection of much needed calcium.

David Wain: I wrote that in the hopes of giving the group an air of legitimacy. I figured if I made up the name, Manhattan Arts Review, then technically I wasn't lying. This was a real article, and it just happened that this particular publication only exists on this flier. And it's credited to my niece, Leslie.

Because The New Group took the work so seriously, not every member was going to be considered up to snuff.

Kevin Allison: Black was known as the Angel of Death. He was Mike Schwartz back then. It was always his job. We called them eleven o'clock meetings. No one in the group had the nerve to kick someone out in the middle of the day. It had to be sometime late at night, in the dorms once everyone is good and drunk. Black would pull someone aside and say, "Hey, you know, it's really not gelling."

Michael Ian Black: I felt like it was incumbent on me to step up and have those uncomfortable conversations. It felt a little cowardly to not do that. I always volunteered to do that. I hated doing it, as anybody would, but I felt like somebody had to. If I was arguing in favor of it, I needed to stand behind my words. I did that a few times. It was always incredibly awkward, incredibly difficult. I don't know that I was the best messenger for these things, but I don't know who would've been any better at it. It's always hard to have difficult conversations with your friends.

Joe Lo Truglio: There was Stephanie Blanchard, and she was in "34 Stuyvesant Place." There's another girl, her name was Sherri Lowenstein, and I think she lasted like a show. I think it was the Brittany Christmas show, and in true "Angel of Death" fashion, as Kevin says, I think Black was voted to literally say it wasn't working at the party after the show. It was completely insensitive, and awful and just regretful. We were just so singularly attached to this idea that we were going to launch ourselves that we had to trim what, in our minds, we thought, was less-talented fat.

Michael Ian Black: I just tried to be as direct as possible. "'We were talking, and this is what we were talking about, and this is what needs to happen." I didn't know any other way to do it. I didn't know how to couch it to say somebody wasn't working hard enough, or they weren't contributing or, worst-case scenario, they were getting kicked out of the group. I didn't know how to do it other than to just do it. I still think it's probably the best way to go about it, but I hated it.

Kevin Allison: There was a plus side and a negative side to everything. On one hand, in our college years, we got rid of some of the folks who weren't gelling so well. On another hand, everyone in the group was left with a slightly paranoid feeling of, "When I'm out of the room, are they talking about having an eleven o'clock meeting about me?"

Michael Showalter: It is worth noting that there were a lot of other people there at the time who were actually in the group at some point, and then usually it wouldn't work out. It was just sort of this strong core group that kept sticking together.

This was definitely not an easy thing to come and be a part of because the core group really did have a very intense connection and a very intense attitude about the work, too. We were like pre-professional. When I went to Brown [University], I was amazed at how little rehearsal we did at the improv group, for example. I was blown away by how not seriously they took it, because with The New Group, it was life and death, and I wanted it that way. So to go to another school and see how the other group did it was like, "What the hell? This is crazy." I realize now that that's what those college groups are. You're not there to rehearse your comedy group all the time. You're there for many more reasons than that. We were always thinking about, "This is what we want to do for the rest of our lives."

Kerri Kenney-Silver: I was all about drama in college. Are you kidding me? My God, the more the better. ... I was more about creating the drama when it came to my dramatic, emotional, Sid-and-Nancy love life.

Kevin Allison: It's been fascinating to see the way some of the people in the group have really grown and blossomed. Everyone used to joke that I would be the first to die, and it's funny, because I feel like, to this day, that's probably still true. Yeah, but Kerri has really, over the years, so many different aspects of her character have mellowed out and become deeper. You know, she's always been just a wonderful person, but back in college, she was kind of a wild girl.

Joe Lo Truglio: Every day that you didn't have class, the next day was like a Friday night. Much of it did involve drinking and watching movies. I got stoned and watched "Popeye" a couple of times, "Buckaroo Banzai." "Brazil" was always floating around. We didn't go clubbin'.

Kevin Allison: [Joe] is a guy on the team who is very, very agreeable, very much a team player, but who obviously has a ton of talent himself and can joke along and bring things to life in a character-y way. I think Joe was never one of the strongest writers in the group. Neither was I, but he was so game. You know there are some people on a team who are good to have there simply because they're so much fun to be with, and they're such a good guy, and you like bouncing stuff off of them. Joe is just the perfect guy for that.

David Wain: Basically, we spent many hours a day together rehearsing and working on our shows as if it were our full-time jobs and that the fate of the world depended on us getting this done well. Somehow that work ethic was there from day one. Also, that we were doing something important and that we are amazing, as crazy as that all sounds for freshmen and sophomores in college. Between hanging out with each other and working with each other, that was a huge chunk of my time in college.

Ken Marino: We loved being around each other. It was our group, our club. When you're a young kid in the city going to NYU, basically your campus is Manhattan. It's not like it was a real campus. You would want to find a group of people that you could spend time with and hang out with and have something in common with, and what we all had in common was we loved comedy. We wanted to create something special and different. I think we would lift each other up. Perhaps slightly delusional, we thought our shit didn't stink. We're awesome. Maybe we lifted each other up too much. We were always there to talk up the group and keep the group going. There was something special about this group and these people, certainly to me.

George Demas: I would feel ripped off if I didn't go out for a long time after the show. In fact, the lines were very much blurred in terms of taking the curtain call and getting out to the bar. We weren't drinking on stage or anything like that, but your coat was on after you took your curtain call and after the group meetings, too. There's acting class in drama school and all that, and you'd get to know people — that's mandated activity — but with the group, you're there because you want to be and you're working over a long period of time. I got to know Mike Black in a very serious way, and to this day I think he's not only a very funny man but a terrific person. He opened my eyes to what drugs were in terms of how negative they are. He'd say, "We laugh off having a joint when the drug trade means that that joint we're having a laugh about equals death in communities in South America." He has a tremendous conscious and is a very smart guy.

Todd, to see what a self-starter really is and to have someone who has an idea and just goes out and does it and forgets about what everybody else says and has his own point of view that he's willing to take a thought and turn it into something tangible, and I know that sounds simple, but it's a jump that a lot of people don't make, and Todd does. Ken Marino's sense of patience with other people, and Kerri's courage to hang around with ten dudes and try and survive, ten dudes who are kind of young, and have a lot of spit and vinegar, and probably are saying some pretty offensive things here and there, her courage in doing that. Every one of them had something. Working with them was just a pleasure in spite of the conflicts that I just had trouble coping with at that age. ... Some of my closest friends were members of the group.

I wish I contributed more writing-wise. You really have to get some writing done because that's kind of the nuts and bolts of being productive in the group, and I really wasn't because my interest in sketch comedy wasn't that great.

Kerri Kenney-Silver: I felt close to all the guys. There's no one I felt distant from. Let's put it this way, if I were stuck in an elevator with any of them, I would've been just as happy. It's Pollyanna-ish to say, but I had ten brothers. They were all very different people. We laughed about different things together. I respected every single one of them immensely, worshipped certain areas of their brains. I couldn't believe how lucky I was to be in a room with so many people that just set me on fire, intellectually, and in my heart, which was comedy.

Joe Lo Truglio: We were at Lower East Side bars, The Edge, Barrow Street Ale House, DBA's, which was on First Avenue. There was a bar called Boo Radley's, which was kind of on campus. It was a bit too fratty. We went there a couple of times. The Dugout was a place on Third and 11th Street. Myself, Kevin Allison, Michael Jann and Ken Webb, we went to The Dugout.

Robert Ben Garant: This place called Down the Hatch was really disgusting, but they didn't card. It was in this weird basement.

Ken Marino: Kevin was just out of his mind and wonderful. You would want to be by Kevin all the time because you never knew what Kevin was going to do. Kevin was outrageous. I remember early on we were at a party, and all of a sudden he just walked out naked it and started talking to people. It was at this packed apartment in Manhattan. He just took all his clothes off in the bathroom and came out and started having conversations with people like everything was normal. He was completely naked. He is out of his mind. I love it. I can't wait to see what he does next.

Ken Webb: He would just go off, and it was brilliant and weird, and Tom would be upset if he heard if Kevin went off and he wasn't there.

Kevin Allison: Yeah, that was my thing. It's so funny because now that I go to these kink events; I'll tell stories like that, and everybody is like, "Yeah, I was the guy who took off all my clothes at parties, too." It's like we're the national gathering of the guys who took all their clothes off in high school.

That was a way of auditioning for me, of being like, "Hey, everyone, notice what a loon I am."

Ken Webb: David Wain would occasionally take out his balls.

David Wain: I sometimes like to pull the sack out, and we had this game where you'd walk down the streets of New York to see who would notice the balls. Sort of pushed the line of just knowing that somebody was going to see it that shouldn't, like when you say something just out of earshot of somebody.

Michael Ian Black: Pretty much for our time at NYU, I don't really remember going to class, but I do remember spending all my time not in class with those guys. We were kind of an inseparable horde, and we did everything together. It was like being in a frat plus one girl. It was a comedy frat, and it was fantastic.

Kerri Kenney Silver: When you left your building, you were just amongst the population of New York City. It wasn't that kind of insulated campus feeling where everywhere you went it was like, "Hey, you're from the comedy group."

Joe Lo Truglio: A weekend or so before the show we were probably out canvassing or putting up fliers or stenciling sidewalks with spray paint with the logo of the show. ... I did the logo and created a stencil. I'd go around New York City, the Greenwich Village area, probably with Ben, and spray-paint all the sidewalk corners.

Robert Ben Garant: We drank a bottle of Jägermeister before we went out, and now that almost makes me throw up just saying it out loud. Ah, youth. It was really, really fun. You couldn't even get away with that now. There are so many cameras. I don't think anyone even said anything to us.

Thomas Lennon: For the record, it was a bottle of honey Jägermeister. It was slightly sweeter, and we drank the entire thing in my basement apartment at 10 East Thirteenth Street. Five of us finished a rather large bottle of Jägermeister. So we were basically hallucinating, running around stenciling.

Joe Lo Truglio: Clandestinely, "Animal House"-like infiltration of all the corners in New York around Washington Square. Probably dressed in black with ski knit caps as well. ... I think people probably walked right over and didn't notice much of it. It was certainly fun. It was kind of like our spy mission that we indulged ourselves in. As with those whole first years of the group, we were completely committed and obsessed with the group, which was great.

Robert Ben Garant: I just think it was so people who already knew who we were would think we were slightly cooler.

It's just recently I've been back and not been able to find them, but up until like five or six years ago, you could still see them every once and a while.

David Wain: In an organic, unofficial way, people started to be stronger writers and stronger performers. I was not necessarily the best at either of those at that time. I was definitely the guy who was good with the logistics and getting stuff done, getting the shows up and running.

Ken Marino: I will say that I've always been a passionate guy. I would lobby for things, sketches that I was excited about. I would lobby for us to get a show going, or to rehearse, make sure we rehearsed things. I like to fix things. I was always up on ladders fixing things. I was a very vocal guy. I was definitely passionate.

Kevin Allison: The group was usually in the mode of sitting around and pitching sketches to one another or actually trying to put them on their feet. I have to say, I often look back and think, so much of it is a blur, my time in The State. Some of it I don't really remember. The fact was those rehearsals and those pitch meetings were always amazingly fun. There was just a ton of laughs to be had in the course of any pitch meeting or rehearsal. They were always high-stakes. The group might not like what you are bringing, but there was always so much laughter.

Kerri Kenney-Silver: We weren't an easy audience for each other. There was a competition. We weren't easy laughers. Also, we wanted the work to be good and authentic and not just something that was a feel-good kind of piece. We wanted to know it was really funny. We were harsh on each other. When somebody did laugh or it did work, it felt incredible because we respected everybody so much. Everybody's sense of humor was so vast; it all came together as one.

Ken Webb: Showalter had a great analogy. Sometimes when a show is coming up and we were overwhelmed, I remember Kerri and I would be the first to be like, "Let's just call it off" or "Let's just push it off." Showalter's analogy was that at some point, Ken Marino would be the captain of the ship who all of the sudden gets rattled and comes out of his wheelhouse and takes the lead and tries to get everyone in line and inspired. That's an analogy I still remember from Showalter. It didn't always have to happen, but every once in a while it just happened.

Robert Ben Garant: NYU is a big waste of money, and I did take pantomime classes. ... Yes, there's a lot of mime in ["The State"]. I did study pantomime and movement with this guy from Canada. We had to master Bird on Your Finger and Walking Against the Wind and Trapped in a Box. We had tests on that stuff. I'm the one who wrote all the mime stuff.

It's funny; I don't remember anybody even pitching any parodies during the college years. Sid Vicious on "The $20,000 Pyramid" is probably as close to a parody is we ever did. It really isn't, but it is a pop-culture reference. Somebody wrote something about being stuck in an elevator with Jack Tripper. I think we did that, and it just didn't feel like us. I don't think people even pitched parodies.

There was an imitation, and the reason we did it was Joe Lo Truglio and Tom Lennon did it at breakfast one day, when everybody was really hung over. I think we were in Woodstock. They started doing Gilbert Gottfried and Christopher Walken doing an ad for Bounty quicker picker-upper. We thought, "This is great. It's a parody, sort of. It's definitely something."

I think we hated "SNL" so much. We were rebelling against all that stuff. At the time, "SNL" was all parody. Every sketch was a parody of some TV show. We just hated it so much.

Michael Ian Black penned The New Group Manifesto, seen on the following page.

Michael Ian Black: First of all, I have no idea why I wrote that. It must have been in a burst of anti-depressant-fueled grandeur. Moreover, I don't know what I had against "Star Trek: The Next Generation," which I think (and thought) was a good show. Finally, the arrogance of the thing just kind of floors me. That being said, I admire my own optimism, an optimism that twenty years in television has slowly worn away from me. I also like point number five, which I think expresses us at our best. We really did think we were onto something kind of new, and we recognized that we were at our best when we did stuff that first made us laugh.

A NEW GROUP MANIFESTO

Over its fifty year life span, television has failed, as a whole, to produce quality comedic programming. We point to: Mr. Ed, Gilligan's Island, My Favorite Martian, The Brady Bunch, The Love Boat, Too Close For Comfort, The Carol Burnett Show, Thicke of the Night, and Punky Brewster. Not too mention the current crop of rib ticklers including Growing Pains, Just the Ten of Us, the New Leave It To Beaver, and Anything But Love.   The above, ironically, represents shows that have been sucessful, and does not include such luminaries as My Mother the Car, and AfterMash.

There have been exceptions to this rule. Beginning perhaps with Your Show of Shows, television has at times come up with fresh, innovative comedic programming, including Laugh-In (on occasion), M*A*S*H*, All in the Family, Monty Python's Flying Circus, Saturday Night Live (also on occasion), and The Simpsons.

But in the last several years televison has stagnated to a new low, marked by the returns of Mission Impossible and Star Trek: The Next Generation, not to mention a Very Brady Christmas. Televison is crying for something new.

Hence, the New Group.

In the light of recent events, we The New Group find ourselves with the unique opportunity to create television, with the power to put ourselves into the homes of twenty million Americans. We like that idea a lot.

We want to fully exploit the medium which burst on to an unsuspecting world with such glorious potential, only to collapse on itself while masturbating to Doc Sevrenson and The Tonight Show orchestra. The New Group aims to bring televison into the twenty-first century ten years ahead of schedule.

The New Group will:

1. Explore traditional sketch format, following in the footsteps of the original SNL and Monty Python.

2. Explore non-traditional formats including film, video, sound, and dance to further extend comedic borders.

3. Write, direct, and produce all of our own shows, ensuring an ensemble which will not be controlled by any one overlord.

4. Make a lot of money and build rockets to Mars.

5. Remain true, first and foremost, to our interests, so that each member never feels obligated to perform for others, but only for ourselves. And if anybody likes what we're doing, then they can come along for the ride, too.

We, the New Group, submit this manifesto to the Gods of comedy currently residing in a small bungalow on Lake Champlain, on this day the twentieth of February Nineteen Hundred and Ninety.

Michael Black as Raphael and Ben as Michelangelo

CHAPTER 8

Teenage Mutant Ninja Hurdles

"Wait a second, you're not going to finish college? Is that the right decision, to be a Ninja Turtle?"

Ken Marino

On the surface, things were going well for The New Group. They were a hit within the drama and film departments, and they started talking about their future after NYU: tours, TV? But then, heroes in a half shell aka Teenage Mutant Ninja Turtles rocked the troupe's world.

Robert Ben Garant: Todd Holoubek was working as a PA for a production company. They produced a big show with Pizza Hut at Radio City Music Hall. It was this giant, sold-out run, the Coming Out of Their Shells tour. They made an album that you could buy at Pizza Hut. The tour was going from New York to Detroit and had a big run in Detroit. The production company realized that the guys on stage were just dancers. All the voices were prerecorded, and the heads were audio-animatronic and prerecorded to go with the prerecorded voices. Nobody in the touring show could do the voices or anything. They realized they needed an advance team to go and do publicity.

Todd said, "Hey, maybe my friends will do it." I think every single person in the group went and auditioned, and Mike Jann couldn't fit in the costume, and Mike Black couldn't really fit in the costume, but he did it anyway.

Michael Ian Black: A bunch of us went thinking that it was going to be a local job, that it would be just the New York area. It would be an easy way to earn some spare change. It was a national tour that they had these promotional turtles to go promote. When we discovered that, everybody was like, "We can't do that because we're in college; so thank you, but no thank you."

Robert Ben Garant: It was so much money at the time. It was like two-thousand bucks a week or something. I was deep in debt from NYU. I couldn't afford it. I was not really happy at NYU. I think Black was the same way. On the subway ride down, Mike Black and I talked ourselves into it. We said, "Let's do it."

Michael Ian Black: We were like, "Fuck it." I had to drop out. I dropped out for what I thought would be a semester and turned out to be forever. That was the beginning of my junior year.

Robert Ben Garant: We told our parents, "We're going to drop out of NYU and go on tour." When they heard about the money, my parents said, "Great."

Kevin Allison: At that point in our college career, we had already started talking about, "Fuck film studies, we've got to make something out of this group." By the time we were juniors and seniors, a lot of us were thinking, no, the future is not in these classes I'm taking in film or theater; the future is in this group of people. We can actually make something out of this group.

Kerri Kenney-Silver: There was chair-throwing and screaming while talking about Teenage Mutant Ninja Turtles. It was like someone was trying to leave the marriage. The marriage was going well.

Michael Ian Black: It was very upsetting to certain people in the group. Ken Marino was just devastated. I remember being taken aback by his reaction because it just didn't seem like that big deal to me. In terms of The New Group, I thought, "You could do a show without us. What difference does it make?" I guess maybe my head wasn't fully around it. Maybe I wasn't as invested in it at that point as he was or maybe some of the other people, too. It didn't seem like I was doing anybody particularly a disservice by taking one semester off doing this. It was a pretty upsetting meeting. I felt like I let everybody down. It was a huge shock that everybody felt that way. I felt like this is a good opportunity, and I should take it.

Robert Ben Garant: Ken Marino freaked. He was so angry that we were leaving a month before the next show was going to start. He really thought it was the end of the group. He was genuinely angry that we were leaving [and] tried to scare us into not going.

Ken Marino: If I recall, I was kind of bummed out because I loved the group so much and I wanted the group to continue doing their stuff. I didn't want anybody to leave because I thought everybody was a valuable piece of the puzzle.

Kevin Allison: I think Ken had a sort of going-away party for Ben and Black, or he intended to, but it became more like a funeral weekend. I'm always the guy in the group who's out of the loop. So I remember thinking, "Wait, Ken seems to feel the group can't survive this, and he's an intuitive kinda guy. Is the group finished?"

I think that was the party where Kerri and I got insanely drunk and moshed in the most epileptic way possible in the middle of Ken's living room, like the girl from "The Exorcist" flailing around on the bed. Like we were vomiting the worries out of our systems.

Robert Ben Garant: From getting the job to leaving was six days. We packed and dropped out of NYU. I lost all my money at NYU. I never graduated. We had just signed leases for apartments. I had an apartment with Ken Marino and Chip Flanagan. He didn't let me out of the lease. So I had to keep paying rent for ten more months.

Ken Marino: When somebody says they're going to go off and be a Ninja Turtle and not finish college, I was like, "Wait a second, you're not going to finish college? Is that the right decision, to be a Ninja Turtle? I don't get it."

Joe Lo Truglio: At eighteen this is such a dangling carrot; you can't blame them for doing it. We were saying — and I think they knew this — "Are you kidding me, the Teenage Mutant Ninja Turtles!?! The New Group is great. We're unique and funny." Of course, I didn't realize at the time that Ben and Michael were having a horrible time at NYU. They weren't enjoying the experience of college. That was the main reason to get the hell out of there. You couldn't blame them.

Michael Ian Black: Just a way to get out for a little while and then come back to this family of friends.

Thomas Lennon: People lost their minds that they would not put the group first, that they would do anything else. We survived, but man, oh man, were people mad about that. I was hurt because I thought there was a chance the group would fall apart.

With Black gone, I realized that I would probably be in more sketches.

So part of me certainly had to be a little bit excited about that.

Robert Ben Garant: They gave us a Chevy Astro van that had these two big, electronic coffins in the back that held all the turtle equipment and the turtle outfits, and we left. I did it for nine months. I think Black did it for like seven months, and he got a job in an off-Broadway play and went back. It was like a no-brainer. It was so much money. I paid off all my NYU debts and paid for an apartment in New York for the next year. I never had that much money in my life. It was great.

Me and Black would go to each city. There was always a Make-A-Wish kid whose wish was to have pizza with the Teenage Mutant Ninja Turtles. You would go and hang out backstage with a kid with leukemia. The outfits looked like the movie. The kids didn't think you were in some kind of costume; the kids really thought you were a turtle. We brushed up and read all the comic books. So we knew every strange trivia question a kid would ask. Kids would ask, "You know when Splinter tied you to that anchor, why were you scared — because you could breathe underwater?" "No, we're reptiles; we can't breathe underwater." You had to know everything about the turtles, all their weird mythology.

We would do P.M.-magazine-type interviews. We would do morning zoo radio tours as the Turtles. It was very surreal. You would walk out on TV live. It was pure improv. Every host would try to throw you, and you had to roll with it.

The helmets were too small. We had these big knots in the middle of our eyes, these big bruises right in the middle of our foreheads, because the helmets were too small. We even did radio in the outfits at first. Four cities in, we're like, "What the fuck are we doing? We're with a bunch of adults, and we are dressed like the Turtles." We stopped doing that for the morning zoos. For the rest of the stuff, we were in full gear. We went through Mexico, Puerto Rico and Canada. We did this huge tour. It was pretty great. I was nineteen years old. So it was the perfect age to do something like that.

He was always Raphael, the brooding turtle, and I was always Michelangelo, the party turtle. I did the surfer dude. We were both pretty good. We took it really seriously. I was out of the costume, and we were on some oldies station, and I was like, "This is the best rock 'n' roll on the dial, dude." He [Black] was like, "Michelangelo would so not like oldies rock 'n' roll." We got into an argument about what type of music our Turtle would like.

Every once in a while I would get a snippy message from Ken Marino that my rent check is due. I didn't talk to anybody else. We might as well have been on the moon — six in the morning until five that night, and you would get in the car and drive to the next town.

Michael Showalter: I seem to remember that a lot of people felt like, "Fuck it, we're not going to do this anymore," and I wrote an impassioned, fifteen-page letter that Joe might even still have, that linked The New Group to the history of comedy. It was an impassioned plea for why we can't quit, and I sent it to Joe with instructions that he read it out loud. "We owe it to history to stay together as a group," which is ridiculous. I mean the grandiosity is just mind-blowing, and I'm fairly certain that letter had no impact on anything. I don't recall what the outcome was. I sort of feel like the group as a whole just took a little hiatus.

Michael Ian Black: When I got back, I was working with those guys immediately. Ben was still on the road, but I came right back into it. ... I didn't learn anything that was particularly applicable to the group. None of my turtle skills really translated to The New Group. Not even all my awesome karate.

Robert Ben Garant: At the time, to be honest, I just thought it was a college comedy group. It was a lot of fun, but I didn't think that would be my life. When I came back, it was still going on, and I was really psyched. I really left without much thought. I left it as easily as I left NYU. This is great, but now I have a job. Hopefully this job will lead to something else. I was and still am kind of winging it. When I got back, and the group was still going, I was sort of surprised and happy.

I got back like the first day of school. They caught me up. I read the program of the show I had missed. I watched it on videotape, and there were a lot of sketches that I would've voted against. It was business as usual. It seemed like we'd been away for a summer vacation. The fact that I missed a show didn't seem to matter that much. I got back into the group and was going forward.

If there were any hard feelings, I think they went away immediately.

Ken Marino: Hindsight being twenty/twenty, what a great opportunity! Why wouldn't you want to tour the country and go to every state in a Turtle costume and get to see the country in a way that you probably wouldn't be able to do ever again?

College. Who gives a shit if you don't finish college? At that time, I was so invested in [the group]. To me, [the group] was my college, was my reason that NYU was so special. I was probably very disappointed and bummed that they were leaving, from what I remember. Again, I was drinking a lot back then.

Robert Ben Garant: On the road, Mike and I started writing a screenplay, sort of autobiographical, of our adventures. We had never written a movie before. We abandoned it about halfway through the tour because we were too tired and busy at the end of the day to write. I found the outline for it recently. It was pretty good. It was coming of age. It was surprisingly indie and intelligent. It was about guys who are with girlfriends they really don't like, at a school they really don't like, and aren't entirely sure what to do with their lives. So we changed to be Rock 'n' Roll Kickboxing Lobsters. The Turtles' message was, "Say no to drugs, guys." The Lobsters' message was, "Drive safely, dude."

Joe Lo Truglio's cover for the "Enough with the Noise" program

CHAPTER 9

And Then There Were 11 (Eventually)

"Black did a typical Black joke. Especially back then, he was playing with this character of the snarky asshole. After I'm about to fall over from the good news, he says, 'So now you can ride the rest of our coattails to success.'"[1]

Kevin Allison on joining The New Group

By the beginning of the 1991 school year, Kevin Allison and Thomas Lennon had already become important to The New Group behind the scenes, and they both became full-fledged writing and performing members in time for the next show, "Enough with the Noise."

Ken Webb: Eventually, I kind of removed myself from the performing side of it because more and more I felt like I'm looking at seven people who could probably do this role better than me.

Kevin Allison: I was supposed to be there just to find out what my cues were for the cassette recorder. I asked the group, "Would anyone mind if I read a script that I'd like to donate to the group?" It was nerve-wracking. It was kind of how I felt before I came out to my parents. "I'm going to do this. I'm going to do this." I asked if I could read the script, and they said, "OK, go ahead," and I read every character. Just to read it was a little bit of a tour de force performance because I got to do all those bizarre voices and everything throughout it and keep the rhythm going. They loved it.

One day, we're walking through Washington Square Park, and Black pulls me aside. He says, "Listen, we've been thinking about it, and you really have a unique voice, and you're always around all of us, and we'd like to offer you the opportunity to be an official member of the group."

Michael Ian Black: I don't remember that. I only remember the bad stuff.

Kevin Allison: I was beside myself. I was kind of numb. I think there was this moment where I was like, should I hug him now, or is that too gay? There was this awkward moment and to break the uncomfortableness, Black did a typical Black joke. Especially back then, he was playing with this character of the snarky asshole. After I'm about to fall over from the good news, he says, "So now you can ride the rest of our coattails to success."

Now I find it very funny, but at the time, it really stuck in my craw. It felt like an omen. He was giving me the good news that I was in the group. That joke also felt like he was letting me know, now that you're in this group, get ready for relentless competition and rivalry.

Michael Ian Black: Sounds like me being an asshole.

Kevin Allison: I think at a certain point Mike had that snarky persona figured out, and then he got married, had kids and all of this stuff, [and] he was able to say, "OK, this is just my persona; I can separate that."

"Enough with the Noise," the last big show of The New Group before the majority of members graduated, featured "Medication," a favorite sketch of members that never made it to television.

Todd Holoubek: I think it will only work in a theater in front of a live audience. You couldn't tape it. That was a live-theater experience.

Kevin Allison: We have this theory, if you're going to do a sketch on the stage for a live audience, one of the best things you can do is make it as theatrical as possible. Make it a real, special effects-loaded or cleverly choreographed sketch to make people feel like they didn't just watch a couple of people talking for five minutes. Not that we didn't have plenty of those sketches, but the ones that we prided ourselves on were the ones where we went, "What the hell just happened on stage?" and "Medication" was the ultimate example of that.

Joe Lo Truglio: It was a restaurant sketch. That was the setup. It was two people and one person who didn't take his medication, and the other two people kind of tell him to relax, and don't worry about it, and these two people suddenly start to speak nonsense, and this premise kind of snowballs where there's this gigantic hallucination.

Kevin Allison: We all ended up contributing so much to the creation of that sketch. I was hugely proud of the fact that I was given probably the most bizarre role in the whole thing. I'm underneath the table, which has a regular picnic table cloth, the kind that is plastic so you can rip through it easily. I'm covered in Queen Helene styling gel, pink gel all over my body, as if it's afterbirth, and I've got an umbilical cord attached to my belly button made out of cotton balls and women's stockings.

We decided to shave my head, so I looked that much more like a baby. The table itself becomes kind of like a vagina, and I spill out of it. I'm wearing like a flesh-colored diaper, so I'm not actually showing my junk, and it's very shortly after I'm born that everything changes and everyone disappears again.

Joe Lo Truglio: Ken Marino and Ben come on stage holding an actual door, and they're knocking on either side of it.

Robert Ben Garant: The sketch gets weirder and weirder and weirder. At the end of it, the waiter has turned into a baseball player who's running around bases on a line of baby powder, and someone is lying it down in front of him as the baseline and sweeping up right behind him.

Kevin Allison: Someone, I think it was Ken, suggested, "Wow, it'd be really awesome to come out on stage with something truly bizarre." I was like, "I know, a pig's head," because someone, as a joke, had given my father for his fortieth birthday, a giant, severed pig's head in a box. I never forgot that visual. "You can go down to the butcher and get them to give you a head." So I went down to the meatpacking district, and they were like, "OK, people don't request this sort of thing, but for like fifteen or twenty bucks we'll give you a big, big pig's head." I would have to do this on a fairly regular basis. One night, I'll never forget, I thought it would be funny, there was this nice BMW outside the theater, like some yuppie's car, and I thought it would be really funny to put the pig's head on it after the show is over. We're all drinking and going out, and I put it behind the back wheel of the car, so when that person backed up he'd get quite a surprise.

Another thing was cow brains. At one point, Ken puts down his top hat on the table, and I'm under the table, and I give him cow brains. People in the audience can't see it's cow brains, but to us it had to be cow brains, and those things stank to high heaven. The pig's head

120

was bad enough, and we're doing this in theaters where it's a hundred degrees backstage.

Joe Lo Truglio: It kind of culminates into this gigantic, climactic climax of people running around and props and lights and sounds that end with "2001's" overture in slow motion. The guy that needed the medication grabs the medication and takes it, and we all go immediately back into our original positions, and everybody's off the stage, and the lights are normal again.

Robert Ben Garant: We put the tablecloth back on; you can't tell that anything weird happened. People who saw that sketch came up to us after and said, "I have no idea how you even did that or what happened, and that was great."

Joe Lo Truglio: It always got a great response from the crowd because it was so involved and so choreographed and just very different from your "premise" sketch. My dream would be if we're still working together when we're around sixty, where that premise called "Medication" would actually be a little more relevant, and it would be kind of a more of an achievement to see sixty-year-olds running around doing all that and succeeding. That would be a terrific State sketch to do at that stage.

Thomas Lennon: I came into the group the same way Kevin came into the group, which was I ran the lights and sound for "Isn't This Our Stop?"

Joe invited me to come [to a New Group meeting]. I've had a lifelong problem with cigarettes. I started smoking at about fifteen or sixteen, but I finally quit the day I joined the New Group. At some point, during that first meeting, I was so fucking stressed out that I went down to the deli, right next to 721 Broadway, where we rehearsed all the time, and I just bought a pack of cigarettes, and I started smoking again. Then, of course, I went on to be a heavy smoker, as was about half of the group.

Two things happened at my first New Group meeting. I was wearing linen pants. (If you're reading this book, you'll realize I had really bad fashion sense.) I was bending over, and Kerri Kenney walked up behind me as a joke and pushed really hard right at my butthole. She did it so hard that her finger actually entered my butthole, which was kind of horrifying. It was one of those weird gags where you're walking up behind, and I don't think she was trying to stick her finger into my butthole, but she did.

Then, about ten minutes later, Ben was standing on a two-by-four that was balancing over a big, heavy paint can, and I walked up and said, "Hey, teeterboard," and I jumped on the other side, and he ended up flying into a wall. He kind of got hurt a little bit. So it was a really strange meeting. I went downstairs and bought cigarettes and started smoking again, and then I would be a chain smoker for another fifteen years. Yeah, so it was kind of a shitty day, actually.

It's impossible to quantify how many cigarettes we smoked during The State. A couple people, Mike Black, David Wain and Ken, never really smoked, but the rest of us were heavy-duty chain smokers. We also drank a lot. I don't know how much that's come up.

I'm not sure why they took me in, other than there was some talk that I might be a good replacement for [George] Demas. I still have no idea why they felt the need to replace George at all. I just feel like the group hadn't fully understood how big an eleven-person group was.

Something was cast in a very early meeting, and somebody was like, "Well, it could either be Tom or Black," and I was like, "Ah, fuck, that's how this is going to go now for a long time. I'm the exact same casting type as Mike Black who is one of the super prolific members of the group.

Out of the gate, it was a real rocky start. My first sketch was called "The Dream Isthmus," which was like a bad "Fantasy Island" knock-off where low-priced dreams could come true, and it was just fucking terrible.

Michael Patrick Jann: [Tom] was so funny; there was no stopping him, no keeping him out of that group.

The State did not raise their collective nose at certain venues. Give the members a stage — or not — and they were there.

Todd Holoubek: Because of the bureaucracy of a school, [NYU] kind of liked you to be a student if you were going to use their facilities. So we started looking outside, and that was where we started doing things like the Strawberry Festival.

Thomas Lennon: We opened for The Toasters one time. We were aggressively putting ourselves out there. Any place that would have us, we would do it. Typically, we ended up doing a show with a drum kit on the stage we would just have to work around.

We did a show on the floor of the sports center at NYU while a basketball game was going on. We did truly strange shows. The Strawberry Festival was a strange show. We did mime and a couple of things. It was not our greatest venue.

Springtime for The New Group

Todd Holoubek: It was pretty wild — like an Earth Day festival. It was just very bizarre, not just to us but the people there were like, "What's this comedy group here doing?" because we weren't doing particularly earth, you know, Gaia-type comedy. But what was really amazing was at first there was this very, not negative, but just like, "OK" kind of neutral reaction or just sort of a, you know, we're more of a curiosity, but by the end of the show, there was like this huge crowd, and so that was, it was one of those moments where we're like, "OK, do the show, and we're in the wrong place," but by the end of the show, we had like this huge crowd sitting out there, and in the end it just kind of worked out really well.

Kevin Allison: It's funny, throughout the entire group's history, I had a real closeness with Todd because I think that, especially when we were on MTV and afterwards, we felt like we could talk about what it felt like to be on the outer outskirts of the power — whatever — dynamic of the group. Plus, Todd always had weed.

Jann was the guy who clearly had an unusual talent for filmmaking. We were all there thinking we were going to become film directors. We all wanted to get those degrees in film and pictured ourselves as sort of the next Scorsese, but Mike was the kind of guy who had that talent for thinking visually. He would make these little films in our freshman year and sophomore year that clearly had a lot more inspired thinking behind how they would be shot and edited. Mike also has this personality where he will stay quiet if he doesn't have anything smart to say, and if he does, he'll say it in a way that is so authoritative that people just tend to just nod and agree with him. It's so funny, I remember we would go to see movies all the time because we were film students, and people would be like, "I thought that was great," and Mike would say, "I thought it sucked," and everyone would be like, "Yeah."

Michael Patrick Jann: I think that's what the education at NYU is. If you want to learn to be a professional, go to USC. If you want to learn how to do it, then come here. Really, you show up, and they hand you your camera, and you're like, "OK, super." "This is how the editing table works. The rest you can figure out on your own." That's literally what we did. We were very dedicated. It was a lot of getting up at five in the morning, getting our equipment, stealing onto the subway because we can't afford the fare. We're going to Coney Island to shoot all day for Joe's music video to a Peter Gabriel song.

Kevin Allison: I was honored and moved that [Jann] chose me to co-write his senior thesis movie. I found out right away that … I was far more interested in performing and writing than I was in directing or having anything to do with a camera, and so I would write these ridiculous character biographies for my little movies and stuff like that, and I think that he was just impressed that I liked to think through a story world like that.

Michael Patrick Jann: The senior film I made with Kevin was called "Shelter." Kerri and Tom played the leads. It was a forty-minute, dark comedy about two people who get married too young and wreck each other on their way to divorce. I begged for money from every estranged relative I could find to shoot it, and it came out really well. But I just ran out of money and couldn't afford to do the postproduction.

Thomas Lennon: I'm positive I could not watch that. To see myself in that movie, trying to be a serious actor, would be like nails on a chalkboard.

Michael Patrick Jann: The rough cut sat in boxes for years, and by the time I had money to finish it, we already had multiple seasons of ["The State"] under our belt, and I just felt like all of us had moved past the student film part of our lives. Tom and Kerri were really so wonderful in it, but the people at William Morris were unlikely to be impressed that I'd finished my beautiful, emotional college art project.

Kevin Allison: I think that Tom was a bit miffed that, "Oh, why did Kevin get to write with Jann and what makes him more — a better — writer than the others of us?" and I felt like Tom was kind of ribbing me a lot at that stage, like, "Oh, you think you're big for your britches now," and in retrospect, it's funny because Tom is a better writer. He has this incredible facility of just having a story flow right out of him.

Michael Patrick Jann: Once they officially asked me to join the group as a regular, full member of the group, according to the sort of democratic principles that Todd had laid down at the beginning, I think I thought we would probably be a lot more successful even more than we really were. I know that sounds like incredible hubris. "Dude, there is no question; we are going to be the best ever," and I think everybody in the group thought that. There's just no question.

Craig Wedren: David was in film school. Tom Lennon eventually was in film school. There were a bunch of film people, Mike Jann. Everybody eventually started needing music. At the time I was in a band called Shudder to Think. We had a very intense, passionate cult following, sort of like post-punk and hardcore from the D.C. indie music scene. When I was a freshman in college and everybody else was sort of still figuring out how to zip up their pants, I was in this band, and we had a record deal. Weekends and vacations, I would be touring. So it was sort of natural that I just became the de facto music guy when they needed music for the student films or if they were doing a black box show. What was the first sketch in the first episode with the sperm and the eggs, the dance? "We need something for Hormones, and we need something original;" so I would just kind of whip something up.

As talk of making The New Group a full-time thing post-NYU began simmering, the troupe made some difficult decisions about its ultimate lineup.

Kevin Allison: The group, in the early days, would make you feel like "Are you up to snuff? Are you really up to snuff?" and if you went into a downward spiral, if you went into feeling too much of a feeling of paranoia of, "Oh my gosh, they're not liking my stuff lately. I keep putting my foot in my mouth," then something starts to get weird.

Joe Lo Truglio: Ken Webb it was, sadly, a mishandled exit, I think. I can't remember the reason, per se, but we kicked him out, and I think Jann at the time was around a lot and also in the film department. He was going to handle the film aspects of the group, and it was a little awkward, I imagine, because both and Ken and Mike Jann and I were in a production team together. So suddenly there was this moment of kind of a switch-out. I remember it being very awkward. I remember feelings were hurt for sure.

David Wain: I know there was a lot of discussion about it, at first about the pros and cons of keeping him in the group, and there was more discussion about how to tell him and how to do it, and it was pretty hard.

Ken Webb: I started to feel less and less comfortable performing, and I was never a strong writer, but I feel like my influence in rehearsals and helping to shape things was always there. But in my senior year I kind of voluntarily said, "I think I want to stop performing for a while." I was working on my thesis project, "The Waiters." That was taking up a lot of my time, even though it's a short film; it was 16-millimeter back in the day.

My wheels were spinning that whole year in the direction of my thesis. I removed myself from that, and then I was living at home. That was also difficult. ... I couldn't afford to live in the city. So my first semester I was commuting back and forth from Yonkers to the Bronx by car. It was like a number of things that were just causing me to drift away from the group. Yes, everyone felt like it [the group] was destined to be famous, and it was. But I never felt like sketch comedy was this Holy Grail for me. I wanted to be a legitimate singer/songwriter. I wanted to make films that weren't necessarily comedy. So, at some point, there was a meeting held, asking me, "So, Ken, what's happening? Are you with us or not?" and I was like, "You know, I came to NYU to make films. I need to focus on this film. If you need an answer right now, I guess I'm not with you." That was a hard meeting.

David Wain: It sucked. I was good friends with Ken Webb. It was a pretty dark time. The first time we really kicked someone out instead of them just sort of atrophying out. It was just sort of a transition from the group truly acknowledging this is hard core; this is not just a college activity.

Ken Webb: In hindsight, I'm still fine with the decision. The only thing that is a bummer is that I didn't realize how valuable it would be to get legitimacy at twenty-three, and by having a show on MTV, those guys got legitimacy and agents, and that's like breaking in. I've never had an agent. I've made a lot of music. I've directed music videos. I haven't had trouble finding work, but I'm still not legitimate.

Ken Webb's senior film, "The Waiters," features several members of The State, including Joe, David, Kevin, Michael Jann (who assistant-directed) and Tom (also the writer). It's still shown to students in NYU's film program.

Thomas Lennon: Ken and I were partners in Advanced Production, where you make one feature film at the end of the year, and he had written the script. I remember Boris Frumin, who was our very intense film teacher, he vetoed it. Boris was the kind of guy who would tell you that. He was like, "It's very bad." He was an intense cat, and many of us studied with him, and the only thing about him, he was one of these guys that was horrible and mean and said horrible things to people all the time, but if he gave you praise, you knew it was real because he was so fucking mean most of the time.

Boris vetoed the script that Ken had written. I had been working on "The Waiters," not even as a movie, almost like something they'd show in an art gallery. It has no structure, little sketchy vignettes, but it ended up doing pretty well, and people really liked it, which was interesting. My mentor is in that film, Peter Hedges, the guy who's trying to move the bunny with his mind. That's Peter Hedges. He's a sort of major writer and director now.

Robert Ben Garant: I got cut out. One of the waiting scenes was a staring contest, and it was me and Pete Dinklage from "Game of Thrones." I bet they all wish they'd kept that in there.

Michael Patrick Jann: Tom's script of "The Waiters" was so, so brilliant — just a perfect idea that popped out of him halfway through senior year. I remember thinking, "Man, that guy is a legitimate fucking genius," shortly followed by its corollary, which is, "and I suck balls." Everybody who works in a high-functioning creative group will back me up: those two thoughts always go together.

Kevin Allison: It was really hard to be in that creative unit, whether it be the Lost Boys of Filmmaking or The State itself, where it was a group of big egos. If your ego was the kind that's not such a tough fighter, it would have a harder time in the room, and that includes myself. So I often found myself commiserating with Ken, in the early days, and later with Todd or Joe, about feeling a little bit like not getting as many roles, not getting as many scripts in there.

George Demas: I had fallen in love for the first time, and it was that kind of overwhelming thing that happens to you. I considered what time I could have to be with my girlfriend and do plays and be a contributing member to the group and get my bachelor's degree. Am I saying that was a great way to make the decision? No, it was a bad way to make that decision, but I did. I was overwhelmed with those feelings and discovering parts of myself that sort of made even my acting career sort of irrelevant. That's kind of where I was at.

Michael Showalter: Ken and George [Demas] were both there from the beginning and were both an integral part of what the group was. So it was surprising to me that they would leave, but I understood as well. But it was like, "Oh, wow! What a bummer!"

David Wain: As we were transitioning from being college students to being pros, when some of us started to graduate, somebody told us we had to set up a corporation. So we had to come up with officers for the corporation, and our big point of the whole thing was that nobody's above anybody else. But I think me and Mike Jann and Mike Black were elected as the officers, purely administrative, to do the paperwork for the corporation. The corporation was like ten people, and Mike Showalter was not in the corporation because he was at Brown, and when he came back to New York after college, he had to prove he was worthy of being in the corporation. It became sort of a running joke, like, "You're not in the corporation; you went to Brown."

The corporation we had was called Jim Burns Productions, which doesn't mean anything. We just thought it was funny to have a corporation name that was somebody else's name. It probably dissolved around the time the group dissolved. For all I know it still exists.

~~[crossed out]~~
~~[crossed out]~~
Sour Milk
Spilled Milk
⊛ Nothing of Major Importance
~~[crossed out]~~
Live Bait
Homo Sapiens
Idiot Savants
Four Stars
Road Kill Revival
Good Night, Johnboy
Just Add Water
Rug Cleaner
Severe Raincloud
Tell It to the Judge
Spacious Firmament
Visible Quasars
Leftovers
Zebra of Flesh
Western Wolf
Closed Shop
Scheme of Things
Hoosiers Don't Hang
Abstract Specifics
Ad Infinitum
Deafening Hum
Chaotic Reality
Sleep On It
Empty Rain
Next of Kin
Abstract Oath
Null and Void

Silent Whistle
Silent Whisper
On Call
How 'Bout. . . .
Opus
Symphony
Toe Cheese
I Spy
Penal Action
Peeping Tom
Peeping Stuart
N.Y.U. Here
Noah's Anderbutts
No If, Ands, or Butts
Unsound Mind
On Sound Mind
Henry's Boring Party
Henry's Boring ~~Day~~ Day
Henry's Boring
Henry's A Boring Guy
Leo Needs A Haircut
Marty's Dirty Socks
I've Got Stubble
Wanna See It?
Endangered Species
Endangered Feces
Wendel's Revolutionary Army
Tension Whistles
Bread and Butter
Don't Go, Stay Home
Christopher John Mowed the Lawn
Yeah, Very Funny. . .
Seconds, Please
Pass the Salt
I Don't Get It

The first list of potential group names, post-The New Group

CHAPTER 10

What's in a Name (Like Tricia's Annoying Friends)?

"We were all really digging our heels in about a bunch of really terrible names. ... I think it always helped to have a vaguely serious name and not be called The Banana Patch Factory."

Thomas Lennon

One of the longest debates in the troupe's history was taking The New Group to The State. It started with a handwritten list — why was Milky Discharge crossed out? — and thus began the deliberation. The illustration at the end of this chapter is the typed list of names bandied about for days and days.

Ken Marino: There was a theater group called The New Group after we were The New Group. They became well-known, and so we had to change our name.

Joe Lo Truglio: I remember really being mad that we had to change the name. We should be what we were from the get-go. Who cares if there's an actual theater company in New York called The New Group? … I think it was a reaction more to people telling us to change it than not wanting to change it. I think there was a pushback on my part not to listen to anyone.

Robert Ben Garant: We knew it was a bad name. At the end of our live runs, we did a big show at this theater, an off-Broadway theater. We were hoping somebody would give us a TV show. Before we did that, we knew we needed a better name.

Todd Holoubek: I know we argued for three days. It wasn't focused around anger because we were genuinely trying to find a new name.

Robert Ben Garant: We had hundreds of names that we went through, hundreds.

Craig Wedren: I had a name. "Call it, Froggy's Your Man," and they were like, "That's pretty good."

Joe Lo Truglio: The last one on the list, that handwritten Bhurris Front, that's Michael Patrick Jann. He really loved that one. He had to scribble that one on after we already printed them out.

Thomas Lennon: We were all really digging our heels in about a bunch of really terrible names. There were a lot of things that would not have survived. I think it always helped to have a vaguely serious name and not be called The Banana Patch Factory.

Joe Lo Truglio: In terms of bland names that don't do anything but I kind of love was, The United States Comedy Troupe. It was really hilarious to me. It's so bland and official.

Kevin Allison: [One of our managers, Steven Starr] sat us down, and we had all been debating for a while, and he was like, "Guys, I got it. This is it," and it was Shock of the New. It's obviously like a marketing statement we're trying to get across there.

David Wain: I remember very long debates, a lot of frustrating campaigning for one name or another. I remember, basically out of exhaustion, we ended up choosing the name Medium Head Root. "We're all tired. Let's just call it that."

Kerri Kenney-Silver: Medium Head Root. We even had posters. Ew. What does that mean? So gross. Ew. It was Medium Head Room, then Medium Head Root. I recently came across some fliers of Medium Head Root. Ew. Weird. Gross.

Ken Marino: There were a bunch of different suggestions. Medium Head Group was based off the name of the character Medium Head Boy, one of the sketches I wrote. That probably was a suggestion I made. We had been debating what the name was. Blackout New Brunswick was one of them. All these silly names. We put a deadline to where we needed to come up with a name. I think Medium Head Root was the topic of conversation at the end of our first deadline. It landed on that.

David Wain: I liked Medium Head, too. I was Medium Head Boy. That was my character.

Joe Lo Truglio: We were that name for two days. I have no idea how we agreed to that. There were so many other great names on that list that I would've went with other than that. That's really surprising that we did that. I wonder if it was a matter of we were exhausted and tired of thinking about it and just picked that. We had that sketch, obviously. It was born from that. It's a terrible name. It's an absolutely atrocious name that doesn't have any cool, punk things about it. It's a failure. It's like an improv group calling themselves Mixed Nuts, which, I think, might've also been on there.

Ken Marino: Everybody went to sleep and came back, and I think everybody felt that probably wasn't the best name.

Todd Holoubek: You know that was the power of eleven, that we could like make a decision and then come back and be like, "OK, wait. Did we make that decision because we just wanted to get out of the room? Was a decision being made because someone's [argument] was really strong, or was it because it was a good decision?" Decision-making is very interesting because your decisions are based on things like what is known, what is unknown, what are the factors involved. The whole scientific theory of decision making, it gets pretty fascinating.

Robert Ben Garant: How it actually happened was Michael Jann opened a newspaper, stuck his finger down with his eyes closed and said, "The State," and that's how it happened. It was at 721 Broadway. I think we agreed on it immediately.

Michael Patrick Jann: It wasn't random. I grew up in Albany, New York, and most of my family worked for the government in education, taxation or wherever. As a teenager, I thought of working for "the state" as the most boring, cubicle-bound, soul-sucking thing that could happen to you. So as we were bottoming out on naming the group, I was avoiding being in the argument over whether Medium Head Root (or Route) was a good name by reading the paper. There was news story [that read], "The state passes budget measure blah blah blah," and I thought, "That would be funny if I could tell my whole family I had gone to art school and was now working for 'the state.'" I pointed my finger at the words in the newspaper and said, "How about The State?" Somehow, mostly because people were tired of arguing about it, it stuck.

Ken Marino: The State, which is equally nothing, but in a great way, I think. The thing about the name The State is it's not necessarily trying to be cheeky or funny.

David Wain: People getting up on chairs and screaming, "The State! The State! The State!"

Todd Holoubek: What was most important was what we did; so our actions gave meaning to the name The State — not to say we could've called ourselves Rhubarb, but I think The State worked.

Kevin Allison: I remember people saying, "Look, it doesn't matter what you're called; once people associate 'Oh, they're funny' with you, they'll latch onto the name." I remember we were kind of attracted to the idea that The State sounds a little bit like this might be comedy that is coming to you from Big Brother, you know what I mean? And MTV kind of ran with that in some of the campaigns, the first TV promos, but there's also that whole state of being. To this day, I still find it an odd name for a comedy group, but I do feel that what we all predicted would happen did happen, where people just began to think we were funny; so they just got used to the name.

Kerri Kenney-Silver: I don't know what everybody else thinks. I feel like I was the one holdout against The State. After hours and hours and days and days of going over ideas for names, I just felt like I gave in. I was like, "Fine. Whatever. Who cares? I hate it. Let's just go with it." My name that I pitched and love, that ever since then I've brought it up to people and every friend of mine says, "God, now that's a terrible name," was Tricia's Annoying Friends, which I thought was so funny at the time.

Thomas Lennon: I was really pro that one. I'm still kind of in favor of that name.

David Wain: Part of the negotiation was, "OK, we can be called The State as long as it's followed by Full Frontal Comedy." That went away fast.

Joe Lo Truglio: It became obvious that that was a bit too long and cumbersome.

1. ~~after school~~
2. ALL TOES COMEDY
3. ANYTHING ONCE
4. ADVANCE NOTICE
5. AUNT BERU
6. AY CALITELLTE
7. BABY DIP
8. BABY SMOKE *ON*
9. BAD BANANNA ON COMEDY GROUP
10. BANANNA COMEDY
11. BARK BOX
12. BHURRIS
13. BLACKBOX
14. BLACKOUT
15. BLACKOUT NEW BRUNSWICK
16. BLEACH COMEDY ROUTINE
17. BLIND OUTY
18. BLOOD AND CHOCOLATE
19. BLUE STUDIO ZOO
20. BLUEPRINT
21. BLUSH COMEDY
22. BORED ROOM
23. BOSS COMEDY
24. BOSS COMEDY GROUP
25. BOXED SET
26. BRAT BOX
27. BREAK THJORUGH BR
28. BRING THE NOISE
29. BROWN HELMET
30. BROWN HELMETY
31. BURN CANDY COMEDY
32. BURNING ITCH
33. BUTCH COMEDY
34. BUTRNUING SENSATION
35. BUY MONKEY
36. BY AND BUY
37. CAFE PARCELS
38. CAN O WORMS
39. CANDY COMEDY
40. CAR BOMB COMEDY
41. CHANGING TIMES
42. CHEAP SDTORIES
43. CHECK IT OUT
44. CIVILLIAN BUZZARDS
45. COMEDIA DEL FARTE
46. COUPE COMEDY
47. DIME ONE
48. DIMENSIA PREYCOX
49. DOOM ROOM
50. EARSPRING COMEDY GROUP
51. EGG SALAD COMEDY
52. ETTIE WILKSON COMEDY GROU
53. FANDANGO
54. FARCE
55. FART VADER
56. FINAL SALE
57. FIRE AND BRIMSTONE
58. FLUSH COMEDY
59. FLUX
60. FOOT FOOT COMEDY
61. FOOTS ON FIRE
62. FRENCH DIP
63. FROGGY'S YOUR MAN
64. FUN DE CIECLE
65. FUNNYBAND COMEDY
66. FUNNYBUN
67. GET MARRIED COMEDY
68. GIRL GIRL GIRL!
69. GRAND OL' OPRY
70. GROUND MUTT COMEDY
71. GROUP FLUSH COMEDY
72. GROUP STARE COMEDY

The final list of group names continues over the next two pages.

73. HAMMISH	109. MEDIUM HEAD HOUSE
74. HATBOX	110. MEDIUM HEAD LAB
75. HEIDI LA FUEL	111. MEDIUM HEAD LODGE
76. HERE'S THE DEAL	112. MEDIUM HEAD LOUNGE
77. HERE, DIAGONALLY	113. MEDIUM HEAD NOISE
78. HOMENY	114. MEDIUM HEAD NOISE
79. HUMAN TORCH	115. MEDIUM HEAD PEOPLE
80. HYPE ROOM	116. MEDIUM HEAD ROOT
81. INFANT TERRIBLE	117. MEDIUM HEAD ROUTE
82. JEHOVA	118. MEDIUM HEAD STORY
83. JESUS OF NAZERETH	119. MEDIUM HEAD THING
84. JIM BURNS COMEDY	120. MEDIUM HEADPAN
85. JOHN 3:11	121. MEDIUM HYPE
86. JOHNNY MATU COMEDY	122. MILK DUDS
87. JOY BUZZER	123. MISSPENT YOUTH
88. JOY RIDE	124. MOM'S SAMPLE PIE
89. JOY ROOM	125. NAILBENT COMEDY
90. LEAVE OF ABSENCE	126. NEW DOOM
91. LORD JESUS	127. NEW GROUP COMEDY
92. LOS ANGELES CLUB	128. NO BRAINER
93. LOST GENERATION COMEDY	129. NO BRAINER
94. LUCKY BABY	130. NO CHUM COMEDY
95. LUCKY PIERRE	131. NOW THIS
96. LUCKY ROOM	132. OINTMENT
97. LUCKY TANGELLO	133. PAY DIRT
98. MAD FOLD IN	134. PAY DIRT...
99. MADAM SKINNYBOX	135. PETTICOAT COMEDY
100. MARKET COMEDY	136. PILBY SOCIETY
101. MEDICATION	137. PILED HIGH AND DEEP
102. MEDIUM HEAD	138. PILLBOX
103. MEDIUM HEAD	139. PINK FLOYD COMEDY SONG
104. MEDIUM HEAD BOY	140. PITTSBURGH COMEDY CLUB
105. MEDIUM HEAD CAFE	141. PORCH HARP COMEDY CLUB
106. MEDIUM HEAD DEPARTMENT	142. QUAGMIRE
107. MEDIUM HEAD GROUP	143. REEL BOUNCE COMEDY
108. MEDIUM HEAD GUILD	144. SACRED COW

145. SELF CONSCIOUS COMEDY
146. SEPIA
147. SHOCK OF THE NEW
148. SHOT IN THE HEAD
149. SISTERS OF
150. SITUATION ROOM
151. SIX TOES COMEDY
152. SMOKE
153. SOBER COMEDY
154. SPIDER LIKES COMEDY GROUP
155. SPOT CHECK
156. SQUAK BOX
157. SQUASH COMEDY
158. STARS AND GARDERS
159. STRONGER THAN DIRT
160. SYSTEM
161. TAKER AWAY
162. THE BIG FINGER
163. THE BITCH COMEDY GROUP
164. THE BLAND BUT COMEDY GROUP
165. THE CANDY COMIC TROUPE
166. THE FRONT
167. THE FUNNYBAND
168. THE GREEN BEANS GROUP
169. THE HYPE
170. THE MAMAS AND THE PAPAS
171. THE MEDIUM HEAD
172. THE NEW GROUP
173. THE SELFISH COMEDY CLUB
174. THE SOUP AND COMEDY BEARS
175. THE UNITED STATES COMEDY GROUP
176. THE WAX TENDON TROUPE
177. THE WHAT'S FURRY COMEDY GROUP
178. THREE HEADS COMEDY GROUP
179. TRALBEE SOCIETY
180. TRUTH OR COMEDY GROUP

David debuts as The Masked Pastor with the lightbulb sleeves in one of his many '80s camcorder comedy sketches.

CHAPTER 11

The Masked Pastor Sneaks into MTV

"When we did 'Molt,' that was our official coming out. 'We're The State now. We're not The New Group anymore. We're not a college comedy group.'"

Michael Showalter

Yay, Todd!

David, Ken and Todd graduated a year before the rest of The State members. Ken hit the road with the national tour of "A Few Good Men" while Todd went to Los Angeles for a bit to see what all the hubbub was about. An old friend of the Wain family, Jon Bendis, was a hot producer at MTV and helped introduce David around the offices there. Bendis recognized David's talent when David was a kid messing around with the family camcorder.

David Wain: A lot of [videos] were under the title Cleveland Rocks, and I would be like, "So, now here's our consultant." I think I used consultant for what I later learned should've been correspondent. Whatever came out of my mouth, I would have to then do that character. "Here he is, the guy with the lightbulb sleeves himself, The Masked Pastor." That was the gobbledygook that came out of my mouth. Then I'd hit pause on the camera — there was no editing — and then I'm like, "OK, what do I do now?" Well, I put on a ski mask that covers your whole face, some sort of other hat on top of that, and then a white sweatshirt, and the sleeves go around lightbulbs on my wrist, and gloves. I'd just talk in the camera. "Hey, hey, hey, this is me, the Masked Pastor, with the lightbulb sleeves himself," and then I would sort of go, "Yes, indeed," and say nothing at all. No skit, no nothing, for no reason. No one's going to watch anyway.

But I showed it to Jon Bendis, who was dating my sister, when they got home, like by force. "OK, I know you want to go make out or whatever, but watch these videos I made while you were gone." They thought it was real funny, the Masked Pastor. So I think I did it again in The Sterile Yak. "Here's the big build up; here he is, the Masked Pastor," and then came out and did nothing. It doesn't make any sense. Thinking about it in retrospect, [I think] it makes even less sense.

Jonathan K. Bendis (former manager and co-creator of "The State"): They were all amazing. ... The Masked Pastor ... it's funny, because he's Jewish. This Masked Pastor is doing this whole thing, and then what happened was he kills himself, and when he rips the mask off him, he's still David, but he's Gene Rayburn, because he was using a golf club as the long microphone. It was just completely like out of fucking nowhere. He made it up. As he pulled the mask off, the name Gene Rayburn came to him. There was no plan of attack on this one.

David Wain: [Bendis] was the guitar-playing, long-haired, cool guy, who was also kind of a comedy nerd and Steve Martin freak. My parents were a little skeptical of him in general. I worshiped him. I was nine, and he was twenty-six. ... He dated my sister for a long time. After they stopped dating, we stayed friends. I would go visit him when I was thirteen or fourteen. Whenever I would go to New York, I got to see behind the scenes at MTV or sneak into "SNL." He was my introduction to everything like that.

I locked eyes with [Steve Martin] for a second when I was backstage at "SNL." I almost had a heart attack. I haven't met him since. It was the most exciting thing in the world. I would figure out how to sneak in. I would sit there. I was in heaven. Looking back, the first couple times I went, I was on such a high. I can't describe it.

Jonathan K. Bendis: When [David] was of age and was going to go to NYU, the family just asked me if I could please look after him, and I was like, "Of course." When he came here, I had already moved to New York, and I was already at MTV.

MTV was attracting a lot of young, untamed types in its early days. While Bendis was spending his nights rocking out in clubs, he had a fortuitous meeting with a wild, young female musician who helped him end up at the fledgling cable network.

Jonathan K. Bendis: One of my bands was playing in a local club in Cleveland. This girl comes up to us and asks us if she can sit in on harp, and we're like, "Absolutely," thinking she means harmonica.

She pulls her truck around the back of the club and asks us to help her literally pull her harp out — and we're talking a harp. This is great; she can sit in with the electric country rock band that we had, and we're totally into this. She did, and it was insane, and anyway she goes on to become the bass player's girlfriend. She is Nina Blackwood, and our band moves out to L.A. She answers an ad for this unknown channel that was about to launch, and it was all music, and that's all we were about. So she flies to New York, gets the gig.

The long and short of it is, I went to visit her in New York and immediately met with everybody, and it just happened. All of the sudden, somebody said, "Hey, can you work on a project with me?" It literally came out of nowhere, and that's it and nothing more, and one thing led to another, and I became the supervising producer and director in news. News was more long-form projects, which is what I still do, rockumentaries and all that. Those are mine.

I just started bringing [David] onto every show I could, to make him money and an opportunity to work.

David Wain: He started hiring me to do little things, light up this thing or shoot this little video thing. I ended up becoming a field producer and writer on projects he was doing at MTV, rock documentaries and specials. Basically, because we were friends, he knew all about The State. ... He recognized how special the group was.

Joe Lo Truglio: Jon Bendis hired us to be camera operators for a documentary he was doing on Ladysmith Black Mambazo. With our 16-millimeter cameras, we were shooting Ladysmith in a studio performance for the special.

Michael Patrick Jann: [Bendis] produced a twenty-fifth-anniversary Rolling Stone special which I worked on for him. "Here's every cover of every Rolling Stone ever. Now, give me fourteen treatments of it and at this length, this length and this length." It was cool. I got to interview Cliff of Cliff's Notes.

There was an AIDS special, and they needed footage of hookers, but they were so freaking cheap, they wouldn't just buy stock footage. Instead they were like, "Call up the kid who's still in college; get him to go shoot some." It was February; it was freezing cold, and they gave me a camera and a rental car and said, "Go find some hookers and shoot 'em because we need 'em." I was driving around all night. ... We were commanded by Corporate America to go get some hookers.

In the end, we wound up getting chased through the Meatpacking District, back when the Meatpacking District was a dangerous place, by a bunch of hookers. I got the shot, though, running backwards down the cobblestone street.

Jonathan K. Bendis: When I finally met all these guys, I knew how I could use them in different ways. ... It was great, but it also put them in the hallways, and back then, with anybody, it literally was you're in a hallway, somebody would see you and go, "Oh, hey, come over here."

David Wain: The other character was Steven Starr who at the time was an agent with William Morris. Since leaving William Morris, he wrote a movie, ["Joey Breaker"], about an agent who was transitioning to be more of an artist.

Jonathan K. Bendis: [Steven] was someone I knew, not somebody I'd hang with. He was an agent. ... At the time when The State wanted to make a move, they needed protection, which is my thing for them. I had run into Steven in the park one day, and I just looked at him, and I said, "I've got a project, and you just might be the right guy to work on it with me."

Steven Starr: They reminded me of the Kids in the Hall, whom I had represented at William Morris. Probably because they were New Yorkers, I found them funnier.

Jonathan K. Bendis: My whole end goal was to protect them, protect their art. Also, I'm on the inside over there, and they really wanted to be [at MTV]. I just needed to protect them from that, more stuff than they'll ever know or appreciate. They may now. Actually, you know what? They do now. There's no way they don't now because their foot in the business now ... they've been through that. It'll make our

145

negotiations back then be like nothing, you know, for some of the deals they've had to pull off for series and films and things.

We'd be their managers, you know, I felt mostly in name, just to protect them because they're the creative force. They're the ones who need to guide what they want to do which included going to MTV. We were shopping it elsewhere.

Steven Starr: Jon and I knew each other from the early MTV days, and he suggested I take a look at The New Group; so I organized a showcase at Fred Fondren's off-off-Broadway theater, The Prometheus. That night, there were so many NYU kids at the theater I almost couldn't get in. An hour later, I understood why Jon was so excited about them, and I agreed to manage and produce the group with him. The thought was to do a slightly expanded version of the Prometheus show over a couple of nights off-Broadway as an audition for the cable networks.

Joe Lo Truglio: Bendis invited Steven to come see the group and [he] was blown away, just loved the energy of the group. He said he was going to get William Morris to come and see us, but I think we had to create a smaller show. It was more of a showcase, a best of. I think that's how it went down. They saw a highlight showcase and then signed us. That was our connection with Jon Bendis and Steven Starr. They both came on as managers/executive producers of "The State" and were with us up and through CBS, for our entire run.

`Around this time Mike Schwartz became Michael Ian Black. Schwartz in German translates as black.`

Michael Ian Black: I never felt like a Mike, and I certainly never felt like a Schwartz. ... and I wanted something a little snappier. I went to Denver to do a play, and their local PBS station filmed that, and it was my first on-camera job. I was thinking, "My name would be on that. So it was time to decide what I wanted to do."... That's awkward when you say, "Hey guys, my name is not Schwartz anymore." It's a little like changing your gender. I'm a woman now.

I think there were some raised eyebrows. It was like, "Yeah,

"Molt" flier by Joe Lo Truglio

whatever." It took years for them to stop calling me Schwartz, which I can understand. ... I didn't want to use my middle name, but I had to for union reasons. There's nothing worse than the three-named actor, but I had to do it.

The troupe began fleshing out a greatest hits of sketches with some new stuff called "Molt" in an effort to get TV networks to take notice. It would feature one of their most ambitious film pieces called "The New Guy," which was filmed secretly at the MTV offices.

David Wain: We did that at like two or three or four in the morning. I had access to the building. We took over a conference room. "The New Guy" was all Mike Jann. He came up with those shots.

Michael Patrick Jann: I wrote [it] with Ben Garant. [The] whole thing went from birth to death all from a point-of-view camera in like two and a half minutes. The first shot was the guy being born with the camera sliding up between somebody's feet, being introduced to life, and growing up and having kids and getting a job, and then ultimately at the end the guy is dead, looking up at a priest at a funeral, mulch being thrown on his face. It's all pretty damn slick for twenty-one years old.

Joe Lo Truglio: The beginning and end of "Molt" were very, very dark. It began with a guy on a bell tower, shooting at people. It went into "The New Guy," and we returned to the guy on the bell tower. And more people start arriving that are pissed off with their lives. I think we had about ten people up on the tower, shooting at people. I don't know who plays it, but somebody comes up with a bomb attached to his chest. I'm sure there is a joke in there somewhere. It ends literally with a boom, and a huge amount of light shined in the audience, and it all goes to black. It was pretty crazy. It was really, really dark. Again, this was the show that was going to get us representation, agents. It was a long show. We tried to make it our concept show. It was basically our Pink Floyd's "The Wall."

Eileen Katz (executive producer of "The State"): I saw "Molt," and I saw the showcase. Those were the first two times I saw them before I brought them in. ... It was a point of view that was distinctive, and yeah, it was dark. But it was MTV; we're supposed to be dark. That's why it just felt very simpatico. As much as they want to think of themselves as subversive, they are so playful, and that's what's amazing about them. As cool and cutting edge and dark as they portray themselves sometimes, there is something so childlike and obsessed with pop culture and playful. I think that's part of their magic — they get it on every level, and they know how to make it work to get their material across.

Thomas Lennon: I don't know what we were thinking. ["Molt" is] a really funny show, but also there's things in it that are like one hundred times darker than anything that's on TV now. Between "Medication" and "Bell Tower," it's like we were really, really hitting heavy for a while.

We were just not going to do anything upbeat or cheerful. Everything had to be very dark, in that era at least. We just so didn't want to be an average group.

Michael Showalter: When we did "Molt," that was our official coming out. "We're The State now. We're not The New Group anymore. We're not a college comedy group." We're a professional comedy group that wants to be seen that way, and these are the members; this is who the core group is. For us it would be like Monty Python or something. Monty Python is Monty Python; there's no way to change that. So we felt the same way; this is the group. No matter what happens from this point forward, this is the group.

Todd Holoubek: By doing "Molt," that was the legitimate path to television. I know that was probably the crux of when it was changing because the '80s were just crazy stars showing up out of nowhere without theater experience, and that's probably because of the ease with which people used video recorders; you didn't really need theater anymore. You had public access. You could be on TV, get camera experience in the home.

Robert Ben Garant: We had this giant, giant show in this off-Broadway theater, and it seemed like nobody came to that. For some reason, we did a show of almost all the same material at Under Acme, this crappy little theater, and that's the one that ABC, NBC and everybody came to, after our big run ended. This terrible stage and sound and bad lights, that was the one that all the prospective buyers saw us at the first time. The "Molt" show didn't really work out. The show two weeks later was the one that everybody came to.

Kevin Allison: At that same time this hotshot was working for ABC as a casting director, and she came, and she did something everyone predicted was going to happen. She was like, "That Marino guy is good-looking. I can give him a contract for being on hold to be a sitcom star," and she did. ... I think she offered Ken something like $50,000 a year for one year for him to be on hold to do something for ABC, but he couldn't be doing anything else.

Ken Marino: I was doing some acting, different things. I did "A Few Good Men," and I was doing some commercial stuff and little things here and there, and I knew this casting director who liked me and got me into something for ABC, and then ABC offered me a holding deal, basically. Back then, you would get a holding deal, and it was like twenty-five grand. And that meant, basically, that they don't have a project for you, but they want to hold you so you can't audition for NBC and CBS and whatever else was around back then, maybe Fox. I remember just talking to the group about whether I should do that or not. My perspective was, because we always considered ourselves an eleven-headed monster, and we really thought that we were going to continue going as a group, and in our head[s] we were going to make movies and a series, and we did get a series on MTV, our own show, but I believe the talk was, "OK, if I say no to this, I hope nobody else, if given this opportunity, says yes to it." Basically, I was like, "I'm gonna say no, but nobody else better do this."

Kevin Allison: Ken was quite torn because this was the second time after the Teenage Mutant Ninja Turtles incident that someone was offered something that would clearly take them away from us.

Joe Lo Truglio: Ken had to consider it because it was money, but I think he so believed in the group. ... I'm sure he considered it, but I think The State he put a little bit more importance in.

Ken Marino: First of all, it was a lot of money, and secondly, we were all living with three to four people at the time or crashing at different people's houses. I don't know how we were surviving on that. You can't do what we were doing then now, financially. It seemed like a lot of money, certainly the most anybody offered me.

Kevin Allison: So he turned it down. That was seen as kind of a crossing-the-Rubicon moment for the group, though Ken made the sacrifice. That should be the precedent from now on, that no one should be considering doing major projects outside of the group while we can still be keeping this group together.

Ken Marino: I think we all loved the group so much that we thought what we were part of was something special. So nobody wanted to mess that up.

Not ready to let it go, though, the Ken sitcom concept became a running gag in The State, with an office pool called "Should I Stay or Should I Go?" and a list of possible show titles including:

- "Marino In Charge"
- "My Dad, the Don"
- "Ken Marino, CPA"
- "Ken Marino DDS"
- "Ken Marino DVM"
- "The Ragu Riders" (Western)
- "Murder, Ken Wrote"
- "The Goombahs"
- "Three Wops and a Little Lady"
- "Our Friend, the Otter" (miniseries)

With management in place, the next step for The State was getting agency representation, and after seeing the troupe perform, William Morris was ready to sign the eleven-headed monster.

Thomas Lennon: James Dixon came into the picture right after "Molt." Steven Starr had actually been head of the talent department at William Morris back in the day. Through his connection at William Morris, he got William Morris interested in us right around "Molt," and they came and were impressed.

Steven Starr: I had worked well with James over the years at Morris. He was passionate about comedy and had solid basic cable relationships. It was a great fit.

Thomas Lennon: I find it very weird that they signed a comedy group that was doing a show like that because it's beyond dark if you look at it now. I guess they felt like we had some heat, and we were well liked in the Village and beyond a little bit. I guess we were starting to have a little bit of a reputation like an indie band might have.

James Dixon (The State's former William Morris agent, now head of Dixon Talent, which represents Jon Stewart, Stephen Colbert, Jimmy Kimmel and other comedy heavyweights): It was obvious that collectively and individually they were a very, very talented group. I think they were really creative, more so than your average sketch group that you would see — and that has been proven now. Look at some of the careers that have sprung out of it twenty years later. They were just really different in a good way. Their stuff was incredibly fresh, and there was talent leaking out of these guys. Some stood out more than others, but in their totality they were very special.

Thomas Lennon: I remember this really epic day. There's something that happens when you sign with the William Morris agency in New York City, and this was at a time when people would still smoke cigarettes in the offices. Basically, we ran into the "Mad Men" up on Sixth Avenue, the old William Morris office. There was an ornate painting of William Morris, the founder of the agency, hanging in the lobby, and then they take you up to sign, literally, the big book. It's almost what you'd imagine Saint Peter has, this huge tome that goes back. I don't know if it goes back one hundred years, but it might, whenever people ceremoniously go sign this big book. They'll open the book, and, "Here's Marilyn Monroe when she first signed with William Morris," and stuff like that. It's really trippy.

Our minds were blown because the person who had signed right before us, just a few marks up the page, was Carrot Top. He had actually cut a clipping of his own hair to put into the book. Right next to where he signed his name, he taped a lock of his red mane. We all raised our eyebrows like, "Guys, this is pretty cool. We just signed the William Morris book three spots after Carrot Top."

On January 26, 1993, the William Morris Agency sent a memo to the company: "The State, our new comedy clients are hot! ... They have done such an impressive job that we are discussing with MTV a deal for The State to develop their own sketch-comedy series. ... With any luck, they can enjoy a success similar to Kids in the Hall."

James Dixon: Yeah, they were raw; they were really NYU students. They were incredibly raw, but they were also fortunate in the timing of where cable television was at the time. People would take a shot on a group who weren't, obviously, seasoned television performers. In fact, that's what they wanted, and MTV back then was taking risks, and I think this group spoke very, very well to their audience.

Thomas Lennon: We were called into [James] Dixon's office, and most of the group smoked, but Dixon, he took it to the next level. He was chain-smoking Marlboro Reds when we went into his office, and he was one of the most intense people I've ever met in my entire life. Immediately, I was like, "This guy, this man is a character. He's beyond just a person; he literally is a persona." He's so the persona of a New York agent that it just blew my mind. I was like, "This guy's incredible," and he was the most relentless person. I was like, "I'm going to write this guy as a character," and I'd like to point out that the character I'm doing is pretty accurate. Dixon is still one of the most powerful people in late-night television. He represents Jon Stewart, Jimmy Kimmel, everybody. He's a huge force to be reckoned with, but as soon as I met him, I was like, "I'm going to do an impression of him."

I remember [doing] Dixon as a priest when I say, "It's kind of a weird thing, not being Catholic or Christian." According to Dixon, he was like, "What are you doing to me, guy? That's going to break my Catholic mother's heart, guy." I wrote the sketch, and I was actually pretty excited about it, and I did not want to tell him about it. I wanted it to be a surprise, and Showalter disagreed with me, and Showalter called Dixon and vetted the idea with him. "Tom is working on this impression of you and is writing a sketch in which he plays you. Is that OK with you?" I remember being kind of mad at Showalter. "Don't, man, you just ruined the fun." I just thought it was going to be so great when he turned the TV on one day and sees that I've made him a legendary character.

James Dixon: I was incredibly flattered. I thought it was great, and he did an unbelievable job with it. I've gotten a lot of mileage out of that over the years. It still lives on, and now with the world of the Internet, it's there forever. Every once in a while, someone will mention that and say, "Wait, you're James Dixon from that State sketch?" It still comes up twenty years later. I thought it was awesome.

They surprised the shit out of me with that, and they did the first one, I think [it] was Power Guidance Counselor, and that began slightly recurring.

Lennon was one of the break-out guys. ... If [the impression] was that accurate, I'm not sure I'd still be in show business. He's kind of over the top, in a good way. It's all for theater, right? I guess they thought I was a character, the way I used to talk to them and deal with people. I guess that's what he took from it, but that's what guys like that do; they take it from a five and make it a fifteen, and that's what makes it funny, right? I was very complimented by that.

Tom wasn't at all concerned that as his agent wielded a lot of power in regard to his young career.

Thomas Lennon: Not at all. Because the thing about it is, I loved him so much. I knew there was no way that he could be mad about my impression of him because I was pretty close to Dixon. To this day, Dixon is probably one of the smartest reps we ever had in our entire lives. He had nothing but good ideas for us, and we were nothing but douchebags with horrible ideas, and he was endlessly trying to wrangle this eleven-headed beast. Out of those eleven heads were coming almost all bad ideas of the way we should operate as a business. We were the least savvy bunch of people you could ever meet, and Dixon was precisely what we needed.

James Dixon: I probably just did what I did, which is give them the best recommendation and advice I could. I obviously knew how to deal in that world of cable and comedy, and when it came to dealing with the network and the deals themselves and the budgets and all that fun stuff, I was pretty skilled, I'd say, even back then.

They were a captive audience, and they were really a terrific bunch of guys, and I had deep affection for them. I still do. I really loved working with those guys, and I'm not just saying that. They were really so fun and pleasant and so appreciative and so kind. It was nice to be able to guide neophytes in a way that you could tell they were appreciative and they were. I was doing right by them, and they knew it, and it was good. ... I knew that world real well, and I think I took pretty good care of them. It wasn't easy to navigate eleven members, how you broke things up, and what they should make and who got what. It was pretty much favored nations, meaning everybody made the same. ... We just kind of went into it as all-for-one and one-for-all.

NYU graduation house band

CHAPTER 12

"You Wrote It, You Watch It"

"The premise of the show was they interviewed people on the street: 'What was the worst first date you ever had?' ... We said, 'This is a terrible idea. Why don't we make up sketches (and) then go cast our friends to say a story that was like the sketch?'"[1]

Robert Ben Garant

A new sketch show was kicking off in 1992, in which MTV viewers would write letters about weird things that happened to them, and actors would perform a reenactment. "You Wrote It, You Watch It" was hosted by Jon Stewart. At a San Francisco Sketchfest show in 2012, Ben, Kerri and Tom showed clips from the show. Kerri said, "This show, it's amazing it was ever on television." Tom called it "an abomination." And Ben said, "You think MTV is bad now? We invented MTV was bad."

Back in 1992, David Wain's senior film, "Aisle Six," was getting some film festival attention, and he tried to parlay that into getting The State's foot in the door at MTV.

David Wain: I was just naturally hanging around the hallways, and that's how they saw my film, and that's how they asked me to become involved with "You Wrote It, You Watch It," which led to me bringing The State into it. ... I was asked if I wanted to be a director on [it]. I had a different way that I thought would work better, which was interviewing people on the street and then intercutting it with their stories. [MTV] said, "No, that's not the way to do it."

Kerri Kenney-Silver: They were going to have different sketch groups perform and act out these letters people had written. David kept saying, "I have a sketch group," and they're like, "That's nice, but this is a network, and we're not doing that."

David Wain: I just went back to the group, and we grabbed our Hi8 video camera.

Thomas Lennon: David really got us our break by pushing for all that stuff. They hadn't said yes to us. ... We shot some sketches for that the weekend of graduation. We shot a sketch called "Anything Goes" with me and Kerri and something else, too. That was our group policy: why wait for them to say yes? They'll probably say no, but just start shooting and doing stuff, and there's a chance that it could happen.

David Wain: In the course of the night, we shot all these reenactments and stole the costumes and presented these three finished sketches to MTV as a demo to what it could be like. They were kind of blown away, both by how fast [we were] and probably how good it was. They were like, "Who are these people?" "This is my group." At the end of the day, we said, "Hire us all as a total unit, as a group, or not."

Eileen Katz: I felt so fortunate to be working with them every day, starting with "You Wrote It, You Watch It," until the day that they told us they were going to the networks. I remember this night so clearly. I was with [President of MTV Productions] Doug [Herzog], and we had just come from a Jon Stewart taping, and we were on our way in a car to a rehearsal that The State was having. I remember saying, "Doug, we are the luckiest people in the world because right now we are working with 'The Show of Shows' for this generation. They're it," and Jon was it. We were working with them at a time that will be remembered.

Michael Patrick Jann: I didn't do any classes my last semester at school because I already had enough credits. So I was more or less lurking around NYU and working as a projectionist there and trying to make enough money to buy tacos to eat to keep myself from wasting away. I sort of made the commitment to myself: "I'm not getting a job as a waiter. I'm not doing anything else. I'm going to work as a director or not at all." And then it happened in six months. Absurd! That's just crazy.

Somewhere in a past life I must've done something good. Among the sort of horrible things, something good must have happened there.

Michael Ian Black: We were arrogant enough that it seemed like the correct next step. It seemed like, yes, this is what should be happening. There was relief that we weren't going to have to break up the band, although I think we all believe that if MTV hadn't happened, we were still going to be doing what we do. We would figure out a way to do it in theaters and become this New York institution or something. Whatever it was, it was woefully naïve.

In the beginning, when we were shooting videos for "You Wrote it, You Watch It," we felt like intruders a little bit. One of the first things we shot was about what it's like to work at MTV. It features us roaming the hallways and the band Dee-Lite having its own office, similar to what ESPN did later with their spots. I think that reflected a kind of wide-eyed enthusiasm and excitement about working there, but it didn't feel surreal because we didn't quite feel employed by them. We were a small part of a small show on the network.

While The State was just getting rolling at MTV, Kerri was dipping her toe in the waters that a lot of actors are drawn to — rock 'n' roll.

Kerri Kenney-Silver: A lot of us already had apartments by that point. I was living in the closet of [my former NYU theater classmate] Nina Hellman. Her boyfriend at the time, who used to be my boyfriend, Craig Wedren, had a bunch of instruments lying around. So we started a band together, [Cake Like]. Everybody had been out of the dorms at that point. It was a small closet but was a very nice closet.

Craig Wedren: Oh, God, it's so much more sordid than that. Kerri and I dated very briefly but very intensely. I was nineteen; she was eighteen. It was a very, very, very, very, very, very intense, passionate, short-lived romance. Then, I started dating Nina, and Nina and I were living together, and I was on tour all the time with [my band] Shudder to Think.

Nina Hellman: Kerri and I, we were always dating musicians and going to see shows. This other couple, Ganza and this girl Pumpkin (yes, her name is Pumpkin), they were starting a band, and at one point I picked up a guitar, and after Craig was like, "You have to play guitar! You have to play guitar!" I came home, and I said to Kerri, "Hey, let's start a band," and she said, "OK, let's do it," and our boyfriends at the time were really encouraging about it.

Kerri Kenney-Silver: Nina and I were both working at this place called The Cleaver Company. It had a bakery, and we did cookie decorating. Nina came up with the name. I think she liked the idea that if you were baking brownies, on the side of the box, it said, "for moist or cake-like brownies." We were always little bakers and crafters and loved doing that kind of stuff. So she thought that would be a good name for us.

Craig Wedren: I was always trying to push them to just get into a room and pick up instruments, like, "Let's just rent a space and bring a bunch of instruments, and everybody can suck, and it would be great," like the Shags or early Sonic Youth. "You don't need to play an instrument. You're all very creative — not to mention adorable — girls. So get over it, and let's do it." We just brought a bunch of beer into a space, and I think it was Eli Janney and me and Kerri and Nina and it could've been Pumpkin Wentzel.

Kerri Kenney-Silver: I loved being on stage, but the idea of singing in a band was never something I thought would happen. We used to go to shows all the time and loved listening to new music. So many of our friends and boyfriends and people around us were in bands, but it didn't seem that we were gonna become one of those people. It just seemed like we were playing house as if we were just acting like those people. We never thought we were gonna leave the practice stage.

Craig Wedren: Kerri and Nina, their music just clicked, and their ideas were extraordinary and extraordinarily unique. I would just kind of hang out and help with ideas and produce the records and just [be] kind of a cheerleader/sounding board.

Nina Hellman: We decided to rent a rehearsal studio, and we started writing a couple songs here and there. We didn't even know how to plug in the guitars, and [Kerri] wasn't even playing bass at that point. She was sort of playing drums. We had a first drummer who left in one day, and then we met Jody [Seifert] who ended up being our drummer, and then Kerri picked up the bass.

Craig Wedren: I thought they were just an incredible band, and people didn't take them that seriously because they were fucking hot and fashionable and didn't know how to play technically that well.

... There's a straight theatrical aspect to their delivery and their ideas which wasn't cool in the early '90s because everything was sort of slacker understated.

Kerri Kenney-Silver: I would just work it around The State, and it was doable, of course; when you're twenty-two years old, you don't have to sleep.

Nina Hellman: It was kind of a hobby that went out of control. We were really just having fun, and one gig led to the next gig. We never really imagined what ended up happening would've happened.

There was another band practicing in the same rehearsal space, and they're like, "We're doing a show at our friend's loft above the Pyramid Club. You guys should do it." We were like, "Uh, OK," and we had five songs at that time. We did it, and that was our first gig, and then somebody else saw us there and was like, "Play at our benefit at Brownie's," which is another club in New York that was pretty popular in the '90s. We played that show.

My friend, Steven Bernstein, he's a jazz trumpeter and a composer; we had played him a little recording tape that we had made. He loved it so much, and he brought a musician named John Zorn who also had a couple of record labels, and this guy Marc Ribot, who's this really amazing jazz guitarist, and they just came up to us after [a show] and were like, "That was amazing; how do you make those guitar sounds? Do you have enough songs for an album?" We just sort of lied and were like, "Sure!" Jon Zorn agreed to put out our first album. It all sort of happened by accident, in a weird way.

He gave us five thousand dollars. We went to a studio in Williamsburg. Craig and Eli [Janney], our boyfriends at the time, they produced it, and we did it in five days. Zorn put it out, and we had this great, really raw album. We hired a publicist, and that's when it just kind of took off because people liked our story. We were these girls who had never played, and we picked up our instruments, and now these really well-known jazz players are digging our stuff. So it was just a good story. One magazine article led to another magazine article. ... Ric Ocasek found us somehow; I don't even know how.

Kerri Kenney-Silver: I imagine that if we had planned it, it wouldn't have gone as well as it did. I think it was the nature of an organic love of music and of each other and what we were doing. People caught onto that, and it was exciting to them and to us. Everything that happened was to our surprise, from the first show to Neil Young's interest to Ric Ocasek's interest. Every single turn was a shock to us.

These are idols of mine for a lifetime and again. ... Obviously those guys don't have a heck of a lot of free time; so I don't believe they were just humoring us. Nor was Rolling Stone or Spin magazine or the fans that came out to the shows all around the world.

Performance is my favorite part of myself. I am at my best and at my happiest and feel most like myself in my body when I'm playing someone else or on stage in front of people. I'm most uncomfortable and feel out of my body when I'm in my normal life. So on stage in any capacity, be it music or comedy or drama, I feel in my element. However, music was a lot scarier because I still, to this day, don't consider myself a musician at all, by any stretch of the imagination.

I think we fit into a genre that was happening, and I don't compare myself to my musician friends of today or yesterday. I never felt like, "Hey, look at us, we're all doing the same thing." I felt like they let the kids come play at the grown-ups' table for a little while but never losing the sense that I was not one of the grown-ups. It was scarier to be on stage as myself in Cake Like than it was to be in character with The State or anywhere else. So I took on a sort of persona on stage with Cake Like to protect myself, and maybe I thought it was a bit more entertaining. I think it was a bit of a smoke screen.

Craig Wedren: They were amazing, and they had the same love/loathe difficult things that all the members of The State had, that thing that if you can make it through your twenties, you can probably work with somebody for the rest of your life, but it's much more likely to implode — which it ultimately did for them.

Nina Hellman: It was all really surreal but fun. Then we signed with Neil Young's label, but The State was going on all that time. So we were very much a divided-focus group. I was doing plays all the time, and Kerri was doing The State. It was hard to lead this double life because both of them were doing pretty well, but we couldn't devote ourselves to touring, which is what really makes a band successful.

Kerri Kenney-Silver: [Acting] was always my first priority and the same for Nina in her acting career and Jody in her fashion career. So when Mom pulled up the station wagon and said, "OK, summer's over. Time to go; we're moving," it had a natural end in that sense. It was very sad. What kind of music would we still be making today if we were in the same town? I know we would be. That's how it ended. We decided the show needed to move and we needed to move for our careers, and that was that.

Elliot Roberts at Avant Records, Neil's label off of Warner Brothers, he always reminds us, "You owe us another album," lovingly. We would love to, and I think people would dig it, and I think it would be a really cool thing to do. It's like The State always talking about wanting to do another show; we would love to. It's a lot of people in a lot of different parts to the country.

Cake Like ended up recording three albums: "Delicious" on John Zorn's label, Avant, and "Bruiser Queen" and "Goodbye, So What" on Neil Young's Vapor label. Cake Like actually existed throughout the MTV "State" years and into "Viva Variety." The band split when Kerri moved to Los Angeles in the late '90s but did reunite for drummer Jody Seifert's wedding about ten years ago.

Kerri Kenney-Silver: [Back at MTV], we had an office, which was also a closet. So I was living in the closet and working in a closet. It was at MTV, and they gave us the storage closet. So there wasn't room for chairs because it was eleven people. We would sit on the floor, knees to knees, and we had a lamp. We were so psyched to have an office at MTV that we didn't care.

Eileen Katz: Eleven of them plus their management, it was almost like one of those clown cars. How many of them can you fit into the utility closet? "All right, if we clear out the paint cans and the light bulbs, maybe we can fit a typewriter in there." It was ridiculous, but it was theirs, and they got to close the door. That's all that they asked.

"Can we close the door?" I'm like, "Close the door."

David Wain: They gave us a fifty-dollar-a-week budget for props and costumes. Otherwise, we had our own camera that we used. We have one room for eleven of us with a VCR. That was it.

Kerri Kenney-Silver: I remember them bringing us a big, fat, phone book "Bible" on how to work the editing machine. It was one of those old reel-to-reel machines. I remember being like, "I leave that to you, David." A few of the guys figured out how to work it, and they sat there and did it. It was a true do-it-yourself show. My mom would watch and go, "Hey, that's my lamp. Wait, that's my chair. I need that back!"

Robert Ben Garant: The premise of the show was they interviewed people on the street: "What was the worst first date you ever had?" "What is your best 'Stairway to Heaven' story?" Very frequently, we all sat around and said, "This is a terrible idea. Why don't we make up sketches [and] then go cast our friends to say a story that was like the sketch?"

Ben credits Mike Jann's direction with helping shape the look of MTV in the '90s.

Michael Ian Black: It did feel fast and furious. We were doing everything ourselves. We didn't have a crew. We learned how to operate sound, and we learned how to get props. We learned how to make costumes. We literally did every aspect of the shoots by ourselves. That kind of DIY approach was how we approached our live shows, and transferring that to television felt natural. I don't remember the pace of "You Wrote It, You Watch It" being particularly difficult although it might've been. We did some ambitious things. The pace really picked up once we started doing a television show, mostly in terms of generating material. Once we were shooting, things required however long they required. We would shoot maybe two sketches a day, maybe three. And it felt quick, but it didn't feel hurried. Probably a lot of that had to do with Mike Jann being a good director in understanding how to allocate time.

Michael Patrick Jann: I was really gung ho, like, "Oh, yeah, we're getting this shot," putting myself on the hood of the car. I lit, shot and edited all that stuff and picked out most of the music, too. Not even thinking about it, like when you're that age, you don't really have anything else in your life.

There were a lot of decisions that I had to make on my own, and coming into the group late, it was sort of a benefit and continues to be a benefit in that I'm perfectly comfortable making lots of decisions on my own and not second-guessing myself which, in a groupthink environment, can sometimes create tension. Ultimately, I think it was a good thing for the group, and it continued on through the series to a certain point of deciding how to do things — because this is my thing. I would certainly have an opinion about writing, but I wouldn't tell Tom, "No, write this sketch; don't write that sketch." Everybody was sort of like a free agent in the area that they were good at.

Eileen Katz: There was so much bad dreck out there and so many bad scripts to read through and so many endless nights in clubs where you just kind of wanted to slash your wrists. Then you see The State, and it's like, "Oh, my God." They are insanely prolific, original writers. They can write jokes. They can create an arc. They can have a beginning, a middle and an end.

I know that sounds really silly, but I'd worked with a lot of other comedy groups who went on to do great things, too, and every sketch would end with just everybody running into the hills because they couldn't write an ending. "OK, everybody throws everything, and there's anarchy, and everybody runs for the hills." I'm like, "Is that really an end?" but these guys, they were just gifted. How they found each other and balanced each other's strengths and weaknesses and built on each other's creativity, it was amazing.

Watch the stuff now, and it's just smart writing, and they're just consummate performers. They commit to these ridiculous characters, outlandish scenes. It's funny, and it works because they make it work.

Thomas Lennon: We were working with super-antiquated equipment. Video editing machines were the size of two walk-in freezers. The editing equipment that comes on a Mac totally standard is one hundred thousand times better than what we were working with. We were always happy to work very fast. Everyone in the group is compulsive in one way or another. We were happy to do stuff on the fly.

Ken Marino: We pushed all the desks to the wall, and we taped off a four square, and we wound up playing naked four square from time to time. I didn't play naked four square, but I know that Tom, Kerri and I don't know who else played naked four square. And we would just play clothed four square, but naked four square did happen in that room.

Robert Ben Garant: Every step of the way was super fun. Everybody turned it up a notch. Mike Jann went from being this precious "Set your shot" NYU filmmaker and immediately switched gears to "I'm going to make this look like MTV." The shorts that we did for "You Wrote It, You Watch It" defined the style of MTV for years. We always kept a little movement in the camera. MTV really didn't do that until us, all that weird, fast cutting and Batman angles on stuff. I know there's one million music video directors who say they invented that, and a lot of that is Mike Jann creating this cheap, crappy look, but intentional — just a lot of frenetic movement and a lot of fast cuts, over coverage of stuff. Everybody just switched gears.

One of the first things we did was this parody of The B-52s' videos. It's pretty good. It's cheap. There is a shot where Tom is standing on top of a car to make it look like he's flying, very dangerous. It looks like we spent a lot of money on that thing, and we really didn't. Everybody really stepped it up a notch when we got to the shorts. Everybody knew this was a big chance.

Thomas Lennon: There's no trick to that or anything. We drove a car, and I'm standing on the roof playing a tambourine. If we did that in a movie, it would be with wires and safety checks. I just did that. Joe or Ben is driving the car, and I'm standing up surfing on this car. The policy of the group is, if you didn't do it, somebody else certainly would. ... but it sort of set the tone that we were all willing to kind of put our lives at risk if we thought it would make the sketch better. I feel like most of the people in the group were like, "OK, cool, if it's gonna be funnier, fuck it, let's do it." There was a lot of commitment to the group.

Robert Ben Garant: We couldn't have done it if we were union. If we tried to do it in the way you're supposed to with a real crew, each one would've taken a week. Everybody was moving the lights and doing makeup. If we tried to do that with a real makeup person, a real sound person, a real gaffer and a real grip, each one of those things would've taken a week. We did them in ten hours nonstop. We just did everything.

Thomas Lennon: I was pretty proud of my Fred [Schneider impression]. There was some discussion of Ben playing Fred, where there was a tense moment when I wasn't sure I was going to get that role. ... We went to vote, and it was super-awkward when you'd be voting in front of a group of your friends.

Michael Patrick Jann: I'm still really proud of our stuff. What we did there was as handmade and as DIY as anything that had ever been on real, non-public-access television before. It's super-crude, made out of passion and some desperation, but some of it is crazy funny. There was no YouTube or Funny or Die then, so it had a pretty original feel for TV comedy. I'm also proud of it because it captured the spirit of the group, the voice and the feeling. It's probably not hall-of-fame material, but you know, it was way funnier than "120 Minutes."

Doug Herzog (then president of MTV Productions and current president of Viacom Music and Entertainment):

There were a bunch of sketches that were just really funny, and the whole thing was kind of fascinating to me in that they were all just out of NYU. ... Tom Lennon is doing this B-52's Fred Schneider imitation, and they just immediately made an impact — enough that we decided to give them a show.

Joe Lo Truglio: It was also pretty exciting because we were finally getting paid to do something on TV. There was a lot of growing pains then because, remember, we're suddenly finding a role within The State on TV, as opposed to The State in a black box theater. ... I remember that we worked very hard. We seemed to not rest at all. I think there were some growing pains trying to figure out what the roles were going to be, if we all were going to direct every sketch, if there were going to be two main directors or three main or if there were going be any number of directors. That was tough because, at the time, none of us knew what our strengths would be. I feel like all of us wanted to do everything.

When we were doing theater, we were all directing, we were all writing, we were all performing. Just from a logistical standpoint, that was too time-consuming to do on television. It was hard to come to terms with what your strengths were. ... That was where we started to figure out who was what.

I remember getting along with the other directors [on "You Wrote It, You Watch It"]. There were ten directors, us being one of the ten. I feel like there was a somewhat notable director that ended up doing some moderately well-known things. There wasn't really any conflict with the other directors. ... We were so green as to how to do this. You're wanting to figure out what your strengths were among the people who may have also wondered the same thing. That was a little tricky.

Thomas Lennon: That was sort of handy with about half of us coming out of the film school; everybody could operate all the equipment. Pretty much everybody could edit; everybody could operate stuff. ... The film school [at NYU] fucking kicked my ass; the film school was really hard. It got us on a schedule of us constantly generating material. So I actually feel like I owe a lot to the NYU film school.

Todd, left, and Tom, third from left, with two unidentified chickens

---

Kerri Kenney-Silver: Some things that we've done I would be less embarrassed if it was a porn that had made it out. ... No doubt they were ambitious. Ambitious doesn't always equal good.

"Bad Date" from "You Wrote It ..." is a precursor to The State sketch "Dreamboy" and both star Kerri and Kevin, who also wrote them, and he plays the douchiest of bags to hilarity.

Kevin Allison: He was an arrogant guy with a goatee and slicked back hair, who speaks as if he's really educated and sophisticated. All he's doing the entire time is insulting her with his nose up in the air. It was kind of like "negging," before the pick-up artist trend popularized that concept. It came about because the girl we interviewed [on "You Wrote It..."] said, "I went on a date with this guy, and he was terrible. He seemed to think he was going to impress me by insulting me." We set up in a little room, me and Kerri at a table as if we're in a restaurant having a date. We would just run the camera, and I would think of some crazy shit to say to her. The one I always remember, I say, "Oh, I'm sorry, am I kicking you under the table?" And I lean in and whisper, "In my head I am."

Kerri Kenney-Silver: "Bad Date" is really funny. That's Kevin. That really is truly funny. Oh, my God, I remember when he pitched that. It was like, "Bam, brilliant!"

Thomas Lennon: It runs the gamut. I think there's stuff that totally holds up, and it's hilarious, and then every once in a while we let down some bombs on "You Wrote It..." for sure.

Robert Ben Garant: Those were just gags. What was great about those was we didn't have to write the stories but just come up with the big concepts. We really were just reenacting the stories that people told us. It was just jokes. We were just thinking of jokes, and we kind of shined. I think the fact that we had to write them really fast really helped us. Who knows what would've happened if somebody would've seen this and said, "We want you guys to write a movie." I think we would've broken up over the process of it because I think it would've been too much stuff for all of us to agree on.

Even eight years after the group, when we got the movie deal, it fell apart because we couldn't agree on a movie. At that time, it was just the idea of writing jokes. Mike Jann threw in a slow-motion "Raging Bull" joke. If we had time, we probably would've argued and not done that, but we had to do it. It was really fast turnover. ... You had to do stuff even if one of the group or half the group didn't like it, just because we had to produce tons of material. ... Another great thing about that was because we produced so many so fast, we had to split up. Some people were there at the Fred Schneider piece. A lot of the group wasn't there. A lot of our best happened when the whole group was not there.

I think you can certainly [see] our enthusiasm. There's no nerves. Nobody's nervous. No matter how stupid they are, it's really confident. When you look on Funny or Die or College Humor and you see a lot of young college groups, you can tell the ones that are nervous. A lot of them are just a little intimidated. We were not intimidated. Those are pretty balls-out.

Eileen Katz: It was all of our first experiences. That was the beauty of MTV at that time. It was kind of like we're fixing the plane and flying it at the same time.

Kerri Kenney Silver: "Wrote It" was like a blink of an eye. Our involvement was short-lived. The show was short-lived. Everybody had other jobs, I believe, most people at least. I worked at a catering company called The Cleaver Company in Tribeca, and I worked in the bakery section and kept working there all through "The State" mostly because I loved it and could work night hours making cookies and stuff. It was really fun. Most people had jobs here and there, and by the time "The State" was well underway, most everybody left their jobs, and that was our full-time thing.

Michael Showalter: I didn't really have a strong opinion about ["You Wrote It"] one way or the other, but I liked the idea that it was like a real job, sort of, like it was a professional gig. When you're starting out, you're just trying to get jobs. You don't care what they are, and I thought that we did a really good job of taking their basic premise and turning it into our own thing and making it our own.

That was like boot camp. Up until that point, we were a stage group. We were doing videos, but it was the first time that we established ourselves as being proficient in the video medium. That had a lot to do with Mike [Jann], and the vocabulary of MTV, we sort of knew that vocabulary pretty well.

*A State cast photo for the pilot with co-manager Steven Starr, left,
and guest star Meat Loaf, center*

CHAPTER 13

The Pitch and Pilot

"We were so cocky; at age twenty-two, we were like, 'We're the funniest people. You guys have no idea what you're talking about. Leave us the fuck alone, or we'll walk.'"

David Wain

MTV wanted to see several ideas for The State's forthcoming sketch show, but what the members had already shown MTV on stage was the show they wanted to do. Still, they had to assemble several ideas to please the network.

Here are highlights from The State's pitch:

■ The Basic Idea: Each week begins with a group of eleven characters in a situation — different characters each week. This situation is visited again in the middle and end of the show. The rest of the show is linked to this spine by overlapping characters, themes, locations, graphics, and other transitions a la "Molt"... all related to the theme ranging from literal to contrived ... The concept takes advantage of this large group...

■ Possible Series Titles:
    o State: Eleven
    o The State and You
    o The State: Camera Ready
    o The State: Such Monsters
    o The State: Full Frontal Comedy

■ Our strength is our cohesiveness, our ensemble — so to establish early strong the idea of this group as a unit unlike "SNL"

■ Each half-hour has a thematic grounding: the next step beyond Python

■ Cliffhangers: Before commercials, no matter what's happening, there comes a major cliffhanger, which ends negatively when we return from commercial

■ Contract notes:
    o Make sure we still own our material
    o Make sure they have no hold whatsoever on the name "the State"

Todd Holoubek: When you're a television executive, you're like, "Show me what you have." So we did, and it was the same with "You Wrote It, You Watch It." We showed them what we could do, and they were like, "So..." and we did it again, and I think it made everybody feel better because this was the beginning of the working relationship. It would've just been arrogant to say, "No, why do you want us to do a show?" That would have just been stupid. "OK, you'd like to see what we can do?" We've got to do a show, and we hadn't really put on a live show in a while, and so we just made this great, really awesome show.

David Wain: MTV people came to us and said "OK, let's talk about what 'The State' would be." "'The State' would be a sketch show." They were like, "OK, give us three different ideas of what type of show you would like to do." We said, "We don't have three ideas. We have one idea." We sort of decided to pitch them three ideas. The first one was the show we wanted to do. The second one was some weird, I forget what it was. The third, we decided it was just improv. Whatever somebody said, let's just go with it, and we made up something.

We knew that there was no other pitch. We would have links between the sketches, touchstones, runners that we would keep going back to throughout the episode. That's what we ended up doing in the pilot. ... One of the things I find interesting, thinking about it now, it just couldn't be a more different landscape. There were very few groups. There were very few cable channels. It was a much more casual situation. The people running MTV were all in their twenties. It was a totally different situation. There was no such thing as Comedy Central. There was no Adult Swim.

Doug Herzog: They were very untested. A lot of credit goes to Eileen. [She] was the first person to ever say to me, "You should pay attention to Jon Stewart; he's great." She was also the first person who brought The State to our attention. So a lot of props and credit to her.

At that time, MTV hadn't really dipped its toe too much into the comedy waters. There had been "Remote Control" already but nothing like a sketch comedy show. That was an exciting project for us, and you knew they were going to be cheap, which was always important to us back in those days at MTV because we didn't have any money. They were self-sufficient. They would write and perform it themselves and, to a certain extent, direct. This would be a great sort of one-stop shopping. We thought about doing our own "Saturday Night Live." "What's its reason for being? 'Saturday Night Live's' reason for being is it's Saturday night; it's live; it's New York City. So this group was an organic group that came together at NYU, and they were an entity in themselves, and it just seemed to make sense.

Todd Holoubek: It was very weird when your dream comes true in your early twenties. It was excellent. It was very bizarre to plan it and actually see it really, really come together. It was very different than "I'm going to build a deck in the back of the house" and then do it. When I was very young, I remember meeting a VJ from VH1. He said, "What are you going to do when you graduate from high school?" and I said, "I'm going to move to New York and be an actor," and he got a great laugh out of that. That was the attitude that a lot of people have. We would joke about it. "New York actor? How many tips do you get when you're serving coffee?" And that's what you're up against, this global stereotype of actor in New York.

So to get there was panic and elatement at the same time — and a little bit of imposter syndrome. "Hey, wait a minute, we shouldn't have let these guys in here." When you think about how other celebrities got on television, you have this picture of their story, and it's all fabricated by the movies, right? So, when it actually happens you're like, "Wait, this isn't how it's supposed to happen." But it is. You do good work. You meet the right people. You sort of follow your heart, and it paid off! Usually following your heart doesn't pay off like this. A lot of time following your heart loses you friends, you know, because you're not toeing the line. We followed our heart; we did what we thought was best, and it worked out.

Because it was MTV, and they hadn't done any real live-action television like this, it felt very much like an experiment. For all practical purposes, we're like a music video station. Oh, were we wrong!

David Wain: I had watched MTV since it launched the summer of '81. I was a huge fan. I visited MTV the first time not too long after that, and I remember meeting Nina Blackwood. Bendis is buddies with Nina Blackwood. I remember meeting her and Martha Quinn and Alan Hunter, seeing that original set, and being beyond starstruck and blown away.

Michael Ian Black: Oh yeah, I watched a lot of MTV. I was fascinated with MTV. I auditioned to be an MTV VJ when I was eighteen or something. Obviously, I did not become an MTV VJ, which I have to say is probably a good thing.

They were just getting into original programming. In their minds, sketch comedy looked a certain way. Although we disagreed, we couldn't articulate really what we thought a sketch comedy show should look like, other than just start making the sketches we wanted to make.

Michael Patrick Jann: MTV was kind of bullshit. Of course, it was the greatest thing ever when I was a young teenager, and it was like, "Oh, my God, Madonna or Dexy's Midnight Runners, the Human League," all that visual aesthetic that you'd never seen before, but by the time we graduated from college, they weren't even into hip-hop yet. They were still dragging their feet on that. It was a lot of Wilson Phillips.

We were our own thing. People were into rock; they weren't into comedy. It wasn't cool; it was to us. I think we were lucky in that nobody gave a shit. There was no such thing as [Upright Citizens Brigade]. There was UCB literally, the original four: Matt [Besser], Matt [Walsh], Amy [Poehler] and Ian [Roberts], but there was no anything. There was a small, underground comedy thing that was just starting to happen. There was sort of the Rebar scene, where you would see Marc Maron or Todd Berry, and everybody would get up and do their sort of I-just-wrote-this-down-in-my-tiny-notebook routine, and people got involved, and that was just starting. ... We had to make up our own thing because there wasn't anything around.

Michael Ian Black: We were making enough money to live. New York was expensive, but it felt cheaper than it does now. Nobody was making any big money. I was bringing home maybe five hundred bucks a week or something. Maybe less. That's having your own television show. It wasn't a lot of money.

The members of "The State" were essentially hired hands for "You Wrote It, You Watch It," but this new show was going to be all theirs, and they were very protective of their brand of comedy and not used to answering to anybody in regard to material or style.

Michael Showalter: It was definitely some validation of what we believed, which was we were a really good sketch group. To have that platform was some validation of that. It also fueled our collective ego. ... We were destined to all meet the way we met and come together the way we did, and it was destiny that we were going to go onto MTV and make our own show. That was always somehow predetermined, and we were just living it out.

Joe Lo Truglio: I think we were so worried about being just another sketch show; that's where we got real uppity about it, about not doing the things the other sketch shows were doing, not realizing, of course, that's the formula for a sketch show, and that's what made many of those shows popular and memorable. At the time, you just have this overwhelming, blinding desire to do something so different because you just don't want to be another "blank." I think that's why we were so sensitive to it.

Doug Herzog: I'm sure there were conversations of "Do we need all eleven? How about this guy? What about that guy?"

Robert Ben Garant: To be honest, we were real assholes. Looking back, as a forty-four-year-old guy who's done a lot of television, [the executives at MTV] were great. The freedom that we were given, and the opportunity they gave us, and how weird they let us be on the show, and how they didn't make us put a star in the group, or they didn't cut people they didn't like, knowing all that now, I'm like, "God, we were real pricks to those guys." At the time, we hated them. Any note they gave us, we thought they were crazy and insulting us. We thought we knew everything. We really didn't think anybody should have any opinion at all. They should just let us do what we do, and we hated them. We really genuinely thought they were idiots. ... We were wrong.

Michael Patrick Jann: One of the best things you can learn about in show business is you're going to work with/for people that you don't agree with. You can either be a dick about it — which everybody probably has at some point in their careers — or you can be like, "I don't care how much I disagree with your note or how much I dislike you, I will still come up with a way to take that note and make it gold." There's a phrase, "How do I spin this shit into gold?"

Todd Holoubek: In a way, they became new members of the group. We had a producer. We had an executive producer. We had two agents. All of the sudden, they became other voices in the group. So it just got louder.

You're dealing with a lot of opinions. They were like, "This is what the network is looking at; this is our focus." In many ways, we stood our ground, and instead of having the network dictate what we should do, we presented our interpretation of what they were

Sample logos by Joe

asking for. We worked very hard to keep our own voice. It was very hard to keep your own voice when you're working with a major network, because you want things to go well; you want your career to move forward. It's one of the interesting dualities of being in that position.

And, on a side note, I think the main theme of "Lord of the Rings" is that once you gain this sort of power, you start to fear losing, as opposed to never really having it before. Not that we were like Sauron, but his whole incredible fear of losing his power is what made him try to find the ring because that was ultimate power. We did not have ultimate power by any stretch of the imagination. You know when you're in college and you're basically producing your own shows, you can tell anyone to fuck off if they don't like what you're doing. That's why you're in school. You experiment and do things that work, and some things don't, but when you're on the network, shows will disappear for no reason at all, right? At times it was very uncomfortable because we weren't used to having three more voices in the group — one of them being a major cable network telling us where we should drive our writing, directing and acting. But we were very fortunate to have enough voices that we could balance it out.

Michael Patrick Jann: I really liked and respected Doug, probably at that time mostly in a conceited, twenty-year-old way. "Well, they were smart enough to give us a show; they can't be all bad."

Doug Herzog: This executive, Joe Davola, famously was always pestering them for catchphrases which led, of course, to, "I dip my balls in it."

They were part of the MTV audience; so that again was how it worked at MTV. We were looking for people who really reflected the audience, and they certainly reflected a part of the audience, no question about it.

They had a more eclectic approach, for sure. Back in those days, MTV wasn't making a lot of original programming. What little we were making was very much MTV-centric. The voice was very much MTV's voice in the shows we were making. The State had its own voice, and I'm not sure we completely understood that or even accepted that early on.

There was definitely a surreal quality to some of their stuff and sort of scatological ... I thought it was out there. I couldn't quite wrap my head around some of it. [Some of it] was right on the money. I'm trying to program a network and get ratings, right? I was definitely coming from a more conventional standpoint in that regard, but I could appreciate it all, for sure. ... I'm ultimately a little more "Reno 911!" than I am Stella.

Kevin Allison: I just rewatched the movie "Amadeus," which I first saw in '85 when it was released, so I would have been fifteen years old. It really struck me, rewatching this movie, how I remember being so passionate about how fucked up it was that the powers that be didn't realize that Mozart was just a total fucking genius and give him all the money — despite the fact that he was out of control. There just must have been something in our youth that gave us the impression that there is a big-moneyed structure, and a lot of it might have been the early "SNL" folks, just hearing their stories and knowing that they had to continuously face fights with censors over what they were trying to do there.

We just came into it with fists swinging. I don't think anyone in the group approaches projects that way anymore. I think that we're very much, "Let's find common ground with whoever we're working with and do our best to make things as fresh and original along with that person." When we first came in, we just assumed that they were imbeciles, and they were the powers that be, and, unfortunately, I think that attitude harmed me more than anyone else in the group because I continued to feel that way. I really adopted that as a persecution complex, which is why I got so riled up about Mozart again the other night. I felt like I was the guy in The State who was even more misunderstood by the powers that be than anyone else. I think anyone [else] in The State, if they heard me saying this now, they'd be like, "Yeah, Kevin always did feel put upon by the fact that some of the executives at MTV or agents and managers didn't get him."

Robert Ben Garant: Nobody really liked Kevin's work, and I don't mean within the group — but the executives. People didn't like Todd's stuff, and they really didn't like Kevin's stuff to the point where the suggestion came out that we shouldn't write the author's name on the top of the script. Some of us fought and were like, "No, no, no, people need to know who wrote it because we all have a different style, and we think that you read them slightly differently if you know whose voice it is." It was so some of the people's work would get through.

Michael Ian Black: In a certain way, it was hard to fit in at a corporation. It was hard to feel like you were part of the Viacom family. That almost feels oxymoronic to say, the Viacom family. They tend to treat people pretty badly. They're very exploitative of their employees. To sort of fit in at that structure was uncomfortable for us, but also it flew in the face of our own self-definition to warmly embrace corporate life. Part of who we were was to reject the idea of working for the man, even though we absolutely were. We really felt it was incumbent on us to give the finger any chance we got, which is right, I guess, for a punk rock sketch comedy troupe but also totally hypocritical.

Kerri Kenney-Silver: I always felt a combination of freedom and restriction. I think some of it was self-imposed because we liked the idea that we were fighting against the man, even though we were on MTV, and we were the first comedy show, we could kind of do whatever we wanted. I think we liked the idea of feeling like we're doing out-there stuff for America. It had been done in England but not as much in America, certainly not in our generation. "Laugh-In" was silly and wacky but maybe a bit more linear than what we were doing. I think it was a combination.

Robert Ben Garant: [Our first producer, Jim Sharp,] was really the George Martin of The State, very genuinely. I think that our show would've sucked without Jim Sharp. He had just done "Almost Live!" in Seattle, which was another sketch show, which we saw and we hated because we were too cool for the room.

Jim Sharp: We produced sixty-five [episodes of "Almost Live!"] in two and a half months, so I was a little burned out and ready to stay home in Los Angeles. I got a call from MTV saying, "There's this sketch group, and they're really young, and they're really green. They haven't really done television; they've done a lot of theater and off-Broadway." They did "You Wrote It, You Watch It."

In their very aggressive and proactive way, they approached MTV and said, "Hey, we can do way better than this" and they did. That actually really fits, that kind of confidence or arrogance. Call it what you want.

They said, "We want to do a sketch show," and I said, "No." "Can we send you a tape?" I said, "Sure." My wife and I watched it, and my wife goes, "Whoa, these guys are kind of special." I go, "Yeah, that's kind of interesting." I had a job in L.A. that I was up for and really wanted, and it was being delayed so I went out there and met with them. I was the thirteenth producer that they interviewed. I remember saying to MTV, "Wait a minute, they haven't done this, and they're gonna make the decision?" and they go, "Yeah, well, you know..."

My lawyer called me that night and said, "They called, and we're gonna have the job offer tomorrow. They want you. They're so sorry it's been delayed." So I went into the meeting with The State with the job I wanted in my hip pocket. So I didn't pull any punches. I don't think I was abusive or a jerk or anything, but I had the job I wanted back in L.A. The meeting went OK except they kept asking me about creative control. The question would be, "Well, you know, who would have final say?" And I said, "Well, I'm very collaborative; that will be the process. It's your show. It's your voice, but if it came down to it, somebody has to be in charge, and that would be me." Then they proceeded to ask me that same exact question three or four more times, and I again explained it would not be an issue. I was there to really help them with their vision, but somebody has to be in charge, and that would be me. It really did not go well after that.

Robert Ben Garant: We did an interview with him during the day, and the thing I remember very distinctly is we didn't really know what a producer even did. Michael Black explained to him what we needed from a producer, and what [he] said was, "We really need somebody who's going to go out and get our props and stuff so that we don't have to do it." At the time, we were like, "Yeah, we don't have to get our own props anymore, man." Looking back on it, I'm like, "Jesus Christ; we're so lucky he didn't walk out of the room."

Jim Sharp: I remember leaving and going to a bar, waiting for my wife to pick me up, because she was in New Jersey. I got a phone call saying, "Listen, they want you to come back without MTV in the room. They want to have some pizza and beer with you. I think we got off track." I went back, and it was a much different vibe, and I ended up doing it. What happened was, I got back to L.A., and the offer that they made me was a really strange low-ball offer — the show I wanted — and we actually thought it was a mistake, and it wasn't. So I went to New York and did the pilot [for "The State"].

The pilot for "The State," which featured a cameo from singer Meat Loaf, was linked by a recurring sketch with all eleven members in an elevator together.

MTV PILOT

Chair Wrestling

Elevator I

Hormones

Ride

Cerialist Commercial

Elevator II

Sid & Nancy

Capt Monterey Jack

Simon Says

Fire!

Link

Elevator IV

Joe Lo Truglio: I remember how excited we were. It was our first foray into having a celebrity working with us. ... Meat Loaf, he's from Connecticut. I think he knew Kerri's dad, Larry Kenney. I think there was a connection with Kerri. It might've been Steven Starr who actually got him to do that. By coincidence, I learned that Kerri knew him. I might be confusing the connection. ... We were like, "Holy smokes, Meat Loaf is in our pilot." This was one of those projects that a lot of pressure was on us. This was our shot. This was our chance to have a TV show. It was the first of many times the group tried to create a runner in the show. We wanted to have some glue that held the sketches together. The elevator sketch was what we used. We were always trying to walk the line of being like Monty Python but not like Monty Python — being different, being the same. We were figuring out what exactly our show was going to be. We wanted to be seamless. We wanted there to be a flow, and we wanted the ideas to kind of run into each other. Sometimes it worked, and sometimes it didn't. I remember a couple of instances that I loved where it worked.

Michael Patrick Jann: I was super-happy they gave me a chance to direct that show, and they didn't need to do that. [They said,] "Here, go do this." I'm not sure that they were sure that I could do it or

Jim Sharp was really sure, and I always give them props for basically starting my career by saying, "OK, you can direct the pilot."

Robert Ben Garant: When we were doing our live shows, we would barely have enough material to fill the show. I don't think we said no to much material. I think the pilot is almost entirely trunk stuff. Sid Vicious on "$25,000 Pyramid," "Hormones" and "Chair Wrestling," those were all from our stage show. The elevator thing, somebody said, we needed to do a piece with all of us in it. We didn't really have one. All eleven of us crammed into an elevator seemed like a good idea, just for the audience to see this is the eleven people of the show. Looking back, I don't think that was a great idea. I don't think that was necessary. I think if the pilot was a little faster and funnier, it would've been better. I wrote the elevator things. Those were the only new material in the pilot.

"Hormones," we knew that was one of our best sketches. The Sid Vicious thing, that was the only imitation that we did. MTV wanted us to do celebrity imitations. Sid and Nancy, even though they had been dead for twenty years, those were our only celebrity imitations. It seemed like we all agreed pretty quickly what our best trunk material was. I don't remember us fighting much about what made it into the pilot.

David Wain: We shot "Ride" for the pilot, and I remember we had this wide-angle attachment that we put on a Steadicam Junior, which was this consumer-level thing you could put on a tiny camera that made it glide. We ended up using that all the time in our second-unit sketches. It made it look kind of cool even though the image quality was so crappy. "Ride" was one of many examples where we ran around with that camera with the wide angle, swooping around. It was also one of the first ones where we realized, "Oh, we can just grab the music and build the sketch around a really great song."

Jim Sharp: We did a pilot. It wasn't great, and they would tell you it wasn't great, but MTV still believed in them and saw something. So they gave us a first season. Once the trunk material ran out, I think it really took off. I've seen that so many times, where they have all this material they've done over the years and they say, "This kills every time. It's never failed us; it's bulletproof." But there's something about trunk material, it just doesn't quite pop, because it's been sitting around for so long. Once that was all gone, man, they rolled up their sleeves and put their heads down and just started writing like crazy. That first season wasn't perfect, but I think toward the end of it, they really found their groove.

Steven Starr: Eileen and Doug were rooting for us, supported us with a great crew and the freedom to create whatever we wanted. We couldn't have asked for a better lab to launch a comedy show. Despite endless games of foursquare and a brawl with the crew from "Beavis and Butt-head," we delivered some great, fresh television.

David Wain: We were very resistant. We were very young. We were so cocky; at age twenty-two, we were like, "We're the funniest people. You guys have no idea what you're talking about. Leave us the fuck alone, or we'll walk." The truth is that somehow we were kind of right on some level. All the executives were in their twenties anyway, and they were like, "I guess these guys know what they're doing." They paired us with this great producer, Jim Sharp, who was not intimidated by us in the least and was very awesome. He was a guy from Seattle and very mellow. He never got riled up. He had nothing to lose, but he was also not afraid to tell us when to pipe down and when to stop making trouble. He also helped us to really discipline our work. He was really, really essential to the show.

Jim Sharp: I just tried to put them in a good position to be successful. They're good guys; they're smart guys, and they want to be successful. They recognized that they haven't done this before and that television is new to them. They cared a whole bunch about the material and jokes, but they were open to work with me as far as shaping it as a TV show.

David Wain: He kept saying, "More jokes, more jokes. If I don't see five jokes on a page, then I'm ripping it up." It was one of those great qualities that I really value in a certain style of producer, which was he was sort of a quiet guy and kind of quietly behind the scenes got everybody going, and you didn't even realize how much he was making everything better. The creative look, feel, format and content of the show was all from us, but he, like a great producer, facilitated getting it to reality.

Jim Sharp: I came up as a joke writer. I was a four- or five-joke-per-minute guy. Maybe I taught them a little bit about that, but I'll tell you, they taught me about performance. They taught me that sometimes the material might not be A-material; it might be B or B+, but the performance can put it over the top — the performance can make it an A. There were times they'd come in my office and say, "Look, we know you don't love this. Maybe you don't even get it, but you need to trust us. We can make this work." When they did that, they were almost always right.

David Wain: I think he impressed us the very first day we met him. I know he impressed me because he put on no airs. He was very Seattle. He was just like, "Yep, this is what I've done. I would be psyched to do this with you guys. I think it's funny stuff, and let me know," and somehow that really made sense to us.

Jim Sharp: There was a learning curve for me, too, because the kind of stuff they were writing was not topical, necessarily. It was not political, and that's kind of where I came from. It was a lot of smart absurdity.

Ken Marino: We were so young and cocky and didn't know how it really worked. So we just sort of made up our own rules, I think. Other than our parents taught us to be respectful to people, we didn't know that we needed to listen to anybody. We were like, "No, this is how we want to do it," and we'd get all huffy if we were given notes or something. "We're twenty-two years old. I think we know what we're doing, so less notes please."

Michael Patrick Jann: [Jim Sharp] was always a really great guy, and he was very genteel in his manner. We made fun of him mercilessly, and he was very nice about it. To this day, we still bust out pretty good Jim Sharp impersonations when we all get together. It sounds a lot like Kermit the Frog — like if you could imagine Kermit the Frog bursting in the door and going, "Guys, you can't smoke pot in here; we're gonna get kicked out of the building!"

He didn't sound like [Kermit] at all. He has a very slight Northwestern accent, and we decided to take that to full Kermit the Frog. The one time that he actually came in and yelled at us was because we were smoking pot in our offices. ... The thing that made it OK to us was that the pot had been left there by the security guards. It wasn't ours to begin with. ... We walked into our office, and there was a giant, old-school ashtray full of roaches and pre-rolled joints. It was like, "Hey, our new office!"

Doug Herzog: I think Jim Sharp took the brunt of it. I loved hanging out with them. I remember Showalter would come up to my office, and he remains very passionate about what he did. He would lead some of the battles. He was pretty outspoken.

I have great memories of all those guys. Marino was a sweetheart. I loved hanging around with him. I remember Tom Lennon smoking furiously outside the building. I would always catch him smoking cigarettes out in front of 1515 Broadway, or for a while there they were up at 1775 Broadway, where the old MTV office is. [I was] always fascinated with Michael Ian Black. [He] always had something to say but always kind of from the backseat, in that now it's become his trademark style.

They were pugnacious, right? They were the upstarts, and while we weren't that much older than them, we were the adults. We were probably in our thirties; they were in their twenties, and, quite frankly, with all due respect to all of us, [I'm] not sure that anybody knew what they were doing, but we were doing it, and that was the fun part.

Eileen Katz: I tried to be as honest and respectful as any talent I worked with. If I'm working with them, it's because I truly believe in them and I kind of hope that I can act as their champion to help them get it across. I hope they knew that I, with every fiber of my being, believed in their talent. I believed in what they wanted to do, and all I wanted to do was to respectfully help them get it done. It's like the spoonful of sugar that helps the medicine go down. There's some things I'm gonna have to say that you're not gonna want to hear, but you know what? It's not about how we get along when things are good; it's how we get along and how we figure things out when they're not good.

There were times that maybe they weren't happy about stuff, and to their credit they were like, "OK, we don't agree; we don't like it," and there was grumbling, but you move on. I hope they felt that they got to do more of what they wanted to do than not, and I hope that was part of what I helped facilitate.

Robert Ben Garant: One meeting, we were getting notes from [Executive Producer] Eileen Katz, and we all took off our clothes and stood around the speakerphone naked. We just thought that was so funny that we were getting notes from an executive while we we're all naked around the speakerphone in some office.

Eileen Katz: Oh, my God. Aaaaaaaah! I can't believe that. Oh, my God, I had no idea. Holy shit!

Michael Ian Black: I think Eileen, in particular, really believed in the show and wanted it to work. Having never dealt with a boss before, I think we treated her as an adversary as opposed to an ally. She was the go-between between us and the network. So whatever notes would come down, which we generally disagreed with, we had a hard time seeing their position. A lot of times they were wrong, but there were times when we were wrong. She became the face of the network, and she was responsible for being bad cop. A lot of time, she was good cop, too. We saw ourselves as artists and not corporate stooges. So anything that smacked of the corporate side of things — like their insistence of us creating recurring characters or their insistence for us to do what they would consider more pop cultural sketches — that really rubbed us the wrong way and felt false to us. They were operating under the MTV playbook, which I understand, but it wasn't who we were. It wasn't what we wanted to do. That caused a lot of friction.

Eileen Katz: Recurring characters, that was ongoing. Even I was like, "I don't know how I'm going to tell them this." Think about it, how are you going to tell what I think at the time was the most cutting-edge, creative corral of people, "You know what? We want to cookie-cutter you. We want to put you in a little box because somebody at the network is concerned about merchandising, and you know, we've got to figure out how we can get Ken Marino's balls in 7-Eleven."

It's commerce meets art. It's a business, at the end of the day. Ultimately what I was kind of able to swallow and face them with was the truth. "You want to consider yourselves knee-deep, playing in the league of groups like 'Saturday Night Live'? It's about memorable characters." And it didn't end up happening, of course, but it's always the carrot of:

"Hey, you know what, if you look at the 'SNL' break-out characters and the movies that they went on to do, is it really such a terrible thing?"

As only The State could do, every recurring character had such a "fuck you" quality to it that I reveled in it; they reveled in it. Doug [said], "This is the beast you're working with. You've got to embrace it on some level, and if you're gonna turn around and tell them, 'OK, here's what the network needs,' you've got to be willing to take some of it back." I would love to know, "Are those parts of the show that you like at all or have any affinity for, or do you still just hate everything about that?" I would love to know that.

Jim Sharp: The first year, MTV was looking for a certain kind of show, certain kind of material, and certainly they were MTV. So they were about pace, but that's about the extent of it. To me, it wasn't that serious. Now, where they were coming from, they may have a whole different point of view about that, but I didn't think it was anything crazy. I think MTV really liked these guys and saw their potential. ... They have passion, and they have a high bar, and they're true to what they're thinking and what they believe in.

Michael Patrick Jann: [Jim] walked up to me at some point during [one of the first days of shooting] and was like, "How you gonna speed this up here? We're gonna head into some overtime." I remember alarm bells going off in my head. "Overtime? What the fuck is that? We just stay until it's done; if it takes three days, we'll just do it. What are you talking about?" Immediately [it] was like, "Oh, right, there's people paying money, and the people who aren't in the group get paid to be here, and if we go over..." I was like, "Oh, shit," that's a whole other level of thinking about how to get things done.

He was very kind about it, and he instilled in the group a very "try to do this cheaply" aesthetic. In some senses [that] was great, and we really needed it at the time, but I know for me, it took years to get over the little Jim Sharp voice in my head saying, "I don't know if we need to spend the money on this." I'd be doing a big, international commercial in Africa, thinking, "I don't know, do I want to spend the extra five hundred dollars on a crane?" The other part of me is like, "Hey, asshole, you're supposed to spend the extra five hundred. Nobody cares." You get to a point in your career where people are really more interested in how the thing turns out than how much the thing costs.

Doug Herzog: We had a very hands-on approach. We were making most of the stuff we put on the air. It was done in-house, and so it was very controlled. Everything had to have the "rock and roll attitude." We were always trying to keep it music-centric and pop culture-centric. Then you're dealing with enormously talented people who had a collective voice and then eleven individual voices — a whole lot of voices for us to manage. We weren't that experienced in managing these types of processes, especially around comedy. For the most part, our experience had been doing stand-up comedy shows and "Remote Control," but MTV was not known for its comedy at the time.

David Wain: It was definitely confrontational. We were the young, bratty group, and they were the executives. I think we turned Eileen into our public enemy number one just because she was the executive in charge of our show, and in retrospect, I know I feel terrible about it. I know we slammed her in the New York Times article, and it was totally uncalled for. The more I grew up, the more I realized how entirely one hundred percent she was simply doing her job. Hopefully, she also understood that we were also just being kids.

Eileen Katz: Their managers did what managers should do; they ran intervention, and sometimes that made things more tense than others. … I think their managers were also young managers. They were the first group that they attempted to manage because I know Jon Bendis was a documentary [filmmaker], and Steven Starr was an agent. So it was a different role for them. They were doing what they thought was right.

Jonathan K. Bendis: Some of my arguments flipped out the kids in The State. They really couldn't know what was behind everything because they weren't living it. I was. In trying to protect them — it was a hard thing to do — I was very combative. There was a side of me, whether or not they knew it I don't know, but it was pretty crazy.

Eileen Katz: It wasn't like I was the most seasoned television executive. We were all figuring it out, and it was a new thing, the whole idea of cable, of MTV, of a sketch show like this, of navigating the press, of navigating the audience and each other. But that's what was great about it, and I wouldn't trade that for the world.

Jonathan K. Bendis: I had no problem coming up against Eileen or Doug or anybody just because I didn't care. Because this was their one shot. It wasn't because it was my one shot. It was their one shot at doing what they wanted to do, and they wanted to hold to it. Did I try and dissuade them from going to MTV when we did "Molt" and there were other possibilities out there? ... It was like, "OK, they're an unknown thing, but let's see what can happen here."

Michael Showalter: I always looked up to [Doug, Eileen and Jim]. I wanted to impress them. They were the sort of parental quality there. It was important to me that they approved of what we were doing, but we also pushed them like kids do push parents, trying to get away with as much as we could. But at the same time, if they stopped caring you'd be like, "Why are you...?" You never wanted them to stop caring; you wanted them to continue. You wanted that tension to exist between you and them but for a little bit of a balance you were trying to strike.

I always really, really liked Eileen and Jim. Obviously, he is an integral part of everything that we are. ... We had ideas, and we had a work ethic, but there was no textbook to it, and Jim brought to what we were doing a lot of textbook and a lot of architecture and a lot of guidelines, and having those guidelines allowed us to change and evolve.

David Wain: I don't honestly remember what our big gripes were because I've dealt with so much worse for years. I think [Eileen] was just being an executive. She was like, "Hey, what are you going to write about? Can we gear it a little bit more this way?" I know that she had given us four traits that every sketch should have at least one, which were either pop culture spoof, MTV spoof... There was another thing where we did sort of a "fuck you." "OK, so here's that!" A lot of the stuff in the first season, particularly the stuff that we cut, was just so against what we were wanting to do, but we did it. "Marky Mark," "Grunge Rock Piece," and all this stuff that we knew was going to be dated immediately. We wanted to be Monty Python; we didn't want to do that at all. We sort of met them halfway, but then as the show went along, just like any show, it was successful enough that they started to leave us alone. As the seasons went on, they left us way more alone. They gave us a little more money, and we still sort of kept that "fuck you" attitude. That's the way it went, and we thought we were mistreated at MTV. We did that whole sketch about how we weren't invited to go to "Unplugged." We were the black sheep of MTV, and we would go to the music awards, but no one cared.

Despite being credited as co-creators of the show, Jon Bendis and Steven Starr wore out their welcome at the MTV offices pretty quickly.

Steven Starr: Jon and I were co-creators and protectors. Our day-to-day job was to develop the freest possible creative environment to allow great comedy to emerge. Protecting The State from outside pressures created a natural tension with the network.

David Wain: They encouraged us and also had a very "us versus them" attitude about the whole thing. I think Bendis is a born rebel, and he had worked at MTV for years and years but always taking on that stance of "Let's fuck them over before they fuck us over." I know there was some series of events where finally they were just like, "All right, they're still their producers and their managers, but they're not allowed in the office."

Jim Sharp: I do recall that, them being rebellious. ... I had maybe a little bit of issue, too. As mangers, sometimes they want to be producers. That was my job, so it was a little bit of that. I don't recall them not being welcome at the office. If somebody said that, they're probably right, but I don't remember that.

Doug Herzog: Bendis, he might even have been on staff at MTV. So there's some history there, and then Steven, who[m] we never really encountered before, they added a whole other thing to the dynamic. That was sometimes complicated.

Bendis and Starr, they adopted kind of a weird attitude with us, and we had some moments where we were like, "Aw, Jeez, these fucking guys." That being said, I have a lot of affection for Jon and for Steven, but there were some rocky moments early on.

Jonathan K. Bendis: Rules were being made that were based on nothing because there was nothing that preceded this that they would go, "Well, the last sketch comedy troupe they had..." MTV was just changing at that moment, whereas, before then, anything we wanted to do, we did. I was there at a really nice era of, "Hey, I got an idea." "Well, go do it." It was really great; it was really fun. It allowed me to do stuff. It allowed me to bring those guys on and other people to go, "Let's just have fun," but be creative and smart. And that's what we did. Right in the early '90s, it started to get a little more corporate. It'd been on the air ten years at that point, and they were really catching on. Everything was big, "Video Music Awards" was big and the movie awards were starting, and everything else was happening. It's not like this was a little fly-by-night operation.

David Wain: [Bendis and Starr] didn't really manage anyone before or since us. They were really producers. As managers, they brought us through our most successful period. So I have to give them a lot of credit, but I also feel it wasn't what they really wanted to do.

Kerri Kenney-Silver: It came as a shock to us when the network said, "Hey, how about you get more girls?" I think we looked around and said, "We only have one girl? Don't we have more girls?"

It wasn't a statement. It wasn't a thing. It wasn't a bit. We happened to be the group of people after the drain swirled down. We were the ones that were left in the lint basket that held on and belonged there. One of them happened to be a girl. I think everybody felt that way.

Kevin Allison: We were invited by the William Morris Agency to the 21 Club, one of the most expensive clubs/restaurants in New York City. It goes back to the turn of the [previous] century or something, and at that point we were just determined to be punk rock. At one point, there were some other celebrities being toasted there for something, and I think we kind of felt a little bit like people were wondering what the fuck we're even doing in there, you know?

Robert Ben Garant: I was legitimately uncomfortable. Everyone was in really nice suits. Even if we wanted to dress up, we still would've looked like hobos, but it was free drinks, and at the time I drank gin and tonic.

Kevin Allison: Four or five of us decided, "Let's drop our pants!" I think we were still wearing underwear, but we dropped our pants, and that caused a stir.

Robert Ben Garant: People were sort of ignoring us, but you could tell that everybody was mad. One of those maître d's walked up to us and said, "Gentlemen, this is the 21 Club."

Kevin Allison: That started security pushing us out, and Ben took a painting of a horse, like a foxhunt or something, off the wall and started to walk out with it, and that was the last straw.

Robert Ben Garant: I had read that Harpo Marx, when he was there, stole a painting. So I tried to steal a little, tiny framed picture of a horse, but I got caught. The guy who caught me was the same maître d, and he said, "Sir, I will call the police if you ever come back," and he was totally serious. I gave him the painting and ran and felt legitimately terrified. Yeah, we were a bunch of assholes. The 21 Club was furious at William Morris, and I had to go into William Morris and apologize to my agent and to his boss and to his boss. It was bad. We thought it was funny, and none of us admitted it at the time, but I felt horrible. I think we all might have felt horrible. We always tried to be pretty obnoxious wherever we went.

Eileen Katz: I enjoyed that so much because it was like, "Ha! Not us this time. Now, you can be mad at Daddy, not Mommy."

Michael Showalter: I thought all that stuff was funny, but I wanted people to like us. I always felt bad when I got the sense that we were pissing people off — not to say that I wasn't a part of that; I was, but it was that thing of, "We didn't mean it..." I never really was pushing the rebellion as much as the silliness ... pushing boundaries of what would be considered a funny sketch. That's what I was finding very interesting. The rebellious stuff was very important to what we were doing — and I certainly didn't object to it — but it never felt right for me to do that.

Joe Lo Truglio: Our editing bay was in a main corridor. We were sharing some desks with "Beavis and Butt-head," and I was editing the sketch "Ride," and the volume was too loud. Someone asked me to turn the volume down. At the time, I thought that was disrespectful. I'm sure it was perfectly fine or maybe it was annoying. Like a total asshole, I flip them off or something. "We are part of this comedy troupe, and we deserve to be here." Some garbage that I had in my head.

One of the producers, not immediately, eventually, came up to me and was like, "You need to apologize to Mike Judge," who wasn't involved in the altercation at all, "and the producers. Otherwise, you may lose your job." I just started laughing like an arrogant prick. "I'm not going to lose my job. You're going to fire The State?"

This was the delusion of safety in numbers that you felt like you had that power. That ego. In pure fuck-you-ery, Showalter and I went out to Times Square to some touristy shop and picked out a card. We found a painting in the garbage of a clown playing tennis. I got a bouquet of flowers, and I wrote a check for ten dollars out to Mike Judge. Me and Showalter approached him. Mike Judge was in the middle of something and was so patient, and I very coldly and very defiantly, without any attitude to him, just kind of explained to him what happened. "I'd like to apologize." He started laughing as soon as we handed over the painting. He was way cooler about it than he needed to be. He had no idea about the incident and probably didn't care. I definitely left that situation in the jerk off column.

Jim Sharp: I had a phrase that I'd say to them at the time, "First, get the gig; then be an asshole. Not everything has to be so precious." MTV, quite honestly, they loved these guys and were on their side and recognized this brilliance. They weren't the enemy, but it's easy to get fired up, and it's easy to say, "Yeah, they're screwing with us. This isn't what we do."

It's just a process. We probably go through it today in my position, my chair at Comedy Central. We try not to micromanage, but we're a network, and we want things to be shorter, whatever that is. It's just part of the deal. I tried to fight some of those battles for them, but there weren't really big battles, especially after that first season.

Kerri Kenney-Silver: We had moments. When I look back at those kinds of things, I personally look at us being in the wrong. I remember we got into a fight with the "Beavis and Butt-head" guys because we were playing naked four square in our office really loud, and they were trying to make a TV show, and these new guys come in either smoking pot in their office and getting naked and playing games with the four square ball. It's just so obnoxious. If I were in an office now trying to do a show, and these new kids came in and did that, I would be like, "You need to get them out of here. I don't care how funny they think they are."

Part of me also looks back with a smirk. "Hell, yeah, we did that. That's kind of awesome." If we didn't have that kind of confidence and cockiness, I don't know that we would've been able to create the kind of work that we did that I'm so proud of today. Some of it serviced us and luckily didn't keep us from working in Hollywood in the future.

Robert Ben Garant: We would do mean, not-funny pranks on each other. We would put stuff in each other's drinks at nice restaurants. I think any place where we felt a little bit out of place, we always tried to do something kind of obnoxious.

Michael Showalter: We had rented a house that we crashed at. It was like, "We're going to live in a house for a week and write a ton of sketches and have fun and bond." We did what you do when you rent a house; you cook out, and you buy beer and all that stuff. So there were like fifteen giant bags of trash. There was a van and a car, and the bags didn't fit in the car. So they put them in the van, and the idea was that everybody in the van would take the garbage bags to the dumpster, but the people in the van left all the garbage bags at the end of the road for the people in the car to pick up and take to the garbage. ... It was like,

"What the fuck? Why is that funny? Where's the joke in that?" The joke is, "Wouldn't this be funny? This is a great prank." But there's no humor. … The joke is you were too lazy and selfish to take the garbage out. So under the guise of telling a joke, you made us do it. So we put fifteen giant garbage bags inside a car when they fit perfectly well inside a van.

It was a very merciless environment. It was very much a "There's no crying in baseball" environment.

Ken Marino: We always considered ourselves outsiders, and maybe we used that as kind of motivation to be rebellious or different. We were in our early twenties, and we thought we were the anti-MTV. If we didn't get invited to something, we'd use that as fodder to shield us, to go "See, they don't like us. Let's write something else stupid that they're not gonna like." I think that Eileen and Doug were always supportive of us. I don't think there was ever any huge conflict in that way. I think we just kind of created what we wanted it to be so we can get all riled up and try to inspire ourselves to do something.

Michael Patrick Jann: As a twenty-one-year-old, you're not supposed to respect anything, and we just didn't. I mean, we were nice. We weren't stupid; we knew who was writing the checks and things like that, but at the same time you don't respect anything anybody says when you're that age, and I think that's part of what was good about the show.

Kevin Allison: We would criticize MTV because we thought MTV — and probably still does — fostered this atmosphere of, "Do good work, because you might not be here tomorrow." They were never like, "Oh, my gosh, we've got such a future in store for you guys. This is your home. Let's make you feel supported." It was always, "Keep at it because we fire people all the time."

While The State was prolific, the demands of creating a regular, thirty-minute sketch show were great, especially when the members had to get the approval of not only the network but also each other, their toughest critics.

Michael Ian Black: To spend half a day working on a sketch felt kind of luxurious in a weird way. Maybe because on "You Wrote It...," we'd do things in a couple of hours and be done with it. We were so used to begging and borrowing space and time. If we had to shoot something in an office, what that meant for us was basically breaking into somebody's office in the middle of the night and shooting. Here, we were allowed to be where we're supposed to be. There were meal breaks scheduled and professional people operating equipment. The pace of the writing picked up exponentially. We would have pitch meetings every day, and there were eleven of us, and each person was pretty much expected to pitch two or three things. That's a couple dozen sketches a day that were being pitched — maybe twelve to fifteen on a slow day. It really required an enormous output from us. We rejected probably ten or fifteen sketches for every one that got on the board. The board was our cork board for what we were going to shoot.

Kerri Kenney-Silver: Remotes are tedious. They still are. I'm working on a single-camera show now with no audience. It's a tedious process. You never know if something's funny or not until you see it on TV. Live shows are easier. No matter what arguments or frustration went into the writing part of it, the editing part of the script or dealings with the network, when you got on stage, and it was you and the audience. It was just a performance again. I love that.

Michael Patrick Jann: There was the live stuff, and that was the big, traditional four cameras, control booths, a very straightforward production scenario, where we'd do a bunch of sketches in front of a live audience. That was really fun, and it was a very group-focused enterprise. That was the thing that was most like doing the live shows. We'd get in a room. We'd rehearse. Everyone would have their say. It was very democratic; it was just the same.

Then there were the Hi8 pieces, which were more like what we were doing as the adjunct to the live shows. It was varying degrees of ambition. A lot of it was really simple, meant to be small because there was a lot of, "Well, we're not sure if this is gonna come out." We had the resources to devote to it. I had developed, during "You Wrote It, You Watch It," a way for printing shows that worked really well, and the group was kind of used to it.

Then there were the bigger pieces. Mostly [I] did the bigger shoots with the big crews, which were partially on video, and then every once in a while for every season we would do a day or two where we shot on film. That was back in the day when video really sucked. Having the ability to shoot on film was so massive. It really made you feel like, "Oh, my God, this is so professional and so real. We really have to do a great job on this." Those were always super-fun days for me because it was just so in my wheelhouse and what I enjoyed doing because you got a little bit of extra resources, got to have a bigger scale with the productions a little bit. I was always very proud about how everybody would come together in a way that was sometimes a little more difficult than just doing something live. It's a different discipline to have the kind of focus to be able to do take after take. It has to be funny, and it has to happen right here because of the timing with the camera.

Michael Ian Black: Even though the process of making television in front of an audience is considerably different than doing a theatrical performance, the basic elements are still there. Having an audience there felt familiar. Shooting on location was totally new for most of us both in terms of how you go about doing it and also in terms of how you adjust your performances — how to write for the camera. We had some experience from it with "You Wrote It, You Watch It," but this was on a different level for us. Incidentally, as an unintended consequence, it gave Mike [Jann] outsized power in the group, because he was responsible for directing the majority of that stuff, with some directing duties falling to David Wain. [Jann's] voice became a little bit bigger in the group.

Michael Patrick Jann: I definitely had my moments where I was like, "Nobody understands what I'm doing here. Half of these guys think I'm just in the way part of the time, and I'm not." If I ever came home and complained, I know my girlfriend at the time was like, "You know what, you've got to quit. You just gotta get out of there and do your own thing." I would immediately be like, "Are you fucking crazy? No way! This is awesome."

Todd Holoubek: I think we just sort of looked at the whole list [of old sketches] and tried to find a way to make them happen. That's where shooting part of the show in front of a live audience was really helpful. We took a lot of our old, live material and did it for the live audience. Sometimes some of that old material would work as video; so it kind of came together that way.

Michael Ian Black: We would come in with sketches. None of us had mastered the process of pitching concepts. None of us would've trusted concepts. You wrote something by yourself, or with other people, or one other person, and you would come in and read it. If the group laughed, then that was good. If they didn't, it disappeared. There were very few instances of somebody bringing in a sketch and rewriting it to make it better in the second draft and re-pitching and having it succeed. I can remember maybe one or two instances of that happening. You pretty much were expected to bring it in done or close to done.

Joe Lo Truglio: We would try to write the funniest sketch, ultimately. If someone wrote a really funny sketch, that would definitely make the others do the same. That dynamic became more pronounced or insidious as we got to television. Everyone had a really good work ethic from the get-go. There wasn't a lot of, "Hey, shape up or ship out." If anyone fell into that, that was me. When we got to MTV, I was either smoking too much pot or playing too many video games at the office. I just wasn't as impressive as I should've been. I think Ken and Black approached me. Definitely Ken. "Come on, you've got to do more. You've got to write more stuff." That was the only memory I have of anyone coming up to anyone. It was me.

Thomas Lennon: We went out almost every single night for like eight or ten years. We would basically roll into MTV in the morning, and then we'd get giant egg sandwiches, and certainly the hangovers probably accounted for like fifty percent of my material.

Kevin Allison: The way it usually worked was the person who wrote the script read all the roles and would even read the name of the character before saying their lines, so that you could follow it, which is an awkward way of doing things. But I think that the way that we wrote back in the day, each writer felt that the words were so precious that they would worry that another person just seeing them for the first time wouldn't nail the tone and everything.

"The Bearded Men of Space Station 11," we really struggled with that sketch. In rehearsals, we were having such a hard time with it that we were thinking of cutting it from the live show. The reason was the group could not make it as funny as Showalter could make it reading it alone. It was just so fucking funny the way he read it, the patter, and the Showalter-ness of every character, that we couldn't seem to nail it. I think we did a pretty good job, but we all felt even after it was done, it's still not as funny as just Showalter reading it alone.

Michael Showalter: That's very flattering. ... I certainly don't feel that way. I do remember it took us a little while to get that perfect tone of detachment and exasperation in the sketch, but I think we nailed it. In pitching a sketch, it could be easier to just read it yourself because you could get all of the phrasing exactly the way you wanted it.

Thomas Lennon: The thing about The State was we really fought. We mostly fought all the time. People would get really stressed out. I think that's why the material has held up, because we were not easy on each other.

Michael Patrick Jann: I was a fighter, a fighter kid. So I didn't care, I guess, is what it really comes down to. To my detriment, I didn't care whether I had a good relationship with anybody; I just wanted to do really good work.

Robert Ben Garant: I think most people were really fighting for what they generally thought was best for the sketch. People didn't back down. They felt their comedy was correct and the other guy's was wrong. People really took it seriously.

Kevin Allison: We really did feel that words were precious. I think we got that largely from Monty Python. There are so many sketches like "The Argument Clinic" or the sketch from "...the Holy

Grail," where Palin is trying to get the guards to guard the prince while he's in the room. Just the perfection of the script, of the lines, is so tight, that the group always felt that was the way, to have the words perfect. Other members of the group might not feel the same way, but that's how I always thought.

Todd Holoubek: I think one of the reasons the show remained successful is that we just did exactly the same thing, except we started using index cards. We put the names of sketches on index cards. Before that, it was a written list. Nobody had laptops. Laptops were still like a thousand dollars, and, you know, they had less power than an iPhone, so...

Michael Ian Black: We would do secret ballots on what we thought should be in the show, and the things that got the most votes made the show.

Robert Ben Garant: Eventually, we started voting. Eventually, we figured out a system where majority rules, even if half the group was furious. If the majority voted for something, we would do it. A lot of our arguments were pointless. "This should be a second longer." I don't think any of us today would have the exact same arguments. People just wore each other down. Eventually, somebody just stopped caring and said, "OK, fine. Whatever." I don't remember them ever resolving with agreement. Somebody just wanted something more.

Kerri Kenney-Silver: There were times when one person was too hungover and showed up late or someone's scripts weren't in. We took turns being responsible and irresponsible.

Thomas Lennon: Of the many little camps in The State, one of them was always the marijuana camp, which I was never in. I drank very, very hard during the State years, probably as hard as any other member of the group, if not maybe one of the hardest-drinking members of the group. But I was never one of the weed guys, just because I have a terrible reaction to marijuana.

The expression that weed part of The State always had with each other was, "If you're William, I'm Helen" which meant, "If you're William

Holden, I'm Helen Reddy." It was the weirdest marijuana code they made up. You always feel like you can't quite click one hundred percent when everybody is getting high and you are not. So as a result, I was probably drinking twice as much to try to catch up. When I look back on it now, just in terms of either alcohol or other recreational drugs and eating the worst sorts of foods in the world, I was an absolute disaster area. I actually think trying to live like I lived during the State years would probably kill me in about a year right now, without a doubt. I would either have a heart attack or something horrible would happen to me.

Todd Holoubek: You know you work with people long enough you start to see where they excel. When we would read sketches and kind of rewrite sketches as a group, you could see who was really good with the overall concept. You could see who was really good with dialogue. You could see who had the visual skills. You could see who could come up with an interesting character on the spot. Everyone had to hone their skills, and as we got into television, it just kept growing. If you're smart enough to play to your strengths, you hone those skills; it's almost Pavlovian because you see which skills get you the reward. So you play to those skills.

Kevin Allison: In The State, I always felt like if the joke failed, it was egg on your face, and I took it way too seriously. I observed over and over Ben and Tom. Ben and Tom had the most professional attitude about how to handle things. We always talk about how much creative control we had, especially in the first couple of seasons. MTV, Eileen Katz and Doug Herzog, they would say, "No, no" to this sketch or that sketch. Very often, they were my sketches. Very often, I would do a sketch, and the group would say, "This is crazy and funny and weird, but we all like it." Katz or Herzog or someone up the chain would say, "No."

The way that Ben and Tom would react to that — they would do that to their sketches sometimes, too — they would be like, "OK, back to the drawing board." They might make a quick, little joke about how shortsighted or unfit the big executives were. The executives might have a note that the central joke in the sketch, the premise itself, has to go, [but] certain parts were working. Ben and Tom were like, "OK, they don't get the central premise. Let's see if we can make something out of the rest of it." They would not let it get them bummed out, whereas it would ruin my week. I would be nursing a wound. "They don't get me."

Thomas Lennon: Being in The State was really the best practice ever for writing in the studio system because every single day you had to pitch material. If you didn't get your material in, you would not be in the show at all, and you're pitching to ten other people who were pitted against you. They didn't want you to get your stuff in because that meant less stuff for them. It was good practice for the studio system because there you get shot down all the time.

Kevin Allison: Even as I observed Ben and Tom doing that over and over, that back-to-the-drawing-board attitude, I wasn't able to be in the moment about it. It was only years later when I did start taking improv classes. I became the artistic director of The People's Improv Theater for a while. I'd never taken improv classes, and I can take them for free so I started going through the system, especially because as the artistic director, I should know what this stuff is. My attitude is that classes and workshops are something that you should be humble enough to take at any time in your life, no matter how much you've accomplished. Classes and workshops can be a great thing to do to hone things, to reflect, just to get more practice in a different way. I did start taking those improv classes at The Pit in 2007. When the joke fails, it just doesn't fucking matter. The audience is like, "OK, I didn't think that was funny," but they're looking forward to the next thing that might be, so you just go on.

Thomas Lennon: I recall times the group or I would get very depressed. When none of your sketches get through, you go to a pretty dark place. It was a pretty cutthroat, despite how close we were and friendly we were. The fights were intense and really emotional. People would cry. People would punch each other. Stuff would happen.

Todd Holoubek: Everybody wanted airtime. I mean, that's natural, you know, when you're building a career. This is what you want to do. This is how you do it. You had to build your own niche within the show. Naturally, it just sort of went to, "OK, I need some airtime," which was unfortunate. There was still this "all for one and one for all" attitude. It was still The State. Just like in theater, you know, people want their stage time.

Michael Ian Black: I think the pressure we felt was self-generated, not so much externally generated. I don't feel like we owed MTV anything, which, again, is our arrogance. It was more like a really strong desire to do something important and memorable.

Thomas Lennon: We've always been pretending we were into drama, even when we're doing "Sideways House Family." It's always our version of what we think a serious thing would be.

Todd Holoubek: There were some very weird debates about things. You know there were certain words they didn't want us to use because it would offend viewers. I think "yearning burrito" was one of them. We said that because we don't even know what "yearning burrito" means. They're like, "Oh, no. Nooo!" This is part of growing up, right? You kind of see the nonsensical way of how the world works. People will interpret things in ways that you could never imagine. Like all those people who think those Beatles songs are about them, and they go hang out at John Lennon's house. The fact that they saw something in "yearning burrito" that we didn't, I really wish we could've met that person, because I'd like to find out, "What did you see in those two words?" [It] never occurred to me that maybe we should meet that person, because they may have been very interesting.

Joe Lo Truglio: Music was something that we were all interested in on a certain level, not just musical theater, but music. MTV lent itself to that. So many of our sketches were just scored by popular music, and we were fans of popular music. I think songs really helped define us as a "rock 'n' roll" comedy group — if not literally, at least in spirit.

Kevin Allison: We spent a lot of time while we were on MTV over at Joe's apartment. Joe had an apartment in Hell's Kitchen for a while, and we would go there, and we would get a big jug of cheap, cheap wine, like a ten-dollar gallon of wine, and smoke some pot, and maybe watch some Buster Keaton or some Bruce Lee or something like that, and just joke around and come up with ideas for things. Joe was the perfect host for a creative jam session because that's the kind of guy he is.

Michael Patrick Jann: My desk was always right next to Ben's, and we always got along really well. I was always drawn to Tom and Kerri. Tom, Ben and I used to hang out. There were little subdivisions, and later on I became really close friends with Todd and continue to be, even though he's not really in the business anymore. He lives in Korea.

MTV gave The State an office overlooking Times Square.

Robert Ben Garant: We had this great office on the mezzanine floor of the MTV building, which is where they later shot "MTV News" where it's like floor-to-ceiling windows looking out on Times Square. That was our first office for the pilot. It's a beautiful, beautiful office.

Thomas Lennon: We had the office for a while. It was the headquarters of "TRL" in New York, right on the corner of 46th and Broadway. It was literally the most prestigious office in New York City, and for some reason, they gave it to us.

Kerri Kenney-Silver: That was our office for a couple of years. Every month or so, an executive would come in with a tape measure and be measuring it, and we would say, "What's happening? Are we getting kicked out?" and they'd say, "Oh, no, no, just checking stuff out." It turned out they were getting ready to knock the walls down and build a studio.

Thomas Lennon: One day, I was looking out the window and Todd was checking in about something really heavy, and I saw Cindy Crawford, and I said, "Cindy Crawford." Boy, oh boy, did it make Todd mad that I interrupted his incredibly heartfelt speech for a Cindy Crawford sighting.

Todd Holoubek: I have no recollection of that. I would gladly give up my check-in for Cindy Crawford. To this day, I would be more than happy to give up my time at check-in. In fact, I'm sure I did. Whatever I have to say is nothing … Cindy Crawford!

Thomas Lennon: He doesn't remember how mad he was at me when I spotted Cindy Crawford out the window when he was talking about maybe quitting the group. … I assure you; it was one of the most upset — he must've blocked it out because he was fucking livid with me.

Michael Ian Black: I might've seen Cindy Crawford on the elevator when she hosted "House of Style." I was just blown away, even by somebody like John Norris, who was a VJ. There was Kurt Loder, and you would be like, "Oh, shit, those people are stars." I became friends with Kennedy after a while. That felt like a real celebrity-to-celebrity relationship.

Back in the early '90s it wasn't taboo to smoke on television, and there were many State sketches with heavy tobacco use.

Kerri Kenney-Silver: I think most of us were smokers. There were only a couple who weren't. We smoked everywhere, in the office, until somebody tried to tell us we couldn't. We were chain smokers for sure. Ken Marino never smoked. I feel like Kevin didn't start until later. David never smoked. But all the rest of us, I think, were smokers.

One time I will never forget. Imagine being a non-smoker. When we would go on location, we were always in these fifteen-passenger vans, and we smoked in them. I remember the windows closed in January, eight or nine smokers and the guys who weren't. I remember David Wain was in the very back seat of this passenger van, with his knees against the seat, and he had biking shorts on. His knees are up, and he's asleep, and Tom Lennon was in the front seat, and he threw a lit cigarette out the window, which went out of the van, into the back window and straight down into David's shorts. I will never forget. It's so wrong, but my reaction is laughter. We all laughed so hard. His reaction was hilarious. It's so horrible. It was disgusting … his testicles on fire.

David Wain: I thought it hit me in the face, and I think I was really mad.

Thomas Lennon: It landed in David Wain's shirt!

David Wain: We rode around in vans all the time, and there was a lot of fighting about windows up, windows down and smoking and stuff like that. I remember one fight we had where someone was like, "I'm so fucking hot, you've got to lower the windows," and it was a winter night, and someone was like, "How can you be hot? It's so cold." I honestly forget who it was, but it was like, "Do you want to see the sweat? Do you want to see the sweat?"

The pilot for "The State" wasn't seen by the public until the release of the complete series on DVD in 2009, but based on the pilot, "The State" was picked up for series. The show's 1993 production budget was $1.9 million for thirteen episodes, including $445,200 for talent, which divided eleven ways did not make the troupe rich.

Eileen Katz: I think they're all insanely talented. Every one of the eleven brought something to the party. I don't think it was always obvious to us at the network at the time, but it's the way they looked out for each other. I remember some of the negotiations; there was some flat fee we were going to give talent, and they were like, "That's not enough. That's not eleven. How do you divide that eleven ways?" I remember legal and the network going, "You know what? It's not our fault there are eleven of you." But you know what? They got it, and they were right, and it made us respect the eleven of them.

I think each of them stood out in different ways — certainly Michael Jann and David Wain as directors. Whatever it was that makes that beast called The State tick, each of them was integral to it. No question. I don't know if I'm comfortable naming favorites.

Robert Ben Garant: I remember that it broke down to about three hundred and fifty bucks a week, when we were actually getting our paychecks. ... Our lifestyles didn't change that much between being students and being on MTV. We all had roommates. We all lived in little, tiny places, but New York was not as expensive as it is now. In 1991, I had an apartment by myself, and it was like a closet with a bathroom, but it was five hundred and fifty bucks. I don't think that exists anymore by a long shot. So, yeah, we were psyched. At the time, it was more than it being three hundred and fifty bucks a week. It was a regular paycheck for forty weeks, which, I never had that before. I think the longest I'd ever really worked at one job was maybe a couple of months.

At the time, we joked about how poor we were, but we had money for food and beer and rent. It was awesome. None of us really made that much. Money didn't get much better seasons two and three. We were pretty broke the whole time, but New York was much less expensive, and to us it was a goldmine. Being paid to do that, it was just a goldmine.

Thomas Lennon: We all would go on unemployment immediately between seasons. I remember, after our last paycheck came in from MTV, running into Joe and Ken at the New York State Unemployment Office at like eight o'clock in the morning when they opened. The weird thing is that we made almost the same amount of money on unemployment. The difference was maybe fifteen or twenty dollars.

Eileen Katz: When you have fifty cents to pay people, which I'm exaggerating — we didn't have fifty cents at MTV in those days — and there were eleven of them, you have to figure out how to compensate. OK, we're going to do a sketch comedy show. Here's what a budget is going to be, but that's if you have five principals. This was an eleven-headed beast. How do make them feel like they're not getting ripped off and make them feel valued? This is what MTV probably still is about to some degree, but certainly [at] that point in time, it was like, "We can't pay you a lot, but we're going to let you do as close as we can to everything you want to get your voice out there." I hope that's what they feel they were able to do.

Kerri Kenney-Silver: We wanted total control. We wanted to be a world that you step into that was populated only by these people, and that way it was controllable. Also cheaper, because we were making the show for no money. We were getting paid, I believe, something like ten dollars over unemployment. We were just so happy to be there and getting to do what we do.

Jim Sharp: They would outwork everybody, but they also played hard. We'd go into a big studio every month and a half, and we would shoot in front of an audience ten or twelve sketches, and then the rest was location stuff. I think the balance might have been sixty/forty [live to location]. This studio shoot was big. It was a rehearsal and long days and hours, and you get that adrenaline at the end of it because the audience is there, and they would then go out and party at the bars. Finally, I just had to put it in the budget, allowing for parties. MTV calls me and goes, "What is this? Party? You have a party line in your budget? You can't do that." And I go, "Trust me, with these guys we have to do it. You do not want to mess with that," and that's how it was.

Kevin Allison: To have access to costume departments, to people working on your hair and makeup, to have a staff helping you create these ridiculous scenarios that you otherwise had been working on for the past several years in college by going to thrift stores to pick stuff up, it was like being a kid in a candy shop. It just felt so exciting to be twenty-two years old and treated like a creator, being treated like artists, and having people wondering what they could do for you next to help you create this joke that you thought of.

I remember those first studio audience nights as being so exciting. It was very much like being on ecstasy; it had that feel being so new and so exciting. "Oh, my gosh, we've got three television cameras aimed at us, and we've got a whole crowd of people laughing at us, and we've got all these techies running around helping us with our hair and where we're going to stand." And these are these silly sketches that we started writing in college! ... Every new thing is exciting, and we were constantly joking about all of the stuff. "Holy shit, isn't this cool? We get to do this now!"

The State appeared on the final episode of Jon Stewart's first MTV talk show to promote the debut of the sketch show.

Kerri Kenney-Silver: With Jon, we came up with the idea,

"How about we destroy your set at the end of it because you're going to be gone?" So we did. They let us take sledgehammers and hammers and saws to the set. So we did our interview; they said good night, and we tore the set apart [live]. That was really fun.

Eileen Katz: It was perfect and, again, it was like, "Oh yeah, we're the bad boys of comedy; we're so subversive."

Janeane Garofalo (comedian, actor, writer): The State, I first met them [when] we were guests together on the Jon Stewart show on MTV, years ago. ... The State destroyed the set as a joke. ... Buffalo Tom was the musical guest because that's Jon Stewart's favorite band.

Jon was moving on; they were going to revamp the show, or he was going to do a different type of show. So it was like, "Why not just destroy the set?"

I knew of them from around town. I just remember thinking, "Oh, gosh, so young," because I was nostalgic for being their age. I was under the impression they were still at NYU. ... I was thinking, "Aw, man, I wish I had been in a sketch group in college." I started to do stand-up when I was in college, but I thought that would've been great to have a group of friends built into this thing I was passionate about. Stand-up, you're on your own. I started hanging out with some of the kids from Emerson [College] back at that time in '85. That's where I met Laura Kightlinger, David Cross, some other people, and they were in a sketch group there at Emerson called This is Pathetic. I remember being so envious because I was a social pariah at college. If you could fit in less, it would be hard to do so.

You look at other people and think, "Oh, they've got it all figured out." I remember thinking that about the Emerson kids and about The State. ... I was envious of their youth and their camaraderie.

The State also appeared in some unusual places to promote the show, such as Mademoiselle magazine, where they posed nude with the names of states on signs blocking their pinker parts.

Kevin Allison: I wanted to be behind Ben so I could get a good look at his ass, which was always my modus operandi. We thought that Mademoiselle might be a bit iffy with Mike holding that sign saying "Mademoiselle Rules." Yeah, it was such a trip. You see these pictures, and we're so young, and it lists all of our ages. I don't remember if this was our idea to be naked and holding states in front of us or not.

The State was not insured by Lloyds of London.

Robert Ben Garant: On stage, I would leap in the air and fall on my face. I enjoyed that. It's crazy [that] MTV let us do it, but for the early previews, we did this parody of "The Conversation," the Gene Hackman movie (Super broad, right? Everybody's going to get that. A bunch of stoned teenagers are going to love that we're doing a "Conversation" parody). They let me fall out of a tree that must have been forty feet in the air onto a tiny, little pad. There was no stunt coordinator. There was nothing. Looking back, Jesus Christ, I can't believe they let us do that. I fell out of the tree, and there were two inches of ice on the ground. If I missed that pad, I would've been dead. That kind of blazed the trail for me. People would let me do those kinds of falls. Tom did a really good fall in "Sideways House," too. It killed me that he got to do a better fall than me. He had the best fall on that show. ... I like Buster Keaton. I'm a lot better falling down than talking.

Yeah, I ate a jar of mayonnaise [in a sketch]. It occurred to me years later, when I did the same gag for some other thing, that marshmallow fluff looks exactly the same. You can put marshmallow fluff into a mayonnaise jar and people are freaked out, but you don't actually have to eat mayonnaise. I hit my face and head with an AK-47 for one of the "Inbred Brothers" [sketches], hard enough that I still have the bump right on the hairline. I can still feel the knot where I hit myself with an AK-47. ... I fell down the stairs in a wheelchair once. I would write stuff intentionally that I would have to do something interesting and maybe hurt myself. Like, "Super Robbie" was great, where I just jumped and broke through a window and fell out of sight. Anytime I got to jump out a window and land on a crash pad, I thought I was super. I really, really enjoyed that.

In order to own some original characters, The State created a list and descriptions of them. Some made it to air; others never did, and some are still making their debuts at State reunion shows.

1. **Myrna:** She is an eccentric, middle-age woman who works as a librarian and also teaches her self-esteem class at the Learning Annex. She's extremely enthusiastic about her subject matter and relies on unconventional means to get her point across. "The next time you see somebody attractive whose attention you want to get, make like you got no bones!"

Kerri Kenney-Silver: [Myrna] is a character that still makes me laugh. The whole idea of her was just so stupid. She's this lady who copes with life by, if you get into a fearful situation, you just pretend like you don't have any bones — you sort of fall to the ground. It made me laugh. Apparently it wasn't that funny because I used it in my "SNL" audition, and Lorne Michaels sort of chuckled, and I went away. I thought it was really something at the time.

2. **Captain Monterey Jack:** A gung-ho leader type. A motivational speaker, ex-cop, war vet, ex-con, recovering addict, animal lover. CMJ travels the school system lecturing kids on the importance of all things trivial. He uses '80s catchphrases and "cool" lingo to get down to the kids' level and teach them about cheese or drill presses or whatever.

Michael Ian Black: It came from very, very early on. We'd play a game to generate material where we would just write titles and throw them into a hat. I think Kevin wrote Captain Monterey Jack, and I picked it out. I wrote it based on the title, I guess. It seems stupid, but there were only two elements in the name that I could grab onto. One was Monterey Jack, and the second was Captain. So the first one [I wrote] was about, I think, keeping your cheese wrapped.

3. **Don Law:** A nebbish lawyer with a Jersey accent, DON LAW is the prototypical late-night spokesman. He stiffly moves around his

lawyer's office set as he begs viewers to call his toll-free number. He will do anything from law to cleaning your toilet. "Just call."

4. Hank of Hank's Royale: A gruff restaurateur, he hosts talent night at his tavern, sports a red tuxedo blazer and constantly has a drink in one hand, a cigarette in the other. Enthusiastic about his show, has a constant repartee with the audience. "...right here at Hank's Royale, where the E stands for (cough, hack, hack, hack) entertainment."

Joe Lo Truglio: I wore a burgundy lounge jacket and sounded like Tom Carvel from the '70s Carvel Ice Cream commercials. We did him at Space at the Chase and other bar shows and the Winter on Wheels college tour. A version of this skit idea, without Hank, we did at the last reunion [Festival Supreme in October 2014], with all the recurring characters.

5. Barney Green: The comedian. A guy who spent too much money on "how to be funny" classes. He tells long, rambling jokes that have no punch line. His catchphrases are, "So, that happened," and "So, I got that going for me."

Joe Lo Truglio: [Played by Ken], another phrase said after he didn't have a punch line: "Bah bah bah, what else, what else?"

6. Johnny Matu and His Friend Donny: The world's worst ventriloquist. He talks to his hand, Donny, in a squeaky voice, but does not even pretend to throw his voice. He tells banal stories of his boring life. "So, we're on the plane and Donny says to me, 'I hope there's gonna be a movie on this plane, I hope it's the 'Pretty Woman'.'"

7. The Lobotomies: A family of lobotomy victims; Mom, Dad and Junior. They have huge scars across their foreheads. They have a television show, which basically features them sitting around drooling on themselves and desperately trying to reconnect their brains. "Pleh."

8. Martin: An overly friendly, smarmy guy who tries to make friends wherever he goes. He plays party games in inappropriate places and is constantly and deservedly ostracized by those around him. "My name is Martin and my favorite animal is ... dog. Okay, now you go." He just wants to be liked, and in his over anxiousness to be liked, he is hated and feared.

Joe Lo Truglio: [He was the] star of the "Martin's Best Day" skit, which ends with a surprise confetti balloon fall on David.

9. The Wops: Tony and Joey an Italian Abbott and Costello (although Costello was Italian). Two big goombahs in the Carmen Rissoli tradition. The stereotypical Brooklyn Italian. Joey is fairly smart, is a good put-down artist. He wears anything by Merry Go Round. "If I wanted a wise ass, I'd sit on a dictionary." Unrelated to Joey, Tony is also a stereotypical Brooklyn Italian. A small guy and dumb. He is always trying to put one over on Joey but usually fails.

Ken and Joe Lo Truglio as the Wops were in two New Group sketches: one in which they were sinking in quicksand and the other in which they were drowning at sea.

Ken Marino: It was just taking two kinds of stereotypical Italian characters because we felt we could, because we were Italian.

10. Mr. Paddyshaw: The most eccentric teacher ever to sit in front of a group of vulnerable young minds. Mr. Paddyshaw is a sweet, cardigan-sweater kind of guy who doesn't mean bad, but is completely unknowledgeable, and teaches his classes about subjects such as "shitting" and "cannibalism." Needless, Mr. Paddyshaw has trouble keeping a job. "Now remember what we learned last week, kids. Never stick your fingers underneath your rib cage and pull."

11. The Nowhere People: This is a group of friends who speak in a vaguely European accent and seem to be European, but whenever anybody asks where they're from, they sort of shrug it off and evade the question. They are big fans of American culture and enjoy discovering new things about America wherever they go.

They are always together.

The Nowhere People became Mr. and the Former Mrs. Laupin for the third-season sketch "Laupin Variety Programme."

12. Darnou, Social Retard: A youngish guy, early twenties, who is incapable of socializing the way normal people do. Because of his sheltered life, he has never fully mentally outgrown being ten years old, which hampers him whenever he tries to be social with people. For example, he prefers scented pencil erasers to women.

13. Bob the Pedophile: A pedophile who is completely frank about his psychosis. He is constantly trying to outwit children, who always see him for what he is, a pedophile. He wears tight pants. He uses lame ploys to impress children, none of which ever work. "Don't get me wrong, Will. I am a pedophile — but I'm also magic!"

14. Iggy Ratto and The Rodents: Iggy is a big, hairy, obnoxious poet for our times. He is the lead singer in his band, a rock opera outfit. He is also a storyteller in the Henry Rollins mode, dispensing his tales of urban angst and violence wherever he goes. Excellent at ping pong. The Rodents are his band and amigos, a motley assortment of ragtag wannabe rockers who follow Iggy wherever he leads them.

Robert Ben Garant: Iggy Ratto and the Rodents was a failed experiment that we did before MTV. We tried and failed at a Blues Brothers. We wanted to create a band where we were all a separate persona, like a Jake and Elwood Blues, where we would go on stage and stay these characters and never break character and just be a band, a comedy band but like a real band. But none of us played any instruments; so it didn't really work. The characters were funny, but none of us were musicians at all; so it fizzled. We tried to do one night, and we were like, "Oh, this doesn't really work," and we never really spoke of it again.

15. James Dixon-Agent at Heart: A one-time big-league

agent for the William Morris Agency, James Dixon lost his job in a pissing contest and now is a drifter, taking odd jobs wherever he can find them, but he is still an agent at heart. For example, he might be a guidance counsel negotiating a passing grade for a failing student. An aggressive, no-nonsense, paunchy guy who talks out of the side of his mouth.

16. Freak Master: Boisterous, bombastic, bawdy showman from birth, a showman 'til death. The Freak Master is a classic carnival barker who entreats paying customers to enter his freak house, which is filled with the lamest freaks imaginable. His trademark is "FREE FEARS!"

17. Drambouie Man: A superhero who is an alcohol abuser. He's a pretty fast runner, but he can't run in a straight line. He'll only fight crime after noon when he gets out of bed. By five, he's drinking again. He laughs at inappropriate times or starts weeping uncontrollably and telling people he loves them. He can't stand loud noises.

Joe Lo Truglio: I completely don't remember, but I laughed out loud at the description.

18. Emmett and Lyle Booie: Two inbred brothers who are inclined to self-torture and gambling on it. For example, they might see a rock and bet each other that they can't hit themselves in the head with it. Consequently, they tend to forget things that they either said or did only months ago. They make great moonshine, which people from all over the country come to sample.

Robert Ben Garant: The Inbred Brothers were sort of characters we did on "You Wrote It, You Watch It." I remember us pitching it, and I don't think we ever did anything with that list [of characters] except type it up and turn it in. There's no way that list would've stuck if anybody had actually called us on it.

19. Neil Linder: Lives with his parents and probably will forever, Neil is in his twenties, and he will stubbornly insist that something is other than what it is. For example, he'll describe a movie he just saw about a giant gorilla that attacks Manhattan, but he'll insist it was something other than King Kong.

Joe Lo Truglio: I don't think this character was ever performed, but we planned on putting him somewhere and wanted to legally own him before we hit MTV. I remember the King Kong bit from riffing on the idea with Ken.

20. Roberta: A dumb girl, big, blond hair, pays attention to her clothes and not much else, her slurred R's come out as W's. She is one of those girls who is so dumb that she thinks she's smarter than everybody else and consequently is incredibly condescending to everybody around her. Her standard response to any question put her way is, "I don't know."

21. Breakneck: A white rap trio in the mode of House of Pain – a parody of white rappers who want desperately to be black. Breakneck is from Great Neck, Long Island, and come from an upper middle class background but refer to themselves as being from the ghetto. They sample Billy Joel in their songs. They are passionate about their music but lack any credibility in trying to pull it off. They are ultra-macho, and, for the most part, ultra-wimpy.

22. Gina: A 17-to-19-year-old Hispanic woman, born and bred in Queens, New York. She has a preference for bangles, baubles, beads and nail art. Works in a nail emporium with her cousin, Lupa, and is very committed to her big boyfriend, Mikey.

The ever budget-conscious members of The State found a location to shoot sketches like "Old Fashioned Guy" and still be able to act a fool: Hot Bottom, Pennsylvania, where Ken's family had a second home.

Ken Marino: Hot Bottom, Pennsylvania, is twenty miles north of

Scranton. It's in the middle of nowhere. It's a very small town. It has the main street, which is like three miles from the house. [There's a] small supermarket, a post office; that was about it. I lived on Long Island. My parents moved out there when I was in fourth grade, and we lived out there for about six months, and then they realized they couldn't get any work. So then they moved back to Long Island, but we kept the place. It was a great piece of land because there were three houses on it — but old houses. There was this fifteen-acre pond, and we had a canoe and a rowboat.

When I was in college, I would grab Tom, Ben and Joe, and we would go there and drink and be reckless and silly and have campfires and just hang out. When we started doing "The State," we realized we could go up there and shoot sketches there with Dave's camera. We'd write sketches that took place in this country area because there was nobody there, and we could just run around and act like fools and shoot out there. We shot "Inbred Brothers" there and "Super 8" and a bunch of other stuff.

Michael Patrick Jann: That was the most physically miserable I've ever been. I was crazy under-dressed, and the heat didn't work. I was sleeping curled up on the floor clutching my hands around my balls because it was the only part of me that was still generating heat. And then we got up and shot a TV show. Glamorous.

Ken Marino: This [story] is just a testament to the commitment of our group or the competitiveness of our group perhaps. We had to go three towns away to get something to eat, and we went to this place. We sat down, and anything that could go wrong went wrong as far as how long it took, what the food tasted like, and the service.

David Wain: It was a like a "Twilight Zone." There was no food.

Ken Marino: It was eleven of us. So it literally took two and a half hours to have a burger. We were all super-frustrated. When we finally paid the check and got into the van, one of us just yelled, as I was pulling out of the parking lot, just started screaming in frustration about how crazy that was. Everybody started screaming, and nobody stopped screaming. It was very cathartic actually. We all just started screaming, and it had to be maybe an hour. Honestly, it was crazy-long, and I feel like I timed it. Everybody was just screaming at the top of their lungs and laughing and screaming and laughing and screaming, but without pause for the whole trip, and it was one of the most memorable, most ridiculous, stupid, committed things I think we'd ever done as a group.

There were certain people in the group who kind of dug the camping vibe that Hot Bottom gave us, and some people didn't like the roughing part. I remember one time we drove up there in a passenger van with all of us, and I was driving, and I didn't necessarily know exactly how to get there sometimes. Instead of driving to Pennsylvania, I drove south or something. Basically, I drove away from it and out of New York, and around one in the morning, I realized what I was doing, and I had to turn around. I had to try to triangulate my way toward Hot Bottom, and everybody was really miserable, and I felt terrible, and we got there at four or five in the morning. I turned on the coal stove, whatever the hell it was in the basement, and it all started smoking. It was busted. So we were all just stuck outside with a big, smoking house.

David Wain: Ken didn't even touch on how hostile some of us were to be out there and how "roughing it" it was, and he only made it worse. I know I was bitching about it. His thing was we were all ready to go, and everyone was in the van, and we're tired and cold and want to leave, and he gets into his rowboat and goes for a little row on the lake, while we're all waiting to leave. Everyone's digging in their heels — very classic State behavior.

Ken Marino: [We] stopped when half the group didn't really love going up there. It was like a three- or four-hour trek from Manhattan. I know Tom and Joe and Ben and I really enjoyed going there and acting stupid. So that was always fun.

I was just talking to my parents about it. It sounds glamorous when I say, "There's three houses on it, the pond," but it's not. One was already falling apart; one burnt down, and another one was built by Sears and Roebuck back in the '30s or '40s. I think they've got somebody to rent it out now and take care of the land because they're not there right now. They've just kept it. I've always said to them, "Don't sell it; I want it," but I've never gone back.

Joe and Ben dig the Times Square view from "The State" office.

CHAPTER 14

Season One

"If you post a video of your cat, people all over the world shit on you. This was back when it was just twenty newspapers and thirty TV stations, and they all hated us."

Robert Ben Garant

MTV blasted a press release in December 1993 heralding a "half-hour sketch comedy show that isn't afraid to take a raw, comedic look at today's pop culture. ... Their irreverent comedic repertoire includes spoofs on commercials, game shows, talk shows, rock stars and regular people. Through group sketches and individual character pieces, members of 'The State' give their perspective on everything from safe sex to parent-child relationships.

In one sketch presentation, 'The State' portrays 'Hormones' — a kind of 'he said/she said' regarding what a couple on a date are saying versus what their hormones (brought to life) are actually looking to do. In another, 'The State' presents a rock version of the '$20,000 Pyramid,' featuring Sid Vicious & Nancy Spungeon as contestants."

Reviews appeared the day before "The State" premiere, and they were harsh — and most of them used the troupe's name to bash the show.

"New MTV Series Isn't 'State' of the Art," the Daily News proclaimed in its headline, and the review ended with "This is one 'State' I expect will secede, not succeed."

Newsweek's review by Harry F. Waters didn't seem very open to the concept of absurdist comedy. He quoted Kevin Allison saying that "The State's" primary influence is Monty Python, following it with "Monty Python should sue." Waters' description of the show: "A man serving a gin and tonic to a llama; housewives chasing a giant mouse; a wrestler getting pinned by a crazy chair; and several people frolicking atop a giant yellow pudding ... it's definitely sophomoric."

Even The Village Voice gave the show a C minus, adding the stinger, "Eleven may be a great number for a basketball team roster, but it doesn't work for this group. ... Whether it's a case of too many cooks, kooks, or schnooks, 'The State' is rarely funny."

One of the nastiest reviews came from The New York Post's Michelle Greppi:

"Every MTV executive who gave thumbs up to 'The State' should be given a urine check," it begins. "It's a collection of sketches that could amuse only the crowd that gurgles and coos (or burps) at any movement by funny-looking figures on TV (or their own big toes).

And it's more puerile (there's one rather androgynous woman in the troupe) and unfinished than raw.

What could have been a riotous spoof of conflicting sex urges instead degenerates into a cotillion for butch hormones and a predictable masturbation joke as a punch line."

Robert Ben Garant: I don't remember a single one that wasn't really, really nasty. We did a morning press tour. They put all of us in a room on five microphones, and we did phone interviews with people all over the country, morning zoos, where they asked us, "Hey, guys, so your show premieres tonight. How you feeling?" I think it shows how dumb we were, but I think also how green our executives were. You would never put eleven people on an interview. The fact that there were eleven of us talking to somebody on headphones at once was almost impossible. You didn't know who was going to talk next, and it was just a cluster fuck from the get-go. The Power Pig in Tampa, Florida, read us the USA Today review live on the air.

"This is a new low for comedy," all this stuff, and we hadn't read any of the reviews yet. [He] ended it with, "Remember my name because you guys are going to be around for a long time: "H-E-Y-W-O-O-D-J-A-B-L-

O-M-E," and we were like, "Hey? Hi?" We were all trying to figure it out, and it was, "Hey, would you blow me?!?" and he hung up on us. That was one of the first interviews of the day, and we're like, "Jesus Christ." Later, MTV and Viacom pulled all sponsorship from that station, and I think that guy got fired.

Thomas Lennon: We had no idea that anyone could be so mean. Something probably snapped in a lot of us that day, where we were like, "Oh, there's aspects of this industry that are going to be just horrible."

Kerri Kenney: I think it was devastating. You hear laughter for four years of college, and you become a minor celebrity in your small circle and get a TV show. "Oh, my God, this is really happening." Then when the real world gets a taste of it and they don't like it, it was devastating.

Robert Ben Garant: We thought that they would cancel us. We didn't really know how it worked, but we thought that they would maybe not air the shows. Up until that point, I don't think we'd ever heard a bad word about us. We went right from NYU to our own little theaters to this great process of getting picked up really, really fast. Nobody ever said anything bad about our work before; so we were just totally destroyed — and people were mean. I think they thought we were like The Monkees. I think they thought that MTV put together a bunch of comedians. Not that it mattered, but I don't think they knew that we were eleven people who had worked together. People attacked us like, "It's a bunch of white people." People attacked us because we were so young — that we'd never done anything before. People attacked us for stuff that was so mean, and we were just devastated. It was absolutely the worst, and that was before the Internet.

If you post a video of your cat, people all over the world shit on you. This was back when it was just twenty newspapers and thirty TV stations, and they all hated us. It felt like a big deal when USA Today hated you. ... We didn't even joke about it for a couple of weeks. I think we were legitimately shaken and hurt.

Kerri Kenney-Silver: It wasn't for everybody — not everybody liked it. Comedy is very personal, and I don't know if it was before its time or anything like that. Some people just thought it was shit, and that's fine. But we loved it and believed in it and didn't change as a result of it. There were no discussions about, "How do we get these people to like us? What should we do differently?" We just kept moving forward and believed in what we were doing and hoped that they wouldn't fire us.

Jim Sharp: I've been doing this a while, and this probably ended up being the best two-and-a-half years of my career. It really turned into something.

"The State" kicked off at 10 p.m. on Friday, January 21, 1994, with an homage to CBS' spinning logo from the '70s and '80s, signifying something special was about to begin: the anti-"Saturday Night Live."
"Boogeyman" was the cold open, and the first State member to appear is Kevin, playing a little kid, terrified that there was a vicious monster under the bed.

Kevin Allison: I'm still kind of excited about that. ... I think two episodes begin with the Boogeyman sketch, which kind of confused people a little bit, because they would see the same set up happening at the beginning of an episode and think, "Oh, I've already seen this episode."

Kerri Kenney Silver: That was really fun because it was a live audience shoot, and that was new for us. Yet it was comforting for us because that's what we had done as a group before. It was new for us to

Show 101
Boogeyman
Lenny Lipton Show
Hormones
Hops Plus
Free Your Mind
(Clown/Pirate)
Chip's Party
Hypothetical Question
On-Air Personality
Mudwrestler
Eating and Swimming
Forever

have cameras. It was a bit of a learning curve about holding your marks and waiting for camera movements and stuff like that. We all quickly caught on. ... We always did cold opens to sort of smash you into the credits to catch your attention.

The credits sequence, scored by Craig Wedren and Eli Janney, felt like a thirty-second music video, with frenetic glimpses of the cast of too-cool-for-school twentysomethings.

Craig Wedren: They were just transitioning from music videos all day to original programming. So the mandate, really, with The State was, "The purpose of this show is still to sell records. So you have to use as many songs as possible from the MTV library in the sketch." I was working on a couple different themes with my little sampler. I sampled a bunch of bad-ass shit for what ultimately became the theme song, including a couple of Nation of Ulysses [songs]. Nation of Ulysses was an amazing, kind of futurist-punk rock outfit from D.C., and they were friends of ours, and it's possible even that Eli produced one of their records.

We didn't think that anything was going to come of any of it, and also they were like, "Hey, here's three hundred dollars. Make a theme song." So I just collaged this thing together, and it was happening. It was like a few different beats that I grabbed from something, these couple Nation of Ulysses samples, and then I was playing ukulele on top of it and singing, "No-no-no-no-ooh" stuff. It was definitely a moment where I was like, "Oh, shit, this is really good. I hope they like it 'cause it's kind of weird but maybe it's right." Everything was kind of grungy and alternative at that point. So maybe it'll fly. It's got noise in it; it's a crazy thing.

Eli Janney (associate music director for NBC's "Late Night with Seth Meyers"): Comedy people don't necessarily understand music. That's not their thing, and it shouldn't be, really. They do their thing, and we do our thing. I think they were just like, "This sounds great!" They had no perspective on it. ... It's kind of funny, now I listen to it now and am like, "What the hell is going on with this theme song?" It sounds insane to me, but it does have energy.

Craig Wedren: I called Ian Svenonius from Nation of Ulysses, and I was like, "Dude, I'm doing a theme song for this MTV pilot. Is it cool if I sample a couple of Nation of Ulysses songs?" I don't know whether I downplayed the commerciality of it because he's a very staunch punk rock purist and certainly didn't want to have anything to do with the man or MTV, but I think he respected me enough as an artist. He was like, "Yeah, man." I remember he said, "I don't want to get in the way of your art. If I can do it, it's great." In retrospect, knowing what I know now as an adult, what it takes to clear samples and the kind of permission that you actually need to get, the basic courtesy that I would want somebody to afford me if they were going to be sampling me, I can't even believe. It was so part and parcel with the way we did everything which was, "Yeah, just fucking do it, man, whatever. Kiss somebody else's girlfriend — it's totally cool. Go on tour for a year and leave all your shit in somebody else's bedroom, whatever. We're all friends."

It's so crazy. It's so rude and destructive, that entire era — and wonderfully so. You just kind of blitzkrieg your way through that, but I think back on that I just want to give Ian a hug. Of course, if I had ever made a penny off of it, I would have at least taken him out to dinner, but it was one of those weird things where it was like we were just kids and MTV was a sweatshop. They were like, "We'll pay you nothing, and you can do whatever you want," and we were like, "Cool, great."

I got it all to a certain point. Eli Janney produced one of my favorite Shudder to Think records called "Get Your Goat." I needed some help finishing the theme and polishing it and having him mix it. In retrospect, listening to it I'm like, "Polished? Mixed?" We shoved it in a tin can, in a shoe in a stinky sock and put it on TV, but I love it. So much spirit.

Eli Janney: It all came together in a haphazard fashion. I know Craig is much more meticulous about his composing, as I am now. But having lacked a lot of experience doing it, I think it's more about the energy and the vibe. We just threw a bunch of stuff on and pulled a bunch of stuff off and then were like, "OK, that sounds about right," and sent it to them. "Here's what we're thinking," and they were like, "Great." It's funny.

Craig Wedren: [The lyrics] "Boys and girls" is a combination of a couple different samples I took off this one Nation of Ulysses record called "13-Point Program to Destroy America." I just grabbed a couple vocal moments. There's this one song that has the "boys and girls" bit and a different song where he screams "action," and I just kind of put them together with all these other beats and guitars underneath.

Robert Ben Garant: The credits sequence, that's all Mike Jann. Anybody who says otherwise is lying. One of the pieces we did on "You Wrote It, You Watch It" was "The Cool World," a "Real World" spoof. They selected people to live in Antarctica. Mike came in, and he filmed the globe and a model airplane — cheesy graphics — and edited it together, sort of making fun of MTV at the time. Jon Bendis, one of our producers, he designed the water flowing over the logo.

But the cool, awesome, weird shots of us turning around, that was all Mike Jann. Mike Jann had a real bead on what MTV should look like. I guess he spent a lot of time watching MTV in high school. I remember not really knowing what it was going to look like, but I always had confidence that Jann was going to put it together right. What's great about it is it's really sort of ahead of its time. The shots in five different locations, edited together, really nice. It looks really cool without us looking like were trying to look cool, which is hard. The style really looks like MTV circa 1994, and it works. We're not trying to look cool, but somehow it makes the comedy group look cool without looking like pretentious jerks.

Kerri at "The State" opening credits shoot

Kerri Kenney-Silver: That was sort of my look then. Half the time I was in this punk band. I was always experimenting with my hair, which I could [do], because I wore wigs all the time for sketches, and I lived in the East Village, and that's what we all looked like at the time.

Michael Patrick Jann: You know how I just said comedy's not cool? Well, I just thought with that opening thing, "We're going to be cool. For these twenty-five seconds, we're going to be fucking cool." I had the colors planned and the location planned and the editing, and then Craig and Eli made the awesome song. It was cool to be cool for a short amount of time. It was a nice change of pace.

Jon Bendis owned those [letters that spelled "The State"]. One of his hallmarks was doing interesting graphic treatments with things, and he was very meticulous. That was one of his tricks. Once we had those [letters], we thought, "We'll make ones that catch on fire and make ones that melt and make ones that do this and that. It was neat, and it was fun. He was a fun guy to work with on stuff like that.

Jonathan K. Bendis: We were talking about different ways to do it and different type of printing block and typeset letters, and it was a matter of let's find them and see what we can do with them. When you get the letters, they're going to be inverted because that is what a typeset is. Then [there was] the idea, let's just leave them inverted. Let's not correct them. Somehow what you see is what you get. It was a combination of a couple different heads coming together. It was a great creative process.

Then I transferred it and I started projecting it again, and it's what I project it onto that then causes the texture. If you project it onto a piece of material that's waving, then you get these waves going by. Can you do this in a pull-down menu on an edit assist now? Of course, but that wasn't the fun, and back then the pull-down menu didn't exist. So then I was projecting some of them onto different things, and one of the things I projected Ken Marino onto was Ken Marino's ass because he has no problem, ever, to this day, dropping his pants. But what was so funny on top of funny was I shot it in black and white but by projecting Ken black and white onto Ken's colored ass and shooting it with video; now, I have brought the color back to his face through his ass cheeks. It was just funny.

As with the pilot and in the spirit of comedy heroes, Monty Python, "The State's" first season featured links to sketches with recurring bits. The first episode's sketch (after the credits) is "The Lenny Lipton Show," a morning news show in which the host, guests and even the meteorologist are constantly running through a park. It segues into a commercial for "Crispy Pops" in which a family is seen bolting from their house and darting down the street, as the pitchman for the cereal glides by on skates. That same pitchman glides by the horny couple in the next sketch, "Hormones," the first of The New Group "trunk" sketches to appear on MTV.

Thomas Lennon: We felt "SNL" was doing sketches that petered out, and we just refused to. So we were pretty hard on people with endings. We didn't always nail it, and sometimes we tried to nail it in the transition. As we look back on the series, for the most part, the vast majority of the links are a little bit arbitrary. Honestly, I would look back and say, "You know what, it would be great to just kind of hard cut in between things," because we were often doing stuff that was just not as good as the sketches in the links and transitions.

Jim Sharp: It was their idea. I wasn't sure about it, as I recall, but certainly was open to trying it. The one word I had with them was, "When you do sketch and you do a show that maybe has eight to ten sketches in it, you're going to have to have a kill number. You're probably not going to be able to go ten for ten. We're probably going to have to throw some stuff away. So the links, if they hold you hostage to the next sketch, that could be a problem if the next sketch doesn't work." I think we had some long conversations about that, and ultimately, when we really set the bar high and refused to put B material on, then some of those links, I think, did go away.

Kerri Kenney-Silver: All networks seem to be concerned with it being a cohesive show. The networks, in general, seem to get very nervous with a sketch show for the sake of sketch. MTV was no exception. They wanted to know how we were going to link the sketches. In the live shows, at the end of a sketch, it was lights out. They didn't think that was going to work; so we created these links that would get you from one sketch to another. Sometimes they would work, and sometimes they were very convoluted. It created a format for making the show individual and getting you from one place to another.

Michael Ian Black: I was always on the fence about it. I like the idea of it. It felt like a burden to me. It didn't feel important to me. It didn't feel like something people would really care about, the audience. It was a needless device. There were times when it worked really well. In those rare instances, I really liked it but felt like at times it didn't work out. I was never particularly invested in it. I don't remember ever writing those transitions or helping with the transitions. I just of stayed out of it.

Michael Patrick Jann: If you look back at Monty Python, their linkages are not terrific, and we didn't do animation. It's just from a different era, and the other thing is, it was a huge point of pride that we did endings. That doesn't go with links. In a lot of ways, we probably chose endings over links. Links are easy. Links are a piece of cake. It's whatever nonsense. Some of them are really funny. Python is known for its links. We're known for our sketches.

Robert Ben Garant: I think half of the group really wanted that, and half of the group thought it was pointless. I think originally we did one animated, a direct rip-off of Monty Python, but we couldn't afford it. I think MTV also wanted us to do that; so it wasn't just random stuff. Sketch shows, there's all these weird buzzwords whenever you pitch a sketch show because we've pitched them since. "What is the theme? What's it about? What ties it together?" I think the fact that they were all linked — our producer, Jim Sharp, thought that was a really good idea, to not have it just blackout, blackout, blackout, but sort of bring you from one sketch into the next sketch. I always enjoyed the links. The links were sort of weird and fun. A lot of them, it wasn't the whole group. A lot of the group didn't care about them; so we could go off and shoot them and not have eleven people there.

Thomas Lennon: We would cut to the nuclear apocalypse, and there's a super-weird one of Frank Whaley just dancing on the street, which was always jarring to me.

Michael Showalter: It was like definitely important to me to be getting sketches through the system, as it were. I was definitely keeping score of how many sketches I was getting through, and I wanted to make sure in every episode I had at least one good part. It was competitive; at least for me it was.

David Wain: [Lenny Lipton was] the first day that we were shooting stuff, and we had the amazing realization that we don't have to clean up afterward because other people would do that. It was totally amazing. We're like, "OK, that's a wrap. Now everyone start rolling up the cables and putting everything away," and they're like, "No, you guys don't have to do that. You can just leave," and we're like, "What?" "That's why we have a crew." "Wow, awesome," and that was the first time that we realized, for some reason, that we thought it would be funny to have the Spin Doctors song "Two Princes" [playing] all the time.

Hormones

Though the sketch was written more than twenty-five years ago, it would be considered risqué today. The piece ends essentially with the female lead pleasuring herself after the guy finishes too early.

Kerri Kenney-Silver: It was not written by me, by the way. It was written by Ken Marino. ... That sketch was always such a huge hit when we would perform live. It was a good one to show who we were and sort of showcase the fact that we have one woman. It also shows a female point of view in this fully male-dominated show.

David Wain: On the stage show, it was always my job and Ben's to also take the couch away after the sketch is over. I always forgot when

"Hormones" rehearsal at Festival Supreme on October 25, 2014

we did it on stage. So I would say to myself, "She jerks off; do the couch. Jerk off; do the couch." Even when we did it on TV, I kept saying that; then I forgot to take the couch.

Michael Patrick Jann: That was stuff that was audience-tested. It really worked. It was sort of a learning curve there, the difference between black box theater and the stage. There was some learning that happened there. Another learning curve was learning to be very direct in the film pieces, as well, learning how to be not too oblique about certain things, which you can do in a stage show, because everyone was so keyed up. It's a nice change of pace, but on a television show, it's the other way around. You have to place the audience closer to the characters than you might otherwise. You have to stick them in there.

Kerri Kenney-Silver: It was Ben Garant's birthday, and I sent a group email to The State saying, "Happy birthday to that one guy from that one hormone sketch two decades ago," and he said, "I'll be wearing my Hormones costume at WonderCon and signing autographs for five dollars if anyone is interested."

Hops Plus

A lo-fi beer commercial that shows the downside of nickel pint night

Joe Lo Truglio: That was a shoot that we did on the weekend. It was a day after a night of drinking. It smelled horrendous in there. Horrendous. It was so bad. We were just retching. I remember from that shoot how bad that smelled. It was perfect for that skit. ... It was a Budweiser parody, obviously. We had The Romantics' "What I Like About You" playing in the commercial at the time.

Robert Ben Garant: It was at Down the Hatch, which later changed into Billy's. Filming that piece, we found like forty-five bucks on the floor. That place was so disgusting. We were so psyched that we had this disgusting, beer-soaked forty-five bucks at the end. That was the bar where we pretty much lived. I think we pulled that sketch because Budweiser was an advertiser of the show for a while. ... Because we were implying that beer makes you drunk, Budweiser doesn't want to advertise on our show. That was it. Budweiser thought that made drunkenness not look fun, and they pulled it.

Chip's Party

Two college dudes crash a kid's birthday party, and for them, it becomes the bash of the year.

Robert Ben Garant: I wrote that one. The chemistry of [Showalter] and I is just so hot in that sketch; it's good.

Michael Showalter: Piping hot.

Robert Ben Garant: I think I said me and Show's chemistry was "odd," not hot.

Michael Showalter: I actually felt like our chemistry was pretty hot — a little hurt you feel differently.

Robert Ben Garant: I love that piece. That's like the only Showalter/Ben sketch in the whole season. Also, Kerri Kenney is this sexy, suburban housewife. Is that what we thought moms looked like? She looks like she's this 1970s Karen Black character. Is that what a grown-up looked like to us?

On-air Personality

We see the birth of the Michael Ian Black vainglorious persona. This and the "Hi, we're The State" pieces that followed on subsequent episodes gave Black more notability than some other members of the group, as he seemingly wasn't in character.

David Wain: The first draft of the sketches were like, "Hi, I'm Michael Ian Black, blah, blah, blah," and we were just, "That's not the point, our group..." and we made him change it to, "Hi, I'm an on-air personality." Then we changed it to, "Hi, we're The State." ... I think we were just super into the ensemble to the point of getting threatened by anything like saying your name. It was so weird.

Michael Ian Black: I didn't feel right about it. It didn't cause me enough guilt to stop writing them, because my ego and my guilt were sort of battling with each other. I would have liked it if other people sort of picked up that baton and ran with it a little bit, by writing, "Hi, we're The States." Some people tried, and that just happened to be something that I was good at.

Talking to the camera was something I was good at. Those pieces I think did have value. I sort of took it on myself to keep writing them and to include as much of the cast in them as I could in a three-minute piece. I did feel guilty about it. I really believed in the idea of ensemble. As far as The State goes, I still do.

Michael Showalter: One thing that I really feel was a big breakthrough for us in terms of our creative evolution had to do with what Michael Black was writing — these sketches where it was, "Hi, I'm Michael Ian Black. I'm the real person. I'm actually me. We're these real people."

That wasn't something that was totally in the vocabulary of "SNL" or Monty Python to do that. There was a little of that but not a lot. Those shows were much more about the characters and the sketches. We were seeing ourselves as who we really were as people, and that was something that we definitely did none of at NYU because of the theater thing and the acting thing and the love of sketch comedy. To break that wall and actually do material where it was like, "Hi, I'm myself," was a little bit of a new frontier.

Michael Ian Black: It was uncomfortable at times to do that and to feel a little bit alone, literally because sometimes I was doing the sketches alone, and also creatively alone, because no one else was in the sketches. They might resent me for doing them. The fact is we did them, and we didn't have to. They were easy to produce and were cheap. They cost us nothing but time to make. They were good pieces to do if we were worried about how much stuff we had. If we were going to come up short, it was easy enough to put together a, "Hi, we're The State." That probably helped them survive.

There was something about that kind of blithe arrogance, that sort of not knowing what a douchebag you're being, that sort of purposeful dick-headedness, but without consciously trying to do that. Because the wardrobe is over the top, my performances are over the top. I didn't even like the outfit that the time, but I didn't have enough confidence to say, "I don't like this."

Mudwrestler

A date tries to impress her boyfriend's family by taking on the dad in an impromptu mud match because naturally the family has a non-regulation mud pit in their dining room floor.

Kerri Kenney Silver: We shot that live, which is insane looking back. We had to because it added to the excitement of what was happening. We wanted the audience's reaction, that, "Oh, my God, they're going to mud wrestle on stage in front of a live audience." There's no second take. At the time, that was really exciting.

Robert Ben Garant: "Mudwrestler," I think Michael Black wrote that one or maybe Ken Marino. I did drag all the time on the stage show. We all had to. We never discussed it, but when people were in drag, they still acted like themselves. On stage it killed. Us doing a woman voice or a woman character would've been so strange because we don't really do that. It always killed on stage.

We just acted like ourselves. That carried on into the series. That just became our style. We never really discussed it. On the stage show, we only had Kerri; so every guy had to do a woman tons of times.

Eating and Swimming

Tom and Joe, pre-pool

A PSA looking at the very real danger of not waiting forty-five minutes after eating before jumping in the pool

Kerri Kenney-Silver: Oh, honey, you're seeing us actually almost die. I remember one really horrific day of shooting that will stand out in my mind forever. It was this piece about not jumping in the pool right after you eat. We shot in New Jersey, in January, in bathing suits, in an unheated pool. It was a one-taker. When we all jumped in, everyone's lungs imploded, and people were drowning in the pool. In hindsight, hilarious; at the time it's amazing no one died.

David Wain: Everyone was so pissed at Mike [Black] because he didn't have to jump in the water.

Michael Showalter: We were young, and we were competitive, and we deeply believed that to be good at comedy you had to be fearless. You sort of sacrificed your body for the joke. There was a lot of crazy falling down — [in] "Pope's Visit," spraying shit at each other and dumping shit on us, jumping in a lake and jumping in a pool. That was part of the thick skin. You didn't want to be the one person who wasn't jumping in the pool. You didn't want to be the one that everyone was like, "Showalter just chickened out."

I had had a lot of training with that in terms of my friends growing up in Princeton. "Who's going to have the balls to do a backflip off the diving board?" I just never wanted to be the guy that didn't have the balls. There was a lot of me doing stuff that I probably was scared of, but I would rather do it than be considered a chicken. Being a chicken was not a good thing in my universe.

Forever

A song Tom Lennon performed at NYU gets turned into an "MTV Unplugged"-style sing-a-long, with Kevin Allison sporting a shiner for some reason.

Thomas Lennon: When I look back on State material that I absolutely despise, I think the boner song is one of my all-time lows. There's a couple of all-time lows that didn't really make the air or got cut, like my "Baywatch" sketch, which was wildly reviled at the time, and Jim Sharp put an F on it or a D minus. Jim Sharp would give you like a check or double check. Jim must've been a schoolteacher at some point before he was our producer; he would give us grades on our sketches. The boner song made it through, and it just makes me cringe. I mean there's a ton of State stuff that I absolutely love and could watch all day, but I just hate the boner song so bad.

Gang Fight

Craig Wedren: Again, this is probably the case of just straight-up ripping somebody off because I didn't know better and because I was like, "It's rad; who cares?" I think I took "War Pigs" by Black Sabbath and Onyx's gangsta rap beat and made

Kevin, Todd, Tom, Kerri and David have their souls stolen.

this really fucked up, fun, collage out of it. I was still really obsessed with my sampler; so there's still a lot of collaging going on and proto-score happening.

Doug & Dad

This episode must have been a favorite of MTV execs, because it features three eventual recurring characters: motivational speaker Captain Monterey Jack, Louie (the guy with the catchphrase) and Doug, a surly teen who lashes out against his hip dad, spouting, "I'm outta' here!" with the combined angst of one hundred drama students.

Dude, it's Dad, Doug and Dave!

Michael Showalter: I didn't sit down intending to write a sketch with a catchphrase. I had an idea for a character, and you're sort of trying to crack the nut of the sketch. I saw there was a funny character of this kid who wants to be rebellious, but his parents are cooler than he is — which I think for a lot of kids in my generation that's kind of true. Our parents were civil rights pioneers, and they were at Woodstock, and they were all in their twenties in the '60s. How do you be cool when your parents were in their twenties in the '60s? Anything you've done, they've done it more: the drug revolution, the love revolution, music. Our parents lived through The Beatles and Janis Joplin and The Rolling Stones and Bob Dylan and all these things. We had John Hughes movies and R.E.M.

Many versions of that sketch were just trying to find the joke of it all. In the writing of it, it started to be funny that he would get frustrated and be like, "Forget it. I'm done. You don't understand." He'd get frustrated and leave. That started to become what was funny, and then it turned into a catchphrase, and then I hear a lot of shit for it from the group. It was absolutely a source of mockery. It was not like, "Good for Mike; he has a recurring character." Once MTV wanted more, it was like I was a sellout and a company man and all that shit.

Robert Ben Garant: Doug is a pretty good concept. It's not like the one-joke concept. You can take it in a couple different places.

Joe Lo Truglio: My character wasn't based on any one person, actually. It was my interpretation of a timid, tagalong guy. The paralyzed mouth — so much of your character choices when you're in the sketch show is about having a rubber face, just having a face that looks different than when you're the leader or something. That character, I think, appeared in a video called "The New Guy," which opened "Molt."

I loved Ken Marino's character in that. He just looked terrified the whole time — just had a look like he was going to run and cry at any moment.

Ken Marino: I think all those kids felt like they were misunderstood. Whereas Doug was defiant, my guy, (whose name I forget if he had a name) if asked any question, would have broken down like, "You don't understand!" That was my interpretation of that character. That was my back history of that non-speaking role.

Michael Showalter: [That] was evidence of the "no small parts" mentality of the group. The shining emblem of that [was] no matter how small your role was, even if you had no dialogue, you would try to make something great out of it.

It's like when you're rationing food, you make whatever you have last. There was so many of us that if there was any little part you could get, you would try to maximize it and make it special.

Joe Lo Truglio: I wish we had another sketch of just Doug and his friends hanging out. You never quite knew what they were so pissed off about not being able to do. "Screw this, we're going to do what we want to." That might've been fun to explore.

Just don't walk up to Showalter at the airport and expect him to dance like a monkey and spew "I'm outta' here" for your phone's camera.

Michael Showalter: I never participated in that. I never liked that. I'm not good at that. I try to be friendly, and I try not to be rude or anything like that, but I'm not good at that. ... I started to figure out how to avoid even putting myself in a situation where it would happen, kind of make myself a little unapproachable — just not make eye contact with people as much as possible and give off a vibe that I don't want to be approached, which, you know, is not necessarily a good thing. It's very uncomfortable when someone comes over to you and wants you to perform for them when you're walking down the street.

Captain Monterey Jack (Lights)

Michael Ian Black: He sort of called to mind these tough-love school lecturers who would come around and tell you you're an asshole but why he loved you anyway. It just worked. That was one of the ones I felt like I wrote pretty easily. The character sort of emerged fully formed. I don't remember any of his advice particularly. "Ring, ring. Hello? Who is it? It's cheese." I don't remember much. "I don't know what the Pearl Jam would do with their cheese." He was trying to relate to the kids but would get it just slightly wrong. "Marky Mark and the Funny Bunch." The idea of falling down at the conclusion was definitely a rip-off of Chevy Chase.

Louie

Fans of The State know "Louie" as a parody of recurring characters that backfired because he became exactly what the troupe was making fun of, but his origin story does involve more than ping pong balls.

Ken Marino: David Wain would always have his hands down his pants, and he would always play with his dick and balls. I'm actually not sure what he was playing with; it might have been just balls, might've been just his dick. At that time, he would eat a lot of things. Whatever was sitting around, he would eat those things. If there was something sitting on a desk, he would pick it up and start eating it. If it was somebody's leftover food that was in a tin, he would pick it up and eat it, or if it was even in the garbage, he would pick it up and eat it. He doesn't do this anymore.

Somebody had a thing of peanut butter on their desk, and David picked it up and took his hand out of his pants, and he opened up the jar of peanut butter, stuck his fingers in the peanut butter, and ate the peanut butter off his fingers. I got very upset because that type of thing frustrated me. I was like, "Dave, why don't you dip your balls in it?" and I started kind of saying that.

David Wain: I think I used to just be very gross in general, by putting my balls places, my fingers places and doing weird stuff with food, not like perverse stuff. When I was kid, I had this friend, Josh Smith, and we used to make videos called "Food Beavers," and we would take all the food out of the fridge in my parent's house and make a mess with it and dump it all over each other. I don't even know why. It was really weird, and then we would do an audio track on it, like play-by-play. "Notice how the texture is." It was really, really stupid, but it became a family-favorite video. Anyway, I don't think I was putting my balls in peanut butter, if that's what anyone said.

I just was in the habit of scratching my balls a lot. They were itchy, and then I thoughtlessly would put my hands wherever after that. I'm better now.

Ken Marino: So we started laughing about that turn of phrase ["I wanna dip my balls in it"], and then I said, "That should be the catchphrase that our recurring character says over and over again." They were like, "How do we get it past standards and practices?" and we were like, "OK, he can hold a ping pong ball," and they're like, "That's funny; that's ridiculous." So he just screams it over and over again. In my head, I'm going to play that guy. I think Showalter wanted to play him, too, and I was like, "C'mon man, you got Doug." I remember having that conversation with him in the bathroom, and he was like, "OK, OK," and he gave up the fight for playing Louie.

Kerri Kenney-Silver: One thing that MTV wanted consistently was a recurring character. We really saw ourselves as this alternative group, anti-"SNL," and felt like at the time that recurring characters were sellout. You only did them to make money and to sell product, and we are here to do art and blah blah blah.

That's why Ken created Louie, who dips his balls in things, as sort of a "fuck you" to them. "You want a recurring character? Here's a recurring character." We're going to hammer it home, and he's going to say it one hundred times. It turned out to be a brilliant way of addressing that note.

Ken Marino: I think the original Louie thing was we just had one show that was hyping up a famous recurring character of ours, and at the end we were going to show it, and it was just the guy who says his catchphrase over and over again. We wound up shooting interviews with Iggy Pop and some other people remembering Louie, this recurring character from the '70s. Then we wound up shooting the sketch, and they liked the sketch, and then they were like, "Do more of that." We're like, "How do you do more of it? It's just a guy who comes in and says his catchphrase over and over again. There's nothing to it."

Actually, it wound up being an interesting challenge because we had to think of cool, fun, different ways to bring a recurring character back and that he was just a comment on recurring characters. We did another one; I think it was the Louie with some terrorists at a party, and they love him, but I think the one that really kind of was the fully realized version of a Louie recurring sketch was Jesus and Louie at the Last Supper.

Michael Ian Black: What surprised me was that we were the only ones who seemed to get the joke. That was disappointing to me. People just thought it was funny, but they didn't get the joke of the whole thing, which is that the idea of recurring characters in and of itself was stupid and wasteful and not very creative. They just liked that there was a guy shouting, "I want to dip my balls in it!" In a way, the joke was on us. The joke was very much on us.

Robert Ben Garant: The Louie sketches were all about Louie, but you could tell everybody was having a really good time with their one line in the Louie sketch. I think that's something that made us different. We didn't just phone in the background parts. A lot of pieces were written so the background parts had to be much tighter rehearsed than the foreground characters, which I think is pretty cool.

I think Louie is really funny. "I want to dip my balls in it" is irrelevant. I think there's a lot of different catchphrases that would've been equally funny, but to me, what's funny about is that people are going, "Boy, I wish Louie would come and say his catchphrase." That to me is so great.

Joe Lo Truglio: I love that we were at least trying to have a take on the convention. Even if no one else got it, at least we were attempting to put it out there.

MTV Sports

Kevin Allison: There was this guy named Dan Cortese who had a show at that time on MTV called "MTV Sports." He was just kind of obnoxious, and the show was edited in such a way that it was a barrage. You felt like you were getting punched in the face throughout the whole show, and he was being a goofball. We thought, here's one pop culture reference we can make to this other show on MTV. The pitch was essentially let dress me up as Dan Cortese, and I'll just say crazy shit on a golf course all day. The group really doesn't know how that's going to turn out, but it did end up being a lot of fun. I still have people to this day say they get a kick out of some of the ridiculous stuff I was doing in that sketch. There's no narrative arc. I'm driving golf carts around and pretending that golf balls are my eyes; I'm just being obnoxious.

Antonio

Eileen Katz: The one Tom Lennon character that I wish had become a recurring character was a foreign exchange student sketch. ... That is my eternal favorite. "Oh, please, can we just see him one more time?" Please, please, I want to see how this ends." I was begging, "I need more." That character was comedy crack for me.

David Wain: I can see that as a series now; we should look into that.

Tape People

Michael Ian Black: What we liked about sketches like that is that they did not directly spoof anything. They weren't pop cultural in any real way, but they did speak directly to our audience because they were coming out of abstract experiences that people that age were having. "Tape People" is just a stupid joke about us putting tape on our faces and somehow warning people that it can happen to them, but it's a very familiar setting, which is college RAs talking to freshmen. It was basically a rehashing of that Sterile Yak meeting where these sophomores act like they have all the answers in the world talking to freshmen, but they [the sophomores] are idiots.

Kerri Kenney-Silver: I remember lots of times going off with Michael Black. We were sitting in an office, and there was tape on the desk, and he put a strip of tape on his face and start talking. I said, "Maybe that's a character," just us walking to the office in a funny way and talking in a funny voice. "You should write that." It was very collaborative.

Crackers

The Cracker family enjoys their saltines — and spitting them all over their neighbors.

Todd Holoubek: We did another one, I don't remember the skit, but it had something to do with an assembly line and bowling balls. I had to be a drunk foreman, but instead of whiskey we used apple juice.

I don't know if you ever drank three gallons of apple juice. Try it; it's not pleasant afterward. I think eating the butter [in "Crackers"] was a little worse. On stage, you can kind of fake that because you have some distance. You don't really have to eat the whole thing of butter because nobody really knows. When you're on camera, you know the camera does not lie. Everybody knows whether you ate the butter. We ate the butter.

Doug & Principal

Show 104

Disclaimer

Cute

Ride

Doug & Principal

Don Law

Light Coma

Old Fashioned Guy

Pants

Capt. Monterey Jack (Cheese)

On the Table

$240 Worth of Pudding

Joe Lo Truglio: With Doug, I don't think Showalter wrote that originally with the intention of becoming a recurring character. I could be wrong. I remember it was just a great sketch. My memory of it was that he just wrote that sketch, and then once we put on its feet, it was so easy to make it a recurring sketch because it was all in one room. They had all the friends; they had the father; and everything was set up. I think it started out as just another sketch but an awesome one. I liked Doug. It was always kind of a fun teasing among the group about Louie and getting recurring characters. To Showalter and Ken, that might've been annoying.

I think in general we were trying to deal with the realities of working for a network, the realities of working for executives who had a show to produce. They have their jobs on the line. They were telling us what they've seen work in the past on "SNL" and stuff. They were really to blame. It was a strain figuring out, how can we do both? How can we give them what they want but keep with what the group thought was integrity? In retrospect, I thought it was a pretty good job. We didn't have a lot of them. We had Doug. We had Louie. Bookworm, we had Barry Toink. He would show up now and again. Of course, Barry and Levon and the Old-Fashioned Guy. At the time, it was a necessary evil that ended up turning out to be ironically enough some of the most memorable characters.

Light Coma

One of the most-controversial sketches among members of The State because it bears a lot of similarities to a sketch on "Saturday Night Live" that aired more than a decade later

Robert Ben Garant: That may even use the same name. "Good morning, Glenn." The first line is exactly the same. I think it was Dane Cook on "SNL." I don't know who wrote that one. I think two people could come up with that premise. The first line is almost exactly the same. Sure, maybe that's coincidence, but that's really weird to me. The idea that you wake up in a coma for five minutes, and your wife is remarried; I get that a lot of people could think of that. I was a little surprised because the first line is really exactly the same, which is very, very strange.

David Wain: Famously copied word for word on "SNL."

Pants

When "The State" was released on DVD, it was without many of the songs that scored the show because the rights were too expensive to obtain. Originally scored to The Breeders' "Cannonball," this is one of the sketches that was truly weakened by losing the original soundtrack. Sadly, the only way to legally watch "The State" now is with the new soundtrack. To be fair, Craig Wedren did an admirable job of trying to replicate the songs as best he could and still keep it legal.

Michael Ian Black: We started looking for opportunities, and I think that was the first one, to write sketches to music, knowing that we were going to do these music montage pieces and taking advantage of what we had. What was nice about them was they were unique. Nobody else was doing that, because nobody else could, because we had access to this library. We could use any music that MTV had. That was a tremendous boon to us and opened another window creatively in terms what we could do. ... We had been assured that we could use this music. It never occurred to us that somewhere down the line the rules would change.

Robert Ben Garant: It was a really easy way to get stupid stuff into the show because MTV always liked it because it was music-driven. ... Yeah, this was great when it was The Breeders.

David Wain: I sat there in the editing room with those two VCRs and the controller and pulling out all of the different quarter-inch video tapes that had the music videos on them. We could steal the music from [them] for the show, and [I was] just trying out different things. That's when we found that song by The Breeders. We were like, "Oh, that's cool," and we re-edited it, as we often did. ... Years later, when we had to do the DVD and replace the music, we also had to replace the voices because we never had it separated, and the voice performances completely changed because I don't think anyone could completely recreate what they did that day.

Michael Ian Black: That's just me strolling down Fifth Avenue in my underwear. It sucked. ... I think it's still pretty bold to do that. I wouldn't recommend that to anybody. I remember hating shooting that, really not wanting to shoot that, but feeling like I had no choice. That was one of those sketches that David shot. They were kind of our B-sketches where we would take a skeleton crew like on "You Wrote It, You Watch It" and go out at night — not get permits and not get any permission, just pretend we were students from NYU shooting.

$240 Worth of Pudding

Velvet suits. Big, permed '70s hair. Porny voices.
Tom and Mike Black's Barry and Levon characters
are fan favorites and well worth the amount of
money they spent on vanilla pudding.

Michael Ian Black: It was something that Tom and I wrote together. He started working on a draft by himself with the title. He hadn't gotten that far into it, and I asked him what he was working on. Then we started riffing on it. That sketch represented to me a distinct direction that I wanted the group to move in. I think lot of us felt that way. I remember pitching it to Eileen. We pitched directly to her because we knew she wouldn't get it if we just sent it to her on the page. So we went to her office and acted it out, totally expecting her to be like, "No, I don't know what this is. I don't understand this." To her credit, she thought it was funny from the get-go.

Eileen Katz: This is what's amazing about them. They came into my office, and they start going through it, and I'm blushing because it's definitely a little sexy, what they're alluding to. I don't know what it is; all I know is I'm really uncomfortable and I'm blushing, and it's all about pudding, but it's not at the same time. I'm hysterically laughing, and they're so deadpan, committed to it. "Fine, whatever has Barry and Levon on it, just greenlight it. It's fine. Next."

Thomas Lennon: Eileen was very supportive. She still, to this day, is one of the people who really did the most for us. She was really amazing. So I hope she gets the credit she deserves as a giant supporter of our show.

Michael Ian Black: And we did it. I guess once it aired, I wasn't surprised that people liked it because I'd seen the reaction of the studio audience. I knew that it was weird. I knew that it made no sense on a certain level, and that was particularly appealing to me.

Michael Patrick Jann: Ultimately, when you think about it, "$240 Worth of Pudding" is really about pudding. It has no subtext; that's why it's fucking awesome.

Robert Ben Garant: It's so funny, I remember, Black and Tom pitched a sequel to Barry and Levon that wasn't really a sequel. It was sort of a progression, the next movement in a piece. It was called "The Ricky Jones Show." The State understood it was a sequel to Barry and

Levon, but the network never let us do it. Also, half of the group hated it, but we probably could've pressed it through. We should've done it. It was a musical piece. Tom popped up in the front, with the permanence of googly eyes, and he looks at the camera, and there's a gold camera behind, and he sings the Ricky Jones theme song. Then Mike jumps out in the back and is dancing around in this one-piece parachute pants material jacket with three buttons on it. And he pushes the first button, and the suit inflates, and they're dancing around, and me and Mike Jann get lowered into go-go cages, and we're dancing around, and nothing ever happens. Half of the group loved it, and half the group hated it. That should've been the sequel to Barry and Levon.

Free Your Mind (Smoker)

Kerri Kenney-Silver: They wanted us to spoof their network. When we did, I think it was pretty dark.

James Dixon: Guidance Counselor

Robert Ben Garant: [Dixon] was so psyched. He is exactly like that. I think that's why James likes it. That's the voice. That's the look. That's the hair. That's the chi of James Dixon.

Thomas Lennon: Dixon was riding on the Long Island Rail Road one day, and he was heading to New York. The show had been on for a little while, and there was a bunch of kids from Long Island who were ditching school, and they're on a train with Dixon. They're talking about how they were cutting school, and then

Show 105

God is Dead

Mind Match

Grandma's Potato Chowder

Hot Pursuits

Free Your Mind (Smoker)

James Dixon: Guidance Counselor

Cindy Crawford

Old-Fashioned Guy

On-air Personality (Youth Conference)

Lunch with The State

Missy Von Kimmelman

Louie II

one of them said, "Don't worry about it. James Dixon will get us off. Ha ha ha ha ha!" And they were standing next to the real James Dixon. I know that for him that was a really amazing moment. He called me up, and he's like, "Someone just referenced me, standing next to me on the Long Island Rail Road." I know it was a real proud moment for him.

James Dixon: That is a true story. I was riding the Long Island Rail Road into the city, and it was St. Patrick's Day, where kids would cut school and go into the parade and get shit-faced. I heard "James Dixon" and I figured it was someone I knew from Long Island. Right? I'm looking around, and I'm like, "Nobody. Who's saying my name?" And I heard it again. "Who's saying my name?" There was a group of high-schoolers assembled by the doors, and I heard them say, "We'll just call James Dixon, Power Guidance Counselor; he'll get us off," and I was like, "You're fucking kidding me." So I walk up to them. Right? I pull out my wallet, and I pull out my license, and I go, "Did you just say James Dixon?" and they're like, "Yeah, why?" and I go, "I'm James Dixon," and they're like, "No fucking way. Aaaaaah." They just went crazy. "You're that guy."

Oh, my God. It was great. "Here's my license." I said, "I work for the William Morris Agency; those are my clients." They practically asked me for autographs. It was really fucking funny. I mean, honestly, you couldn't write that shit; it was just crazy. But that shows you the impact that they had at that time.

Lunch with The State

David Wain: I really wanted to do that one because I really loved to overeat as much as I possibly could. We went to Tavern on the Green and ordered shitloads of food and ate it.

Ben

CHAPTER 15

Drag

"I was blessed in that I had
the body of a prepubescent
boy, which translated well to
playing women. I think I did
a fine job, but I just hated
it — hated it on the day of
shooting it and subsequently
hate it every time I'm asked
to do it."

Michael Ian Black

Robert Ben Garant: I was the first one in the group to do drag, I think, on the live stage, and it was in "Crackers," a sketch that I think Michael Black wrote. The Cracker family, and Kerri was already in it as the mom, but there needed to be another girl who came in and then got yelled at. I don't remember why, but I got cast as that, and I just totally didn't play it as a girl at all. The dress that we found was like this weird, sleeveless, farm-girl dress. At the time, I used to lift weights and do push-ups all day long. So I had good arms, and I thought that it was so funny because I had these gorilla arms in this Dorothy Gale dress. I was going out on a date. So I decided to go bowling because when I held the bowling bag, it made my arms even bigger, and it got lot a big laugh. Coming in as Sally Cracker and not acting like a girl at all and no one really acknowledging that I was just acting like me really went well. The audience laughed at it a lot. So we tended to do that.

Joe, who is sort of hot as a woman in some sketches, he would act like Joe. The Pythons, when they were women, it was such a specific thing that they did, and it was so great. We really talked about it, like, "What do we do? We need to have our own approach. We need to have our own thing." We knew always from the beginning that we were going to have to do a lot of drag 'cause we only had one girl. What we decided on was that we wouldn't do anything; we just sort of acted as ourselves.

Kerri Kenney-Silver: I don't think it was even necessity, really. Some guys would come up with characters that were female for them to play. There were times when there were enough girls to play the girl parts, but it's funnier. Joe would do the character in a funnier way. It was never an issue for us. In fact, it was shocking when MTV even brought it up. It's funny now that we were shocked by that, but they brought up all the time. "How about some color or how about other women?" This is who we are. We can't just throw people in here.

It always bummed me out when Michael Black would put on a dress and look better than me because he doesn't have child-bearing hips. I think everybody made a pretty woman, except maybe David. God love him; he does not make a good-looking woman. Very bizarre.

Kevin Allison: The first one I think I did was for the "Lenny Lipton Show," which is in the first episode. ... I was supposed to play a news lady, and I had never done drag before. As a gay man I had never had the desire to do that. Even as a kinkster, I still don't have any interest in that whole cross-dressing thing. In the kink community, it's a trip to me to see how popular it is among straight men. It's all the rage. But it never interested me.

When I got up in drag for the first time I was shocked. I was like, "Oh, my God, I look like — and I started to sound like — my Mom." It became much more pronounced as time went on. One sketch, "PMS," it's causing [Kerri] to have Jekyll and Hyde syndrome. She keeps becoming a slightly different character. Different members of The State keep running out in red dresses as if they're Kerri. In that sketch I'm just Kerri's friend. I swear to God, if you watch that sketch, I've got the short auburn hair that my mom has, and I'm wearing a rather conservative, plain dress like my mom would wear. I said, "I'm just going to go all out and be my mom here. I'm just going to embrace this." I see that sketch to this day, and I'm like, "Holy shit, I really nailed my mom there." It's weird to me that whenever I get up in drag, a part of me just starts veering toward Mom.

David Wain: We're not doing women's voices or trying to make our voices higher. We're just like acting like we normally act, and we just were wearing dresses. I guess we were wearing makeup, too, but I think that was what Python did, sort of? We just decided that since we're all going to be playing women, we'll just play them as other characters and not try to specifically or necessarily act like women.

Michael Ian Black: I hate playing women, and I hate it with a passion. It's odd to me how much I dislike it. I hate putting on women's clothing. In a way, that makes me feel like I was abused in women's clothing as a toddler. I hate putting on a bra. I hate putting on the makeup. I like wearing long skirts because they're very comfortable. The amount of time in the makeup chair I hate. There's something about having breasts that I find so upsetting that I almost can't deal with it. I was blessed in that I had the body of a prepubescent boy, which translated well to playing women. I think I did a fine job, but I just hated it — hated it on the day of shooting it and subsequently hate it every time I'm asked to do it.

Michael Patrick Jann:
Mike's half a girl anyway. Have
you seen his skin? His skin is
ridiculous. ... I know Joe usually
gets the props for being the best
in drag, but I feel like maybe I
deserve a second look at that.

Eileen   Katz: Oh, my
god, Joe Lo Truglio, the hairiest
man in the world, five o'clock
shadow for seven days, in a
wig. That adds a whole other
level, a whole layer of wit and
creativity, and it's just more
sprinkles on top of the frosting.

Joe   Lo   Truglio: I'm
pretty in drag. I think one of
our costume heads used me as the Virgin Mary on a Christmas card
and sent to the cast and crew. I was flattered by that.

Kevin Allison: Everyone agreed that Joe was actually kind of
hot when he put on drag. That's one of those things where it's a little bit
hard to predict how well someone is going to be able to pull off drag. Ben,
it was almost humorous because he did a lot of working out, so he had
a very cut, manly body, and it looked all wrong. We would deliberately
put him in sleeveless dresses to emphasize that, isn't it funny how unlike
a woman he looks? Then there were people like Showalter who would
put on drag and just kind of seemed damaged. We enjoyed it. To us it
was no big deal. We'd seen Python do it, and we were surely aware of
Kids in the Hall doing it.

**Jana Rosenblatt (costume designer for seasons
two and three):** You could really tell how they felt about women
by how they played women. Joe was always fun to make a woman, and
Showalter, even though he was not an attractive woman, always really

took what you gave him and made it somehow respectable. Todd, he did not play that game well. ... His wig was never straight. For him, playing a woman meant disheveled and a wreck of some kind.

Michael Showalter: I really, really, really hate being in drag. I would probably rather not be in a sketch if it meant being in drag. I hate putting on stockings. I hate putting on a padded bra. I hate wearing a wig. I hate wearing makeup. When there were sketches going around that had us in drag, I was the first to volunteer not to be in it. I'm still like that, by the way.

Todd Holoubek: Hard to say. You know, I don't know. That's a very tough one because everyone had their own flavor of drag. When you're in comedy, you see men do drag, and some men play it like a pseudo-female, where they accentuate the sort of feminine qualities; so they look silly. Some men play it as they are; they just happen to be wearing a dress and makeup. Then some people play the character. I always tried to play the character, regardless of what I was wearing. So if it was Game Show Hostess, I was a game show hostess. It didn't matter; more of a shape shifter. The worst part about it was shaving. What a pain!

Tom and Sho

CHAPTER 16

Season Two

"Second season, a bunch of us went to this big strip club in the middle of Times Square. ... The deejay said, 'Hey, I wanna dip my balls in it.' We were like, 'Oh, we've made it.'"[1]

Robert Ben Garant

To launch the second season, The State and MTV made the brilliant decision to take their critical beating and turn it on its head.

Kerri Kenney-Silver: One of the smartest things we ever did was turn that around. True to that sort of "Fuck you if you don't like this" attitude, we made a commercial for the second season with us all walking through a park and kicking rocks and consoling each other. "I Started a Joke" [by The Bee Gees] was playing, and we had all the bad reviews scroll over the screen. The last thing it says was, "The State coming this summer. More miserable crap."

Doug Herzog: Eileen and Joe Davola and myself, the development team, we were pretty passionate about it, and we were a little bit in love with those guys. They were pugnacious yet irrepressible, and we just loved being in the sketch comedy business. I guess we must have felt strongly enough about it — despite the bad reviews and the first-season mediocre ratings — to bring it back.

Then they did that promo, the "I started a joke" promo, with all the shitty review lines, and then all of the sudden people started going, "Hey, the show is getting better." They were the same shows; we were just re-running them, and people were just coming around. I don't believe it was ever a gigantic ratings hit, but I think it got to a place where it did just fine.

Robert Ben Garant: I think that was maybe the first time we felt good about the bad reviews. I think, until then, it really hurt. Then I think that reminded us who we were maybe — that we were punk rock, and everybody's supposed to hate us. ... That was the thing that turned the tide.

Kerri Kenney-Silver: We got a great reaction from that and probably gained a lot of viewers. Kids love that. "Ooh, I'm watching something the grown-ups don't like." That was a really clever way to handle that. ... We turned it into something good and slowly started to get respect.

Michael Ian Black: I feel like most of our peers, people our age, didn't watch television in New York. New Yorkers were going out to eat at restaurants and going to clubs going to see bands. The impact was very gradual. I felt like pretty much nonexistent in New York City, and even if people did recognize you in New York, they would be too cool to say it — which is exactly what I would've been like, too. There was a moment I remember. We would go to this bar downtown on Tuesday nights called Don Hill's, and I remember there being a moment in time when, "Oh, I'm kind of famous now walking in there." That did not lead to me having sex as much as I would like....

Robert Ben Garant: The first time I even had a sense that people were watching the show was the break between season one and season two. I went to visit my parents in Phoenix, Arizona, and I went to a bar and was recognized there. I went to see Michelle Shocked, and somebody in the crowd recognized me. I think that was the first time it even occurred to me that anybody was watching.

The second season, we would walk around in big groups, and people would kind of freak out and recognize who we were. I think it was second season, a bunch of us went, as sort of a joke but sort of for real, to Flashdancers, this big strip club in the middle of Times Square. It's the strip club where David Letterman used to send the guy in the bear costume. I hadn't ever been in a big strip bar before. So I was really nervous, and [while we were] walking in, the deejay said, "Hey, I wanna dip my balls in it." We were like, "Oh, we've made it."

Thomas Lennon: If the show were on now on MTV, it would be an epic. We'd have pretty big numbers.

A.D. Miles, now head writer for "The Tonight Show with Jimmy Fallon" is an early State collaborator who has gone on to work on many of the troupe's movies and shows in subsequent years. He started with them as prop master for the second and third seasons of "The State" on MTV.

A.D. Miles: I had fallen in with some commercial production companies, just being a PA, and worked my way up to the art department and had become a prop master. One of the people that I was working with knew somebody at "The State" and said they were looking for somebody to fill in. It went pretty well so I stayed on with them. My first real friend in the group was Joe Lo Truglio, and [we] became kindred spirits and found we had a similar sense of humor. To this day, he's one of my best friends, and I count him among the most like-minded people I've ever met as far as comedy goes.

They were as cocky as you'd expect some twenty-year-olds who had their own TV show but generously so, if that makes any sense. I loved watching them work, and I think being on the crew for a while allowed me sort of an anonymous front seat to watching their process on the studio shoots and on the remotes, where there was just a continuous, nonstop reworking of the idea and the pitching out of lines and "What about this?" or "How about this idea for the ender?" I just thought that was really impressive, and also it was easy for me to feel comfortable around them because they seem so generous with each other, as far as it was a very large ensemble and everybody had their moment in the sun.

Costumer Jana Rosenblatt also came on board during the second season.

Jana Rosenblatt: My very first interview with them, I'm in producer Jim Sharp's office, and they're all sitting around the room and they were pretty casual. I'd never been interviewed by a room of twelve people, and I believe it was Ben Garant that said, "Well, here's the thing; we are the ones that are funny. We don't want the costumes to be funny; we want us to be funny." And then they wrote skits like "Porcupine Racetrack," dresses made of bacon for "Bacon," "Sea Monkeys," and I'm like, "OK, yeah, I can do that."

I felt a lot older than them. I had to maintain some form of hip and cool, which was a little bit staggering for me. I remember a lot of them thinking that '70s was retro and, therefore, funny and, therefore, good to write with, but I had to live through the '70s. I didn't find it attractive, yet I was having to dig through that history quite a bit. It was actually helpful, I think, that I was older in terms of my visual experience in life. I was really grateful that my husband, who is very musically and culturally knowledgeable, was always much farther ahead. We're the same age, but he was much more clued into what was current. So I would run home with a script full of names of people I had never heard of who happened to be current and topical, and his job would be to find me some kind of visual resource or at least explain to me who they were. It was pretty funny.

Mime Crash

Real cops try to hash out the details of a faux car crash between two sets of white-faced mimes.

Todd Holoubek: Most of us had studied mime. We made jokes about that — not like serious mime; I don't think any of us actually performed as mimes. [It was] part of the curriculum. There wasn't "television acting;" it was theater. [In] some classes you wouldn't even say the word television. That would get you kicked out for the day, you know? Yeah, we had to use our mime, sure. Mimes are also funny, you know?

Show 201 (July 10, 1994)

Ballet I
James Dixon: Power Priest
Choking
Sleep with The State
Piggy Shoes
Nazi War Criminals
Ballet II
Barry Lutz Show
Mime Crash
Ballet III
Service with a Smile

Service with a Smile

Lots of sketch shows do fast-food sketches, but this one became a fan favorite thanks to Ben's over-the-top performance as a cruel manager with three magic words: "Chicken sandwich, Carl!"

Robert Ben Garant: I love that one. I wrote in Central Park.

That's the most sketch-type sketch I've ever written in one of the worst sketch-sketches on the show. It's just a sketch. That could've been on Ernie Kovacs' [show]. I knew that I wanted to yell at Todd. That's one of the sketches that we pitch at three o'clock. I think I wrote that at 2:45, knowing that I wanted to pitch something. That's a classic restaurant sketch. In some ways, I'm surprised it made it through our system.

Michael Patrick Jann: Ben would go off in the middle of the day, to the park or the Met, and he'd come back in the afternoon with his little notebook that he always carried with him, and he'd have three solid, pitchable sketches that he'd write out in two hours. He'd do this every day. It's hard to keep up your self-esteem when you see someone working at that level so consistently, but you can't be jealous when you see how hard he worked. He was always prowling every situation we were in or the situation in his own subconscious for ideas. He'd whip out that little notebook right in the middle of a conversation. No one ever got mad at him for that because we all respected him and his work so much. "Chicken sandwich, Carl" was one that he found out in Central Park one day.

Todd Holoubek: I think that's the one that has never been removed from YouTube. "Chicken sandwich, Carl," which isn't the name of the sketch, I don't remember what ... "Service with a Smile," yeah, that's it. That's a terrible name. Naming things is hard.

That was definitely one that I know stood out just the first time I saw it. I don't know if it was the physicality of it, but it was special.

That kind of worked out with the sort of the Skipper/Gilligan two-member comedy team, you know, Abbott and Costello. I think we had both grown up watching a lot of black and white, old comedy. Old Buster Keaton, Marx Brothers, Abbott and Costello, we watched all of those, so that moment, we knew exactly what was going on there.

Robert Ben Garant: I didn't have the wherewithal to step back and look at what my strong suits were. When I look at "Service with a Smile," I think I should've yelled at people more. That sketch is good. I never wrote other things where I was furious. Looking back, that's a shame.

Get a Job

Avoiding the wacky and surreal, Ken, Kerri, Joe, Mike Showalter and Michael Ian Black perfect a realistic suburban experience of a twentysomething who refuses to work.

Ken Marino: To me, that one was more like a New Group sketch that we would have done in college. I was worried that it was not State-worthy, but I enjoyed it. It wasn't completely absurd, or crazy all over the place or visually interesting. It was just two dudes sitting down and talking. It felt like it was from Kids in the Hall, but I always liked it. I thought Mike Black was really funny in it, and then Joe coming in at the end ... [it] was very blue-collar.

Joe Lo Truglio: It was more of a slice-of-life type of thing than a set-up, punch, which I loved. I loved the garage. It was just a real '70s suburban thing for me — people just sitting in the driveway, and that was kind of the hang. People would come by and drink a couple of beers and just look out at the block where nothing was really happening.

I had a dad character that was my go-to for many of the characters in The State. That one in particular was an amalgam of a couple of my dad's friends and also a couple of my uncles and people in Queens that I knew, that always would punctuate their sentences with a look, a stare-down that was so intimidating but also hilarious to me. They look silly, yet they thought they weren't looking silly. Some of them didn't look silly. Some of them, genuinely I was like, "I don't want to have this guy on my bad side." They're strong, silent, men of few words, who carry just a weight in their looks and their walk. It's chest out, at almost a waddle.

I always wanted to incorporate that stare-down. The other thing,

Show 202

I'm Watching

Pre-school Narc

Get a Job

Jurassic Park

Norwegian Cruise

Battleship I

Copy Shop

Battleship II

Superfriends

Eating Muppets

Hi Brow / Low Brow

that my dad did do, was when he sat down, he would always let out this sigh, this cascading sound that ended when he hit the chair.

Norwegian Cruise

Possibly the best State commercial parody, this one highlights some of the more unusual perks of travel: getting assassinated by monkeys?

Michael Patrick Jann: I didn't join the group as an actor. ... They were fucking competitive. We were a group of friends, but it was definitely competitive, and I was not involved in that competition. First of all, it was never anything that I set out to do. I didn't go to acting school. I had performed a little bit with the group, and I had small parts, but when it got to people really needing their faces to be on screen in every episode, I was like, "Go for it." I was totally OK with being skipped over in that department. I was super-happy to be one of Doug's friends. That was cool with me. I was never bummed out about I'm not in enough stuff. So when I wrote ["Norwegian Cruise"], it was like, "Well, there's only one person in this, and there's no dialogue." I remember in the meeting after I read it, I actually asked, "Would anybody mind if I just did this?" I remember Kerri Kenney screwing her face up and going, "Of course, you can; you don't have to ask."

We shot that on the same day as "Choking." While we were shooting that, I lost my glasses on the beach. I'm practically blind without glasses. So, luckily, I figured it all out beforehand, but I shot "Choking" without my glasses, and my nose was touching the monitor in order to be able to look at what was going through the camera.

Superfriends

Aquaman gets cut to shreds in this DC Comics-themed costumed caper.

Joe Lo Truglio: We had a "Superfriends" sketch, and we cut to an exterior of a suburban house, and we saw Ben run by as The Flash. Then we went into the house for "Eating Muppets." ... It was a transition that I thought was kind of cool. It incorporated some animation and the joke into the next sketch. Those work in chunks. I don't know if the entire show was able to pull it off well.

Bookworm

Joe's recurring character, high school jock Barry Toink, goes to great lengths to remember a nerd term.

Joe Lo Truglio: Any of the sketches that I wrote, like "Bookworm" or "Ride," the two cold opens — the call is coming from inside the pants and the ghost story cold open that were parodies of horror movies — I wanted to be involved in directing. The ones that were more traditional sketches, I felt less inclined to want to direct. If I wrote it, I wanted to kind of direct it. The budding filmmaker came out in those examples.

There was so much collaboration on the second-unit stuff, like "Taco Man." There was a collaborative feeling. We felt like everybody in The State was directing anyway. I always felt like I got my share of directorial contributions during those moments. It also wasn't something that I was that interested in. The writing and the performing were more important to me at that time because that was how I was going to get in sketches.

The strongest voice of the group was the writing and the performing. That being said, Jann and David created the look of the show that is very specific. That only dawned on me much later.

Show 203

Microchip
Bookworm
Down the Pants
Relationship Line
People Really Live This Way
Elevator
State Intro
Phone Line: Carrie
Lois & Clark
Barry & Levon
Phone Line: Plant
Brow

PMS

Intricate choreography makes this sketch shine, in which Kerri goes through many physical stages of her time of the month, as portrayed by most of the other members of The State, all donned in the same wig and dress.

Ken Marino: I tended to write a lot of the big group, visual sketches. ... It started with "Hormones," and I always liked writing sketches that involved the group and had some sort of weird visual thing. I think in some smoke-filled room that I was sitting in with Joe and probably Ben, I was like, "You know what would be really cool, if we all got to play the same character. How do we do that? In a live sketch, how do we make everybody play the same character? Everybody can be a different personality of that person, but it's in front of a live audience. How do we do that?" That was my attempt at that.

Those types of sketches I always get excited about because I just thought they were slightly trippy or slightly more visual than just word play or set-up, joke, set-up, joke. They were bigger. So that's what I tried to do from time to time.

Inbred Brothers

The title says it all.

Robert Ben Garant: Those guys were sort of based on the sketch we did on "You Wrote It, You Watch It," the "Skeet Call" thing. I think those started with Tom making fun of me good-naturedly, being from Tennessee. I had two uncles from middle Tennessee, and they swear those characters were making fun of them, and they loved it. They thought that Emmett and Lyle were making fun of Steve and Randy. Those were great. Again, those were pieces we just went out there and knew that we could think of a minute's worth of jokes that we set to music. That's really fun.

Teacher's Lounge

Another slice-of-life sketch, imaging the conversations that likely really happen when educators get behind closed doors and verbally rip apart their young charges.

Kerri Kenney-Silver: I didn't get to keep any [wigs], and between there and "Viva Variety," the amount of young Chinese girls' hair I had on my head is amazing. The one that does stand out for me was in a sketch called "Teacher's Lounge." It was how I expect I'm probably going to look when I get older, which is sort of that lesbian art teacher, long, gray hair kind of thing, lots of turquoise jewelry, flowing clothes from Chico's. It seems to be in my not-too-distant future.

Show 206

World Records I

Hepcat

Babysitter

Pimple

Teacher's Lounge

World Records II

Dinner: The Kids

Wildtown

Fetishest

Unplugged

1:15:06 PM
AUG 11 1995

MOTOTROME INVIITATINAL

zzzz

MOTOTROME CO-WIZARDS

NEXT WEEKEND...

MOTORDEATH HELL!

There are dozens of State sketches "in the trunk,"
that were never recorded. Here's one of them by
Tom Lennon and Michael Ian Black, including a
storyboard by Joe Anders.

BMX MOTORTROME 1995

Lennon/Black
computer title
Date Submitted:
Version #:
Version Date:

*A home movie camera gets turned on. Two teenage guys, AARON
and JEFF are decked out in full BMX gear. They both have braces. THEY
are on the front lawn of their home with their BMX bikes. As AARON
speaks, JEFF creates his own echo effect. SEVERAL OF THEIR FRIENDS
are hanging around. Most of them have Slurpees. HAIR NOTE: They
should have real short sides and long hair in the back. The whole piece
should have the look of a home video.*

AARON
Good afternoon, ladies and gentleman, and welcome to the first an-
nual Jeff and Aaron BMX Motortrome Invitational 1995! Riding the
Widowmaker, in the red officially licensed BMX gear — Jeff Sherman.

JEFF
And taming the Hell Cate, in the blue officially licensed BMX gear,
Mr. Aaron Finley. Today Jeff and Aaron will be competing for the title
of Motortrom Wizard 1995, performing death-defying stunts on their
BMX bikes set to the music of the one and only-

TOGETHER
Mr. Billy Joel.

AARON
Operating the camera today is my younger brother, Mr. Todd Finley.

TODD swings the camera around to himself and shows us what he is up his nose.

JEFF
Let the Motortrome Invitational begin!

VIDEO EFFECT: In camera chyron: "Motortrome Invitatinal" flashes.

A montage of BILLY JOEL songs start: "Uptown Girl" to present as JEFF and AARON do tons of very funny BMX stunts.

Ideas: Jumping over the dog. KEN chasing somebody with his ass. Lots of wipeouts. Shot of their neighbor sort of shaking his head in puzzlement. Them playing basketball in full BMX gear. THEM having a pantomime light saber fight. TODD taking a whiz. One of them has their braces caught on their bicycle chain. One of them driving straight into a moving car, just hard enough to hurt them. THEM doing the slalom through RC colas. THEM jumping a lit sterno can. THEM. A FRIEND holds the camera, we see his hand holding a cup of Slurpee. He says, "Slurpee bomb!" and lets a bunch of Slurpee drop to the street, where it splatters. A FRIEND making out with some RANDOM GIRL. THEM really mad at each other having a serious fistfight. THEY jump over Black Cat fireworks. THEY parade their bikes with sparklers in the spokes with REAL KIDS from the 'hood. Jousting with rakes. ONE OF THEM actually has gotten knocked out somehow, and others are trying to revive him. Racing around the bases of a baseball diamond. Riding their bikes off a diving board into a pool, and lots of other funny crap. ONE rides into a heavy piece of plexiglass that he was supposed to break through. AN OLDER WOMAN is seriously yelling at them, pointing at their shit on the street. AARON and JEFF nod solemnly. Throughout the piece there are glitches of a birthday party or similar.

Music ends. JEFF and AARON stand together.

JEFF
And now, the crowning of the BMX Motortrome Wiazard. The judges

are tallying their scores ... and here is the result.

AARON unfolds a piece of paper towel.

AARON
We have a tie! Your 1995 Motortrome co-wizards are Jeff Sherman and Aaron Finley.

THEY shake hands.

JEFF
A special thanks to Mr. Todd Finley.

TODD places the camera down and runs between them.

AARON
We'll see you again next weekend for the ultimate BMX challenge: MOTORDEATH HELL!

THE THREE of THEM pose and make cheering noises. After a beat, ONE OF THEM walks to the camera and turns it off.

OUT

Black, Sho and Ken take a break from the road.

CHAPTER 17

Road Trips

"Get in a van, see the country, and essentially try to have sex with people who liked our television show — preferably girls.

Michael Ian Black

Joe Lo Truglio: I believe this was probably May or June of '94. We had shot the second season. So Ken, Show, Black and myself had decided to take a five-week-long trip cross country.

We had a hiatus. We had just worked a lot. Everyone was just taking a vacation off. We knew we were going to do more episodes after a few months because MTV had just ordered a big chunk, and we had done a few of them at this point. So it was like, we know we have a job coming up, let's take a vacation. How about a cross-country trip?

Ken gets comfy in the van.

Ken Marino: We finagled a big, fourteen-seat passenger van and we pulled the back seat out of it and we're like, "Oh, this is gonna be great." We were gonna drive down to Georgia and then New Orleans and then across to Vegas and then up to San Francisco and Portland. It was gonna be fabulous.

Joe Lo Truglio: I think everyone just wanted to do their own thing. I know that Todd and Mike Jann, maybe Ben, went down to Mexico because Todd's family had a time-share down there. I think everybody just kind of split off and did their thing. It was a very memorable trip. We were going around the whole perimeter, down to Baltimore. We hit Athens, Georgia, and we met Michael Stipe there.

We were in some café. He said, "So you guys have a show on MTV." [Showalter] was like, "Yeah, yeah, we do. I hear you're a rock and roll star," and Stipe was like, "Yep, yes, I am." It was kind of a cute, little quippy exchange, and he was very cool. We were down in Athens, and we hit New Orleans, and then we went to Austin, Texas.

Michael Ian Black: Get in a van, see the country, and essentially try to have sex with people who liked our television show — preferably girls. I feel like the other three were a lot more successful in that venture than I was, probably because I didn't drink, and I didn't really know how to do that.

Michael Showalter: Oh, my God. It was very much of a rite of passage. We really drove all the way around the country. We crashed a van. We took lots of drugs. We drank copious amounts of alcohol. We saw all of the great sites: the Grand Canyon, the Badlands, Mount Rushmore, the Hoover Dam, Las Vegas, New Orleans. This was the first time I'd visited any of these places. We drove through Montana and through the Dakotas and into Minnesota and Wisconsin. We drove through Mississippi, Alabama, Louisiana. We went all the way around the perimeter of the whole entire country.

We were just having fun and blowing off steam. We were young; we were partying a lot. A lot of it was having adventures, going to some city and meeting people in that city and sneaking into the quarry. We were in Athens, Georgia, and we'd meet people, and we'd all go to some lake in the middle of the night and all go skinny-dip. It was that kind of a trip.

Joe Lo Truglio: We stayed in Austin for a good three or four days; we loved it. Our M.O. throughout this entire trip: we drove into the new city to go to the downtown area, find or ask someone where the best bar was, and we would go there and try to meet people, where we would find out we would either stay with them if they recognized us from the show, or we would just have a couple of drinks and meet people. We were taking advantage of our newly found, minor, cable celebrity.

You have to remember that we got terrible reviews. The ratings weren't that great for the first season. So it started to dawn on us as the trip continued that more people were watching the show, specifically more college kids were watching the show. We were being bought shots, and people were coming up like, "Where you guys staying?" or "Where you guys gonna crash?" We were like, "Oh, we don't know." I think we might have stayed at a frat house once. I have no idea which city, but we ended up meeting people that were very cool. Once that started to happen after the first two cities, it was like, "Maybe this might be a great way to save money."

Michael Ian Black: It was a very intense trip. We were out all night, every night, driving for hours on end, hanging out with cool people in great towns. It was a great experience overall.

We were the same age as the kids we were staying with, maybe a year or two older, but it made sense at the time. You do get tired at a certain point of listening to the Red Hot Chili Peppers at three o'clock in the morning in some frat house, but it took probably longer than you would think to get tired of that.

Joe Lo Truglio: So we have this fifteen-passenger van. After a couple of towns, we realize people are watching the show. That was exciting, and it was really the More Miserable Crap promo that people had been talking about that we met. So we pull into Austin, and I think we're at Emo's, and Ken didn't drink that night because we had planned to leave Austin and go to our next city late at night, like midnight. Black wasn't drinking and still doesn't drink, I don't think. So I think it was Show and I, and Ken was our DD, and then I guess we wanted to beat traffic.

Ken Marino: Black didn't do any drugs, or drink or do anything like that, so and Mike and Joe, it was our last night there, and they were gonna drink. I said, "I won't drink tonight. I'll drive the first leg until the sun comes up and then I'll wake Mike up and he'll drive the second leg." Joe and Showalter can sleep it off. I drove through the night, and then the sun came up, and I woke up Mike Black. I said, "You OK to drive?" and I remember him going, "No." He was joking around and goes, "Yeah, let me just get some iced tea," because he wanted something to wake him up. So we stopped, and we got some iced tea, and he started driving.

Joe Lo Truglio: I'm in the shotgun; Ken is in the long bench directly behind the two front seats, and Showalter is in the last bench in the back of the van, kind of sleeping. I doze back to sleep, and the next thing I know I wake up to a scream. I didn't realize it was a scream, but I wake up to a scream. I kind of open my eyes, and I'm just seeing the van bouncing all over the place. I'm seeing branches fly by the windshield, and my first thought was, "What dumbass shortcut is Black taking? What is he doing? Why are we not on the freeway?"

Ken Marino: We were driving over small trees, and Mike Black had the cruise control on; so he was doing seventy until we were hitting these trees, and he wasn't hitting the brakes. The van kept pulling itself back to get up to seventy. Every time one small tree went down, there was another small tree in front of it. It's not slowing the car down. You couldn't see the next thing in front of you. We were bumping and moving so much that I flew forward, and Mike grabbed me as I flew back-first into the CD charger.

Joe Lo Truglio: It was chaos. The van was bouncing. Ken has flown forward between Black and I. Black is now holding onto Ken. I'm strapped in but kind of reclined. There's just shock on everyone's face[s]. We're bouncing for what seems like an hour, but we finally come to a stop. Thankfully, we go through a few very small wire fences, over a few shrub brushes, we go down into a ravine, and up the embankment and then finally stop. Silence. We're just kind of grasping what just happened.

Ken Marino: One hundred feet in front of where we stopped was another ravine. If we had gone into that one we wouldn't have been able to get out of it. We would've hit the wall, and I would've went through the windshield.

Joe Lo Truglio: Luckily for us, what we didn't realize, there was a pickup truck behind us that, as soon as we went off the road, had called 911. Shock has really now overtaken all of us. I just needed to get out of the van. Showalter is asking me for a cigarette. "Joe, do you have a cigarette? Joe, do you have a cigarette?" Finally, I just said, "Sho, we just went off the road at eighty miles an hour. I don't know where anything is now. I don't have a fucking cigarette. I don't know where my cigarettes are." I just wanted to get out of the van. Black has gotten out of the van and is now walking around the van just to take a look at the damage. Ken is the only one that's kind of hurt. He went flying into the dashboard, and the cigarette lighter that was out as a charger, and [he] just really hurt his back. So he's now laying on the front bench where he originally started just until the ambulance got there.

Black does the view of the van. The windshield is spider-webbed, cracked. Both side view mirrors are gone. The front axle is now pushed back and has come out because we slammed into an embankment on the other side and just dents and scratches everywhere. The two front tires were busted.

He comes around and leans in the driver's side window, and he's like, "You know, guys, looking at this, it's actually not that bad." This is the shock that he's in. The fifteen-passenger van that is on MTV's dime is totaled.

A Texas state trooper has now arrived and is literally out of "Smokey and the Bandit." I mean, it's the hat; it's the mirrored sunglasses; it's the swagger; kind of a gut over the belt — literally out of a movie. He's like, "Yeah, boys, how ya' doing? Mornin'." Black sees him and raises his hand and says, "Mornin' to ya'." The guy's like, "Mornin'. Everybody all right?" He was very cool. As much as he looked like that guy from the movie that was going to bust balls, he was quite nice and kind and compassionate, and I think what helped is that this is like eighty-thirty in the morning, and it didn't appear to be, nor was it in actuality, any type of drunk accident. It seemed to be someone had fallen asleep.

The ambulance is there. He makes sure everyone's OK. We leave the van there. A tow truck is coming at some point. We all get into the ambulance with Ken, and we go to the nearest hospital which is in Sonora, Texas. We're like the only people in this hospital. It's the smallest hospital in the world. The nurses are the sweetest people in the world. Ken goes to get an X-ray, and it's me, Black and Showalter in the waiting room, and that's when the weight and the magnitude of what almost happened really sinks in, and we all got pretty emotional.

Black, of course, felt horrible, and there were hugs and like, "Oh, my God, we were so lucky."

Ken Marino: My back went into spasms because the charger kind of went into my spine. My seventh vertebrae got swollen or shocked, so they had to take me in an ambulance to the smallest hospital I've ever been to. It's like a six- or eight-bed hospital in Sonora, Texas. It was just me and all the other beds were empty. ... I stayed in the hospital for two days, and it was my intro to cottage cheese. I learned that cottage cheese was delicious. If you ever really want to get into cottage cheese, try the cottage cheese at some weird, random hospital in Sonora, Texas, because it's really delicious.

Michael, Ken, Joe and Sho

Joe Lo Truglio: This was one week into what was going to be a five-week trip. "What are we going to do? Are we going to bail, or are we going to move forward?" "Let's do this; we're going to keep going."

Michael Ian Black: That kind of ruined the trip for me, as it would, when you almost kill your friends.

Joe Lo Truglio: [MTV was] so gracious, and the most important thing to them was whether or not everyone was OK. The insurance covered the van. We had also borrowed a video camera because we were gonna maybe shoot some stuff, and I think that made it through OK. They were just really, really cool.

We ended up having to rent the next car. Out of the five weeks on the road, I think we spent between seven and ten days at a hotel, motel or sleeping in the park. The rest of it we were just crashing on people's floors and couches and stuff.

Ken Marino: The rest of the trip was phenomenal. We went to the Grand Canyon. We stayed there for a good twenty minutes and were like, "This is great; let's go to Vegas." We went to Vegas and gambled for a good amount of time and then made our way up to San Francisco, Portland and went to the Badlands and did some adult things.

Joe Lo Truglio: We did allow Black to get behind the wheel again.

While Ben, Michael Jann and Todd hit different locales on their road trip during the same hiatus from "The State," it's interesting that both adventures climax with run-ins with the local authorities.

Robert Ben Garant: I think that trip very much tells you the different personalities of some of the members of the group, because we loved drugs too, but we sort of fled the limelight and other people went to the heart of it.

Michael Patrick Jann: We drove from Wisconsin all the way down to the Yucatan in this giant, white Suburban. Todd and I started down. We picked up Ben in Tennessee and hung out with his uncles, Steve and Randy.

Todd Holoubek: We kind of hung out in the mountains. We went running through the woods. It was really incredible. We met [Ben's] uncle, [and] his uncle's like, "I've got some guys you wanna meet." We go to this dirt road, we meet those friends, and then those friends are like, "Oh, we've got someone we want you to meet," and then we were further off the dirt road. There was no road, and we met this family. There wasn't even a grid back then, but they were off the grid. They showered in a waterfall. Off the grid. This guy took us on a running tour of the local mountain paths. For him it was like his backyard so he just took off.

Michael Patrick Jann: Uncle [Steve], I'm not kidding, took us out to a storage space before we left and opened up [a] lawn-size trash bag that you use when you have a maple tree in your front yard. It was full of dope. He just reached into it and pulled out handfuls and handfuls of weed, stuffed it into a giant lunch bag and said, "Here, for the road." We went off with a natural bag of weed and had this incredible road trip.

Robert Ben Garant: It must've been at least a pound. It was huge.

Michael Patrick Jann: We went to Memphis, and we accidently wound up being at Graceland on the night of the candlelight vigil.

Todd Holoubek: We just pulled into town, we looked around and you just knew something was going on. "Oh, look at all these Elvis impersonators." We thought that was normal, but then you started to see tents and festival things. Everyone's got candles and singing, and everybody around you is crying and weeping. It was definitely one of those moments that's etched in my brain. I will never forget standing with thousands of other people holding a candle. Somehow, we all knew the words; we sang along with everybody. It was one of the most surreal things I think I have ever done.

Michael Patrick Jann: Then we went down to New Orleans, and some friends of ours, Craig Wedren, actually, who did the theme song, his band [Shudder to Think] was playing on the second stage of Lollapalooza.

We got to New Orleans, and walked in the French Quarter. God, there's so many bars, so many places to go. We had no idea where we should be going and we spotted two or three girls and were like, "They look cool. Let's just follow them wherever they go." It wasn't like we were stalking them, we were just hoping they would go into someplace cool and lead us, inadvertently, someplace cool. I guess we didn't do a very good job of following them because they turned around and were like, "What're you doing?" We spilled the beans. "We're just looking for someplace cool to go," and they were like, "Oh, we just moved down here from the East Village two months ago," so they were actually from our neighborhood. We had a great time.

They owned a secondhand shoe shop down in the French Quarter. We wound up spending the day with them and part of the next day. We called MTV 'cause Lollapalooza was in town, and we're like, "Can we get tickets?" MTV hooked us up and put us on the Smashing Pumpkins' list. That was like, "Holy shit, we have a TV show, right. We can do cool things." And then we told them, "We're going to Lollapalooza tomorrow," and they're like, "Oh, great, we're going to go there, too because [the bassist in Smashing Pumpkins] D'arcy came into our store and put us on their list, too."

We went out to Lollapalooza in the morning, not really thinking through entirely, "OK, now we have just walked into our audience." The people at Lollapalooza, that's who watches "The State." There is nobody else who watches the show except for this entire group of people. We walked in and we saw Craig [Wedren's] band play on the second stage, and then wherever we went it was like, "Ah, ah, ah!" people pointing. People started coming up to us and asking us for autographs. It was incredible ... a guy handed me a twenty dollar bill and just said, "Sign this" and I'm like, "You gotta be kidding me? You're gonna want to spend this. My autograph is worth nothing."

Robert Ben Garant: I think even if we hadn't been famous, we still would've been the Willy Wonka of that Lollapalooza. We were just handing out marijuana.

Michael Patrick Jann: We caused such a stir just walking across the fairgrounds that they took us aside and said, "Look, we're just gonna set you up in a booth over here." People just lined up to have us sign stuff at Lollapalooza. The three of us are sitting there, just saying hello to people and signing their whatevers. As this is going on, our girls that we had met came up and saw us at the table and they said, "Wait a second, who the fuck are you guys?" That was the best thing that ever happened with a girl you just met. "Oh, we have a TV show. We're superfamous. We just haven't mentioned it the past three days because we're cool like that." Then we very reluctantly left New Orleans a few days later.

Robert Ben Garant: That was the first time I had really been to New Orleans as an adult and I really, really loved it. It seems like I go back to New Orleans every chance I get.

Michael Patrick Jann: We know we're gonna have to cross the border the next day, not even thinking, "Oh, we're in Texas. We can go to jail forever." Just thinking, "Well, we can't go across the border with all this weed," so we pulled into South Padre Island. It's one of those places that MTV does spring break now. This was before there were phones or Internet so we just got an actual map map, and we're trying to figure out, "OK, we'll pull over here; we'll check into a hotel, and we're just gonna smoke all this weed tonight." We got in our hotel room and rolled up giant, cigar-size, Cheech and Chong, Bob Marley joints and walk out of the hotel room to go down to the beach. Now it's night. We get two steps out the door, and there's a cheerleading convention going on of high school cheerleaders. Teenage girls all turn around and go, "Oh, my God, you're the guys from 'The State'," so that was also fairly awesome.

We finished [the weed] on the beach, cheerleader adjacent.

Todd Holoubek: Then we just drove along the coast. We went through the border, no problems and then our entire world changed. The roads suddenly become unmaintained roads, like rustic landscape. Some of it was like driving through like desert. But parts of it were jungle as you went to higher elevations. I have this really distinct memory of driving late at night and seeing fire ahead of me, and it turned out to be a series of burn barrels to mark the road.

I had "On the Road" and "Fear and Loathing in Las Vegas." We all took turns reading and sleeping in the back seat.

It was really surreal because you're living by a whole different set of laws there. We made it down to Tampico. ... We basically stuck to the coast of the Gulf of Mexico. I took a left turn. You weren't supposed to take a left turn. The police pulled us over. I was living in terror because you hear these stories of how they'll just take your car and be like, "It's ours now." I was like, "I don't know what you're saying. I don't understand." He was yelling, and I had documents for the car, and I had all the paperwork and everything; it was legal, and then he saw the paperwork, everything was legal, and I was like, "But I don't understand what you're saying. No comprende," I knew enough to say. I knew I had taken a wrong left turn, but the entire city was like no left turn, like to navigate that town was ridiculous.

Michael Patrick Jann: In a couple days, we traveled through the jungle, got down to where the houses were. We got down there and our unit production manager, Rich, flew down to meet us and he smuggled the drugs into Mexico. He came on the plane with his own hash. We came home to Todd's house, and Rich was just perched on the front steps. He didn't tell us he was coming. He just showed up and we spent the next few days with him.

Todd Holoubek: We made it to the houses, and it was I think there was a full moon out that night. We went swimming and chilled out for a day. ... It was like an old Bogart movie, like "Key West" or something. We had a deck of cards. We each had a bottle of rum. It was raining, and the rain was just ridiculous. Then the sun came out, and we were like, "Awesome, let's go for a swim." It wasn't that it had become sunny, that was the eye of the mini-hurricane. We're out in the water, and the other side of the eye passes. "Get back into the house!"

We got a little bored one night 'cause there's not a lot to do down there, and that's the beauty of it. ... We heard there was a place that had music and dancing, and I don't know where music and dancing turned into, "Let's break into Tulum," but we had this bottle of spiced rum so that was it. We got in the truck, and at that time Tulum was this ancient wall with a very small doorway. "I know the back door. I know the secret entrance."

Michael Patrick Jann: That night we were sitting there smoking hash and we're like, "You know what I wanna do. Let's go down to the ruins that are five minutes down the road," which are sort of an architectural treasure of Mexico. I'm told nowadays it's very difficult; you can't even get near them now. But at that time it was just like a thing you could more or less walk straight into and walk all over, 'cause the area was not developed. We were gonna sneak into this architectural treasure zone of Ocamora. We park the car; there's a small village before you get there, and we're like, "Let's get out, sneak around behind these huts and get in there."

Robert Ben Garant: Tulum is on this really cool beach; so we went there just to smoke dope and go swimming. The stuff I would never do these days, but we were young and foolish and gung-ho about everything.

Michael Patrick Jann: We took bats in case an animal came out of the jungle after us, which is what we were thinking. We're carrying a bat in our hands as we're walking through the complete darkness, skulking through, super high, and we get about halfway from where we parked the car and the jungle to where the ruins are and all of the sudden all these flashlights go on all around us. It's basically a group of Federales, soldiers with machine guns pointing them at us and talking to us, and none of us really speaks any Spanish. "What are we doing exactly?"

Todd Holoubek: It didn't occur to us that they would have some kind of security, because all the times I'd been there nobody was there.

Michael Patrick Jann: Our production manager, who's from Houston and spoke that kind of Spanish you need to get by in Houston, goes, "Donde esta a la discotec?" They all looked at us, and they're like, "Si, si, si," and then they give us directions. Apparently there was a discotheque that was five or ten minutes away through the jungle that was hard to find. "Have a great time, boys. Go on your way."

We went straight home, in a fucking sweaty panic.

"The Pope's-a-Visit" may be the messiest State sketch ever, but it's only the troupe's sixth favorite. After a vote with all eleven members, their Top 10 are:

1. Porcupine Racetrack
2. Taco Man
3. Cutlery Barn
4. $240 Worth of Pudding
5. The Jew, The Italian and the Red Head Gay
6. The Pope's-a-Visit
7. The Bearded Men of Space Station 11
8. Pants
9. Cannonball Run Bloopers
10. (three-way tie) Hot Dogs, Monkeys Do It and Tenement

CHAPTER 18

Season Three

"'Porcupine Racetrack' is indicative of one kind of sketch that I tended to have the most success with, which was writing something from beginning to end in less than twenty minutes."

Thomas Lennon

Season three of "The State" saw many fan-favorites debut, including "Porcupine Racetrack," "Taco Man," "Bacon" and "Monkeys Do It." The growing number of viewers who were beginning to recite choice bits of dialogue had no idea this was the beginning of the end.

Ken Marino: We got rules at the beginning, but we didn't pay that much attention to them. We were just doing what we wanted to do, and I think as the seasons went on, we just got more comfortable doing a TV show. I don't think it had anything to do with, "OK, now let's break out the absurd stuff." I think that's just the stuff we would always do. We were doing weird stuff in college. I don't think our voice changed too much. I think it was consistent and sort of in a vacuum, and I think that's what made us a unique voice because we didn't really pay attention to anybody or anything else. We were just, "Let's do our stupid thing, over and over again." The arcane muscle got better as we kept using it. I don't think we were paying attention to what anybody was telling us in the beginning. We were just doing what we wanted to from day one.

Kevin Allison: There was a hell of a lot of frustration in the group while we were on MTV because we never felt that they promoted and supported us enough as far as getting the word out. So maybe midway through our run, we put our own money together in a pool to get our own publicist. I forget the guy's name, but he's now a huge publicist in Hollywood. And he was not able to do much for us either.

I finally see Comedy Central seeming to get out of this groove. All those Viacom channels seemed to be in this groove for a couple of decades of "We'll throw some money at some very fresh, original show, but we're not going to throw any money into promoting it or helping it sustain itself. We're just going to see if it gains a cult following, and if it can sustain that for long enough, then we'll start to champion it." They kind of did for "Beavis and Butt-head," which is why we had a jealousy thing about them. "Beavis and Butt-head" had preceded us very briefly, but it had quickly gained a following. So they really owned it. They were like, "This is our show," whereas The State never got that.

Publicity came in the form of a New York Times article, released two weeks into season three of "The State." In it, Executive Producer Eileen Katz has high praise for the troupe, but the members are quick to bite the hand that feeds them, as a chunk of the article details the battles The State has over content.

MTV pushed for parodies of current TV shows like "Blossom" and "Beverly Hills 90210," and in return The State offered a parody in which hunky "90210" character, Dylan, is actually Bob Dylan. According to MTV, the audience for "The State" wouldn't know the legendary singer-songwriter. It became an ongoing joke for The State to then hide Bob Dylan references in many future sketches.

"The kicker is, two weeks ago, MTV gave us tickets to see 'Bob Dylan Unplugged,'" Kerri Kenney-Silver was quoted. "It's interesting MTV has a very low opinion of its audience," Michael Ian Black said to The Times.

Bendis chimed in, too, to rally against MTV, and Katz tried to find some middle ground in the piece. "I think with my instincts going toward one end and their instincts going toward another end, together we've found a place that's a recipe for success," she was quoted as saying.

To defend The State's organic creation, rather than being pushed together via a network, Kerri said, "If MTV had cast the show, we'd look more like a Benetton advertisement."

Despite the fact that TV comedians sometimes joked about the networks they were on — David Letterman had done it at two major networks by this time — MTV President Doug Herzog was not amused.

In a memo to Bendis and Starr the day after the NYT piece ran, Herzog wrote:

"I just wanted to let you know how distraught we were about the NY Times article. The comments made by both the group and management were inappropriate, unprofessional and in some cases, erroneous.

"I feel that over the course of our relationship, MTV has been supportive, nurturing and open minded. Of course any relationship, especially a creative one, is going to evolve over time. There will be some rough spots along the way, and we've definitely had ours. But talking about them in print is amateurish. Blaming MTV for poor reviews of unsuccessful programs is appalling. And to single out Eileen Katz in any of this is absolutely unconscionable. She is without question the State's biggest single supporter. Her tireless efforts on your behalf have been a major contribution to your success thus far. She is the reason you are on the air, period. For this reason alone, you should all be ashamed of yourselves.

"Finally, you need to know that you've disappointed a great many people here. People who work hard every day to help make your show successful. I'm sure we'll find a way to put this behind us. But, we need to do so with greater respect for one another's roles, and a greater degree of professionalism."

Steven Starr: That was just a bit of showbiz positioning. A bit of "Young Upstarts Meet The Powers That Be." No more, no less.

Doug Herzog: I only vaguely remember it, but I'm sure we were upset because we took our press very seriously in those days, ... Part of the thing was they were trying to make us into "the man" all the time, and that was a very uncomfortable place for us to be because we were the guys that weren't the man. We were the upstart network who was thumbing our nose at everybody else. Now, we have these guys who come in who think they're fucking more badass than us or more rock and roll than us? They were like, "Yeah, you're the man; you're trying to keep us down." There was a lot of that. We were young; they were really young. I would go as far to say they were kids.

Kerri Kenney-Silver: We were just crappy. Who does that? We were kids. How dare you? I still have a relationship with Doug Herzog today, and I forgot about that. That's probably always in the back of his mind, "Spoiled brat."

We were so insulated in our world, and when one of us would get on a soapbox about something and somebody else would join, we felt so powerful. ... You don't do that; that's your employer. If that were my son doing it to his school or his employer, I would be mortified.

Kevin Allison: We really regretted that. In retrospect, you know it was so funny. When "Reno 911!" the movie was released, there was a party in Tribeca, and Eileen Katz and Doug Herzog showed up, and we were all chatting afterward and laughing about old times, and Kerri came up to me, and she was like, "Gosh, Eileen Katz is just a person. What the hell were we thinking?" Back when we made that show, she was a young person, too. There's just this authority-figure thing. "I've got to rebel against whoever's got the power, the gatekeepers."

Kerri Kenney-Silver: That was just sort of our attitude, which was really dumb in a lot of ways at the time, but I think we thought we were really hot shit. "What are they going to do, cancel us?"

God, I can't believe I said that. That's really ballsy. It just goes to show you that we really thought that was our launching point. It certainly wasn't the end of us or the bulk of our time together. That was going to be the tiny beginning. In a lot of ways, it has been, which is interesting. It just doesn't look the same as it did before, but we all still work together in different combinations.

Doug Herzog: I've now made a pretty good career in the world of comedy development. That was one of my very first experiences at it. You learn to trust the voices. If you're going to try to nurture a voice, you gotta let the voice have its say and say what it needs to say and do what it needs to do. A lot of stuff was very MTV-centric, built to sort of trumpet the MTV brand. This was not. This was about a collective, comedic voice. It was like wrangling cats on a lot of levels. I think some of the folks who worked with me had a great learning experience, as I assume it was for them.

Eileen Katz: I'm sure Jim Sharp had a big role in doing this. I would say the majority of the time, I was with them, whether it was pitching stuff or we were shooting stuff or going over plans for the next season, promo campaigns, they really had a unified front. How you do that, at that age, with that many people, I don't know. But I have to say, I honestly don't remember a time, to my face directly, that I saw infighting or jealousy or bickering. I knew obviously it was going on, and I knew that Jim was steering that ship, masterfully, but again, given their age and experience, they were really consummate professionals.

The Jew, The Italian and The Red Head Gay

A sitcom that plays up the stereotypes of its title quickly morphs into a musical-theater explosion.

Show 301 (December 24, 1994)

Beardan High

Boy in a Barn

The Jew, The Italian and The Red Head Gay

Blueberry Johnson

Let's Move Out

For Chelsea

Just the 160,000 of Us

In The Bathroom

Ken Marino: Dave and I liked to break off and write stuff before the writing meeting. There was a time, it was [me, Dave and Kevin] sitting in a room, and we were like, "Let's write as many sketches as we can, as quickly as we can, to bring into the room," just trying something different. We wrote all these short sketches like, "Where's the Mousey?" One of them was "The Jew, The Italian and the Red Head Gay," and I just

The State channels "Godspell" for the finale of
"The Jew, the Italian and the Red Head Gay."

love that it became something much bigger than what it was when we wrote it. We thought it was the stupidest, dumbest thing that nobody would respond to.

David Wain: We pitched it as a joke, pretty much, and then spontaneously everybody started going, "'Red Head Ga-ay,' let's actually do that!" A lot of the best stuff, I think, was that sort of progression of, "Wouldn't it be dumb if we did this? Obviously we won't." "No, let's actually do it."

Ken Marino: When we read it in the room, somebody suggested coming back out and doing the "Godspell" ending, and we were like, "Oh, yeah, perfect, that's it," and everybody was on board, knew exactly what that was going to be, knew how it was going to look. I think it looks exactly the way that it was written and brainstormed in the room.

The two "Monkeys Do It" sketches utilized the "Wop" characters Joe and Ken performed during The New Group years.

Monkeys Do It

An Italian family conversation sketch proved so popular it spawned a sequel and could have further spun into its own sitcom.

Ken Marino: It was sort of based on holidays with my family, the second [sketch], the one with all the meatballs. "Monkeys Do It" started with "Let's watch monkeys do it," which I think Tom or I said, and then we were laughing about it. I think that's the sketch that Tom and I both attacked. Maybe it was Tom and Black; I don't remember. It's all a blur.

There's the mousey.

Where's the Mousey?

Dinnertime scenes are a sketch-comedy mainstay, but The State's knack of making the ridiculous hilarious shines through here.

Kevin Allison: Jack Benny, his most famous thing was just this silent glance toward the camera. That was not The State's style. The reason we were so big was we felt like our humor was smart and maybe a little nuanced as far as what the thinking behind the jokes was. We often felt like we had to tip our hats a little bit to the audience to be like, "This is funny," by upping the presentation of it with our voices and our body language.

We would act a little bit bigger and broader and louder than what was necessary to show an American audience this is funny, even if some of the ideas in the dialogue are little bit more nuanced.

I think when we were doing in-front-of-a-studio-audience stuff, we were still in the mode of we've really got to project stuff so the people in the back of the house can see what's going on.

Tom as Tammy

Tammy Wilkins: Notebook Artist

Tom takes aim and skewers the art world and the silly things middle school girls scribble in their notebooks.

Thomas Lennon: It belies a weakness of my sketch writing, which is I was always doing these things that are like fake documentaries.

It's a lazy kind of writing because you're like, "Here's the character I'm going to do, and since I haven't written a structured sketch around it, I'm just going to have someone tell you facts about that character." I like "Tammy Wilkins." I think there's funny stuff in there, but I don't really like my performance as her character, which is with the weird braces and stuff. That was sort of a sketch-writing crutch that I was leaning very heavily on in those days because I did it a bunch of times. The nice thing is that it was very different.

The Bearded Men of Space Station 11

David and Ben during a "Bearded" break

Robert Ben Garant: I think anything that we did that was quiet and strange, I think those are the ones that we're all the most proud of. The ones that were really not super-obvious, jokey ones, but the ones that were really, really odd. Those are certainly the ones that I'm the most proud of.

Michael Patrick Jann: Although I am bearded and have been for decades, [it's] something I had zero to do with. But I hope if Mike Showalter ever doubts his own talent, he looks at that and says, "Nobody can do what I do." So freaking good.

David Wain Open

Michael Patrick Jann: In terms of people appreciating what you do in the group, I remember there's that "David Wain Open" where he says, "I edit most of the show." I swear to God that just about murdered me when he said it, and it made it to air. "Arrgh, that is so unfair." I was terminally, emotionally hurt by that.

I get it; that's the joke, but you know later on, I missed "Nirvana Unplugged." Everybody else went but me because I stayed back in the office and I edited.

Also, on that particular day, you can see in the background, the sketch we were doing is the kids with the drugs, something smoking, public service announcement. I had the flu that day, like a serious one hundred and four degree temperature and still shot all day long. [I] was in that sketch, and then in the background he's saying, "I'm the one that puts the show together behind the scenes." Ugh.

Freaks

Ken's showmanship as a barker propels this non-freak freak show, a sketch that goes back to The New Group Days.

Ken Marino: I think that probably we should have shot it as a remote or a single-camera thing. I don't think it ever translated properly when it was shot for the show. I thought the set kind of looked ratty. It was a fun, black-box theater sketch, but when we did it on the show, it kind of exposed a lot of the things that I don't think were fully realized or particularly good about it. That is a classic sketch that I was involved in where I tried to bells-and-whistle it. If I jumped around and acted out of my mind and was loud enough, maybe people wouldn't realize that the sketch was just mediocre.

Joe and David (as Medium Head Boy) in "Freaks"

I've watched that one recently, and I think in the middle I was just like tap dancing or something. Honestly, I was just crossing the stage and just trying to flail about as much as possible. I guess maybe that was partially part of the character, too, because he was trying to make things much more of a spectacle than they were, but I think the reality was that was me trying to make the sketch more of a spectacle than it actually was.

The Funeral

Ken's spin on taking pranks too far is a Season Three highlight.

Ken Marino: I always liked the visual stuff, and I always tried to build something around a funny image.

Yes, it's a little creepy seeing The State like this.

Asides

In this author's opinion, this is one of the best State sketches ever, as it has everything: breaking the fourth wall, turning high school archtypes on their ear and great lines: "I want to be Buzz's bitch!"

Michael Showalter: I had done a play in college that was called "Stupid Kids" that was sort of influenced by melodramas, teenage James Dean movies and stuff. "Come on, Boffo; we're gonna go under the tracks." It was a very beatnik way of talking, "Hey, daddy-o," that kind of stuff. I think I was in a little bit of a phase of writing theatrical dialogue. "Asides" was like, "I'm Buzz, and I'm a rubber burner!" It was very high-falutin', melodramatic, teen dialogue.

Panama

Van Halen's "Panama" is the perfect tune to watch The State take over an MTV Christmas party's cheesy music video machine (It's a shame the original tune was changed for the DVD release.).

Michael Ian Black: We were very insular. I think we were kind of intimidated by the machine of MTV. We never quite felt like we were a part of it. A lot of the sketches had to do with resentment. We just never felt fully welcomed into the fold. We always saw ourselves as outsiders. They basically had a green-screen set-up, and they would play music, and they would record you dancing to the song. It was a typical office Christmas party, and we recorded ourselves lip-synching to Van Halen. We thought it was so stupid [that] this would really make a good end credit. So we used it.

Dreamboy

This is a remake of a "You Wrote It, You Watch It" sketch, and once again, Kevin is brilliant as a prick you'd hate to be stuck with on a long road trip.

Kevin Allison: What was so funny about that sketch was I don't know how to drive. I have a phobia about driving, so I've never learned. The group was kind of frustrated with me because they're like, "Kevin, wait a minute, you come up with this premise and you sold the group that we should do this, and now you're not able to be in the fucking driver's seat. It's supposed to be a ride share." I said, "No, it all makes sense that I'm forcing her to do all the driving anyway." We did do some takes in which I'm driving. We're in this wooded area, and I drive right off the road into the trees, and Kerri is just screaming, "Oh, my God, he's gonna kill us!" while I'm trying to act all arrogant and everything. David was in charge of the camera, and the only other person there was Showalter. He just wanted to be the guy who would be there to help me think of new bits. He was just hiding on the floor in the back of a car. That was a super-fun shoot because we were all just laughing all day long.

Ben, Tom, Ken, Black and David have musical theater in their hearts.

Porcupine Racetrack

Kerri Kenney-Silver: "Porcupine Racetrack" and the ones that everybody was a part of and had dances attached to them, "The Jew, the Italian and the Red Head Gay," we love those. It harkens back to our high-school theater days. Everybody had a little soft spot for that I think.

Thomas Lennon: "Porcupine Racetrack" is indicative of one kind of sketch that I tended to have the most success with, which was writing something from beginning to end in less than twenty minutes. I think three [o'clock] was the pitch time, and so that was what I'd call the category of a 2:15 p.m. sketch, knowing that the group meeting was coming up. I was always sort of a musical-theater-type person.

Recently, when we performed live, we lip-synched to the entire opening of "Corner of the Sky" from "Pippen." It was one of those last-minute things, and I was like, "I want to pitch this to the group, and let's see how they react." Whenever it's musical-theater stuff, the answer is always a hundred percent, "Yes, let's do that." There's never any pushback because I think all of us at some level are sort of musical-theater people, but "Porcupine Racetrack," including all the melodies, was written in less than twenty minutes, in a stream of consciousness right before the pitch meeting.

By the way, it is true that the first time we wanted to do it, it was vetoed by the network. They were like, "No." Too silly or too old-fashioned. It's very old-fashioned. There's certainly nothing cool about "Porcupine Racetrack." It was not the sketch for the MTV generation, but apparently it was.

Eileen Katz: See? I hate that. Really, come on! Tell me that you've been working on this since you were seven, and you were honing and crafting and every word was like a Rembrandt. You know?

Thomas Lennon: For some reason we were one-hundred-percent yes on it, and they were one-hundred-percent no, and it was one of times that we were just like, "You know what, we're going to do this one. This one's not really up for discussion; we're just going to do it."

Eileen Katz: I think the compromise was a credit-roll thing. It's comedy; it's a subjective thing. If I may use the pun here — if things were going to stick in their craw about certain choices, there were just certain things that I was like, "I can't; I'm not the end-all expert on everything." I was just kind of like a controlled stop checkpoint in the comedy process for them, and I just didn't see it. I was like, "OK and? I know you can do so much better."

Ultimately, it was just compromise. It's a give-and-take, and was it my favorite sketch? Probably not, but you know what? It's just the absurdity and ridiculousness of what a point of contention it became. It was like, "I'm going to die on the sword for the porcupine sketch," and we're like, "Are we curing cancer here?" To their credit, this is where the respect comes in; there were definitely things where I would say, "You know what, it's not my favorite. I think you have stronger stuff." They kind of respected that, and if they said to me, "You know what, we want this; we'll fight for this," it's a compromise. I have to sit back and respect that and say, "OK, I might not get it, but I respect you and your taste, and if it's that important to you, go for it. It's four minutes in a twenty-two-minute show."

Thomas Lennon: Later it was scored by Theodore Shapiro, who is a major Hollywood composer. He set my melodies to a giant orchestration, but it was basically fully formed right as I pitched it. It was one of those times that you just felt really good. If something was an absolute slam dunk that everyone agreed on, then it was a just a very good feeling because it would almost immediately go on the board.

The boards would get moved around in sort of a passive-aggressive Risk game where something would be up on the board; then it would get moved over. It would get moved down. It was certainly a lot of politics in getting things on. Although, another very obvious thing about "Porcupine Racetrack" is that every single person in the group has a moment in it. So I might have been pandering to the group a little bit.

That was when Mike Jann really would shine — filming stuff like that. We threw a lot of production value at that piece. I'm always touched [that] high school kids will do perfect recreations of "Porcupine Racetrack." They're kind of eerie. There's one where they recreated the entire thing, without the sets and costumes, but with the harmonies, and it's really pretty amazing.

Michael Patrick Jann: I loved it from the first time Tom was humming lyrics. I was so jazzed to do that because I was a huge fan of the Arthur Freed musicals on MGM. I was a massive student of that style and Vincente Minnelli and wanted it to be like that. The second he started humming, I partially saw it happening in my head. I was like, "It will be half 'Guys and Dolls' and half 'My Fair Lady' ascot racetrack. We were able to rent 'Guys and Dolls' costumes from a road show.

It was a big production number, and it was this thing that I was certainly proudest of at the time. This has to be perfect and awesome. The visual, the sound, the color, the costumes and the set, all of that stuff has to be great in order for this to work. ... [I] had the full support of the production like, "Yeah, kid, great. Go to town."

I was able to work really closely with Jana [Rosenblatt], our costume person, and Ruth Ammon, a truly brilliant production designer, to put together this one-day musical shoot. I had it planned out exactly down to the frame. We were able to shoot that from basically setting up and lighting, and we're choreographing it as we were going as well. We did the whole thing, soup to nuts, in one day, but I had it absolutely super-planned, like every little piece of how ... people were going to move, except for David's dance, which was more like, "OK, David, there's eight bars...."

David Wain: The Catman was when I was a little kid, like nine years old, or even younger, maybe. There was a little cat mask with cat whiskers at my house. I put the mask on, as well as a straw hat and a white bathrobe. I would basically sneak out of the room where my family was having dinner, and then I would just put on all those things and just stand there in the doorway in that outfit and wait for my family to notice me. Then I would just stand there, and they would be like, "Oh my God, look at that, the Catman!" I wouldn't say anything, and then I would run away as fast as I possibly could. I would rip everything off and run back as myself, and I would say, "Did you see him? Did you see him? Was he here?" When I told The State about that, they, Tom in particular, started calling me Catman, to this day.

Contrary to popular belief within The State — or at least with Tom — the dance that David performs in "Porcupine Racetrack" is not the Catman dance.

David Wain: I was just bummed because nobody gave me anything to sing in "Porcupine Racetrack." They were like, "Oh, you'll do a dance move." There was actually a choreographer there through the whole thing, and so he showed me a little dance move that would make sense for the genre. Of course, I couldn't even do ten percent of it correctly. I think we did it twice. I did not intend to fall down, but that's what happened, and the rest is history.

Michael Patrick Jann: David's sense of humor is, without a doubt, the sense of humor of a little kid whose parents have just come home from a night out. His entire voice seems to revolve around, "I, I, I, I came up with this funny thing; you wanna watch it? Aaaaaah, it's really funny," and the parents going like, "OK, David, thank you." "You want me to do it again?" "OK." That's David Wain's baseline voice, and that's exactly what that dance is.

["Porcupine Racetrack"] took fifteen minutes to edit. We got in, scrolled through the thing. Everything was like, "Use the last take," and it was bam, bam, bam, and they just fit together like next, next, next, next, next, next, next, next, done. ... When I watched it back after having assembled it for the first time on the Avid, I practically burst into tears I was so happy.

Race

An innocent father-son race turns dirty and has a delicious twist.

Michael Showalter: "Race" is my ultimate moustache sketch. [Putting on a moustache] literally makes me feel older and more macho.

H's & M's

Looking like extras from a 1970s Vincent Price horror flick, Kerri, Black and Showalter divide the rest of the gang as to whether "Merbert Moover" is funny.

Kerri Kenney-Silver: That was another one that made people mad. Some of my favorite sketches that I wrote are the ones that made people furious. Michael [Black], Michael [Showalter], and I thought that was so funny. I think everyone else, it made them angry at how stupid it was. We just had the best time. We just pumped it up, until the set got bigger and bigger, and the costumes and hair took two hours. Everybody was like, "We're spending all this time on this stupid sketch. Oh, my God." We were wetting our pants and trying to get through "Merbert Moover." I really can't wait to sit with my son and husband and see what holds up and what was truly just stupid. In my mind, it will always be funny.

Ken Marino: I don't remember thinking, "Oh, 'H's and M's' is great," but there was fighting and arguing, debating about whether things are funny and should they go into the show or shouldn't they. I think at a certain point, if this group of people thinks it's funny, let's do it. I don't quite get it, but let's do it.

Michael Showalter: I wouldn't put it in top twenty favorite sketches, but I like it because it's so stupid; it's barely anything. It's almost not even anything. ... It's a similar vein to a "Froggy Jamboree" or "The Waltons" or some of those sketches that are really, really, really deconstructed. I think that's kind of where it's coming from. It's a little bit of a think piece.

David Wain: One of my absolute favorites is "H's and M's."

Slinkys

Toy-store employees provide the ultimate sales pitch for the toy that's the hit of the day when you're ready to play.

Kerri Kenney-Silver: It went dark and weird at times, but I think that is a testament to all the personalities coming together. What was beautiful was someone would write a sketch in their voice and not know how to end it, and someone else would say, "All of a sudden, they just fly out of the scene like birds." I certainly never would've thought of that. You put those two things together, and you've got this new, unique voice. It works for rebutting the room.

David Wain: It's a Showalter/Kerri combo that makes me laugh.

Eileen Katz: My god, Kerri Kenney, the Lucille Ball of our time. What else can you call her? She's a comedy chameleon, smart, and funny and sexy but can pull it back ten degrees, and she still just delivers and delivers and delivers.

319

Hot Dogs

David Wain: Our production company is named after that. We were going to call it Hotdog Missile Packing Facility, but we just shortened it to A Hotdog. At the end of "Wanderlust," you'll see it says, "An Apatow Production in association with A Hotdog."

Tenement

The State had appeal for multiple audiences. If there were junior-high kids watching MTV at that time and they hear Ken Marino saying "poop," they're going to giggle, but then there's the theater people who will get a kick out of this attempt to remove all the foul language from a gritty working-class scene.

Ken Marino: "I took dum-dum from every freaking Mickey" ... I forget. They were all fun. I'll tell you what I did like, "Poop, poop, poop, poopy, poop, poop, poop," just the angst and heartache that had to be put into that. I enjoyed that.

Kerri Kenney-Silver: That's a really smart sketch. And kind of timeless.

Robert Ben Garant: I remember writing it, and afterward Ken was tense because he thought it was his idea. I honestly don't remember the details of that, not bullshitting or glossing over something, but I do remember that he was a little upset. We never talked about it, and he never spoke to me about it, but I could sense it. I love that sketch.

Ken Marino: Ben and I, and Joe and Tom, we would frequent a bar called the Barrow Street Ale House, where we wound up closing the bar a lot of the times. We would walk out of that bar at five in the morning, and it would be light out. I had this idea about a sketch that was all curse words but as if they were done on TV, inspired by watching Spike Lee's "Do the Right Thing," where, instead of saying "Motherfucker," they went, "Mickey Fickey."

[Ben] got excited about it, pulled out his pad, wrote down the idea, which was not "Tenement." It was just the concept, but I was excited about it. Then, in the next pitch session, Ben came in and pitched this sketch, "Tenement," exactly how it was performed. It didn't have to be changed a word. I was bummed out because I thought we were going to write that together. I was also bummed out because it was so good and I didn't get to write it with him, because I had pitched it to him several nights before at the bar.

I immediately approached him and told him I was bummed out about it. So when he says that we didn't talk about it but he sensed something, the reason he sensed something is because I went up to him right afterward and told him I was bummed out about it. He said he felt bad, he doesn't remember, which I completely understand because we were deep into one of our drinking nights.

Robert Ben Garant: I know this is sort of boring, but we had really bad makeup artists for the first half of one of these seasons. That's one of the sketches. So if you look, we were all really pale, and we had these weird rings under our eyes — really bad, sort of Joel Grey "Cabaret" makeup in almost everything. When I look at "Tenement," that's kind of all I notice.

One of the things that we used to do a lot live for our NYU people was stuff that was really smarty-pants but stupid at the same time. We'd do a joke about "Waiting for Godot" but really silly. They were really silly jokes but for the smarty-pants in the audience, and I think that "Tenement" is one of the only ones of those we really got away with on the air. "Missy Von Kimmelman" was another one which was like a Laurie Anderson sketch that they actually let us do on MTV. They would argue, "Nobody's heard of Laurie Anderson," but the fact that they let us do sort of a '40s group theater parody on MTV, I'm really proud of that. That turned out great.

Fuzzy pineapple was from "Scarface." The very first scene when he's being interrogated in the room and they're like, "Where'd you get that scar, Tony, from eating pussy?" When you see that on TV it's, "Where'd you get that scar, Tony, from eating pineapple?" And he says, "How am I gonna get a scar like that from eating pineapple?" It's so funny, but that's a real one. So fuzzy pineapple is my favorite one.

Monkeys Do It II

Robert Ben Garant: We got to hire opera singers. I thought that was really great at the time; we had a sketch with real opera singers in it.

Taco Man

Kerri Kenney-Silver: My favorite sketch of all time is Kevin Allison as the mailman who delivers tacos. I don't know why. Since then, we've run into a couple of people with taco tattoos on their arms because of that sketch. I don't know why that sketch kills me. David Wain as a woman, "Bye, mailbox," that just kills me. It's just the one of the sketches that goes on forever, just talking and talking. The more you talk, the less funny it gets, and then it gets funny again.

Robert Ben Garant: "Taco Man" only happened because nobody else was there. It was one of the rare days where they went off on like a B unit. So nobody was at "Taco Man" who wasn't in "Taco Man." It was just Kevin and David and Black. That was purely those dudes, and nobody got to argue about it. Nobody got to say, "Hey, that doesn't make sense; the mailbox walks off." Nobody got to argue that it needed a stronger punch line, and so I think that's one of our greatest sketches — and it only happened because the committee wasn't there.

David Wain: "Taco Man," we were shooting "Lincoln Logs," another sketch, and we were just sitting around on the porch of that house, me and Kevin and Black; we just sort of said the lines and pretty much typed them out as they were said — didn't need much revision.

The thing about the second-unit pieces is that we didn't need quite the same level of everyone-on-board. I think that's because they didn't cost us anything, time- or money-wise, really. So we could take more swings with those. "Taco Man" was definitely an example of, "You guys want to go over there for an hour while we're shooting something else and say some lines into the camera? Give it a shot."

Thomas Lennon: It was my idea for the mailbox to walk away. We were shooting it, and the mailbox was not nailed down or dug into the earth, and I said, "Why don't we have the mailbox just walk away?" Everybody's like, "Yep," and that was another way we knew The State was a good, functioning unit. I can silly-pitch, "Hey, what if the mailbox walks away?" and everybody's like, "Yep," without [a] one-second delay. Everybody's like, "That's the only thing that could happen right now." That was the only logical move is that mailbox walks away, and we said, "Goodbye, mailbox."

Sal & Frankie

Joe and Showalter are hysterical as two gruff old-timers who wave to passers-by right next to the highway, rain or shine.

Kerri Kenney-Silver: I love that. That was our acting-school training being put to good use. I think they were beautiful characters that were fun to watch. I love that as well.

Joe Lo Truglio: It holds a special place, too. Show and I wrote that. I felt like that sketch really captured the energy of the idea of when Mike and I thought of it. I love nonsense. I love nonsense words. It's just one of those cases where it made sense and fit in uniquely to the character and the sketch, as opposed to just being a non sequitur. I love that it was on film. I love the look of it and the pace of it.

I think Ken Marino is terrific in that sketch as the mayor, who was uncomfortable being interviewed and not really sure where he should look. It's a subtle and absolutely genius take.

I am able to tap into those types of angry, grumpy people well. I remember being so excited when the group wanted to do it. It was just character-based, and we really didn't have an end. That was something the group really prided themselves on was that the sketches had endings. Some had good ones, and some didn't; that one purely was just character.

Michael Showalter: Every season or so [Joe and I] would collaborate on a big sketch, and "Sal & Frankie" was one of the main ones. It was a really fun shoot. Every couple of episodes, we would shoot something on film, and that was a big deal; that was exciting. ... At that time I was very much wanting to be an actor. Now, I look back, and I see even then my passion was much more in the writing. But at the time it was an opportunity to be in a movie and act on film, and so it was exciting — kind of an honor.

Cutlery Barn

Kerri Kenney-Silver: I remember half of the group was angry with us when we pitched it. They were like, "You know what? Fuck it. Just do it." Half of us were adamant that this was the funniest thing that ever happened. The other half just gave up and said, "Do it." It's still a bone of contention to this day. That kind of thing just makes me laugh. It's total nonsense. It reminds me of some of the animation that I enjoy today, "Uncle Grandpa" or something. Some of the group was into nonsense, and some of the group was anti-nonsense. It had a reason. I just wasn't one of those people.

It was originally called "Pottery Barn," but they wouldn't let us say that. One of the reasons we got it in the show was because I was on

crutches. We had done a live show the week before, and in the final credits sequence on stage in front of the audience, we were all slam dancing, and Michael Jann had on steel-toed combat boots, and he accidentally kicked me in the knee. I walked right into it. He's a big dude. I tore the entire meniscus in my knee. There were very few sketches I was able to shoot. I'm on crutches in that scene, just standing there, and I just lean my head into the frame. That might be one of the only reasons that thing got shot.

Thomas Lennon: That's a weird one. I was always on board with "Cutlery Barn." I was never a fan of "H's and M's," which is like jazz to me. Ultimately, that is the strength of the group, material that got through that half of us were strongly against. Nothing got through that people weren't passionate about. So if it got through, there was definitely enough passion about it. The other thing that would happen was people would really bring their A game if they knew that half of the group didn't like something.

In the original script that Showalter pitched to me was, "The special of the day is spaghetti with fried poop." I was like, "I'll tell you right now, there is zero chance I will support this sketch if the special of the day is fried poop. If you change it to bumblebee, I'll support the sketch one hundred percent." That was the only time I really remember making a deal like this on a sketch.

The use of the word "poop" in that sketch made me absolutely hate it so much that it tarnished the entire sketch for me. ... These are the sort of life-and-death things that we were battling about. The use of the word poop over the use of the word bumblebees was a giant deal-breaker. To that camp's credit, they deferred to me on that, and they also knew they would get my vote.

Michael Showalter: I don't think fried bumblebees is any funnier than fried poop.

Thomas Lennon: Bumblebees is a million percent the right call. One of the times I felt like I was a great writer was when I came up with bumblebees for that because it totally takes the sketch to another level.

Kevin Allison: The last fifteen episodes, we started to get a lot weirder. We were really enjoying that. The sketch where people's faces come onto the screen where everyone is talking in these froggy voices, that is definitely not something we could've ever done in the first fifteen episodes.

Michael Patrick Jann: The way that I thought at that time was I don't want anything else in my life; I just want to do this. This is what's important to me. This is what's meaningful to me. It seems silly when you go back and you look at something like "Cutlery Barn," and you're like, "Right. So you decided that you weren't interested in love or your future or your emotional stability or your relationships with anybody because you were super-dedicated to the idea of which should be funny, when the guy says, 'poop or bumblebees.' Or, you know, 'Bikini Fun Roller Team,' figuring out that set and those lights — that was more important than your own emotional stability."

Cannonball Run

The State recreates the end credits/bloopers note-for-note from the Burt Reynolds road movie classic.

David Wain: I know memory is fuzzy, and I don't want to be self-serving, but I do think it was my idea. Growing up, my friend Stuart and I watched "Cannonball Run" over and over and over again, and I was particularly fond of the credits. I think it was my idea because I know that I pushed really hard to do it. It was a lot of different locations. It was a lot of stuff that had to happen. So I figured out a system where we would do a shot or two at the end of every other shoot during that season. I had a home video Hi8 camera, and I was like, "Hey, come over here; we're going to do a little piece of 'Cannonball.'"

Show 310

Hitchhiker
Terrorist Situation
Leonard Harris Show
Permanent School Record
Free Market Economy
Beach
Fragments
Billy's Play
Coffee Family

David plays Jack Elam as Dr. Van Helsing, which is perfect because the doctor was always sticking his finger in everything.

Robert Ben Garant: I think that's my favorite thing we ever did, to be honest. I think it's the funniest thing that we did — like, of all the State stuff, that might be the one that I still enjoy the most. ... I feel like me and Joe were part of who started that concept, but I don't remember who else was there. I feel like that might have come out of being pretty stoned. I feel like it might have been Jann; it might have been Tom, but I really don't remember.

Certainly everybody that was in that sketch really grew up with "Cannonball Run." It was one of the first sort of naughty movies that I remember watching. My parents were sort of OK with me watching it because it had Burt Reynolds in it. I watched that movie over and over and over again, and I think so did a bunch of us. I feel like Jann and I bonded over that movie. We also had a little VCR on set. So we'd watch it and do it, but I feel like everybody kind of knew it already.

Joe Lo Truglio: One of my favorites, we just re-created it. I can understand why Adam Scott and "The Greatest Event in Television History" is so fun to do because re-creating shot-for-shot things that you loved as a kid is its own type of drug. People pay a lot of money to help you shoot this thing that you just saw one million times as a kid and fell in love with. It's like nostalgia crack.

When we were shooting it, we had the real "Cannonball Run" credits to get every gesture, every pause, every inflection, and then we re-created the singing chorus of children over it.

It's not surprising that movie was watched so much by David and myself and a few other people in the group. You can tell in that movie that they were just having a good time. It was a party. That's certainly a tenant of how David did his movies and The State worked. It really was about this energy of fun and goofing around that definitely bled into all "The State" and post-State projects.

Thomas Lennon: "Cannonball Run," I recall being the most fun we ever had shooting anything. I never had more fun, even to this day, than shooting "Cannonball Run." It was such a blast to shoot that thing.

While it was popular among the cast, it did not end up on The State's lone compilation VHS titled "Skits and Stickers." The strange and frustrating thing about that is the artwork for the cover of the tape is an illustration of The State as characters in "The Cannonball Run."

Thomas Lennon: They were like, "It might be a copyright infringement issue because you're just doing it word for word."

Robert Ben Garant: Nobody would have said anything to us if it had been on that videotape. That's the thing that was really corporate stupidity to us. The whole cover was this big, expensive "Cannonball Run" parody that's not even on the tape. It's so fucking annoying.

Prom

The State attends a real high-school prom with fans of the show. Antics ensue. Luckily, no lawsuits were filed, and David perfected his Chewbacca impression.

Todd Holoubek: We met some really amazing people. ... It was a favorite because it was such a surreal experience.

Ken Marino: I remember picking our dates up and then going to the prom, and I don't remember what we did there or how much we made a spectacle of ourselves or how much we drew focus. It was pretty obnoxious to do it, in hindsight.

I don't know if that was "Wouldn't it be funny if we did this?" I think we just did it and hoped something funny would come out of it, and I don't remember if something funny did come out of it.

Kerri Kenney-Silver: It was scary. It turned out to be really fun, but I remember thinking, "Oh, my God, what are we doing? This was on paper, and now we're doing this." The kids were great. It sort of reminded us that we were getting older because we were quite a bit older than the kids. It turned out to be a sweet night, and we had a decent piece out of that as well.

Show 311

Great Moments
Prison Break
Sideways House Family
Super Robby
Mr. Flemming's Arrival
Prom
Inbred Bros.-Army
Borscht Boy
Walton's Theme

Show 312

Blinking Contest
Dentist
Sci-Fi Laboratory
High Plains Magic Fairy
Jerry's Audition
Bacon
Kiss My Grits
Last Will & Testament
One Camper

Bacon

Ben's bacon obsession includes him in a dress made from the pork product.

Robert Ben Garant: People remember Bacon Guy. "Bacon" is really strange. Did we ever complain that they wouldn't let us do stuff on MTV, and yet "Bacon" got in there? I think it's a testament that they didn't have the reins on very tight and were really letting us do anything we wanted. I'm very proud of that one.

I look at "The State," and I'm always a little baffled; I never just talk normal. I wish I could go back in time and just say, "In some of these, you can just talk normal if you want. You don't have to put on a weird voice." I have the weirdest voices, even in the sketches where I'm supposed to be just a normal, suburban guy.

Adventures of Young God

The final MTV State sketch to air is a tribute to cliffhanger serials, this time starring a young, yet already white-haired-and-bearded, God.

Robert Ben Garant: I wrote that one. Mike Jann's vision was that sort of weird rear projection stuff. That wasn't my idea. I wrote it as sort of Indiana Jones. I think in my head it was going to be black and white and really sort of cheap-looking, but he came up with that concept, and I think it looks pretty cool.

A weird thing would happen on sets when everything was super-expensive because we weren't used to waiting between takes and having to do new camera set-ups. So for "Young God" and "Porcupine Racetrack" and "High Plains Magic Fairy," things that were really shot well, people would start grumbling at about eleven in the morning. People would start walking around and complaining. So it created this weird vibe on the set.

Anytime something looks great, those were some of our worst days on the set. People would start grumbling about Mike Jann and grumbling about how slow we were going, and I think some of the stuff that really set us apart were those really beautiful-looking sketches. Jann would have to fight us to stay focused on those days because we didn't like going slow.

Michael Patrick Jann: I don't remember anybody being crabby, and I think it was probably because I was so focused on what I was doing. I was also such an interpersonal dumbass at that point in my life that I just didn't care. "Go ahead and be crabby; we're still doing it!"

Show 313

L.A. Open

Dixon: Jedi Talent Agency

Tough Choices

Gas Station

Gunter Brothers

Desert Extras

Real Estate Broker

Adventures Of Young God

Farewell

Hi-lite Reel

The State for hire

CHAPTER 19

I (No Longer) Want My MTV

"You put the blinders on and feel like you could go into that trench without your targeting system on and still just nail that torpedo and go to (a) network. We did not blow up the Death Star; the Death Star blew us up."

Joe Lo Truglio

Season Three was split into two parts, and by the time the second half of the episodes were filmed, The State knew they would be the last for MTV. On March 15, 1995, Steven Starr sent a resignation memo to MTV on behalf of The State.

"After long deliberation, we have elected to move beyond our relationship with MTV Networks when our contract expires this August.

We'd like to take this opportunity to thank you and your associates at MTV for your ongoing support of The State over the last two years.

It has been a remarkable experience for all of us, and we'd like to thank Eileen Katz in particular for her commitment on our behalf.

We look forward to delivering the final seven shows with the same enthusiasm and creativity as the last nineteen."

The State's management was in talks with ABC, and the golden carrot being dangled led the members to believe that they would have a legitimate opportunity to take on "Saturday Night Live" head to head.

Eileen Katz: They were breaking up with me. You know the speech, "It's not you; it's me." I personally was so disappointed, but that's what MTV was about. At that point in time, there really wasn't the money to do holding deals and to give them the opportunity, "Stay with us for five years, and we'll throw you a movie." That machine just wasn't in place. You can't hold talent if you can't promise them anything, and you can't certainly hold them back. Part of me felt, "OK, we did our job. They're that good now that the networks want them." Isn't that the payoff, that something you work on is suddenly viable and enviable and somebody else wants it?

Steven Starr: I was ambivalent. We had a great run with MTV, twenty-six episodes, and they offered us an expansive, long-term commitment for more episodes. But while we loved Doug and Eileen, the budgets were brutal and a deep restlessness had set in. There were tensions inside the group about staying; that there was an opening to compete with "SNL," which was struggling, was deeply felt, and the consensus was to make our move. So I asked Morris to talk to CBS and ABC, to see if they could assemble major markets on Saturdays at 11:30 p.m., and both networks expressed great interest.

Todd Holoubek: We always followed our heart, and we did what we thought was right. And in a lot of ways those negotiations were like, "Look, we're not making a lot of money." A lot of people still had roommates. We were a huge presence on the network and going on vacation was like, "OK, we're still budgeting." We wanted more budget to produce the show. We had more ambitious ideas. It wasn't just, "Hey, we want more money." It was, "We'd like our show to grow. We'd like to turn the show into something greater than it is now. We'd like to be able to eat well," and then when they said, "No." We said, "OK, then we can't do that." I don't think they were expecting us to walk away, but there was also some buzz in the air because as soon as those negotiations happened, we started meeting with the other networks to see what was possible.

Ken Marino: We were fairly cocky in thinking that we were doing something really interesting and really funny and something that would be more appreciated on a bigger network. That was some sort of confirmation that we were good as we thought we were.

Michael Ian Black: We knew MTV wasn't going to pay us a fortune. We also knew that there were eleven of us. At the same time, we felt like, that is your writing staff, your actors, your directors, your editors, your producers. We all felt like we were getting ripped off from the beginning. In the beginning, money wasn't our primary concern. At the end, it became a sticking point. Had MTV paid us what would've been a reasonable salary, there's a good chance we wouldn't have left.

Joe Lo Truglio: I thought it was time. When you have the success that we had that early, and we felt we were really in the zone and creating great material, you've got a distorted sense of your destiny. And you kind of put the blinders on and feel like you could go into that trench without your targeting system on and still just nail that torpedo and go to [a] network. We did not blow up the Death Star; the Death Star blew us up.

"We've been on MTV for two years. We were together five years before that. We have seven years of experience, and we know what we're doing, and let's make it happen." In hindsight, that was the wrong decision, but you can also make the argument of, who knows where the quality of material would've been if we had stayed at MTV another three years? Who's to say that the dynamics of the group would've changed, and we would've gotten on each other's nerves too much, and we wouldn't have been able work together, as we did later, many years later. There's other damages that could've happened.

What was nice is that we certainly didn't jump the shark. The kind of silver lining on us letting our ego demolish the TV show was that we went out almost on top.

Kerri Kenney-Silver: I think we always thought [MTV] was a good fit. I think we always felt at home there. Certainly when it was brought to us by our agent/manager that CBS was interested, that's exciting, especially because we thought MTV was losing interest. "Are we going to get canceled? We better hop on this available opportunity."

Michael Patrick Jann: I didn't feel the same [pressure as the others] because there was no competition. I directed the show. David did an occasional piece. Nobody else was competing with me for what I did, and I was definitely fine with that. I had a unique position in the show and in the group. There definitely was more tension going on. Certain people felt like they were carrying too much weight, and they wanted more acknowledgment for it.

Truth of the matter is we didn't make any money back then. "God, I hope the show gets picked back up and we go into production before my unemployment runs out." We all lived in Manhattan. [It was cheaper then] but not that cheap. ... I lived on Joe Lo Truglio's couch. I lived there. I didn't have any place else to go, and that was a super-cheap apartment. It was literally falling apart around us. I moved out shortly after the ceiling literally collapsed on me while I was sleeping on the couch. There was this crack in the middle of the night, and the ceiling is falling down on top of me. So I had to find a place. It was time to go. I'm sure Joe was happy to see me leave.

Kevin Allison: After about thirty episodes, we were feeling like, "OK, MTV pays us diddly, and we really do feel like we are funny as hell, and we feel like we're used to creating sketch comedy for TV. Maybe we should try to fly the coop? Maybe we should try to get on the networks? Maybe Fox?" We did a lot of talking with our managers, "What should we do?"

Jonathan K. Bendis: I didn't want them to go to MTV at first. That would be my biggest thing, but I was already there for ten years. I didn't feel that this was the right move for what they wanted to do, and they called me on that one. There wasn't a point of fighting that one. It was like, "If that's what you want and they're going to throw a deal at us...."

As far as them leaving MTV, my memory is that they wanted out. It's for a couple reasons. There was never going to be more money, and they couldn't afford to exist on a MTV salary and pay the rent. Also, this was MTV in '95, and MTV was big, but it wasn't big in the comedy field. Things were shifting, but it still took many years before it was really gonna shift, and obviously Comedy Central took over for that part.

They wanted out, and this deal came, and it was like, "All right, this is a crapshoot. MTV is willing to sign on again, or we're going to go into the unknown." I didn't lead them either way on that one, so that would've been stronger stuff maybe coming from Steven, I don't know. I'm positive that nothing would have come out of my mouth in a strong way either way. ... I was more about protecting their creativity than making deals.

Robert Ben Garant: I don't want to totally shit on these guys, but they gave us really, really terrible advice at the time. We just wanted to be really, really big. We thought that we could be bigger than on MTV. Our numbers were really, really small there, just because MTV's numbers were really, really small. For some reason, we had this dream that if we got to network ... but there wasn't anybody around saying to us, "Hey, you guys, if you go to network, you're not going to be able to do this kind of material. It's not gonna be the same." Our managers should have known better. I guess it should've also occurred to us. So we can't one hundred percent blame those two guys, but we just wanted to be bigger. Looking back, if we stayed at MTV for another couple of years, we would've been much, much bigger. That would've been the right way to get into movies and albums and everything, staying at MTV. Nobody ever had the conversation with us, "Hey guys, sit back, look at where you are. You're doing this great, weird TV show; it's on MTV; this is a great opportunity, and you should really, really enjoy it."

Kerri Kenney-Silver: It was never told to us at the time until after we signed our CBS contract that MTV wanted to keep us on for more seasons. We were given the impression that we were done there. That's one moment in time that we all look back and think, "What would've happened if we had stayed? If we had known the information we were supposed to know and we had stayed." I don't know what would've happened. Maybe it would've made a difference. We certainly would've made more money.

The belief in the world is that we were fired from MTV, which we weren't. We were just not told the whole story. It's kind of a shame that people's memory of us is that we were canceled. We took a risk without knowing the facts.

I believe [our managers'] intentions were good, but they were young, too, just sort of starry-eyed with the possible chance of moving to a major network. Even to this day I have some anger about it. That was a pretty shitty thing to do.

Michael Showalter: I actually recall wanting to stay at MTV. A long time has gone by, and that was a crazy time, but I was feeling we were in a good place and kind of wanted to stay. I was kind of willing to keep fighting through all of it. I was frustrated, and it was [an] extremely contentious environment, but I didn't want it to end. I think I was very afraid of different people, afraid of it ending. There was always a feeling of the end lurked around the corner, that certain members of the group were going to get famous and leave, sort of like what had happened on "SNL" with Chevy Chase. There was for me a feeling of wanting to keep the band together, so to speak, but you could feel it coming apart at the seams. It was like a something-had-to-give feeling.

I remember it was Doug Herzog, and he basically said, "We want to keep you guys on." They made us a big offer, and we said, "No." I definitely remember that.

Todd Holoubek: I think it was a good idea to stay for one more season. I think it would've changed the future in a lot of ways.

But we're all growing, right? We're all getting older; we were hoping for a little more cash. We wanted to be able to afford our lives a little more. Money comes into the situation. At that time, I was really thinking about what other things are out in the world. What else is happening out there? There was a whole world going on around us at that time. Negotiations didn't really work out. I think if they had said yes to what we were asking, we would have stayed. They said, "We can't do this," and we said, "OK, and neither can we. We can't continue like this." Then it was very amicable. ... We were like, "OK, we will go elsewhere."

Michael Patrick Jann: As long as I had the opportunity to continue to make stuff, I was good with whatever it was. ... When they offered us whatever that deal was, I remember thinking, "That's too long." Not a good idea. There was already a little bit of tension over stuff, and I can imagine things would have gotten to the point where ... to continue to just make that amount of money, fuck, I think it would have taken us until we were almost thirty.

If you talk to anybody who's ever been in a band, especially at that time, if you have a chance to go major label, you go major label.

Kevin Allison: I think we were so offended that they weren't valuing us more, that we thought, "Fuck this, it's time to move on." In retrospect, we were in our mid-twenties, and because of what happened with "The State," I had to spend my late twenties and my entire thirties making almost no money at all. To have stayed there, getting low pay but continuing to build this brand in this creative entity would have been blatantly obviously the smartest thing to do.

Ken Marino: They offered us some more seasons, but I feel like we thought we were going to go on to bigger and better things. So we all wanted to move on. We thought we had the knowledge at that point and the kind of experience of doing it for three or four seasons. "OK, let's now try to go somewhere where we can make a little bit more money and we can be seen by more people." I think we also felt like we needed a change of scenery. We were certainly a cocky group, and we certainly made our mistakes. I don't know if we burned our own bridges, but we made some mistakes, certainly.

David Wain: I remember so well when we got the news that MTV was making us a really nice offer to stay — a budget increase, a salary increase — and we didn't even think about it. We were like, "No fucking way; we're hot shit. We need to be on CBS." How absurd it feels now to say that, but we thought we were destined to be on Saturday night, up against "Saturday Night Live" until "Saturday Night Live" gave up, just like The Sterile Yak gave up. I think that was in our heads. When CBS gave us that song and dance, "We're going to get you on late night," we were like, "Hell, yes, let's go." I remember our agent, James Dixon, sitting with us, very emphatically and gravely, sitting with the whole group and saying, "Guys, I don't think you should do this. I think you should stay here at MTV." I think that we considered that our resignation of defeat to do that, instead of what I would consider it now, which is building on a really good thing.

Being naïve and also having that "We want to roll the dice and go down in flames" mentality, which we did, but then I suppose it could have worked, but it didn't. A chain of events could've happened where we ended up on a bigger network and became a hit show, but in retrospect, no way. Are you kidding? No way! It's really interesting to think about that, but, yeah, it was a real mistake.

I can't think about what could've been, and who knows, maybe staying at MTV could've been terrible for some other reasons? Maybe we just would have been bored. The truth is we were already like getting antsy, and the group was already starting to have the feel of splintering. If we had stayed for that next season, it might have been tough, but we just don't know.

Joe Lo Truglio: I thought moving to the network would've forced us to up our game even further, and that was very attractive to me. I think I underestimated how productive it is to stay in a rhythm and a momentum where your creative control is really strong and powerful. MTV was really leaving us alone at that point and trusted us and, besides all the bumps, really knew that we knew how to make the half-hour TV show for cable television that was really funny. A couple more years of that might have helped us really cruise into network, but I feel on a logistical and production level, we were ready. We knew that we'd run into some bumps creatively and we'd have to tailor our material a little bit, but I felt that our talent would be able to surpass that. In terms of maneuvering network, and this is where we were really naïve, I thought we'd be able to get around that enough to create a show that we were proud of.

Kevin Allison: We had a hell of a lot of creative control. We were spoiled and didn't realize this is profoundly rare. We should have stayed there many seasons beyond that because of having carved that niche for ourselves.

The people that should have done that for us were our managers, Steven Starr and Jon Bendis, and frankly, I think that they were new at that, too. They were new with managing a creative group. I think that maybe they had too many disagreements between the two of them and they made some unwise moves. They should have been thinking, "We should just keep these guys working even if they're not getting paid all that well. Just keep them working as long as possible."

Michael Ian Black: It was a combination of things. First of all, we weren't making any money at MTV. There were eleven of us, and we were taking home like four hundred bucks a week, which isn't a lot of money for having your own television show. It didn't seem like that was going to change anytime soon.

We were fighting a lot, and I think the idea of taking on "SNL" was a rallying cry for us. We felt like that was competition we wanted, and, honestly, we felt like we were better than them and that we deserved that shot. We also had two managers who were really pushing us in that direction and one agent who was telling us not to go. He was absolutely correct. It was a debacle.

Dixon thought we should stay, but he didn't make a very good case for it. I wish he would've made a stronger case.

Part of it is that we would own the show, we'd all make money, we'd be in the big time, etc., etc., etc. A lot of it had to do with their own egos. A lot of it had to do with the fact that they were kind of banned from our MTV show because they caused a lot of trouble. They were sort of tough for our producer, Jim Sharp, to get along with, and he basically said, "Don't come around anymore." A lot was about them wanting to get back in the game, and they were filling our heads with nonsense, basically.

It sounded great, but we were just too young and dumb and inexperienced to know that we were committing suicide.

Somebody saner should have said, "It doesn't make any sense for you to be on the 'Murder, She Wrote' network." Somebody should have said, "This doesn't make any sense."

Nobody wanted to listen to [Dixon], and I think he allowed himself to be swayed, too, because from his point of view it was a big move and it would have been a huge paycheck for him, too. I think he allowed himself to be swayed, but he was the only person saying "Don't do this." He just didn't say it loud enough.

Doug Herzog: I remember being pissed and unhappy and upset. I was like, "What are they doing? If you're going to go anywhere, really, CBS?" That just seemed like the worst idea to me.

There were a couple of more seasons to do on MTV, but keeping a group that large together over a long period of time is probably unsustainable. It probably just moved up the timetable on when they were all going to start to break off and start things on their own or in smaller groups, and that's what happened. They've done very well.

Robert Ben Garant: I was just kind of tired of it. I was tired of arguing with each other. I was tired of sort of feeling like we were still Double-A ball, that we still weren't in the big time, and I was tired of fighting. I really thought we should either make it big or stop. That's just naivety; that's not how it works. You're not just an overnight, huge megastar. If we'd gone to network, that wouldn't have happened. Even if we had a great big hit show, we still would've been struggling.

I was just tired of it. I was tired of the fighting. I was tired of the pace. I was tired of arguing, and we all had this weird idea, this brass ring that we could grab and suddenly we would be as big as "SNL." I guess that was all of our dreams, to be that big. I think that was the head that we were coming from, and it was totally up our ass. It was really not a smart decision at all or even really a smart way to be looking at our career at that point. It was a big mistake leaving MTV.

The rumor was that before we left, MTV offered us sixty-five episodes, which would've been like five years. They offered us sixty-five episodes to keep going, not with huge wage increases, but with wage increases every season, and our managers passed. If that's true, if they really did offer us that, then I know for a fact it was never brought to the group. The group was never told that MTV made that offer. I don't know if MTV really made that offer or not. I really just haven't bothered to dig into it, to ask around, because the past is the past. We didn't hear that rumor for years, but years later, after CBS had already failed, David Wain, I think, heard from somebody at MTV that actually was the case. Maybe it was just a rumor that went around MTV, but if that's true, that's horrible. I think if we had heard that, we certainly would've discussed that and maybe would have stayed. I don't know if it's true or not, but if there was really an offer out there, we should have taken it, and we should have stayed at MTV.

I hate to rag on our managers, but I just want to be honest. I think our managers are supposed to be the marriage counselors to a certain extent, and they really weren't doing that. I think our managers were the ones who kept talking about "the big time." They kept talking about how we're going to get a network show and so much money. Instead of our managers being like, "Guys, one step at a time. You've got a great place. You've got a lot of freedom here." They never said that. They just kept talking about "the big time" in a way that made us feel like, "Yeah, they're right, we're not there yet." I think if we had good managers, I think we would have been together for another two or three more years. I think that we would've stayed on MTV. I think we would have had a different perspective. I think we liked Steve and Jon more than we liked Dixon, probably because we'd known them longer. We gave them credit for where we were at MTV. Dixon wore a suit, and the other two guys wore rock and roll T-shirts. I think that we were listening to the wrong guy. James Dixon was giving us really good advice, and we did not listen.

James Dixon: I think history proves that I was correct about that, as a matter of fact, because they made sense for cable; they weren't broad enough for broadcast television. It didn't make any sense to me. Why do you have to be on broadcast television to validate yourself? Who made that rule in the business? Look at Jon Stewart; he kicked everybody's ass from Comedy Central. Right? He didn't need to go and replace David Letterman. He carved out his niche, and it worked for him. The platform shouldn't matter that much.

Thomas Lennon: You know, it's one of these things that I'm so embarrassed now because when I look back at it, it's the simplest decision we could have ever made in our entire lives, which is we could have listened to Dixon and stayed at MTV for sixty-five more episodes on the air. We would be one of the all-time legendary shows. At the time, I just can't believe I was so stupid that I thought there was some upside to taking us to network TV. It shows how incredibly naïve we were and how cocky and arrogant because I legitimately thought that that we would be a hit on network TV. I had very little doubt about it. I've never really ended up on network TV on a show that was a hit until I was forty-four years old, which is now, and I'm back at CBS. Basically twenty years went by before I was back on. I had to grow into being the CBS audience, apparently.

To their credit, Starr and Bendis were incredibly persuasive people, especially Steven. ... Starr and Bendis had a very good bedside manner with what we wanted to hear business-wise, and they were very good at holding our hands. I think another thing about Starr and Bendis was we felt like we were a rock band or a punk band and they were kind of like our cool road managers. They felt like cool guys, and it felt cool to be listening to them, and we knew that Steven knew the business and Bendis was very rock and roll, and it felt like cool friends of your older brother that we should listen to.

Eileen Katz: They did amazing, great things, and whatever their network experience was, I hope that at the end of it, they walked away feeling that what aired was what they wanted and who they were because that's all we ever wanted to give them the platform to do.

Todd Holoubek: I don't remember being entirely for leaving MTV. I remember being like, "Let's not get too crazy; let's not get ahead of ourselves." MTV was still figuring out, how do you deal with eleven people? Nobody knows how to deal with eleven people. Five you can deal with but eleven? That's ridiculous. That's probably the one thing that has stopped us from doing movies and such because people are like, "There's no way we're going to pay eleven people what we would pay five people."

But I knew the value of the stability of MTV. There was this other opportunity looking at us. So we're like, maybe it was time. I wasn't opposed to leaving MTV. I knew there was security in it. Even if it was such little money, it was steady money. I will always take steady money over the one-shot big money. That's just good financial planning.

The State was told that ABC was interested in a late-night comedy program so this would be the chance to take on "Saturday Night Live" head to head.

Michael Showalter: I remember going out with all the people at William Morris to this really nice restaurant and this private room, and we're smoking cigars and drinking whiskey, and them saying, "We got this great deal; you're gonna do a series." I think it was a late-night thing. I think it was exactly what we wanted and we were like, "Oh, my God." ... What happened was, we had that big celebration and then didn't hear from anybody for a long time, and they were like, "We're working on closing the deal. We're working on closing the deal," and they never closed the deal.

Joe Lo Truglio: At the last minute it seemed the affiliates wouldn't commit to the network that they would run the show. I think that's when the network said, "Then we can't do this because we need you guys to put the show on."

Jonathan K. Bendis: A lot of agenting going on. It was just talks.

Ken Marino: I think we were like, "OK, what's the next thing?" William Morris was telling us, "Don't worry about it. The ABC thing fell through but we'll find something else." Then they got us this CBS deal, which, on paper, was nowhere near as exciting as the ABC thing. But we thought, "Well, we'll try. We'll do what we can because that's where we are right now." I don't think any of us felt like we could go back to MTV, and I don't think anybody was thinking that's where we wanted to be.

Todd Holoubek: CBS was looking for a younger demographic, and when they got us, I think they got way more. They were like, "This is what kids are like? Holy crap! What about more 'Murder, She Wrote?'" I think they had no idea what they expected.

Todd Holoubek screen shot from 1989

CHAPTER 20

And Then There Were Ten ... Again

"Second to (mentioning), 'Chicken sandwich, Carl,' (people ask) 'Why?' They just come up, and they're just like, 'Why?' and then after getting fired from CBS, they would come up and say, 'I blame you!' I'm just like, 'How do you even recognize me?' I was like, 'You watch too much TV, son.'"

Todd Holoubek

The State moved to a new office on 26th Street to begin working on a CBS Halloween special, which was to be the first of several specials before moving to a regular, weekly time slot. Members of the group started discussing who was ready and not ready to be a prime-time player. While The State was birthed as a democratic one, the shift was beginning toward the Orwellian. A hierarchy of writers started to form and the less prolific pens — including Joe, Kevin and Todd — were seeing their roles diminished.

Kevin Allison: If you look at a certain sketch with "The State" called "Origami," you'll see that I'm reading the book "The Power of Positive Thinking" by Norman Vincent Peale. I'm playing a high-schooler, and I'm reading this book, but I was literally reading "The Power of Positive Thinking" at that time because I was so stressed out about "What is the future of this group going to be, and am I going to continue to be a member of it? Am I going to survive in this group, and is the group itself going to survive?" I turned back to my religious roots, and I started to do a lot of praying.

Michael Ian Black: There was a lot of tumult in the group at the time. Showalter was kind of spearheading this movement to delineate responsibilities a little bit more accurately. The group had operated as a meritocracy and almost a commune for so long, going back to our college days, that it was a real sort of tension in the group about what our ideals were and what was actually occurring.

He basically wanted to create a security council with these writers, of which I was one, and I kind of allowed myself to get talked into it even though I knew it never felt right to me, but I also knew that the group was just kind of threatening to break apart at that point because it was just hard. It was a lot of pressure. It was a lot of tension. People were fighting a lot. Even had we stayed at MTV, there's a big chance we wouldn't have survived that long. I know I wasn't happy. I sort of directed my unhappiness at the group. I wasn't mature enough to understand that the problem was with me, not with them.

Michael Showalter: I felt that under the heading of "something's gotta give," there was a portion of the group that was doing a lot of writing, that was doing a lot of heavy lifting. You want to feel like you're given the tools to set your wings and fly. It wasn't so much excluding someone else as it was like wanting to be handed the baton, in a sense. Let's acknowledge what's true, which is that this group of people is generating an enormous amount of material that's getting produced. So let's incentivize those people to want to continue doing that. It wasn't so much about the people who weren't; it was, "Let's incentivize [them] to keep doing this and feeling good about it and not feel like they're doing all the work but not getting the credit that they deserve or the compensation they deserve." It was an effort to move the needle in that direction.

I also felt that we were at this crossroads of the game changing and we needed to try to stay afloat. From my vantage point, things were starting to rip apart at the seams, and it was sort of a "What adjustments do we need to make to change with the times?" You can look at this as a negative, or you can look at this as a positive. For me, for the people that weren't being included in that whatever we called those divisions, it was "Now, you can feel less pressure to be generating material." I remember Kevin in particular feeling undue pressure. Kevin, he's a phenomenal writer but didn't generate as much volume as some of us did, and he felt pressure to do that. What I saw is that it was affecting his confidence, and it was affecting his day-to-day mood. Part of the idea was you don't have to feel that pressure now. You're not being asked to carry the load. Now, there's some weight taken off you. You don't have to feel like you're not doing your part.

On a larger scale, as I've grown in this business, I'm a big fan of do what you do well and let people do what they're good at and encourage them in that. Writing sketches wasn't what was getting Joe out of bed in the morning. Why are we pressuring Joe to write sketches all day? Why are we putting pressure on Joe to feel that pressure when it's not necessary? But because of the history and because of all of the interpersonal stuff, obviously it was a failed experiment, but it was also a very short-lived experiment. We never got much of a chance to workshop that. If we had a season's worth of shows, I think we might have come out the other end with something that was working for everybody, but we only had one shot at it, which was that CBS special.

Kevin Allison: There were a couple members of the group, I think it was mostly Mike Black and Michael Showalter, if I remember correctly, who thought that "If we really want to take this group to the next level, maybe we should acknowledge the fact that some members of the group write a lot more than others. Some members of the group seemed to be more in the alpha position than others. Maybe we should create a hierarchy. We should say there are head writers and there are mere featured players." It became absurd because it created a lot of nervousness and ego-bruising.

One of the ideas was that if a person was a mere featured player, I think they did not have the right to vote whether a sketch should be allowed on the show, and they did not have the right to pitch [sketches] to the group more than one time a week whereas everyone else would be meeting daily and pitching every day and have a vote as to what actually ended up getting on the show.

It was so awkward that it was just three of us out of this group of eleven that were basically being told, "No, you can't come to the daily meetings anymore." And now, your pitching to the group is going to be much higher pressure because you only get to do it once a week and everyone's going to be looking at you like, "Oh, one of the mere featured players wants to pitch something. Let's see if they can make it through the hoop."

Obviously, it created a lot of stress and worry for me, Joe and Todd. I think there were other members of the group who felt very torn about the whole thing.

Michael Ian Black: I don't think it was about ego. It was a sense of discontent with the process and feeling like we were kind of lying to ourselves, that there was a better way to do things, but if we embraced that, it would cause a lot of hurt feelings. The truth is, of the eleven of us, there were probably five or six of us who wrote eighty to ninety percent of the material, but we were still acting as if everybody contributed equally. We would have these pitch sessions, and five or six of us would present material, and some of us wouldn't have anything, and some of us would present something either half-baked or not very good. It felt like a charade.

In retrospect, so what? In retrospect, who cares? It's been working for us; why rock the boat? But I think part of the resentment was about those people who are contributing to the writing having an equal say in terms of what gets on the air. Is that fair? Our minds were restless. We were always looking for problems.

Kevin was pretty resentful because he was a slow writer, and he couldn't keep up with the pace. He would work for two weeks on something, bring it, then it would be met with a shrug, and then he would be like, "Fuck it. What am I doing here?" They were different processes. When you're spending sixteen hours a day with somebody, those little things start to grate on you. As we became more successful, we became more insular, and those problems kept rubbing up against pretty tender areas.

Kevin Allison: I understand where the folks who had the idea in the first place were coming from. They were coming from a place of feeling like this group has so many members and we waste so much time arguing about whether or not this sketch is going to make it or not, that person should be cast in that sketch, can't we make this terribly cumbersome process of trying to run an eleven-member group streamlined a bit?

Can we make it a little bit easier for those who really are writing a lot of great sketches and bringing them in efficiently and consistently to be getting more personal attention? But that clashed a bit with the group's original philosophy of everyone's voice being equal.

What makes us special is the particular chemistry of these eleven people. We're all like family; we're all like brothers and sisters, and that's why there's an organic chemistry in this group that should not be fucked with.

Joe Lo Truglio: There would be a group that were the main writers, and everyone else was focused on performing and other directing contributions, and they'd certainly have a say in the writing, but it was kind of differentiated to a handful. I think it was motivated by efficiency and volume. I think Black, and Ben and Tom certainly would've been in [the main writer group] with Showalter, maybe Ken. It felt a little weird to me. I know I wasn't for it at all. I think that's why Todd left. ... I think that just was completely antithetical to what the group was up until that point, which I think is why there was such pushback on it.

In the defense of those guys that wanted to do that, I think part of it was not wanting to fuck up this very big network chance to usurp "SNL." We were going to network now. We really needed to fine-tune the way the group worked, play to our strengths. I think a lot of that was just nerves, of being scared of failure. That was one idea of how to prevent that.

It felt like we had made a mistake or focused on the wrong thing in terms of what was going to make the CBS show work. It just felt bad, icky. It didn't feel right. The gut feeling on it was this doesn't feel like this is the correct path for The State. Bands break up, or people leave bands and stuff, but it felt like we wanted the show to work more than the group. It wasn't a fun time.

Ken Marino: I think certain members of the group felt like, "Hey, we're doing more writing, and that's our strength. Let's make that a separate thing." It was just kind of an evolution, and I don't know if that went over too well.

I was one of the people who wrote a lot. ... I would, at times, muscle some stuff in that maybe wasn't the most popular stuff. My passion helped get things through. There were certain people in the group who were hungry in the writing, and there were certain people who that wasn't necessarily the thing that they were best at.

Joe worked great with other people. For my money, a line reading of a funny line from Joe, hands down, he was the best at that. I never was like, "Oh, where's more sketches from Joe?" because I knew that Joe was showing incredible stuff as a performer. Kevin had such a unique voice. He wrote shit, and a lot of it just didn't get in because it was so far out there — and that's saying a lot for The State because we did some weird stuff.

Todd wasn't necessarily writing as much, and he wasn't in as much, and I'm sure he felt like he was maybe being pushed out a little bit. I don't think any of us tried to comfort him in any way on the contrary. That was a sad time for the group, and it must've been incredibly hard on Todd. I certainly felt shitty about it because Todd was somebody that we all cared about. Nobody would argue that without Todd the group wouldn't exist. Todd's passion and need to create this thing is what made it happen and then all the sudden, in a way, it was like we became kind of this Frankenstein monster that was in danger of killing Dr. Frankenstein, and that was a bummer.

Robert Ben Garant: That was sort of a frustrating cycle of, we knew [Todd's] heart wasn't really in the show, but he never really said he wanted to quit. At one point, he did a check-in with us where he really told us that he's been exploring other things. He never really said, "because The State isn't that fulfilling to me." We never put together that The State is not fulfilling to [him]. My young kind of mind was, "If you're into all these other things, you should re-devote yourself to The State or get out." We were just so slammed with trying to get material out, and we needed eleven people to be hauling ass; so we weren't the most sensitive people in the world. I look back, and I think we heard not with supportive friend ears but with professional ears.

I remember when [Todd] was kind of talking about the whole season that he really hadn't written very many [sketches], but he'd learned to play piano. I remember being pretty mad. I didn't say it, but I remember being like, "This is our fucking job. This isn't a commune. We're all being paid one-eleventh of this; we need all eleven pistons to be firing just to keep up." I remember not feeling supportive but being pretty angry that he was still there if he wasn't gonna commit to us one hundred percent. Not the most supportive friend mind but just a practical mind. I could tell that this wasn't what he was into anymore. We all kind of knew that, but he was coming from a place that was still this sort of "friends doing this as a club." It wasn't that anymore. It was a real job.

Todd Holoubek: I had just gone camping in Maine for two weeks, and I canoed by myself from Millinocket, which is in the middle of Maine, all the way up to the Canadian border, along the Allagash. The Allagash is one of two rivers in America that [flows] from south and north. I canoe this, and it's just me, my bag, canoe, paddle, just me. Just to get my head together. We had left MTV. I just needed two weeks to just try to see into the future. You can drink water out of the river as long as there isn't a dead moose or anything there. It was absolutely beautiful, and when I came back I had gotten far enough away from New York, the hermetically sealed bubble, the day-to-day everything of what it would be like to keep working on it, and something inside me said, "This is not where you want to be, and it's time to try something else. The world is a big place." ... I just up and said, "I'm done." I had to figure out what I was going to do next. I hadn't really planned on it.

I think I told them one at a time. I think their minds were on the CBS special at the moment, and they were like, "OK, see ya'. I gotta get back to sketch writing." We had just gotten new offices so I didn't really have anything there. I went in my own direction and didn't go there anymore.

Joe Lo Truglio: I felt that the group had come this far, and Todd's in this group, and it just didn't seem like we were going in with the original DNA, into a forum that we wanted to be at full strength. That being said, I know that Todd did not feel comfortable with the kind of re-shifting of roles with CBS, and that the idea that there'd be a core writing group also didn't sit well with me. I wasn't in that core group.

I think the idea behind it was actually a very good one, which is to play to the members' strengths. We had been together for a long time. We knew who did what very well, and just on a logistical level, it did make sense. On a more visceral level, it felt like we were trying to meld the group in a way that for seven years, we were trying to fix something that wasn't completely broken. It could've been more efficient, but I felt that it wasn't broken enough that that had to be made. Again, I don't think there was any ill will or lack of confidence in everyone's writing abilities, I think it was a matter of streamlining and playing to everyone's strengths.

Thomas Lennon: It's hard to describe the bad, psychological effect that had on the group. I think that was a really bad precedent that we set, but I think that Todd got excluded. ... It was a vicious cycle, I think, because the more [Todd] felt excluded, the more he detached and vice versa. It certainly did feel like he had one foot out the door, but I also feel he had been getting nudged toward that door for a long time and not really taken seriously. Todd was never one of the cutthroat members of the group, and the group, if you look at us, it's a bit of a shark tank. It's a comedy group with basically eight alpha males in it, which is insane, but that's what we were.

I felt like it had been coming for a very long time, and probably the vicious part of me thought the group was a little leaner and a little tighter without him because he had never been a really strong voice since founding the group. That said, something about it certainly felt a little bit icky. We basically kept nudging the creator, founder of the group into a corner, into a corner, into a corner until he basically was like, "Fuck it. You guys are sort of a cutthroat bunch of people, and I'm sort of a very Zen, pot-smoking free spirit, and you have kind of stomped on me for so long that I'm going to quit." I felt two things, probably a little bit icky about that aspect and that also that the group was a bit sleeker and stronger without Todd. We hadn't really been close in a long time. That said, I can't say it's something I've ever felt great about — mostly because it was Todd's group; Todd put the group together. It doesn't feel great that that happened, but at the time, if I'm being honest, I was probably one of the people not making him feel very welcome in the group 'cause I was all about, "We gotta be a fucking machine. We've gotta be so much funnier than everyone else." We had a sort of take-no-prisoners attitude. It was a pretty harsh environment, and I particularly felt bad.

Michael Showalter: It seemed to me that [Todd] was drifting. ... I wasn't particularly sentimental about it. There was so much going on around the time of the CBS special, like the boat was sinking. I was neither passionately in favor of Todd being part of the group nor was I passionately opposed to it. At the same time, we were all fighting for our own survival in a way. There was a lot of survival of the fittest, and part of the reason why I wasn't sentimental was because I was someone whose head had been on the chopping block for a long time. For me, there was a little bit of like a "fuck you all" feeling. "You've hung this over my head for so long that I'm an outsider and that I should feel lucky to be here." So I had my armor on from day one. From day one of returning, after being at Brown, I had armor on. I had my sword out. I had my helmet on. I was fighting for my own feet in the group. I was not going to be worrying about other people.

David Wain: As every single person in the group started to become more individually confident and individually finding their voice, it became harder and harder to submit to the group of eleven on everything, every time. I know that to varying degrees, various members of the group were like, "I don't want every idea I have in my life to go through a vetting process of these other ten people from my cult." I understand that in retrospect, but I was less like that at the time. I was still feeling like, "the group, the group, the group" and very excited about [it]. ... Ken had potential acting opportunities, and everyone was starting to feel like there is an outside world; there is something outside the cult. What we knew was that the minute anyone tries to juggle The State and anything else, it's over. It's just too hard. As we've tried to do State projects in subsequent years, just gathering up people that have other stuff going on is impossible.

Todd was always a really tough topic because he started the group and he was, therefore, very much the soul in a lot of ways. But he wasn't writing the best sketches, and he wasn't a big actor in the group, and he wasn't directing or anything. So he started to become sort of distracting, not contributing. None of this was his fault; he was just on a different drummer. Really. I think he, as we've seen, was destined to go a different direction. It was just one of those things where he started the group, but then he evolved into sort of being an outcast within the group. There was a lot of consternation and discussion like, "Does he fit in?" It was just clear that it was not working out, and he left. That was also just another piece of the puzzle of the downfall of the group. I think clearly the glass was breaking.

Michael Ian Black: I was pretty unhappy for a lot of it. I think it had a lot less to do with what was going on with the group and a lot more with what was going on with me. I just wasn't comfortable enough in my own skin to enjoy what I had. I was too young and too immature to appreciate what was going on. I was also mature enough to know that about myself. I should be enjoying this, but this is a really great opportunity. I chastised myself for not enjoying it more. I couldn't. I was just constantly in battle with myself and feeling sort of insecure and unhappy.

Todd Holoubek: At a crossroads you have to make a decision, right? I thought we were going to go to CBS and that was going to be like super-stardom at that point. I think at that point, that was when everyone was like, "OK, this is where we're going to do it." So when I walked away, it was when the reward seemed to be the greatest. I was giving up a lot. In fact a lot of people, second to [mentioning], "Chicken Sandwich, Carl," [ask] "Why?" They just come up, and they're just like, "Why?" and then after getting fired from CBS, they would come up and say, "I blame you!" I'm just like, "How do you even recognize me?" I was like, "You watch too much TV, son."

You know some people watch too much TV; this guy watches too much "State." He probably only watches "The State." He's that weird guy that hangs out in front of John Lennon's house and thinks all the songs are about him. I guess when it looked like the time to reap the most benefit from the path of that group was when I chose to leave. I never really thought about it that way until now. OK, I'm going to go kill myself.

Robert Ben Garant: It would come out in little spurts. Somebody always wanted out of the group forever, like from the beginning. There was always at least one of us that was very seriously considering quitting the group. I remember once Tom was really, really considering dropping out of the group. This is when we were on TV. So we hired a stripper to come and strip during the morning pitch meeting. The stripper came in dressed as a secretary. She brought her boom box and set it down, and then she stripped for him, and then gave him a forty of Budweiser, which is what he drank at the time, and we did that for him to stay. We did that to show him how much we loved him and say, "Hey, look, this is fun. This is not horrible." That was the way that we reached out, and we talked to him about it, and he changed his mind. There was always a point where somebody wanted out of the group.

I never, ever considered leaving the group. There were times where I was really pissed and mad, but I had this total "all for one and one for all" vision in my head of us doing this for as long as we could. I had a pretty specific vision in my head of what we were going to do was like Monty Python. I thought we were going to do the show for a few years, and, for some reason, in our heads, doing it on MTV didn't count. MTV was the warm-up, and we were supposed to do it on network. I think it was just our obsession with "SNL," but I think we all thought we need to do the show for a couple of years on a network. At that point, we would break up, and then every year do a movie. I thought that's exactly what we would do. I really think that was the plan for our lives.

So I never really thought about dropping out, but I was ready for the group to break up. I didn't want to quit, but by the time we got to CBS, I thought, "OK, we better make it really, really big, or we should break up and start trying our own stuff."

I was just sick of it. I was sick of the meanness. People were mean. The general fighting about material I didn't mind. I was kind of used to that, and I thought most of the time it was pretty constructive. But people were getting mean toward the end. People were saying things that were vicious, cruel, and it was just like, "fuck." One kind of really mean comment at me or at the group or at somebody else really took the steam away from me for a few days, and I was just like, "Why the fuck am I doing this? I should try to get a job somewhere else." That's what got me. It wasn't the constant bickering; it got ugly toward the end. It wasn't arguing for hours and hours that Monty Python had done this before, but toward the end people felt like they were working harder than other people; people thought they were better than other people.

Michael Ian Black: Everybody loved Todd as a dude but felt like Todd really wasn't helping the cause, other than just by being a great dude, which he was and continues to be. Some of the animosity was being directed his way. That was causing him to retreat into himself.

Joe Lo Truglio: [Todd is] the voice of reason — the voice of truly coming back to the whole vision of the group, and that plays in very subtle ways. It's like when you bring in a vet to a locker room that provides his teammates with the principles of the team and the values that should be placed above other values. Todd clearly was the soul of the group because it had grown and flourished in such a way that it was planted by him.

That was the vision — to make sure everyone had their place and their voice, no matter how big or small, and I think that was one of the things that Todd struggled with at the end was that it started to shift a little bit too much where some voices were heard more than others. But that's also an inevitability of a creative group. It's not democratic; the strengths aren't evenly distributed, and that's just how it works. What I think Todd brought was a centering of sorts and when we got to "the big time" to remember where we came from and what it was about.

The pressure was on for us to deliver on a level that none of us had experienced, and so the perfectionist nature of all of us had to prioritize in some way what was going to be sacrificed to make sure that we did not blow it when we got to this point. I think everybody knew the origin and the principles that the group was based on and knew that Todd represented that, but we had to make a call. It was a very difficult time. We were young; we did not have the kind of savvy and guile and kind of nuanced compassion that you need when you're in a situation like that. You overlook these small things that really are the glue and the gas that keep the engine running. Never put glue in an engine. Let me just say that; that's never smart.

Kerri Kenney-Silver: I'm the kind of person, to this day, where if I go to a restaurant and the first time I go I order a taco, and I like it, I will only ever order that taco. And if they take it off the menu or they don't have it that day, it affects me greatly. I like comfort, and I like regularity. Not to mention that Todd was one of my very best friends on earth. He was one of my confidants and best friends. I'm not comparing Todd to a taco. I don't like mixing things up. I like when things stay the same especially when it's something that's important to me as a human being, as a dear friend and partner.

That was a really intense, hard time. The group was changing. The landscape was changing. Everything was changing. Things got lost in the mix of it. It was just like he was in the office one day, and he was not in the office the next day. It was hard. It didn't feel right. It still doesn't feel right talking about it. He was a family member. I still have completely mixed feelings about it. It's still emotional for me to think about. I don't have any definitive response to it, other than it rattled me.

Todd is one of the most positive people you will ever meet in your life. Todd would put a positive spin on anything. He is incredibly intelligent. He's a thinker and doer, and he's so innovative. I'm thankful that I can do comedy because I sure as shit can't do anything else, and Todd is doing light installations. His go-get-edness and his brain are just limitless. It's so inspiring. I would expect nothing less from Todd, of course. Of course, he feels this way because every day he's comfortable in his own skin and expanding himself and moving forward. He's kind of the opposite of me in that way. I'm a bit of a moper and remembering-the-way-things-were kind of person.

Things happen that are good despite my efforts. I've been very lucky considering that's my outlook. He's not that way; he's the complete opposite, which always drew me to him. Everything he's done has been a success. I feel like it's probably the best thing that's ever happened to him so he could move forward and find all these different amazing things he's capable of excelling at.

He had days like anybody else that just got to him. It was a relationship, and it was working, and it was twenty-four hours a day. I don't mean to say he was some Pollyanna about everything. At a certain point, this one-headed brain started to separate itself. His started to go a different direction than ours. I don't know if it had to happen or if it's just part of the history. I think ultimately as human beings, it was the best thing for him and maybe for the group.

Ken Webb: When I heard that Todd had left or was asked to leave or whatever happened, I had a clear thought that the group had lost its soul and that Todd really was the soul and that the group didn't have a complete understanding of the entire organism and it kind of killed itself. ... Like Ringo, if somebody else drummed, it wouldn't be The Beatles, and even though Todd Holoubek wasn't their largest performer, his spirit was a backbeat to the group.

Todd Holoubek: No one ever tried to talk me into anything. I did what I felt was right, and I think at that time a lot of people were really focused on the show, and in a lot of ways I think we knew the size of eleven was a hindrance at times. What we forget to look at was that was what made things work. So it was a blessing and a curse, and I think we could all tell. My heart was starting to move elsewhere. It was starting to become a really weird place for me to work. Plus, what did I want to do with my life? There were plenty of opportunities to stay in the entertainment field. There were other agents who were ready to represent me. "Come and produce this. Start another thing over here." I had good street cred. I had started something that rocked. In this industry, those are the guys that make things happen, but I wanted to get away from it all; I was so burned out. I didn't really know what or who, I just needed a complete refresh and really needed to recharge my batteries, figure out who I was. All that time as one of eleven, what identity is mine?

I think everybody had hard feelings. If I hadn't left, I don't know what would've happened. Leaving took a lot of courage, to walk away from a hermetically sealed bubble. I think that's what gave everyone else the confidence to maybe step off. In a way I feel bad; I left right at the beginning of that Halloween special.

Michael Patrick Jann: Everybody realizes Todd's not dead, right? He's a very successful artist living in Korea. He's both alive and cooler than all of us.

If you go back to the thing that Todd talked about right at the beginning, when he started the group, about it being democratic, about it being a group endeavor and not a "me, me, me" endeavor, when it stopped being that, then it was time for it to end. When you get to that point, it either needs to evolve or it needs to end, and so for The State, it kind of did both, in like it ended that there was no more The State, but then there was "Reno 911!" and there was "Wet Hot American Summer" and there is et cetera, et cetera, all that other stuff continues to be, and that's the evolution of The State.

"The State's 43rd Annual All-Star Halloween Special" kicks off with a big song and dance number and an ironic career death joke, with the members hanging in effigy in the background.

CHAPTER 21

A Poke from the Eye Network

"I think we thought we were the hot group from MTV that everybody knows and now here's our big special. I remember Alan King did the intro, and we were psyched to have him, but he did not say the thing we wrote for him. 'I know funny; you guys don't know funny.'"

David Wain

The State intended to inject some vigor into the old-lady network, CBS. If the Halloween special did well, State members would get more specials later in 1995 and '96. If those ratings held or improved, the troupe was going into a series.

It seemed like a chance for David to once again put the smack-down on Goliath. From The State's outline for the CBS special: "The show will be fast-paced, highly energized, and will have a choreographed chaos; not unlike the charged feeling of old Saturday Night Live or The State's live theatrical performances, which got them laid a lot."

When "Saturday Night Live" attempted a bit of sabotage to the Halloween special by luring away musical guest, Blues Traveler, The State countered by adding indie darling, Sonic Youth. For guest spots, State members called in favors done for Jon Stewart and Denis Leary and somehow ended up with classic jokester, Alan King, to open the whole shebang. (Perhaps this was a nod to CBS' current demo?)

It was all shaping up to be a State fan's dream. The problem is State fans had no idea it was on, and those biddies who tuned in at 10 p.m. on a Friday expecting to see Angela Lansbury foil Mickey Rooney's murder scheme on "Murder, She Wrote" were bewildered. Otherwise, "The State's 43rd Annual All-Star Halloween Special" was largely ignored, and the prospect of a 44th disappeared like fun-size Snickers after the kids go to bed.

Ken Marino: We knew we got a consolation prize when the CBS deal happened because we thought we had ABC. We thought we had a big fish, which was the number-one network at the time, and it was a much better deal. We were gonna do a series, and then what we wound up getting was, "No, no, no, you don't have the big fish, but here's this piece of shitty boot that we found on the bottom of the ocean. See if you can make something good with that."

Robert Ben Garant: I think a lot of people when we got to CBS, and before CBS, were not motivated by The State anymore. I think people were being motivated by "What's in it for me?" I think it shows. The lack of interest that we show in each other's material by that point, I think, is pretty clear.

We were just dysfunctional at that point. We all wanted it to be big, but I think that we were all totally being assholes. We were all being selfish. All of us we were really beaten up, but I think we thought the CBS special was going to be great. I just think that we were at our worst. We were not the commune we [once] were. I don't think because we were at CBS, I think because we'd been doing it so long that people's heads were not in the game.

Michael Ian Black: There was a lot going on internally that was sort of ripping us apart. I was always aware that that was going to happen. I was always aware that success was probably going to fuck us up more than failure did.

It was like when a couple decides to have a baby to save their marriage. This will be new worlds to conquer that will allow us to rally around something and sweep the problems under the rug. We were always talking about those things. We always thought The State would be our careers and this is what we would do for the foreseeable future forever. Of course, there would be movies, and, of course, there would be network television, and, of course, there would be books and whatever else.

Ken Marino: I think that we were very much like a band, and at a certain point there's a tipping point. You create, over the course of years, a niche for yourself within the group, and then it almost becomes a parody of itself. It becomes too extreme or people get older, and they start to go, "You know what, I'm not OK with that personality trait of yours." I'm sure that everybody had their own version of that, but that being said, I think that everybody truly loved each other and cared about each other, but it became very much a dynamic of a family where it's, "I love you, but right now I don't like you."

Did I feel that way? I got frustrated creatively probably more than I got frustrated personality-wise. If I was passionate about something I liked, I would fight for it even though clearly we moved past it, and I think that probably drove people a little nuts.

The State did have big ideas for the foray into network TV. Here is their pitch to John Pike, CBS' then head of late night programming:

Mr. John Pike

June 12, 1995
CBS ENTERTAINMENT
Los Angeles, CA
(via fax) 213 653-8276
RE: "THE STATE" —NETWORK FORMAT
Dear John,
You'll find attached a broad-stroke format designed for the CBS Halloween Special. It is predicated on a one hour/six act structure. This design could easily carry over into a weekly series, and/or a series of one hour specials. I'll emphasize that we consider this format to be in development, and open to discussion.
A few words of explanation:
1.) CELEBRITIES — We are most interested and eager to bring a number of promotable celebrities onto the show. And while we see the talent pool as a reflection of our hip and young sensibility, we are wide open to utilizing celebrities that appeal to a broader audience as well, providing that we can use them in a creative and unexpected fashion.
We will integrate them into the sketches as appropriate, and we've even designed a Second Stage (see Act Four) as a weekly slot for a stand-alone external talent showcase.
2.) MUSCIAL GUESTS — We want major musical acts to fill two performance slots in the show. In the case of the Halloween Special, the possibilities include ideas that range from Pearl Jam performing a cover

of "Boris The Spider," to a Green Day or Live performing one of their hits. Depending on stature, we would either book one band or two.

3.) STUDIO SHOOT — Under the following scenario, we will be shooting in the Studio a minimum of Five (5) Live Studio Sketches (five sets), Four (4) Home Bases (one set), Two (2) Musical Guest Slots (one set), and One (1) Second Stage performance (one set). This will require a minimum of Eight (8) interior sets to be constructed.

4.) REMOTE PRODUCTION — We intend to shoot a minimum of Five (5) Remote Productions, which will be shot on 16-mm film.

5.) LINKS — We intend to shoot a minimum of three (3) links, which will be shot primarily on Beta Video.

I emphasize the word 'minimum' because we may find ourselves shooting shorter, (and therefore more), sketches.

PRODUCTION VALUES

Our MTV show, as good as it looks, needs to look better if we are going to attract and impress a network audience. Here are areas that require greater support and money.

1.) FILM — We must shoot all remote production on film. We feel that we can continue to use Beta for links only.

2.) PRODUCTION DESIGN — Sets, props, materials must be upgraded. Ruth Ammon is a miracle worker, but her crew has been ill-equipped and we need to give them the means to make us all look fabulous in the network circumstance.

3.) ADDITIONAL TALENT COSTS — For the first time, we are inviting non-State talent to guest on our shows. This costs money. Musical guest costs may include rehearsal, etc.

4.) MTV vs. NETWORK — While we greatly appreciate that CBS will allow Starr/Bendis to supply a non-union production, thereby saving us certain fundamental costs, let's remember the fact that we will have start-up and one shot costs that are usually amortized over many shows in a cycle. A produced open costs money. Also, let's not overlook all the free music that MTV was able to make available to us, as well as the free office and overhead.

We see this as a pilot. We hope the network supports us in a way that will allow us all to best reflect the very unique talents of THE STATE. We are critically acclaimed and poised for stardom. With enough money to execute the show, we can create a franchise that will serve all parties for years.

John, this Saturday is our last live taping. We have a great deal of press coming, (Details, Mademoiselle, Interview, GQ, Rolling Stone, New York Magazine, Newsweek), and it is imperative that we be in a position to exploit this opportunity to announce the deal.

Toward that end, I've asked William Morris to be available to finalize our negotiation immediately. Please make this the same priority at CBS. And thanks for all of your help!

All best,
Steven Starr
SS/gg
encl.   *cc:*
THE STATE

Mr. Jon Bendis

Mr. Lou Weiss

Mr. James Dixon

Thomas Lennon: When we were working on the CBS special, I turned twenty-five years old, and the group took me out to the Barrow Street Ale House, which was one of our major stomping grounds. Barrow Street was like the unofficial West Village bar of The State, and 7B was the East Village bar of The State. The following morning is when we were working on the CBS special. I was so hungover and so violently sick from alcohol poisoning that I was basically lying on the floor under my desk at our office on 26th Street — and my parents came to visit.

They saw me lying under my desk, curled up in a ball with the stench from the night before. Keep in mind, none of us drove at the time. None of us had cars. So you were basically free to hit it as hard as you could until you blacked out, and I frequently did. My mother, very nicely, went out to a deli down the street from our office and got me a big thing of Pepto-Bismol and a huge thing of water, and I perked up and wrote some sketches for the CBS show.

Michael Ian Black: I think we all felt good about the material we were generating. We were doing good work. I remember we booked

Blues Traveler to be on the special, and then they bailed at the last minute, and we replaced them with Sonic Youth, which we were psyched about. Nobody said, "Hey, guys, Sonic Youth doesn't really belong on CBS in prime time." Somebody should have said that, but nobody did. It was stupid from start to finish. We had no business being there.

Kevin Allison: Because we wanted to go to a big pond, we didn't realize quite the extent to which they just wouldn't care. We thought we knew what it was like to be part of a big organization where the executives really aren't all that concerned about you personally, but to go to CBS, that was a whole new level. In fact we were a little bit spoiled. In retrospect, people like Eileen Katz and even Doug Herzog over at MTV, we did have a pretty good relationship with those guys. They did actually end up giving us a lot of creative control after a couple of seasons.

It would've been very wise to continue building those relationships. Going over to CBS, [there] was very little interest in who we might be and what we might have to offer. The whole thing felt doomed from the start.

Michael Patrick Jann: I don't know if it was a good experience. It wasn't great. It was OK. It was different. It was weird because we didn't have Jim [Sharp] anymore, and that was probably a mistake. ... Here's the thing, it's hard to talk about it in terms of we should've done this, we should've done that because the point of it is it was a fucking doomed enterprise. If we stayed at MTV, it would've gone sour, I think.

The ABC thing just didn't happen. ... CBS came to us, and they were the "Murder, She Wrote" network, and they were like, "No, no, no, we're doing a new thing. We're rebranding. We're going young. We're going after kids, and you're our beachhead. We're landing you on Normandy to be our beachhead into the younger audience. That's what we're about from now on. That's our thing, and you're A-number one, and you're gonna be our 'Saturday Night Live.' You guys are gonna be that thing."

We're like, "Fucking great. Awesome. First thing we do is a Halloween special? Super." We get barely into this thing, and they're basically, "Yeah, well, we changed our mind about that. Instead, I think we're going to do more 'Murder, She Wrote,' and if we could somehow convince James Garner to come back and do more 'Rockford Files,' maybe we can get that going. But you guys finish that thing."

Robert Ben Garant: I was the head writer. I was credited on that show as the head writer, and, to be totally honest here, and I've never said this to the group or anything, I think at that point I was writing about forty to forty-five percent of the show. I don't think I wrote the best stuff, to be totally honest, but I wrote the most stuff. I think the volume of material I wrote allowed us to do a TV show. I don't think all of it was bad. I think most of it was good, but I don't think I wrote that many great sketches. It was the padding that allowed us to have these shows.

Everybody else could write brilliant stuff, and I wrote the stuff that made the show twenty minutes long. I was the TV writer, and everybody else was kind of like geniuses. The other thing that I did was I really helped sculpt material that wasn't quite ready. I genuinely enjoyed that. I really enjoyed if somebody came in with a half-idea. I would say, "Oh, let's do this. What if the plane is going down? What if you.....?" I did that all the way to the end, just because I really, really liked it. I was able to take some sketches that maybe would've gotten thrown away and say, "Hey, we already have this set. Why don't we change the location to this, and we can do the sketch for free."

When we got to the CBS special, I said, "Look, I'm writing a vast majority of this stuff. I'm sort of script editing, to a certain extent. When this is over with, nobody is going to know that I wrote a lot more than everybody because I was casting other people in my stuff." "Eating Muppets" and "Talk You," I would write material and knew I wasn't a strong enough actor to pull off my material. Everybody else cast themselves as Doug and cast themselves as Old-Fashioned Guy. Everyone else was really represented by how much material they were writing because they were in everything that they wrote. I didn't do that. So I said, "I want to be head writer. I want people to know that I'm writing more than it looks like on the show," and everybody agreed. I don't think it was even a fight. People thought that that was right.

Thomas Lennon: A lot of my material made it into the CBS show, and I feel a little bit like that was because it was more mainstream. I'm not necessarily proud of that idea. I was getting better at the politics of getting my material through, but a lot of the CBS show is stuff that I wrote. I don't know if that's a blessing or a curse. It got nice reviews, but I don't think it's one of our better shows, technically, on a lot of fronts.

David Wain: What, in retrospect, were we thinking? This was going to win over people? I think we thought we were the hot group from MTV that everybody knows and now here's our big special. I remember Alan King did the intro, and we were psyched to have him, but he did not say the thing we wrote for him. "I know funny; you guys don't know funny." He said whatever he wanted, and we had to edit it down to something that made sense to us.

For six weeks during the making of the CBS special, writer David Lipsky was with The State penning an article for Details magazine. It was intended to be a profile of an emerging voice in comedy, but it became something else entirely. David Lipsky is the author of the bestselling book "Although Of Course You End Up Becoming Yourself: A Road Trip with David Foster Wallace" and was played by Jesse Eisenberg in the 2015 movie "The End of the Tour" based on the book.

David Lipsky: [The State] was cerebral comedy without being the least bit cerebral.

When I went to my editors at Details, they didn't know who I was talking about. I said, "It's that show on MTV. It is their highest-rated show right now after 'Beavis and Butt-head.' It's a great show." No one had heard about it, and I said, "Let's just do a piece on them. I think they're going into their next season." They said, "The only way you can do it is if you do it as a participatory piece because no one knows who this group is." Then when I walked in, I found out that they were going to CBS.

They were doing this unbelievable foolhardy deal with CBS. ... At that point, I was fairly new to being a journalist, but for anybody who knew about how the entertainment world worked, that was the worst deal they'd ever heard of. It was the kind of deal you get in a monkey's paw story where they're trying not to have it work. "If it goes OK, we might give you another special." How are they going to get a show from that? It was insane.

Kevin Allison: It was at a fever pitch when we moved to CBS. I remember telling the group this, and I remember the journalist was in the room when I said to the group, "I've really turned to praying a lot," which is weird, you know, because it's not hip and cool. But what I was praying for, especially during CBS was, "Oh, my God, let us survive this." I think we began to suspect that if this special didn't do well, we might not get another even though we were contractually set up to. There was all that angst about "the head writers versus featured players" thing that was going on. So there was just a lot of stress, and I became very prayerful.

Thomas Lennon: I think everybody thought it was really cool to have a reporter around. It made us feel like we were this rock band and he was sort of a rock writer — and cool. I think everyone wanted to be liked by David.

Michael Patrick Jann: I don't know why we had a journalist with us all the time. That made me uncomfortable the whole time. Not a good idea. ... He was an OK guy. I stayed away from him as much as I could. I was like, "I don't want to have anything to do with this. I don't want to be mentioned." I had at least the presence of mind at that time. I was not a good people person. I was liable to say something stupid. I'm still liable to say something stupid, but I was liable to say something dumb at any moment, and I knew that about myself so I stayed away from him.

Joe Lo Truglio: It was because of the proximity and access that he had while we were working on the CBS special that he was able to write that article. It was a mistake on our part. We tried to keep the reporter out of those meetings — and we did. I think what happened was our desire to be completely forthcoming and honest with our process. Remember, at this point we thought it was going to be our coming-out party to the mainstream. We wanted to keep the integrity of our group, which was we are anti-authority and we're punk and we do things our way. We don't like the man. We won't let the man push us down. We've been around for a long time. We speak the truth, the comedy truth — all of those pretentious, lofty things.

David Lipsky: They couldn't be relaxed because they didn't know what CBS wanted. They kept saying, "Is this a CBS sketch?" Everything about it was wrong. If they just waited one more season, they could've had a huge audience, and they could've negotiated for a much better deal.

Kevin Allison: [David Lipsky] seemed like a nice enough guy to me, a little idiosyncratic, hard to read at certain moments. We would joke around a lot about how Lipsky would sometimes say things that seemed socially inappropriate to say to us, like, "I just wonder why you guys did that one sketch because it's so miserably unfunny." We'd be like, "Oh." But then like other [times] he would talk to us as if we were just a bunch of geniuses. He was a really idiosyncratic character, and I kind of liked him. He definitely really liked us. He thought there was something really special about us. I don't know how other members of the group feel about him now because of that article.

Michael Patrick Jann: Then the whole Pike thing happened.

One paragraph of the Details article about John Pike's alleged racist comments got a lot of attention:

"...according to people at the meeting, Pike quietly sizes up the group. He notices, he says, that he doesn't see any black faces. This is something the group should consider — black faces would help attract black audience. Pike then flatly explains that research shows there are three reasons why African-Americans are an important part of the late-night demographic: First, they have no place to go in the morning — no jobs — so they can stay up as late as they like; second, they can't follow hour-long drama shows — no attention span — so sketches are perfect for them; third, network TV is free. When they leave the meeting, the group is clearly shaken. One of the members confesses, 'He just described the three reasons why I would be watching the show.' (John Pike responds: 'I would never have said any of those things.')"

Michael Patrick Jann: We're just a bunch of kids who have a little TV show, and nobody really knows who we are. When we came out of that meeting, and he did say those things, and then we were totally, "Wow, that's a crazy thing for that guy to say out loud. That's so racist. That's the kind of shit you don't say in public," and there's a reporter standing there.

I remember John Pike as someone who didn't seem to understand what we were doing and didn't really support the show that well. I'm sure he was a nice guy.

Kevin Allison: He did say shit to us. It was a particular time in history where it's like, "No, dude, it's not cool to say that kind of shit anymore." When he first walked into the room, I think he said something like, "I saw one of your episodes last night. Was that supposed to be funny?"

That was his way of trying to break the ice. He had kind of an Archie Bunker-ness about him. "I'm an old, grumpy, Republican man, and I'm going to joke around with you." He wasn't warm. Let's put it that way.

Todd Holoubek: Unfortunately, I was there for that conversation. ... I remember coming home from that meeting. This guy was your stereotypical television executive, like any movie you saw in the '70s or the '80s that had television executives, this guy was it. ... We sat there, and he explained what television was for. And I think that's all in the article so I'm not going to go over it. It was very weird because we had all committed to going to CBS; so we all were in the "want it" mode, but I remember going home and sitting there that evening and being like, "Did he really say that?" Because no one said anything in that moment, like it just washed over us. It wasn't until maybe six hours later, I sat there and was like, "Did that really happen? Wow, it happened. That guy actually said that." It's like watching an old-timey movie where that was the culture of the time. The next day I talked to Mike Jann or somebody, and I'm like, "Did he really say that?" and Mike's like, "You know, I think you're right. He did. He did really say that."

It was really weird, the power, the Reality Distortion Field. We come in, we're all like, "OK, yeah, yeah, that's what television's for, yeah, yeah," and then six hours later you fall out of that hypnosis, and you're like, "What? What was that?" It was a very shocking moment, and I think maybe it was another push toward getting out of television for me.

David Lipsky: I had come up loving "The Jeffersons" and "Good

Times," which are both CBS shows. It was weird to me that someone at CBS was speaking that way because I associated CBS with progressive stuff like Norman Lear and "All in the Family" and "Good Times" and "Maude" and "The Jeffersons." So that was what was really strange to me about that.

It put me in a bind just because I loved [The State] and didn't know what effect that would have on them, but when [the Details editors and I] sat down and talked about it, it was like, "This isn't just a story about The State. This is about television...."

Author's note: John Pike did not respond to requests for an interview.

Michael Patrick Jann: There's a sort of groupthink that goes on with that group of people that when they get outside of their own, when you get outside of your own echo chamber, it's difficult to realize that what you're saying doesn't make sense except to the other people in your echo chamber. If you hung out with enough executives, you'd heard lots of stuff that as a regular person you're like, "Huh, really? You really think that?" But I have a career to watch out for so I have to dial it in.

Joe Lo Truglio: We thought this article was going to be the canvas that painted us for a wider audience. In that desire, too much was said. That's how it all got out.

Kevin Allison: The way I recall it may not be accurate, but I thought a few of us gave Lipsky bits and pieces of what Pike said on the day it happened. I remember that we were so raw and shocked and unsure of what was going on as we spilled out of the meeting and into the hallway. There was a sense that CBS might not happen at all because this guy we'd just met with was such a bad fit and Lipsky just happened to be there during this car accident kind of moment for us. I remember over the years people have said, "Oh, so and so was the first to tell him most of it, but so and so was also there." I think it was basically that Lipsky started picking up pieces and, over the next couple months, got a few of us to corroborate. Like, "Yeah, two different members have agreed he put it this way. Will you at least not say that he didn't?" It was like Woodward and Bernstein in "All the President's Men." "I'm not going to ask you to say, 'Yes, he said that,' but if you're silent, I'll assume that you're OK with me running this."

Thomas Lennon: Other than all the insane humbug that happened with that, it was kind of a good article.

`The State didn't have time to dwell on the politics of CBS, the members had a show to do and had to hope (and in Kevin's case, pray) that people tuned in.`

Ken Marino: It was no more pressure than we put on ourselves for anything else. That's what the group was, and that's what always made it work, which was whether we were doing a show in a little, black-box theater or doing a show and having this big break with CBS, I think we treated it the same way. "This is fucking serious shit. Let's write the funniest stuff, and let's do it the best we can." I don't think there was a fear that we wouldn't write something funny. I think the fear was, "Will anybody see it?"

Robert Ben Garant: I think a lot of stuff happened during the CBS special. People started fighting for stuff that was theirs, not necessarily because it was good but because it was theirs. That happened a little bit. I didn't want to come out and be a hard-ass just because I had the title of head writer. So I think I took a backwards step at even making suggestions. I think I did it less at the CBS show than I had done at MTV just because I didn't want to suddenly have it like, "Oh, my God, he's the head writer; he thinks he's the boss." I think I took a little bit of a step back as far as saying what my opinion was.

I remember very, very early in the process, we had a pitch meeting and David and Ken pitched a sketch that was a pun joke about a wedding. They saw a sign that says, "Wedding parking," but it was WEEDING, and they're dressing the bride in a gown, and they go and get water dumped on them. And they pitched it, and it didn't go well. Everybody was kind of silent, and I said, "Ok, next. Who's got something else?" and we kept going. Marino really tore into me that I wasn't giving his sketch a shot. "What, we're not going to talk about that one? We're not going to discuss that one?" I had to kind of defend myself and say, "Well, OK, let's talk about it. Did anyone like that?" Nobody did, and I said, "OK, do we need to talk about it anymore, Ken?"

He was really, really mad at me, and we kept going. Then, twenty minutes later, Showalter stood up and said, "That was wrong. What just happened here was wrong, and we need to talk about it because that was bullying, what you just did." It was this thing that had never really happened before, and after that I was done. I was thinking, "It's not worth it to me to get treated like shit in here."

I stopped writing for the show. I didn't really care. Somebody missed a meeting once. We had ten o'clock meetings, and they missed it, and the next meeting I said, "Hey, could everyone be here on time for the meetings?" and I got reamed for that. I was called an alcoholic, literally, in front of all these people, and yeah, I drank a lot, but I was reamed for telling people to be on time. That was all during the CBS special. I swear to God, I was like, "Fuck it. Fuck these people."

CBS Halloween Special

Alan King Intro
Opening Number
Manzelles
Jefferson
Celebrity Interviews
Ros Fanaroff
Lawn Ornaments
Jimmy Tries Pot
Desi Arnaz Tribute
Capo, Louisiana
What Am I Saying?
State Memories from Around the World
Boiler
Fourth Wall
Sonic Youth
Hold Me
Sued by the Beatles

I was like, "If this fails, great." I'm not crazy about the CBS special, and I'm the head writer of it. I don't think there's a single sketch in it that I love, and there's some that I flat out think are pretty lazy, and that's just where I was at the time. It was really, really a brutal process.

David Lipsky: It was clear to me, and I know that some of the other people were sore about that, but I said that Tom and Ben were the most talented writing team there. It didn't surprise me that they did the most. They just were amazing to me, someone who grew up as kind of a comedy snob. Those guys were just fucking first-rate comedy writers.

David, center, warms up the live audience before the CBS Halloween special, flanked by Kevin and (good sport) Todd on cue cards.

Michael Patrick Jann: [CBS] had the audacity to give us freaking notes. There's a piece of that sketch, "Boiler," where there's two people having an argument over a fence. There's about twenty-five seconds torn out of the middle of that that made that sketch brilliant, and it was literally forced out by an executive coming into the editing room and saying, "Shorten it. It's got to be shorter. Shorten it." We're like, "Where?" That sketch got neutered to me. He couldn't understand that the repetition of it was part of what was funny about it. He's like, "He keeps saying the same thing over and over again." I was like, "Exactly." I still think that sketch is really good.

I think the "Manzelles" sketch is one of the best sketches we've ever done. It's unfortunate that nobody's ever seen it, although if you work in advertising, you've seen it, because that's the sketch that got me into the commercial world. I cut a version without the puns in it.

David Wain: I think we knew it was done even before we finished the editing. ... We knew the writing was on the wall, if not just completely over. ... What we were told and what we thought was we were going to do four specials, and then after that it would go weekly on Saturday nights. That's what was in our heads, and then the whole thing went up in flames.

Michael Patrick Jann: It was coming to when it was going to air, and they were talking about, "We're not going to promote the show at all." That was where [we] were like, "Ooh, it would be better if we had a Lorne Michaels" someone who could negotiate that thing. That's just not who Bendis and Starr were, obviously.

It's 1995. "There's this thing called the Internet. You should promote it. Get it out there." This is the Internet in 1995, what does that even mean? "I want you to go sit in AOL."

Ken Marino: It was an older-person network. ... I remember the TV Guide coming out for that week, and the cover of that week was Halloween specials, and it had Roseanne's show and all these things and a bunch of shows that weren't even Halloween specials. I guess they were because the people were wearing costumes, but it wasn't really a Halloween special. What we were doing was a Halloween special, and we weren't even in the TV Guide! I was like, "Oh, OK, they don't give a shit about us at all." I believe the only thing that had worse ratings than our show that week was "Dweebs."

Jon Bendis, Michael Jann and Craig Wedren gave The State's opening credits a Big Three network overhaul.

Jonathan K. Bendis: We built The State as a massive rooftop sign, looking almost like a Broadway theater marquee. It was huge. I think we shot that on 16-millimeter. Michael Jann was directing that. I was shooting again on Super 8, and so we combined them.

Craig Wedren: As you can well imagine when you get that level of idiotic genius, testosterone-fueled, competitive, you know, privileged white snarkiness in a room together, it's not pleasant. It was great for me because I was never in it. I kind of had the best role because it's like I was kind of considered a part of the extended group and was always creative with everybody equally and got pretty equal respect and love from everybody without any of the bullshit shenanigans that people had between each other.

The show opens with the devil, played by "Games of Thrones" actor Peter Dinklage.

Thomas Lennon: I was the one who had asked Pete to do that. Looking back, I don't know how great I feel about it. He was like, "Look, I would never do this for anybody but you guys." The lyrics when Pete comes into that song are, "The dwarf you just saw, he's working for free. It was the last favor we could pull in the show biz in-dus-try!" And then he goes, "Hahahahahaha." In hindsight, I don't know if it's our finest hour to ask Pete to do that, but I remember I was the guy who made that call to ask him to please come do that.

Ken Marino: I thought the opening number was funny in theory, and I think that the way it was executed was less. You felt the budget of it, and I think if we had to do it again or if we had a little bit more money to put behind it or a little bit more know-how of how to shoot something like that, it would've been better. I stand by the lyrics and the idea of it. I thought it was funny. "Manzelles," you can't get better than Showalter in a one-piece deer costume yodeling.
I did like "Boiler." I thought "Boiler" was fun.

David Wain: We stole footage of Sting that he had shot from something else in order to make it seem like Sting was doing an interview for us in the Halloween special, but he really wasn't.
"Ros Fanaroff" is one of my favorite sketches, where the woman is directing her own show, but it's like a three-camera, so she's like, "Camera one, camera two." How bizarre and then like, "OK, now here's Sonic Youth." "What the fuck kind of show is this?"

Kerri Kenney-Silver: I thought the show was good. It was different. It didn't feel as comfortable as The State's original show did. There

"Manzelles" remains a State- and fan-favorite sketch, despite the fact that the only way to see it is via a bootleg recording. The Halloween special only aired once and has not been released on home video or digitally.

were so many cooks. It felt like the stakes were higher. We made choices that were more commercial, but I think we were little fish in a big pond and didn't really know the right thing to do. We didn't want to piss anybody off, but we also wanted to stay true to ourselves. It was a bad mix.

Ken Marino: If you watched it with a bunch of other episodes, you'd be like, "That was great." I think you would like it as an episode. As a special, I don't know if it was fully realized. We tried a lot of things. It was pretty ambitious. I do think maybe because it was our first big swing for CBS and that the pressure of, "If this special goes well, we get another special but if it doesn't, we don't," that made us really over talk the value of each sketch to the point where it was like, "So, what's getting in there?"

Michael Showalter: I think there's some really good material in that show, but the negativity just started to invade everything, and I'm not into that. I was never into the, "We suck; no one likes us." I never liked that. I hate that. I hated the whole, "We're a piece of shit. The world thinks we're stupid. Nobody's watching the show. We suck. Everybody hates us." I never felt that that was true. So there was this feeling of if the group is determined to burn itself down, then I guess I need to jump onto a boat and float away. I think I was someone who was a little bit glass-half-full. "Hey guys, we've got an opportunity here. Let's try to make it work."

Michael Patrick Jann: I was really proud of it actually because it's really good. Literally some of our best work, and then it airs; nobody saw it. If you see tapes of it, in New York there was a storm warning in the middle of it running across the bottom of the screen. I remember going out and drinking fairly heavily and thinking, "Well, I wonder if there'll be a review in the paper the next day," getting the newspaper and, of course, there's nothing in the newspaper because, first of all, TV reviews don't work that way. I don't know what I thought I was doing, maybe a Broadway show or something like that, like it was the '50s. "I hope Walter Winchell writes about us."

The New York Post's Michelle Greppi trashed "The State" when it appeared on MTV. Less than two years later, she gave the troupe a four-star write-up, also for the Post, this time heaping praise on The State's CBS prime-time special, calling it "genuinely inspired," "raucous" and "hipper than 'Saturday Night Live.'" Greppi at least acknowledged her prior review at the end of the piece but refused a retraction. "That was then. This is wow."

Michael Patrick Jann: In some way, that's the verbal

equivalent of throwing a handful of glitter in the air.

Thomas Lennon: We all went to Showalter's girlfriend's house to watch the CBS special, and there was a huge thunderstorm warning in New York that kept coming across the bottom of the screen. It was just a strange harbinger of bad things coming. Every five minutes, "Beep, beep, beep, severe thunderstorm watch for New York City."

The Halloween special got a six share in the ratings. Today, having six percent of all TV watchers tuned in to your show at the same time is pretty good, but not so much in 1995. Four days after the special aired, The State was finished at CBS.

Thomas Lennon: We were [at] work relatively early in the morning. Kerri and I, because it was close to Halloween, wrapped ourselves in toilet paper like mummies and stripped down to our underwear. We came in to be spooky and surprise the whole group and when Kerri and I came into the room going, "Wooohoooohooaaah," the group was already on the phone with CBS on the West Coast. ... They were canceling us. They were dropping us from the other specials we were going to do, and it was one of the most awkward pieces of timing.

What's interesting is they canceled us at ten o'clock in the morning on the East Coast, so that means on the West Coast, they got up early and went into work early, just to cancel us.

Steven Starr: Jon and I produced the CBS special full on, hands on. In theory, we entered the relationship believing we were seeding the field for a run at "SNL" in the spring or fall. But Pike's commentary on how we should reform the group, how we should rethink our audience and our comedy were so inappropriate that we came away from it feeling under siege. So while I believe the show is a damn good hour of The State, it turned out to be our last.

Kevin Allison: It was kind of a gray day, and Bendis and Starr revealed that they had gotten the phone call that we were fired from CBS. I remember we went to a place where you can hit a baseball out of a thing down by the Chelsea Piers. Then I went back to my apartment, and I literally laid on the floor and felt my body shaking. It was like my body knew and my psyche knew that my life was going to change dramatically now, and this group probably wouldn't survive, and my faith in God just totally went out of the window for years, where I was just like, "Fuck you! What was all that praying for?"

Michael Ian Black: We were shocked. First of all, the network lied to us, and they said, "You know, we're giving you four specials," and four turned into one when the ratings were terrible at 10 p.m. on a Friday night. We were just so stupid that when the rug got pulled out from under us, we were all shocked. We couldn't believe that show business wasn't a truthful place. ... Individually and collectively, we've all learned that lesson over and over and over again.

I was pretty devastated because in that moment, it didn't feel like the end of The State. We knew that was a possibility, but there were other things going on. We had a record deal, and we were talking to movie people. I don't remember what the state of the book was at that moment.

Todd Holoubek: I started taking temp jobs to pay my bills. Like six months later, they got fired from CBS. So they were all hanging out at a bar nearby. I went down there, and I just hung out with them for the evening ... just kind of helped take the burden off by being another family member in the room. I think we were at a place called Ace Bar in Manhattan. It's still there actually. Ace Bar has actually become a staple, but it's very dusty now. ... Everybody was like, "Oh, what are we going to do?"

Kevin Allison: Long story short, after the CBS special, not only did the group feel frustrated with how we are having a hard time making it to the next level after MTV but we were feeling a little bit frayed with one another. Do we all have each other's back? Do we really feel like this eleven-person chemistry is a sacred thing, or is this becoming more about so-and-so wants to become famous?

Ken Marino: I think that the CBS special was, ultimately, the beginning of the end of The State as far as us getting paid and working on a show together. It was the beginning of us starting to either vocally realize or just in the back of our heads realize that we're probably gonna have to all get other jobs because there was no place to go. We couldn't go back to MTV. ABC was no longer an option. Fox had "Mad TV." NBC had "SNL." CBS we were done with, and so there was nothing else. I don't think CW existed; neither did UPN. So there was no place we could land. It wasn't like there were five thousand cable networks.

Jonathan K. Bendis: It was a really low point, and everyone was really dejected. It was a matter of if something was really around the corner. The bottom line was they couldn't afford to pay rent on what was happening, and, believe me, any pittance of money that I would take or Starr would take, it was one ounce, and it was barely cab fare. We wanted the thing to succeed, and it wasn't about us making money. We'll take a pittance for our efforts, and you guys gotta make as much money as you can. So we shopped some things around, but nothing was biting.

It really did feel like, "This is it," as far as this run is gonna go, and it was a drag. I was continuing on with all my productions and stuff.

Steven Starr: Once the CBS relationship hit a wall it was over to me; everything that followed — the book, feature development, the album — felt like Stations of the Cross. To the question of what if we'd stayed at MTV? What if we'd gone with ABC? It's so easy in hindsight to imagine another outcome, but we'd all had a profound and amazing experience together, and it was time to let go. And so we did.

Ken Marino: There's a lot of blame, finger pointing at Bendis and Starr. We made our decisions. We all sat in rooms for hours and hours, contemplating what was going on, what we should do and ultimately we made every terrible decision. They advised us, but to somehow point the finger at them and make it seem like those were the guys that fucked up our career, I think that is off base.

The Details article by David Lipsky called "They Died Laughing" came out in January 1996. The first-person piece goes into behind-the-scenes details as to how the writer essentially became

a member of The State during the making of the
CBS special.

Michael Patrick Jann: It's about him! ... I get it. He showed
up to this thing, and it didn't work out the way he thought it was going
to work out. So he had to write that story, but he mostly wrote the story
about himself. I guess that's his style of journalism. I don't know if that
continues to be popular or was popular at that time. Oh, no, it continues
to be popular; it's called a blog now.

The paragraph about Pike's alleged racist comments
toward his audience got a lot of attention. CBS
immediately began an internal investigation.
The New York Times quoted Lipsky in an article
on January 17, 1995: "I heard it from several
sources, and reconfirmed it myself, and the
magazine's fact-checkers reconfirmed it again."
Pike told Variety magazine that the paragraph
was "a totally unfair characterization."

Jonathan K. Bendis: Hollywood Reporter and Variety [both
had] two-page spreads in the middle of the magazines. You would open
them both at the fold and just the million signatures in defense of John
and saying, he's not a bigot; he's not like that. ... I think Michael J. Fox's
name is one of the names that jumps out at me right now.

Michael Patrick Jann: I know some people took out a nice ad
to say what a nice guy he was, but I also seem to remember Bob Newhart
was part of it. I'm like, Bob Newhart? I love Bob Newhart. I don't really
remember the rest of it. It was just another thing that happened. To be
perfectly honest, I feel very little about it.

Todd Holoubek: Those ads those guys took out really blew me
away. I don't think we realized who we were talking with. We had no
idea who this guy was. Ed Asner was on there and I loved "Lou Grant."
I loved that show. I think "Mary Tyler Moore" to "Lou Grant" was one

of the most amazing spin-offs I'd ever seen. It went from a comedy to a drama. I was so upset that Ed Asner was on that.

Michael Ian Black: I remember getting a kind of wild thrill out of it and sort of feeling like, "Well, he said it." If it's public knowledge that he said it, then I guess I don't really have a huge problem with it, and if he loses his job, I guess I don't have a huge problem with that either. At the same time, I didn't feel bad for the guy, but I felt bad that we had kind of betrayed a private conversation and made it public. I felt bad about that, but at the same time I sort of felt like, "Well, fuck the guy."

Todd Holoubek: You don't say what's happened in a meeting. They have paperwork; it's called a confidentiality agreement. I think CBS took the right approach which was, "don't sue," because it would have just drawn more attention to what he had said, because what he said was wrong. But they could have killed everyone's career right there and then. Maybe it helped that William Morris was our agent because the possible reverberations were just ugly.

Robert Ben Garant: We were given the [Details] article in advance, and we wanted the Pike thing taken out. Whether it's true or not, the writer of the article, Lipsky, said, "If you don't have that in there, then this article is not going to be in Details magazine because that's juicy. Beyond that, I don't think Details magazine cares enough to put this article in," which was probably bullshit really. Looking back it doesn't make that much sense to me. It's such a long article, and they spent so much time and money on it that I bet that was bullshit. I bet that was a lie, but at the time, I think the group was torn.

I think a lot of us knew that what Pike said was wrong but thought that was a shitty way for it to come out. If we'd gone in with the agenda of, "Yeah, let's tell the truth about this guy," then I think it would've been different than somebody drunk went off, and this writer was there. I think that's bad. Our team decided that article should go in, and we should leave that thing in there. I think we really all felt like shit because of it.

I also think it turned the tide of, "Hey, root for The State!" to, "What? Fuck these guys." There was a sort of heroicness to us before, and I think that article and the Pike thing really sort of took away that "cool" thing. I think even if we had gone in and said, "Hey, we're going to say the truth about Pike, even though we're shooting ourselves in the foot at CBS," I think that would've been cool, but the fact that it went out so lame, kind of hidden in this other article and we weren't really clear about where we stood on it, I think it took the cool mantle off of us.

Michael Ian Black: It was just a final shovel of dirt on our grave.

Kevin Allison: I think the group feels like we got a guy fired. No one really feels good about that. On the other hand, he was kind of a prick.

We went out of the small pond into this big pond with people who just weren't interested in us. Les Moonves, he was literally being hired to be the main guy at CBS as our Halloween special was taping. He's got ideas on how is going to reinvent CBS. CBS was in real trouble at that point in its history. Quite frankly, I heard a rumor that he never actually saw The State special. I think his reaction was, "I'm not interested in thinking about a sketch comedy group."

David Lipsky: Maybe my anxiety about the fact that there wasn't going to be a State anymore was wrong because they would've broken up maybe a year or two later anyway. In the meantime, they all ended up going out like comedy soldiers into the media world and changing comedy individually over the last years. ... "Wet Hot American Summer" is now everybody's memory of summer camp. Splitting them into individual State cells, maybe that ended up working better.

Kevin Allison: We might have been doomed there whether or not we had John Pike behind our backs. The lesson when you do start playing with corporate entertainment, there's going to be the shadowy figures that are making decisions, and you never even get to see them or know what their reasoning is.

*Ken, Jann, Kerri, Black and Tom working hard
on The State album in the Bahamas*

CHAPTER 22

The Album, Book and almost the Movie

> "They gave us this huge sack of money and said, 'Go make an album and bring it back to us.' We went there and just drank for weeks and vomited these sketches onto tape — which I still think is one of the funniest things we've ever done. "

Kerri Kenney-Silver

When the Details article came out, the media was all over the allegations of John Pike's racist comments at CBS, even though that was only a small portion of the piece. The State had trekked to the Bahamas with producer, Eli Janney, to record their "lost" comedy album, "Comedy for Gracious Living."

Eli Janney: They came to me and were like, "We have this budget but it's not enough budget for us to take any money home." I had been reading about this studio in the Bahamas called Compass Point where "Back in Black" was made and all these Rolling Stones records were made. This legendary studio down there. I was like, "Well, we could go down there and just blow the whole recording budget on the recording, instead of trying to take any money," and they were totally into that idea.

We rented two condos right next door to each other, which were across the road from the studio. The back of the condos was on the water. They were pretty modest, little condos, but one of them was owned by Robert Palmer, and I think the other one was owned by Chris Frantz and Tina Weymouth from the Talking Heads.

Ken Marino: I think it was the beginning of the end. That's not to say that the group was going to officially disband or that we were going to say, "Let's not do this anymore," because I think time has certainly dictated that we all love working together and will continue to do so until I guess we retire or aliens get us. But I think once the CBS thing happened, going to the Bahamas was like our getting away from it all because we did have that offer to do a record. So we're like, "Let's get away. Let's do this and see what happens." It just so happens it happened during the John Pike thing.

Kevin Allison: We went to this place where Talking Heads and, I think, Bob Marley had recorded albums, even though its heyday was beyond it. We're in this game room in the recording place that has a foosball table and an air hockey table and all that kind of stuff, and CNN is on the news, and they're talking about it, and I remember I was just feeling like, "Holy shit! It's a nice thing that we're here." I think that we

Ben and Tom

were unavailable for comment for a couple weeks.

Joe Lo Truglio: I think the most rock 'n' roll thing about that whole event was, when the article came out, we were recording our album down in the Bahamas. When the hoopla hit, and it was on the [Howard] Stern show and a couple of outlets in the news cycle for a moment, the culprits were out of the country and could not be reached for comment. ... That was to me the most exciting thing about that mess-up. We just couldn't be reached.

Michael Patrick Jann: As a joke, I left a "no comment" on my answering machine or some type of version of, "At this time, I have no comment on the matter," on my outgoing message, and they quoted me on that, the Post or the Daily News.

Ken Marino: I don't know how it would've affected us if we were in the country, but it was certainly nice to be in a really beautiful, tropical place drinking cocktails and recording really stupid sketches, as opposed to hanging out in New York and reading that article and hearing how we fucked our career up.

Thomas Lennon: When we were in the Bahamas recording the album, we had to get on calls where we were deposed by an attorney at several points. I guess there was going to be a lawsuit against us ... or against somebody, maybe against the magazine. We all got separately put on the phone, and we sort of passed the phone one to another and talked to this lawyer. I think the distressing thing about that for them was they couldn't disprove anything that was said. Certainly, something that someone said to us in a private meeting should not have been publicized, and that's not an ethical thing to do. That said, the thing that was printed was pretty horrible ... it was pretty dark patch but I remember all of us thinking, "Oh, fuck, did he say that?" "Oh, I guess," and none of us really remember and certainly none of us, to my recollection, had remembered saying it to [David] Lipsky. Yeah, that was a real bummer.

Kevin Allison: I don't think that anyone came to the Bahamas with very much material. If people came with material, it was probably sketches they had written for MTV, and they thought, "Oh, this might work in an audio format." I think we did most of our writing of the album down there, and the album is one of the most improvised things that we've done, too. It kind of shows that none of us had any improv training. ... It's really funny to hear how some of those improvs are so messy and insane. One of the rules of improv is don't establish yourself as an insane character right from the beginning because then where does it go? We were pretty much off of that rule right from the running.

Eli Janney: Every morning, we'd have this group meeting. They'd talk about which sketches they wanted to do, and we'd go into the studio. ... In between, I would work on sound effects for the sketches and stuff like that.

I think like most comedy collections, there's amazing stuff, and then there's mediocre stuff. Everything wasn't killing, but there was stuff that was making me laugh so hard while we were making it that I was like, "OK, we're good." Also, we were recording more than we needed for a record. I figured we would get back to New York and then turn it into a record with all the material.

Robert Ben Garant: I think that we didn't know we were done. We thought this was a stumbling block and we would go forward. ... I think we felt that the album would be really big and the movie would be great, especially when we were just starting everything.

I had no sense of, "This is it. We're done. Nothing is ever going to happen to us again." Without the TV show every week, Warner Brothers, I doubt they even listened to the album. We should have been smart enough to figure this out, but we weren't. Wouldn't it be great if our managers would've been smart enough to figure this out? There's nothing on the album that you can play on the radio. ... It didn't occur to us that we could've done a Louie-type of thing or a Doug-type of thing or like "The Hanukkah Song." There's no "Hanukkah Song" on it.

Nobody sat us down and said, "OK, the way that you sell an album is that you have tracks that they play on the radio and people listen to those tracks on the radio and buy the album." Steve Martin had "King Tut." We didn't write anything for the album to be played on the radio, and if somebody had said that to us, we would have said, "Oh, of course," and we would've written like four really funny, stupid songs. But we didn't do that at all.

In fact, that's our manager's job. Our managers should have done that. So that's fucking annoying.

I think if you listen to the album you can tell how little we cared about the other people's material. Who's on [the] mic is probably the only ones who were in the room. I think we were all like, "Great, do it." People would rather just record it than argue about it.

Ken Marino: I actually think that we tried to make a funny album. It was a first swing at a certain way of making it. We'd never done it before. When I got back and listened to it, I think that it's hit and miss. There's funny things and not-so-funny things. Is it a fully realized album? No.

I guess we tried to do [the dance club song] "Illegal Rubbing." I think that that was the song that was on there. We didn't have a band there. We weren't writing songs. We went there to do sketches and then "Illegal Rubbing" kind of came up. Tom had written it and said, "Let's try this,"

"Comedy for Gracious Living" tracks

1. *Barbershop Tourettes*
2. *Jailbreak*
3. *Skip This Track (They were drunk.)*
4. *Illegal Rubbing*
5. *The Late Mr. & Mrs. Balloon*
6. *The Kendalpants Manor Affair. A Sherlock Holmes Mystery*
7. *Zucchini Bread*
8. *Laurie Anderson Song*
9. *The Koo-Koo Koach ™ in "Half-time Hilarity"*
10. *Glass Eyes*
11. *Disclaimer*
12. *International Farting Mice*
13. *Animal Sounds*
14. *Bald*
15. *Houston*
16. *The Uncomfortable Adventures of Doctor Shrinkyballs*
17. *Kerri's One Second Noise*
18. *Goin' Off*
19. *These Are The Things We Love*
20. *Timmy the Tugboat*
21. *Steve*
22. *Which Would You Rather Do?*
23. *Stadium Seats*
24. *The News from Central Minnesota*
25. *Something Terrible's Happened*

and we did it. We never had the wherewithal like, "You know how this comedy album could work was if we had this one song and that people can put out there and be aware of the album and then buy it." Of course, that makes complete sense, businesswise. We were just trying to do funny sketches, audio sketches. One of my loves was listening to Cheech and Chong so I wanted shit like that.

What was great about the Bahamas was it was our last little, "Let's go away and celebrate what we've been doing for the last five, six years and try to create some stuff, because this could be it."

Eli Janney: It was just an amazing time to be down there. Our assistant engineer there was local, and he was like, "You guys should walk up the road here, and go this far, and then go to the right and there's a little beach there that nobody knows about." At night they have those luminescent sea creatures there; so we'd walk up there, and we'd turn out our flashlights, and the water is just glowing with all these little creatures. It's crazy!

Thomas Lennon: From my end, I was probably fucked up all day long, every day, drinking a lot. I don't really recall how it happened, but at some point Joe Lo Truglio and I, we went to this nightclub called The Zoo in Nassau, where we ended up hanging out with some girls and then oh, my God, I don't know what happened. It was just the worst, truly debauched time.

Kevin Allison: The Warner Brothers record, that was pretty filthy. That did have some really blue language in it and some really X-rated, R-rated stuff in it.

Michael Ian Black: Yeah, we had a great time in the Bahamas. It was very fun, and there was, I think, still a fair amount of optimism in the group — and then very quickly that all came apart.

Eli Janney: I think it was more like executing a vision of what they wanted to do as a comedy record, not, "Hey, how can we sell this?" ... Honestly, looking back on it, I think Warner Brothers was like, "Here's a very popular show on MTV. They're now transitioning to CBS. ... If this show does well on CBS, we have something that's going to sell itself."

Kerri Kenney-Silver: They gave us this huge sack of money and said, "Go make an album and bring it back to us." We went there and just drank for weeks and vomited these sketches onto tape — which I still think is one of the funniest things we've ever done. It all feels like an inside joke. It certainly was not our best work, but it was our most fun work. Low stakes.

When we brought it back, the woman we were working with originally was gone, and there was almost nobody there to hand it to. The person we did have listened to it, and they were like, "What the hell is this?" We never got a call back. "Do we have to give the money back?"

The album caused Kevin Allison to flash back to

one of his passions as a kid, audio recording. In fact, love of audio has been a boon for Kevin and his popular podcast and live show, "Risk!" which is covered in a later chapter.

Kevin Allison: I just felt a real freedom while we were doing the album. I felt like the album was one of the projects we did where I got to shine the most. I just felt particularly comfortable in that format. I loved doing it. So I really enjoyed that time. We were drunk pretty much the entire time. We were drinking sweet rum drinks the entire goddamn time. I remember Ben, in classic Ben form, found some cliff to jump off of where no one knew if it was established, if you were going to paralyze yourself, if you jumped into the water from there. Of course, I was like, "Well, if I go to the cliff-jumping thing, I'm not going to jump off the cliff, but maybe I'll get to see Ben's butt."

Joe Lo Truglio: The Bahamas was such a scary, delicate time because the group's future was so uncertain. ... In the movie version it's like the rope being pulled taught and one strand pops and then the other couple of strands pop. ... I don't know if it was for that reason, but Kevin thrived in this chaotic time. Kevin came on to the scene in a very dramatic way, his own comic voice, even though it had been peppered throughout the entire group's history. I find it interesting that it's at this time when the group is completely in tatters. No one's facing the inevitable truth of what's going to happen after this, which is we're probably done. I just thought that was kind of interesting. Like Kevin, boom, there he was!

It's probably no small irony that [Kevin's Koo-Koo Koach™] piece is a pep talk.

Kevin Allison: I think that we left there thinking, "We've got a lot of material that's just too fucking weird, and we've got some good stuff, and hopefully we've got enough for a fifteen- or eighteen-track album there." I think today, listening to the album, there's probably about five tracks that we wish were not on there, just for being a little bit too whatever. But some of it is really fun. The one that sticks out the most to me is the coach monologue where I give the half-time speech because that was really, really unfiltered Kevin comedy. I remember Ben made a little gesture to me after I recorded it, like someone hitting a ball out of a park. I felt really good about that, and I would do that monologue for years afterward. That kind of led into my believing that I should be a guy up on stage doing a character alone, which eventually I decided to drop for telling true stories.

Thomas Lennon: It's funny, we actually became like a band to break up like a band, which is we went into the recording studio.

Bits of bootlegs of the album would appear from time to time online leaked by members of The State to fans. "Comedy for Gracious Living" was eventually released with little fanfare on Rhino Records in November 2010.

Thomas Lennon: I had a terrible time on the record. I have almost no material on the record at all, and I don't think the record is good. I'm not proud of it. I'm not really surprised that it got shelved for a long time. I think if it was good it probably would've come out, but it's not our finest hour. It's one of our lower moments, actually.

Eli Janney: I felt like we put a lot of work into it, and I thought that it was a really good record.

The State also had a book deal. A faux travel guide of the U.S. made sense if only because of the troupe's moniker, but their hearts just weren't in it. The book "State By State with The State" was initially called "Road Kill." Their idea is as follows:

"Travel tips, essays, arrest forms, short stories, points of interest, cartoons, recipes, overheard conversations, drinking games, photographs, one pop-up page, and totally made-up facts from across and about the United States of America.

The concept for the book is simple: The State visits all fifty states and reports back what they see, hear, touch, taste, and smell. The book takes as its spine the classic travel book, but whereas the editors of those books actually go out and traverse the entire length and breadth of the country in search of hidden treasures off the beaten path, The State is just going to write about the stuff that interests us and our generation. Namely cool bars, weird freaks, motorcycle gangs, the strange things old people say, bands nobody's ever heard of, odd foodstuffs, lame-ass things to do, bizarre happenings, and getting laid. And what we don't know, we'll just make up.

For example, you might read about some amazingly funny adventure that happened to us at this incredible bar in Austin, Texas. Don't expect to visit this bar the next time you're in the Pan Handle. Chances are, it won't be there and nobody will have ever heard of it, because we'll have made the whole thing up. On the other hand, a lot of the material in the book will be entirely true, culled from the six weeks we're going to be spending on the road during our upcoming winter college tour.

The book will be laid out according to state, each chapter beginning with introductory remarks about the area, and then quickly digressing into assorted, absurd adventures. There will be no attempt made to present sucky states in a favorable light, and certain areas of the country will receive much more coverage than others. For example, there might be twenty pages about the Badlands of South Dakota versus a paragraph about the entire state of Connecticut. Peppered throughout each chapter might be road games, recipes, handwritten messages, and doodles. You might get to scratch and sniff Gary, Indiana. Maybe there's a centerfold. As indicated, the book will have a significant amount of graphics. Each page will have a distinct graphic identity, but the design will retain a cohesiveness throughout.

Another idea for the book is to create the impression that you're buying a used book. We would do this by creating handwritten notes in the margins, phone numbers, funny to do lists, etc. Part of the fun reading "Roadkill" will be piecing together the personality of the person who owned the book before you through the silly messages that person left behind.

Part parody, part "Choose Your Own Adventure," part Gonzo journalism, "Roadkill" is a different kind of travel book, because it's more than a travel book. Nobody's ever seen the country quite like this, *because there is no country quite like this.*

Ken Marino: We got this book deal. We sat in a room and [said], "How do we do the book?" We're not gonna do it the way we do a sketch show where we all sit and we rehearse stuff. Everybody just write stuff and hand it in.

Thomas Lennon: We never really committed to the book in the way that we probably should have. The book now feels very thrown together. There's some brilliant things in there, but there's also a lot of filler.

Michael Ian Black: I know I wrote something called Patch, Who was Hell with His Fists. ... We divided the country in quadrants or quintets or whatever, and I wrote a couple of those, I think. And then some other stuff, but I couldn't tell you what.

I was pretty burnt out, and I feel like a lot of the other guys were, too, which is probably why we felt like it would be best to just go off and write our own stuff and throw it into a big pile. I think it was just easier at that time to squirrel ourselves away.

Michael Showalter: The book is our "White Album."

Kerri Kenney-Silver: There was no collaboration. We all picked the state, wrote it and sent it into someplace and put into a book. It was kind of the laziest thing we ever did.

An original and bizarre running piece in the book is a comic strip by Joe Lo Truglio about a man who murders his family, goes on the run, and his story/confession is told via the different small-town newspapers he ends up at under a different alias.

Joe Lo Truglio: Super-dark. If the group had been under a bigger microscope, that might've been something that wouldn't have gotten in there — not because it was so dark but because it was so layered and complicated. Not right in your face, here's the joke; here's the premise.

[You] really had to put the pieces together. That was the good fortune of us doing the book. At that point, everyone was over each other and wanted to just do whatever they wanted to do and have the editor put it together. That was kind of a happy accident. That was something that could sneak by the more critical eyes.

Robert Ben Garant: The book, oy! The book is just, "Can we make it enough pages?" I don't think people even read each other's material. Me and David sort of compiled it.

There were times where we sat down with the [editor, Mollie Doyle] — and I've never been this embarrassed — [she] read (and I won't say which one it was) one of the stories to us that was so fucking bad and just not funny and stupid and vulgar and looked us in the face and said, "Seriously, guys, that's the best you can do?" I was just like, "Fuck! We suck." I couldn't argue, "No, it's great because this, and this and this," I just sat there in this big, nice office thinking, "She's totally right; that fucking sucks."

It was hard, but nobody cared. We didn't care at that point.

David Wain: I was very enthusiastic about it not being over. I really wanted to do whatever we could — let's go to the movies!

I guess anything could have happened. We could have become like Lonely Island and just been doing cool stuff, but we didn't. With the eleven of us, that big of a group, we had to have a pretty huge home base of work in order to keep the whole thing going. So that was not in the cards.

We did write that book, which I really loved, and we did make that album, which I really loved, and we developed all these movie ideas about these different characters.

Todd Holoubek: I don't think I've actually ever heard the whole album. I don't know if I have a copy of it. I don't even think I have a copy of the book. ... That actually, I think was a little weird. I was like, "What? Nobody saved me a book? Gimme the goddamn book already! What are you guys doing?"

Michael Patrick Jann: I had a bunch of things spread out through [the book]. I was doing commercials already at that point. There's this thing about my apartment as a place to stop by when you come to New York. ... That was the one thing I wrote for the book I was like, "That's fucking funny," and it's also incredibly accurate if you thumb through it and find it.

Ken Marino: The passion we had like we did [for the] live shows, that certainly wasn't there with the book. There's funny things in the book, but it's just kind of State vomit. We all just said, "Blech. How about that?" and then we're like, "Yeah, sure, put it in the book."

Jonathan K. Bendis: [If] CBS still picked up on the show and they're going down to do their album, it would have been a different album. It would've been a different book. Everything would have been different. It's interesting to look back on it now, in context, to what it was.

Kevin Allison: The next thing we decided to focus on was movies. Let's do what Monty Python did when they stopped making the "Flying Circus;" let's make a movie. Let's make our "Holy Grail." What we essentially did was we made the same exact mistake again. Instead of going with a smaller pond, we aimed for a bigger pond.

We were talking to this guy at the time, Cary Woods, who produced a lot of big, independent movies for various people. He had produced "Citizen Ruth" and the movie "Kids." He was kind of a big deal as far as producing indie movies went. He was interested in creating a project with The State. I think maybe he even produced "Scream" and "Swingers" [and] those other movies that Harmony Korine made. He was involved in a lot of really interesting indie projects in the '90s. It would've been a great idea to work on something with him. At the same time we're talking to him, Bendis and Starr get us talking with Disney.

We started saying we need creative control. We don't want to come to Disney unless Disney agrees that we're a creative entity. They were like, "Of course. Of course." We started pitching ideas to them, and they hired us and gave us some sort of contract for three movies, but first we really had to sell them on one of them.

Michael Ian Black: I remember getting excited about this one insane idea that we had. It may have had to do with a marching band on Mars. Disney wanted us to write an "Animal House" version of a marching band movie which, in retrospect, is a perfectly reasonable thing for Disney to request, but we didn't understand why they were asking us to do that because it clearly just wasn't who we were. It was just a total misconception of who we were from their point of view. So we just kind of looked at them like, "What are you talking about?" I think we definitely liked the idea of writing a movie, and we were flattered that a studio wanted to be in business with us, but Disney and [a] marching band, we were like, "This doesn't seem right."

We would've been the members of the marching band, I guess, going up against, what, the bad marching band? I don't know what we would've been going up against — the squares at the school who didn't like our punk marching? I don't know. The ideas we came up with were all totally absurd and surreal and way, way out there, and the guys from Disney were looking at us like guys from Disney would look at us when you come up with those ideas. So that went nowhere.

Kevin Allison: At one point, we pitched them one, and they were like, "No, no, no, when we said 'Animal House,' we meant in scene three of 'Animal House,' the rebel guy meets the cute, blonde chick. Have a rebel guy meet a cute, blonde chick — only in space." They wanted us to do a cookie-cutter movie, and we were like, "Holy shit, we told you from the beginning we need to be organically The State."

Michael Ian Black: We weren't capable of writing something that could exist in the mainstream at that time. ... We could not have written a movie that Disney would have found acceptable. We were literally not capable of doing that. At that time our sensibility was moving further and further afield of what mainstream comedy was doing. The stuff that, to us, were the greatest successes were the things that would have found no home anywhere on network television or in any movie studios. We were getting more and more absurd and silly and bizarre. It all made sense to us. It wasn't absurd for absurdity's sake. We felt like we understood what we were doing. We felt like it was funny what we were doing, but we may have been the only ones in show biz that felt that way.

Here's a sample movie pitch from The State:

THE PITCH - THIS IS THE FIRST STATE MOVIE AND HERE'S WHY:

OPENING STATEMENT
We were given this script. Our reaction was negative, but what we liked was an opportunity to make a great high school movie with a good device and to make it...
-- have a totally State sensibility
-- have a plot and a structure
-- funny, edgy, '90s outrageous and unlike anything else
-- a completely new script with improved, fleshed-out and new characters (that no way resembles the original)

SO YOU'LL SEE why this is absolutely the first great State film.

What is this script about and what is the world of this script?
Simple and Universal: It's the State's versions of the classic high school growing up falling in love movie (love triangle) — but it's in The State's world where the rules are stretched to the very limits — anything can happen.

Tommy loves Midge. Midge has a crush on football quarterback Bobby. Will Tommy win Midge back?

What's funny about this?
We've taken a strong simple accessible plot and put it in the bizarre anything can happen State world ... and classic funny high school moments. State PACING, constant jokes on all different levels, outrageous CHARACTERS.

Like what happens that's outrageous?
--main character's best friend is Iago from "Othello"
--Boy Scout camp flashbacks a la Viet Nam – horrific nightmare memories

--in a jealously attempt Tommy marries a 53-year-old lunch lady named Dotty
--huge sword fight at the end between Tommy and Iago
--The Gay Sailor Picnic – huge MGM musical number...

Who's the main character?
Tommy's a guy whose girlfriend breaks up with him — Boy Scout story, gotta overcome his wimpiness.

Who's this movie for?
The original script alienated young people by parodying '50s health films as the main joke.

When we first read this script we felt it was something that appeals to no one — this one appeals specifically to a younger generation. It is high school — not intellectualizing. From twelve to thirty-four. Hip sound track, hip cameos — the first great high school comedy of the nineties. Layered levels of humor.

What is this film in a sentence?
The classic high school love story set in a world where the situations are taken to the absurd degree of outrageousness. The Holy Grail of high school movies.

How would you compare this to "Clueless?"
It's not nostalgia like "Dazed and confused." It's over the top.

Michael Ian Black: It felt like, at that time, that everything was going nowhere, including the album, and then we had the book, and that felt it was going nowhere. I don't know; it felt like we were checking off boxes.

Thomas Lennon: We pitched a couple different things. One was called "Beer Runners," where Earth can't grow hops anymore so they send a ragtag team into space to get hops to grow. There was a crappy murder mystery one.

The last day that we had to pitch, the executive's name was Scott

Immergut, and we were meeting him for lunch in The Rotunda, which is the executive dining room in the Disney studio. The night before, me, and Jann and Ben had gone out, and we ran into David Cross at a bar called the Three Clubs on Vine in Hollywood. He sent us a couple of rounds of tequila shots. I'd never been a person who drinks shots, but we did them. I was so fucked up that I got behind the wheel of the car and then turned the car into the curb and told Jann, "I can't drive this vehicle." Jann somehow got us home. I don't know how he did it to this day.

The next morning was our lunch pitch, and the three of us chugged a bottle of Pepto-Bismol that we got the gift shop at the Universal Hilton. Then we went into the Rotunda, and we all had chicken Caesar salad while the room was fucking spinning. [We] couldn't function, literally looked like death and probably smelled horrible, and this poor executive got to hear us pitch "Beer Runners" while we could not hold a knife and fork and keep the room from spinning. It was the worst hangover I've ever had in my entire life, and we're eating chicken Caesar salads on plates that have Mickey Mouse on them. It was really, really disturbing.

Kevin Allison: I think we were pitching the movies for a year, and [Disney was] just not biting. They were also not paying. We were having a hell of a time actually getting these paychecks from them that they owed us. It was so demoralizing, and more and more months were passing by, where the world was not seeing output from this entity called The State. In this world of entertainment, if you're gone for a few moments, forget it.

We were feeling more and more like, "Oh, my gosh, what's going on?" All throughout the years we had this unofficial rule that no one in the group should take on work that could become big enough that it would really take them away from working with the group. A last resort was we started pitching some shows to Comedy Central ... but I think at that point we were just too frayed and not feeling like we were on the same page.

We could have gone back to MTV. I remember suggesting that at one point. Once the Disney ship was becoming ugly, and once CBS had exploded and we were feeling like, "What the fuck has happened to our careers?" I think we really could have still gone back to MTV. After all, they're used to being months of hiatuses before another batch began airing.

Thomas Lennon: Ultimately, The State movie, people just stopped showing up. The people that kept showing up were Jann and Ben and me because there wasn't anything sexy about it. It was sitting around Jann's apartment and outlining stuff and throwing ideas out.

Robert Ben Garant: I think that David and Showalter went off to write "Wet Hot American Summer" while me and Jann and Tom were writing The State movie at his apartment.

Thomas Lennon: Twenty years later, Ben and I are still writing. Ben and I are writing two movies right now; so that circumstance led to the rest of my adult life.

Michael Showalter: I think you had to at least pretend to have a thick skin. I think that it's possible that part of the reason that we flamed out was how hard it was to have a thick skin. After a while you just can't take it anymore. The inherent tension and volatility that was present — that was also passion and determination and all these different things — it was a battle. Every day was a battle, and I think there was a pretty heavy burnout. There was a "I can't take this anymore" feeling.

One real advantage of having a singular boss is — as much as it kind of creates a hierarchy and hierarchies come with their own problems — when every single person is equal, there's no governing body. That governing body has the ability to move things forward in a way you just can't do when every single person is a sovereign nation unto themselves and has the ability to filibuster, and "It's my right to argue for this joke all night long if I want to." It was like we really stuck to that. If you really believed passionately about something, there was no way to stop you from endlessly arguing about it.

Robert Ben Garant: I think we were sitting in Eli [Janney's] apartment, and I don't remember what we were discussing, but somebody — it might have been Ken — was in L.A. auditioning. I think at that point I realized, "Oh, this is it." It was after all this other stuff had fallen apart. "Oh, we're not a group anymore. We need to get jobs. We need to get individual work. This is not an all for one and one for all thing. We're done."

I had to switch my brain from, "Stuff for the group, stuff for the group, stuff for the group," to "What do I do? I need a job. I don't have much money." I think that may have been when it hit me.

*Black's Johnny Blue Jeans character serenades
the Swimsuit Squad on "Viva Variety."*

CHAPTER 23

Viva Variety

"It was basically a Eurotrash
'Hee Haw.' What if 'Hee Haw'
came out of Belgium
and it had a nice run?"

Thomas Lennon

The State was without a nation — or at least a network. While the Big Three were not an option, the expanding world of cable was still a possibility, and it so happened that their former bosses from MTV had traveled to a sister network, Comedy Central. It could have been a laughing matter, but a former, manic "State" sketch was about to shatter the group.

Eileen Katz: Doug [Herzog] went over [to Comedy Central] as president, and he brought me over as executive vice president of programming. Literally, we walked in the door, and the third phone call we made was to those guys. The first was to electricity; the second was air-conditioning, and then it's, "OK, I got The State in."

Robert Ben Garant: I don't know if anybody else remembers this; after we got canceled on CBS, we pitched another show to Comedy Central, to Doug Herzog, and it was a show where we played everybody. It was this town where everybody was played by eleven people, and at the end, [we] revealed that it was a Martian colony, that only one of them was alive, and the rest of them were robots. That's why everybody looked alike because they were played by these ten models of robots.

Thomas Lennon: I do remember, slightly, a weird, "Twilight Zone"-y type of thing, when what we should have done was episodes of "The State."

Robert Ben Garant: We pitched it, and it was a horrible, horrible pitch. While we were pitching in the room, it was like "Twin Peaks." It unraveled like a mystery, even though it was just a sketch show. In the pitch, Ken Marino argued with me that I had mistaken something. I was moving forward, "And then this happens, and then this happens and then..." and Ken goes, "No, no, no, no, that doesn't happen yet." And in the pitch, Ken Marino argued with me that I was pitching it wrong.

Ken Marino: Whether he was nervous, or whether he forgot or whether he didn't think it was relevant, Ben skipped the set up to the show we were pitching, and I tried to just bring it back to try to remind him that we need the set up. There was no arguing, and there was no fight in the room. It would be like telling the second half of "The Jerk" without knowing [Steve Martin's character] was born a poor, black child.

We went in there, and Ben was supposed to be the point person telling it, and he skipped the first half of the story, thereby unintentionally sabotaging the rest of the story. I was just trying to remind him that you need to tell the first part of the story for the second part of the story to make any sense.

Robert Ben Garant: We didn't pitch it anywhere else except for Comedy Central, and they stared at us like we were bananas. They passed in five minutes. That might have been when I realized, "Oh, we're done," when we couldn't sell something, when we came crawling back to Comedy Central and begging for work and they said, "no."

In the season three sketch, "Laupin Variety Programme," Tom and Kerri played Mr. and the former Mrs. Laupin in a nonsensical take on anything-goes Euro variety shows. There was a talking cuckoo clock, a vegetable cart-crashing ape man and Ben as an Adolf Hitler-type character.

Robert Ben Garant: "Viva Variety" was a sketch. So we were backstage [at MTV] with Jim Sharp, who was our producer at the time, and we were talking about what a fun show this would be to do. Just joking, but me and Tom and Jim Sharp were backstage saying, "We should just do this show — the band, the dancing girls and just do this."

After the group broke up, we were all thinking about stuff to do, and Tom said to me, "What if we really had a conversation with Jim Sharp about really trying to do this show?" I thought, that's a great, great idea. In my head I still had this concept of The State will go forward, we'll all do these little individual things, we'll all do "Fawlty Towers," and we'll all do these weird, little, strange side projects, but the group will keep doing stuff. I knew nobody's hiring the group right now. I knew that the group was done.

[Tom] pitched me "Viva Variety," and I said, "Yeah, that's pretty funny. Let's see if it can happen." Jim loved it, and I think the pilot was a su-per, super easy sell because it was all the same team. I don't know if I'm allowed to say this. I think that MTV loved Tom, they loved Kerri, they loved Mike Black and they loved me. I didn't think in those terms at the time, but looking back, they loved us, and they liked other people in the group a lot, too, but they had issues with a lot of the other guys. None of us four said anything really shitty about those guys in the press, and other people in the group had, and nobody else in the group fought for material that wasn't so good. The four of us were four of the workhorses of The State, and we were pitching to people who knew that. We were pitching to the same executives who saw the material, saw the names on top of the sketches and who wrote the sketches; so they knew. They had favorites, and we were four of the favorites; so it was a really quick no-brainer, and they were trying to do variety shows at the time. It was a pretty quick green light.

Jim Sharp: It really started with the sketch, and they were the guys in the sketch. They're the ones that created it and wrote it and were the characters; so it wasn't so much that I thought I should pick these four guys to do something with. It was really starting with a sketch that they did.

Thomas Lennon: To me the idea was, you just landed in Europe with jetlag and you turn on the TV and go, "What the fuck is this?"

Kevin Allison: The group did start pitching some stuff to Comedy Central, but I think at that point we were just too frayed and not feeling like we were on the same page. Basically, what happened was a few of the members of the group went to Comedy Central without letting the rest of the group know and pitched the show "Viva Variety" there. [They] came back to the group and said, "While the group was trying to think of a show for Comedy Central — and Comedy Central didn't seem so interested, and we all felt so demoralized — a few of us pitched a show to Comedy Central, and it looks like they want it."

Thomas Lennon: We were in a very strange place. There was nothing really going on with the group.

Michael Ian Black: I wanted to work with those guys specifically because I felt like we could do it. We could write and perform it, and it would be very streamlined, and there wouldn't be anything extraneous about it. It would be very small. That's what I was really looking for that moment.

I never felt like The State was over. I felt like, "Let me do this thing for a while, and let everybody go away for a while and do what they're going to do, and then at a certain point, it will make sense for The State to come back together."

I think the reason I wanted to jump into "Viva Variety" so quickly was because it felt like a way to make a clean break — or at least a break even if it wasn't a clean break, to streamline everything I didn't like about The State into something I could like.

Robert Ben Garant: We told everybody, and I believe it was when Marino was on a conference call from Los Angeles. We said, "Hey, we're going to pursue this as another show. Is that OK with everybody? We're really gonna try to do this." I think that we were up front and honest and said, "We're really gonna try to do this." I didn't think it was a fifty-fifty chance. I didn't think it was definitely gonna sell, but we were definitely gonna try to sell it. I don't know what everybody else thought, but we got — I swear to Christ — we got verbal permission from everybody.

Ken Marino: The nail was in. Because that was announced to the group — and I feel like it was announced in a group meeting — I know I was like, "Oh, that sucks, because that means that that's it; we're done." I probably was emotional about it.

Anytime we would write a sketch, we would always say, "It was The State's sketch." So if it was brought in to the group and pitched, it was a State sketch, whether Tom wrote it or Kerri wrote it or I wrote it or five people wrote it and worked on it and made it what it was, it was always a State sketch. The idea of making "Viva Variety" felt a little icky. I know it did to me. In hindsight I don't think it needed to be, but it was an emotional time because it was the end of something that I thought was pretty great, something that I loved deeply and we all put a lot of passion into.

"Viva Variety" was a State sketch but the truth is that was completely from Tom's mind. Much like most of the sketches that Tom wrote, they didn't have to be touched. He wrote them, and we did them, and they were brilliant, and so it wasn't necessarily fair to Tom to be like, "Well, that's ours!" Yet there is an argument that it was fair to say that it is ours because that was the deal. It was just a wonky time, and I think the ickiness of it was more about the fact that the group as we knew it was coming to an end. ... The focus and the anger and the sadness and the frustration was filtered through, "Hey, you're taking a State sketch, and you're gonna go off and do it with four people. That's fucked up." The truth is it was about something other than that.

Joe Lo Truglio: There was a deep sense of betrayal. The intensity of the betrayal was unwarranted. The intensity of it was very dramatic for sure.

Ownership credit was such a huge issue for The State. From the beginning we always wanted it to be, The State wrote it, and the reality of how the industry works is that that's just not right. "Laupin" wouldn't have been "Laupin" without the other people in the group. We were wrong. I'll say that the group at the time behaved in a way that was unprofessional. I think they all paid us money to be allowed to use that sketch. We were so new to this idea of breaking up and new to this idea of truly going out as individuals and creating something for ourselves, it was scary. None of us wanted to be left behind.

"You guys are going to now have success and have money off something that we all created, and that's unfair." Life's not fair, and certainly this industry isn't fair, and everything changes. The rest of the group was also at fault in terms of trying to inhibit their creativity, their desire to grow as artists. I think we all learned different lessons from that.

Kevin Allison: That was a totally devastating moment for the group because it was very clear that finally that boundary had been crossed. A few members of the group are going to be working on something that would take them away from the rest the group to the extent that the group probably couldn't continue doing anything as a group. It was a period of shell shock really. There were a few months there where a lot of us didn't know what to think or feel. We all knew,

"Holy shit, it's time to find survival jobs."

Michael Patrick Jann: I would imagine that because we had all sort of grown up together and moved straight from college into TV and having our own show and going through that, in some ways our growth was retarded. Dealing with that, we probably didn't handle it very professionally. We probably handled it more like pestilent college kids. I don't remember minding one way or the other whether they did it, but I do remember thinking when someone brought up, "Yeah, they should pay us all two hundred dollars," it was like, "Great. Yeah, great idea." In retrospect it's, "What the fuck were we thinking?" We should've just said, "Great. Have a good time," but instead I think everyone was worried and thought they were being left behind. I did a little bit of work on "Viva Variety." All I could think at the time was, "I just want to move on. I want something else."

David Wain: Maybe I was more naïve about it, in a bubble, but I was pushing, pushing and thinking we were going to make it work until "Viva." There were those of us who were not in "Viva" that were very upset when we found out that they were doing this project that was a spin-off of our show at Comedy Central without us and unbeknownst to us. I felt blindsided and obviously excluded and unhappy, and it was not a happy moment in our history; there's no question.

I certainly cannot vouch for or remember all my behavior at that time. I'm sure I probably said things or did things that I would regret now because I was so angry, but the overall big picture was, yeah, we were really upset that they did that because it felt like they were single-handedly and definitively ending the group forever. On some level, I feel like maybe they felt that that's what had to happen or doing the group a service in a way. ... I know I ended up doing the audience warm-up for the "Viva Variety" pilot.

Michael Ian Black: It was terrible and all self-inflicted. I was of the mindset of feeling resentment that we're not this college comedy club anymore. We're all professionals in the world, and as a professional, I want to make decisions based purely on professionalism and not on these friendships. In retrospect, I don't disagree with that assessment, but I don't agree with the harshness of that assessment, in the oneness of that assessment, because ultimately the friendships are much more important to me than a TV show, but in that moment I needed to assert myself in a different way. I needed to make a break and hold myself accountable in a different way. I think I handled it badly. I don't like the way I did it, but in the moment it felt kind of imperative to me. To not do it would have meant limping along with The State for I don't know how long. It could've been a year or two years of fruitlessness, limping along with something that I wasn't that happy to be involved with at that moment.

Michael Showalter: That it was not something that we decided as a group that was so damaging. ... They asked me to be a part of "Viva." ... I was not comfortable with it. I just couldn't wrap my head around it.

"Viva Variety" was the nail in the coffin. That was [the] absolute point of no return because my feeling was that after the whole MTV thing and the whole CBS thing that we could at least fold our ears back and lay low for a bit, take stock of the situation and talk about what, if anything, could be next for us. I still had some hopes for becoming Monty Python and making a movie. I did feel, and had always felt, that unity was key to that, that the core group needed to stay united. If the core was to break up and break apart, then the group as such could not exist anymore because even after CBS we did do a record, and there was serious talk of a movie deal, and we did the book after that. We were still doing stuff.

Ken Marino had an agent and was getting auditions. Auditioning for a commercial was a big deal for us. Even though we had our own TV show on MTV, we do not exist in the larger context in the entertainment industry on any level. So auditioning for a sitcom was a huge deal. It's funny because I think about the way the business works now; I would like to think it wouldn't be like that, but at that time we were in a total cocoon, and some group members were starting to pop and get real opportunities outside of the group. I, in particular, feel like Ken and Kerri but also Michael Black ... that was creating a lot of paranoia, a lot of distrust and fear. Fear, really of who's going to pull that first brick out of the foundation, and I think that, for better or for worse, "Viva Variety" was twenty bricks at once.

Thomas Lennon: At the time, it was basically felt that I killed the group and that's how I felt, and everybody was fine to let me feel like that. And they weren't necessarily wrong. The only thing that's different is that in some way [now] the group is still alive; so the murder of the group didn't quite stick.

Kerri Kenney-Silver: I was terrified. I thought, "My family is falling apart. This can't happen." When Tom called me and said, "Michael, Ben and I are going to do a pilot for the sketch "Laupin Variety Programme" that we did on The State," I said, "Absolutely." I didn't want to lose that family, and it was a great idea. I was one of the lucky ones. There was a lot of pain and anger at that time. There still may be some lingering because it was like a divorce. It came suddenly, and no one knew what the future was going to be, and then here's a good chunk of the group finding success in a similar home. It was a weird time. It was a dark, weird time, but "Viva" was a blast. ... We had most of the same crew. It felt very similar but still with the big piece missing.

I was in a better position than Tom and Mike and Ben were because I was not a producer-creator. They just hired me. It was hard for people to be angry with me because any one of them I think would've said yes, had they called. Maybe that's not fair to say. This is one of those times when being the only woman maybe was a benefit to me because they need the girl, and I was the only girl. I was very lucky, probably the luckiest of all because I didn't really get the brunt of anyone's anger, and yet I got to work and stay with my friends. It felt horrible. It felt really, really horrible.

Michael Ian Black: It was painful for everybody, and certainly we are the ones who instigated that pain. In retrospect, I don't think we should have done it. It wasn't even so much that we broke off to do a thing or took a State sketch to adapt. Those two things combined, I think, were really hurtful to people, but at the time, I felt like it was important for my own sanity to just do something else and to get away from this larger group and to live my life as a professional as opposed to living my life as a member of a college club. To me, what that meant was, rightly or wrongly, striking out and making a deal somewhere.

It seemed to me that the group was done or at least going to be on a long hiatus. We'd lost our network thing. We weren't going back to

MTV. There was no movie opportunity for us. We were adults now and we had adult responsibilities. I felt like this is the time to do something. The more diplomatic route would've been to strike out on my own or sell something on my own, but I don't think I had the confidence to do that. I think all I knew were these other people, and I saw an opportunity and felt like I should grab it. From a business point of view that was probably a good decision. From a personal point of view it was a bad decision.

At that point I was so burnt out of The State. It wasn't that I didn't care. My desire to do something else outweighed those considerations in a way that they wouldn't today.

Joe Lo Truglio: I think those guys had to pay each of us some money because it was a State idea. A lot of that, certainly on my part, was coming from, "I don't know what to do now."

David Wain: I was twenty-seven years old around that time, and I felt like, "Had I peaked? Is that it?" And people were like, "Oh, yeah, 'The State,' I remember that." I was like, "Oh, boy."

Robert Ben Garant: When it got picked up for pilot, it got as nasty as it's ever been. They really, really thought that we had pulled a fast one. They didn't sue us but threatened to sue us. They wanted us to pay to buy their rights to the show, to the material, and when trying to come up with a sum of what that fee would be, at the time I think it was twenty-seven hundred dollars to each of them, I think times three. The three of us had to each pay that to each of them. At the time, it was more money than I had. At the time, it just seemed like a huge, huge amount of money. In trying to decide what that number should be, Ken Marino was very clear they wanted it to also be punitive, that we'd done something wrong and that we should pay something extra because what we had done was wrong.

People were really, really mad. We signed the check, and I honestly didn't speak to some of them for years. Actually, some of them, my relationships with them have never been the same. We didn't talk for years and years and years and years, and I know somehow all eleven of us feels like we got fucked. They feel like we fucked them, and I feel like they fucked us. Everybody feels like everybody turned into monsters right then. I think all eleven of us feel that way — really, really shitty.

I think almost everybody was on "Viva" at some point. David did warm-up and was in the thing, and Joe was in the thing, but it took a long, long time for that to pass us and I don't think one hundred percent. My relationship with some of them has never really quite been the same.

Todd Holoubek: I don't even know why we had to sign off on it because MTV owned everything. ... I don't think that was about, "Oh, you're using State material." That was a little bit like, "Oh, you got a show." It was a bit like, "Aw, shit, these guys are rocking" because everybody wants to do well.

I don't remember anyone being really upset, but I wasn't in the mix at that time. I was like, "Right on! Do it! Keep the love alive." If anybody was upset, it was probably the same thing as the Mutant Ninja Turtle thing 'cause nobody knew really how to deal. Do you take the whole State and put it in a box and put it in storage and just start fresh, or do you use it to build your career — and why not?

If I had some material from that show that somebody was like, "I want to make a TV show out of this," why not? The idea is that you split off, and you keep doing things and then you start evolving. ... If everyone on the show could've taken a sketch to a different network somewhere, the way a plant sort of shoots its seeds all over, new plants grow, to me that was kind of the idea, right? Go, take the material, use it. It was something that Tom had written. It wasn't like he was taking "The Jew, The Italian and the Red Head Gay" and making it his own version. That was something he wrote. If John Lennon wrote the song, the guy should be able to sing it whenever he wants, you know? Oh, he can't 'cause he's dead, but you know what I'm saying. I was lucky enough to not have to get into that. I think it was more family squabbling than legal. Again, I don't know everything that was happening there. Maybe there's a whole other side of it that I was not privy to.

Kevin Allison: The first "Viva Variety" taping came around. They invited the rest of the group to the taping, and what happened was we all got there, like seven of us together, and we're sitting there in the bleachers watching this go down, and it's the same studio we used to use. They have the same makeup people, and they have the same camera people, and they have the same art people.

We are watching what feels like a night of State sketches being taped, only with seven of us in the bleachers. There was a meeting about a week or so after that. I said, "Sitting there that night felt like the Judas kiss. We're supposed to be supportive of having watched this thing we've spent eight years creating, now being done by all but seven of us. We're supposed be patting you on the back, when in fact, we all feel like we've lost our careers."

The guys who were working on the show did not like hearing me say that.

Robert Ben Garant: When it was filming, everybody was in the audience. Everybody came to watch. I was so, "Hey! I'm so happy you're here," and I could tell that they were in a real funk. Since then, I've spoken to Joe about it, and I know Joe was thinking, "Oh, wow, we're moving on, and I'm not in it." I remember him being really crushed there. David Wain brought a lawyer. He brought a lawyer and sat next to our lawyer, which after the wrap at the bar, it dawned on me because at the time I was still thinking about the pilot. But afterward at the bar I was like, "Oh, David Wain brought a lawyer." It didn't even occur to me that that was weird until after we wrapped.

David Wain: I'm pretty sure that was my girlfriend at the time, who happened to be a lawyer.

Kevin Allison: I remember tears were shed. People were saying, "Well, I guess that's it. I guess it's over." I was riding in the cab with Mike Black and Kerri Kenney away from the thing. Mike was saying, "I'm just surprised that people got that emotional about all of this. I'm surprised people took all of this that personally and were shedding tears." Then Kerri looked at him and said, "Mike, it's because we're like a family. It's because the members who are not doing 'Viva' feel like they've been disowned by their own family." What happened then was that there were a lot of raw feelings between the members of the group. I think most of it is now water under the bridge. In retrospect now, I can say, the guys who went and did "Viva," it's really hard to blame them about it entirely because we were starving. There's an element of self-defense to it. There's an element of, "My God, I'm a performing artist. I don't know how to do anything other than performing arts, and we do have these contacts, and nothing seems to be happening with this group of eleven. This group of eleven seems to become too demoralized, too dysfunctional to really be getting things done.

Thomas Lennon: It's weird to think now, "Oh, my God, this is the nail in the coffin of The State." The show that is actually a tiny footnote in our careers together. I'm sure it seemed very significant at the time but if you list our credits, it's the one that no one ever mentions. That's sort of fascinating, the thing that was a devastating thing to a lot of the group is so not even thought about by anyone [else].

Joe Lo Truglio: I had a nervous breakdown, a legitimate one. It was just after the group broke up. We were all still hanging out. I went to a bar. I was with Black and Ben and could have been a couple other members. I suddenly got a strange feeling I've never had before. I felt detached from everyone that I was with. [I] felt like I was in a bubble. It was almost a visceral reaction. I felt like I wasn't me. I was like, "Sorry, I've got to go." I left the bar and sat on a curb and completely broke down in tears. This was out of the blue. It wasn't like I was bummed out that whole day and thinking about it. It literally came out of nowhere. There was the subconscious thing. A deeper part of me realized that my identity with the group was now over and I had to create a new one for myself and had absolutely no idea how to do that yet. My success and my comic voice was through the filter of The State. I was now in the position of, "What am I doing?" The dream of being a serious director and film actor on any real level was done at that time for me. I didn't know what I was supposed to do.

I went to a therapist for a month just to talk about redefining myself as an actor and as a writer. What was I going to do? ... We all ended up working with each other, but that marriage — at that point had gone on for eight years — was over in no uncertain terms.

Kevin Allison: For years, I was waiting tables and catering and later working in publishing and doing anything I could think of to try and keep my rent paid. I can't tell you how jealous I was of the guys on

"Viva Variety." I was so filled with jealousy and resentment and self-loathing, just upset about what happened. I heard a line somewhere, "They had built the house, but someone else took the keys."

I remember thinking I felt that way. I had helped a group of people build a house, but the keys had been taken away and now I couldn't get into it. On top of all that jealousy and resentment and self-loathing, there was also the tendency of mine to be the black sheep, the guy who goes off into his own universe, the guy with so much social anxiety that he's not used to socializing with other comedians. One of my greatest regrets in life is how poorly I dealt with the group's breaking up.

Kerri Kenney-Silver: I think it took a while for people to be able to fraternize again and be OK with it. Again, we were working crazy hours, and I was still doing the band. I was too worried making albums. I didn't really have much time for that kind of thing anyway. Obviously, it all came back around.

David Wain: It's not like we stopped being friends. That's what's so weird. We're family. We never stopped being family, but it was just a really rough moment, and it was around the same time Stella was happening, too, and Mike Black was part of both. It was a very weird moment, and then, of course, at some point "Viva" moved operations to L.A., and therefore Tom, Kerri, Mike and Ben moved to L.A., and that divided up the group even more or ended any thought of any real reunion.

Robert Ben Garant: In the pilot, I was a bad guy. I was like Hitler who was trying to shut down the show, and Tom had a daughter in the pilot who was Sara Winter, a big TV actress now. After the pilot, they sat us down and said, "Look, we love this concept; we love the show. Lose you as a character. We don't like the daughter, and we don't like you." At the time, it never even occurred to me that they were wrong. They were one hundred percent right, and I think as a twenty-five-year-old kid, I was like, "I totally, totally agree. I'll be much better served if I'm behind the camera. I'll be much better as a writer. My character does not work." I remember they looked at me like, "Oh, fuck," like they really thought it was going to be a fight, and the fact that I just genuinely agreed that I was not a strong enough performer to make the show work, I think they were impressed. They loved us, and they gave us a lot of fun freedom on that show.

Thomas Lennon: I would love for people to see the actual pilot of "Viva Variety" compared to the series "Viva Variety" because the pilot is bat-shit crazy. ... It's got a whole animated sequence of rock and roll foosball men. It's got a whole puppet sequence called "Land of Reality," which is where Mr. Lapin would go to East Berlin, and he would smoke cigarettes with this little horse that was a heroin addict, and it was just a war zone that he would go to, like Mr. Rogers. A lot of the edges got sanded off by the time it made the air. It had become a much more sensible sort of show; it was still fairly silly.

"Viva Variety" toned down the manic energy of the "Laupin Variety Programme" sketch a smidge. Tom's and Kerri's characters got first names, Meredith and Agatha Laupin, and their shtick became slamming each other like a Eurotrash Sonny and Cher. Their companion/punching bag was Black as the clueless Johnny Blue Jeans, who attempted to be the epitome of American cool but came off more like Fonzie with a learning disability. All three spoke with an indeterminable European accent Kerri dubbed "the nowhere people."

There was also the Swimsuit Squad, because every variety show needs a cadre of scantily clad female dancers. "Viva" featured college rock acts such as They Might Be Giants, Ween and Reel Big Fish, past-their-prime celebs who made sense, Evel Knievel, and those who did not, Charles Durning?, plus real sideshow-type acts and fake ones — Ben and another bald dude play piano with their penii — and you have the gist.

Comedy Central ran original episodes of "Viva Variety" from 1997 to 1999.

Thomas Lennon: It was basically a Eurotrash "Hee Haw." What if "Hee Haw" came out of Belgium and it had a nice run?

Michael Ian Black: There was something to us that was very funny about doing a fake European variety show and taking all the weirdness of not just European variety shows but particularly "Sabado Gigante" on Univision, the sort of freewheeling five-hour parade of nonsense every Saturday, then translating that to American television. It seemed like a really funny opportunity in a way to do things cheaply on purpose and badly on purpose — to sort of do the outsiders again. The whole idea of that show is outsiders looking in and desperately wanting to belong. That's how we beat ourselves.

Thomas Lennon: It was a sketch comedy show being hosted by recurring characters, which took it to a slightly different level. I'm always amazed how many people have never heard of it, ever. The details about "Viva Variety" are inaccurate online. For example, there's more episodes of "Viva Variety" than "The State."

Doug Herzog: "Viva," definitely [a] fantastic show. ... I wanted to do a variety show, and they came in and pitched it. I'm like, "I want to do this; it sounds great." I loved that show. ... Back in the MTV days, I got to know Michael Ian Black a little bit, certainly Showalter, Marino, Tom, Ben to a lesser extent, Kerri a little bit. David was a little bit more of a mystery to me and was really fun to watch him emerge over time in a lot of different ways. Ultimately, I got to know all those guys better, at least those four guys working on "Viva Variety."

Thomas Lennon: Something happened the very first week of "Viva Variety" that threw me. I realized that I was gonna be the straight man and Johnny Blue Jeans was the much more fun character to play.

Black's wardrobe for "Viva Variety" involved a lot of denim and translucent polyurethane, but boy did he have a fantastic mop of rockabilly hair!

Michael Ian Black: In the beginning [the Johnny Blue Jeans hairdo] was all me, and then in the last season I asked for a wig because it was such a pain in the ass. I think the character was really good. I liked wearing all the pleather. It was the first time professionally that I was able to live in a character for a long time, and it was really fun. I felt like I could do anything with that character. I knew him really well, and that provided a lot of freedom, and it was great. I thought that Tom and Kerri were great.

Kerri Kenney-Silver: I loved it. I love that character. The negative part of doing "The State" was a good character that you love, that was it, you do it for three minutes, and you are never going to do it again. I loved it. It was different for me because it was a glamorous role. At the time, I was model-size, and I was able to wear these one-of-a-kind couture gowns and have my hair done up into a working water fountain or a real birdcage, and then still be able to do comedy in front of an audience. And we had live bands. We had Run DMC, Mighty Mighty Bosstones, Sonic Youth.

Thomas Lennon: Doug Herzog is a real music aficionado, and he was always looking for a cool way to have music in shows. ... The line-up of bands for "Viva Variety" was incredible. It was just the list of everybody you would want that was around at the time.

Michael Ian Black: The whole reason we wanted to do it was to streamline production. Streamline the writing, streamline the arguments, streamline all of the difficulties in navigating an eleven-headed beast. From that respect, it was just so much easier because it was just the three of us, me, Tom and Ben writing. Kerri was more like an actress on it.

At the same time, I hadn't worked out for myself whatever was going on with me during "The State." I remember being in really black moods for a lot of it. I wasn't able to fully enjoy it, and I don't know what that was other than literally not being on antidepressants. I literally think that was the issue. So the same kind of things that were affecting me in "The State" were affecting me on "Viva Variety." Even though there were times that I had a lot of fun with it, in particular hanging out with the monkey doing monkey sports, there were also a lot of times where I was so in my own head that I couldn't get out.

Thomas Lennon: The circumstances writing "Viva" were nowhere near as fun as writing "The State," because it was me, Ben and Mike in a room. ... There was times where Mike Black would come in, and sit at his desk and not really talk to me or Ben almost all day. Our office was the most depressing place you could imagine. It was a windowless room in the basement of the studio at 106th Street and Park Avenue. We didn't see daylight ever when we were doing that show, and it was the opposite of "The State" where we were up in these fun offices in Times Square with everybody goofing around and having the time of their lives. This was definitely more like a job, and it was not the funnest time, but I'm proud of the show.

Jim Sharp: It was a lot easier. Sometimes four against one is a lot easier than eleven against one. We were just working together very well. Everybody knew their role and what we were trying to do, and it was just being more experienced and more focused. That was just a really great run. I did two years of it, and it was just a machine as far as the writing and the producing and what we were trying to do.

Eileen Katz: There were some real gems on there. ... It was not a big, broad breakout, but it was the perfect satirization. If "Sabado Gigante" wasn't a satirization of a variety shows enough, this took that to the next level. I felt that it was a little self-indulgent. I loved their twisted perspective, and you kind of put it in that Ben-Kerri-Tom machine, and out it came. It was fun and big and broad and over the top, but still the smartness and the subtlety of what they bring to everything was there. It was a joy. My God, the costumes, over the top.

They were a little older and wiser. We were a little older and wiser. You know what, when you buy "Viva Variety," you better know what you're buying. It's like if you don't get it at the checkout counter, you're never going to get it.

Robert Ben Garant: It was before "The Daily Show." We were before "South Park," so the bar was very, very low at that time. There wasn't that much pressure [for] great ratings [on Comedy Central].

Tom and Kerri as Mr. and the former Mrs. Laupin flank "Viva Variety" guest star, Kathy Griffin, in a "Wizard of Oz" sketch.

Kerri Kenney-Silver: Our favorite thing in "The State" was to do song-and-dance numbers. We got to do at least one every week. So it was a dream job. It was so much fun. Probably my favorite show that I've done to date.

Robert Ben Garant: We have these [dancing] girls. We didn't know what to do, and we decided to start writing musicals. After [episode three], there was a song in every single episode. These women [were] doing this wonderful choreography, and Tom and Kerri and sometimes Mike had to sing and dance with them. It felt like we were on "The Dean Martin Show" or something.

Michael Ian Black: Most people in "The State" are big theater fags. We're kids who wanted to sing songs and put on shows. So with "Viva," that's what we did every day, and it was really fun. It was unfortunate that I discovered that I'm an even worse singer than I believed myself to be. So recording songs for me was torture. I just couldn't do it because I was terrible at it. We had this great composer, and Ben wrote most of the songs, and he was quite brilliant at it. I wish Ben would buckle down and write a Broadway musical because he would be fantastic. Of all his gifts, lyricist might be his finest. The whole putting on a show thing every week was really fun.

Kerri Kenney-Silver: We went to Vegas for two episodes with [Nell Carter] when Tom and I got remarried, and she was the high priestess who married us.

Thomas Lennon: I remember during those Vegas specials being just about the most stressed I've ever been in my entire life. If you've never lived in a casino for a long time, a hotel casino, don't do it. It's not great for your mental health. At this point, I'm probably smoking almost four packs of cigarettes a day.

Michael Ian Black: We got a lot of older people; those are the people who needed the money. Adam West is still with us. Ben Stiller is still with us. Dick Clark lived for many years after he did our show. Eartha Kitt lived many years after she did our show. Walter Koenig [of "Star Trek"] did not.

Author's note: he's still alive.

Michael Ian Black: Oh, he his? My bad.

While Comedy Central allowed a sketch in which Mr. Laupin's grandfather was part of Hitler's comedy basketball team — an Aryan nation Globetrotters, if you will — a bit about a board game called Find the Lindbergh Baby was nixed.

Michael Ian Black: Why they would pick that, of all things, is crazy to me. A lot of times in TV that kind of thing feels arbitrary from everybody else. The standards and practices people seem to understand why you can't make a joke about kidnapping the Lindbergh baby, but Hitler jokes are fine.

It wasn't like the baby was going to be offended. The baby died.

Thomas Lennon: The "Dunkwaffe." Not everybody thought that was a good idea but I remember thinking that was a great one. They play against the filthy gypsies.

Production left New York for the West Coast for the third season.

Thomas Lennon: That [show] got us to Los Angeles and put us where we are now. I know for myself and I'm pretty sure for Ben, neither of us ever had any intention of coming out West. I assumed that I would live my life and die in the West Village in New York and never, ever leave.

Jim Sharp left to go produce a show for Magic Johnson called "The Magic Hour," which ended up being sort of a game-changing flop. ... This was the first time that I felt very untethered on that show because Paul Miller and Kimber Rickabaugh came in and became the producers. When they came in, I realized, "These people don't get my sense of humor at all. I actually don't even think they like this show or get what I think is funny about it." I liked them as people, but I never felt creatively like we clicked at all. Suddenly, I felt like a stranger on my own show and it was a pretty bad feeling. That's how we headed into what would be the third season of "Viva." I felt very much like they felt like it was Kerri's show. I guess I felt resentful of that. I wasn't surprised that the show sort of petered out that season. I think from the time that we lost Jim, it started sort of a downward spiral.

By the third season, TV comedies are typically in their groove allowing for them to get a little weirder and edgier.

Thomas Lennon: We took definitely the opposite path, which was our pilot was the weirdest thing we ever did and then we got more mainstream-ified until the end.

Kerri Kenney-Silver: God, I don't remember exactly how it ended. ... I don't know how much more that show could've gone on, honestly. It was a miracle to me. It was great. I loved it, but still the concept was very out there. I think it had a really nice run for what it was.

Michael Ian Black: I think "Viva" was good. "Viva" never became what I wanted it to be. I still don't know creatively how I could have made it better. There was a lot I liked about it. I like its free-spiritedness. I like its absurdity and the surreal aspect of it. We did insane things, all of which I think are really good. It never quite gelled for me the way I wanted to. I still don't know why.

We did like forty episodes. We ran it into the ground, which was nice. I never felt like it lived up to what I had in my head for it. I couldn't even articulate what that was. It was a fake European variety show that featured insane guests and crazy vaudeville acts and cool bands and ludicrous sketches — and yet I wanted all of it to have been like another fifty percent of that, an even bigger carnival of asinine-ness.

It wasn't a question of expense; it was about creatively trying to find it, and I felt like we never got there. I felt like we came close a few times. We did some things that I really liked, but no single episode, to me, ever quite fully gelled as the definitive "Viva Variety" episode. There's so much about it that I like, and I'm glad we did it, and I think we did some really funny, original stuff, and yet I feel like we never quite got over the finish line.

All the elements individually were great. Where I felt like I came up short was in the writing.

Kerri Kenney-Silver: I can't believe the network let us do that. I still look back and say, "Who the hell said yes to that?" I don't know. I think it's kind of brilliant in a way. I wish they would play it again. The music thing, just like "The State," it's impossible. You're never going to get the rights to all those acts.

Robert Ben Garant: I had a VHS of it that got lost in one of my parents' moves. I don't have it, so I would love to see it.

Thomas Lennon: Recently, I did a popular show on Australia TV called "Noches Con Platanito" which means "Evenings with Little Banana," which is a Spanish-language show. I was standing there with a guy in clown makeup throwing fruit at girls in bikinis, and I was like, "Oh, this is 'Viva Variety.'" We owe everything to "Sabado Gigante," which was at the time a giant influence.

Ben, Black, Kerri and Tom reunited for a live "Viva Variety" show at San Francisco Sketchfest in 2012. A fan, Robin Williams, popped backstage at the Eureka Theater to say hi.

Robert Ben Garant: You meet a lot of famous people, but Robin Williams, there's just something about him that feels so much bigger than anybody else I've ever met.

The wounds from "Viva Variety" started to heal slowly.

Robert Ben Garant: We would get together in twos and threes gradually, you know. I never really had hard feelings with Joe, and I never had odd feelings with Todd or Jann. I think with some of us it was never even a ripple. We got together and talked about it pretty quick. By the time I saw David, Sho and Ken again, it had been years, and so we've never really talked about it. But by the time we'd gotten together again, we'd all done so many things in between "The State" and "Viva," and when we next met, it was fine. They all did the "Reno" movie, which was great. A bunch of them were on "Reno" before that, but a bunch of them sat around the table for the "Reno" movie, and that was the first time we officially all were together at all. We broke bread and then never discussed the past at all except in good ways.

Joe Lo Truglio: There's an operatic Greek tragedy inherent in it — the tragic flaws of arrogance and being destroyed by it, the rising from the ashes of humility and collaboration. ... I'm so grateful that we were able to weather the storm and be very close now. It is truly amazing. I don't use the word often, blessed, but I do feel that way. It's a special thing.

Sho, David and Black's nightclub act, Stella, at Fez

CHAPTER 24

Stella

"It was a little bit like finding Nina in the Al Hirschfeld drawings. The black dildo is the Nina of Stella shorts, much like Jim Stansel is now the Nina of every single David Wain project."

Paul Rudd

As "college radio" in the '80s turned into "indie rock" and then became (oxymoronically) mainstream "alternative" in the '90s, the birth of contemporary live comedy started around the same time in New York, and, of course, members of The State were there.

Michael Ian Black, Michael Showalter and David Wain were all experimenting with solo stand-up in nontraditional venues like Rebar and Luna Lounge in New York City. The three were looking at new ways to tell jokes, avoiding the trappings of observational humor that eventually strangled stand-up comedy in the late '80s and early '90s: Airline food! "Gilligan's Island!" The missing dryer sock!

"Not only did I want to not be put into that box, I couldn't do those kinds of jokes even if I wanted to," Showalter said.

Michael Showalter: It was all very purposely experimental. ... My entire stand-up act was to the person who stole my sweater the last time I was here. That was my whole act, and it was trying to appeal to their sense of humanity. It was fun, and we were all getting really into that.

David Wain: When we were shooting "The State," we were going to Rebar downtown, and we were doing bits and hosting. We were always trying funny performances, and that's where we got to know Janeane Garofalo and Louis C.K. and Marc Maron and Todd Barry.

Michael Ian Black: You would go there, and there would be all these established comedians or up-and-coming comedians experimenting with form and storytelling and trying different things. For them it was a way to work out new ideas, but for people like the three of us who weren't stand-ups, you would work on this new stuff, and when it was over you'd have no place to take it. It was sort of like it was dead. We thought maybe there was an opportunity to create a more professional room that would work in concert with Luna Lounge and with whatever other alt rooms were springing up. That was the impetus. It came directly out of doing stand-up or some form of stand-up.

David Wain: We got booked at Brooklyn Polytechnic [Institute], and we thought we would each go up for a few minutes and do something and then we would maybe do something together. They basically dragged these tech students out into this brightly lit fluorescent room with chicken wings in the back and forced them to sit and watch. A magician opened up, and then we came out. It couldn't have gone over more like a thud.

We called it Midnight Expressions. We each realized that whatever we had planned had to be shortened a lot and just get out of there as quickly as we could. It was a disaster. So I'm glad we kept going after that. The Fez show, I think the first couple shows we hosted and then bits in the middle we each went up and did our own little piece. We realized almost immediately that the real juice was the three of us kind of screwing around on stage. Then we did that every week for a while.

The trio found Fez, a funky club that would host jazz combos and assorted eclectic acts. It had the nightclub vibe that felt right to them for anything-goes comedy. The first show was January 15, 1997, and featured State mates, Kevin and Ken, as well as Janeane Garofalo, Marc Maron and Stephen Colbert.

David Wain: We were thinking this kind of comedy should have an actual home for a real show and have a band and people are all dressed up ... a fun evening that people could go week after week. ... We didn't have a name and the booker, Ellen, at Fez was pregnant, and we asked her, "What's the name of your kid going to be?" and she said "Stella." So we called the show Stella.

Michael Ian Black: Riffing and writing scripts — that evolved into this comedic vocabulary that became Stella.

Michael Showalter: We would tell each other our ideas and run our ideas through each other. I was never as serious about that kind of stuff as a lot of other guys. Looking back on it now, I never took it as seriously as other comedians for whom really getting their bits perfected was what it was all about. I was throwing lots of things at the wall. Also, it was sort of social, somewhere to go and hang out with people. ... A.D. Miles and Leo Allen and Eugene Mirman and Janeane and the [Upright Citizens Brigade] and people like Jon Benjamin, Todd Barry, so many. It really was like a whole scene.

The UCB, before they were a theater, when it was just a comedy group, they would always come on and do something very, very elaborate and innovative. The sketch would start, and then it would morph into five other things. Someone would be heckling from the audience, and you'd find out the person heckling was a member of the troupe, and the sketch would change into something else, and it would keep building from there. It would always involve breaking the fourth wall in some way. In general, that's what I remember about the performances of everybody. It was always playing with the fourth wall in some way or another.

I remember people like Janeane Garofalo would come on and be really confessional. She would have her notebook right out in front on her stool for everybody to see, and you could see that she was literally just reading little thoughts and scribbles out of her notebook and disclosing, in front of everybody, what was on her mind that week and where she was. It was very interactive.

Janeane Garofalo: I was drawn to it out of necessity. It wasn't like I was getting tons of stage time on main stages in mainstream rooms. It's just hard to do that but especially if you're not a comic who tells structured jokes. I don't really have the discipline. I don't have very many structured jokes per se. I never have, and that's not any moral stance I'm taking or any anything; it just happens to be, for good or for bad, just the way I do stand-up and always has been.

Wednesday nights, Stella at Fez was one of the greatest times — just a fantastic show that I was always very happy to participate in. I participated somewhat at Rebar, Luna Lounge and then definitely much more regularly when they were at Fez.

First, I thought they were gay, which is not a criticism. I remember thinking, "Well, here are these three very comfortable gay guys," and they are not. Again, let me be clear, that is not a criticism. ... I just remember thinking, "These are the three coolest guys in the world and so comfortable with their sexuality." Of course, they are not gay, and even if they were, who cares?

Funny is funny. I don't care what the genre is — if it's a duo, a trio, a single person, if they're doing it with music. Whatever it is, good is good, and mediocre is mediocre. They're very good and also very personable, very likeable and very intelligent.

Zak Orth (actor, Stella performer and frequent State collaborator): I was completely in awe of [Stella]. They were so on top of it, they had such an amazing juju going on, they were really cool and they were really stupid and they were completely in control and they were hysterically funny.

Michael Ian Black: Colin Quinn was there a lot. Louis [C.K.] was there a lot. Todd Barry was there a lot. Stephen Colbert and Paul Dinello did a really memorable thing where they rented bassoons and tried to play "The Devil Went Down to Georgia" on bassoons — possibly even double bassoons, whatever those are.

Zak Orth: That is the hardest I have ever laughed in my entire life. I made a complete ass of myself. I was like, I was just howling, clutching my stomach, crying. It was the most ridiculous, sublime thing I've ever seen.

He knew the patter. He knew all the, "Well, the Devil went down..." He knew all that shit but then when it was time to play the bassoons, they had just rented them fifteen minutes before and neither of them could play it, and they were both just cracking up but still trying to get through it. I have no idea how it went over with the rest of the audience, but for me, I know it was "Showtime at the Apollo." I was standing up in my seat just screaming. Thinking about it now just makes me giggle.

I remember being Bill Clinton [in Stella]. I think my exit line was, "I'm going to go down to Veselka and people-watch." ... I remember there was this sketch where I was a German scientist in a lab coat and I was saying all of this German and Yiddish up on stage. I was the same way then as I am now, which is just a total utility player. If they've got some-

Stephen Colbert and Paul Dinello boast double bassoons at Stella.

thing for me to do, I'm totally game, I'm totally down to do it. They'll just stick me in wherever they've got stuff. They've written stuff for me sometimes, and other times they're like, "Oh, Zak will do this."

Michael Ian Black: There was this comedy duo, a rap duo, called Cracked Out that was, I think Jon Daly and Brett Gelman, that used to just crack me up so hard because it was the most hardcore, sexual, misogynistic, over-the-top rap that was also really good. It was so filthy and so funny that it never ceased to make me laugh.

You'd have drop-ins. Mitch Hedberg was there once or twice. Jon Stewart I think came once.

Joe Lo Truglio: I did a character called Joey Adams at Stella, which was a riff of a Borsht Belt comedian. ... [Showalter came] to me with a clipping from the New York Post, all these really bad jokes like,

Rick Roman or like Shecky Greene. Sho said, "Listen, I have this idea for a character where you would play this guy and he would tell these jokes." It was embracing the kitsch of these terrible jokes in a mid-'90s setting. I think it was a character that Showalter always had an affinity for and was cool enough to be like, "Hey, I have an idea for you." When "Wet Hot" came along, that was his opportunity to really embrace this character that I think he wanted to do since Stella.

Showalter as Alan Shemper in "Wet Hot American Summer" practically steals the climax of the movie.

Joe Lo Truglio: I did another character called Penis Pants, [a] blue-collar male prostitute. "Oh, yeah, whatever you need, Jerry. I'll fist ya'. I'll do it from behind. I'll do it in your butt. I'll do it in a dog's butt. I'm just a regular guy."

Michael Showalter: Jon Benjamin always did extremely experimental stuff. Sam Seder and Jon Glaser, the joke [was] there was almost no joke. There literally was no joke. It was almost like they were trying to get booed off stage or something. They were trying to get the audience upset that they were on stage for so long without making a joke. Everyone was always trying to think of the new, funny way to do humor that was different and conceptual.

A.D. Miles: It was as close as someone just starting out could feel what it must be like to be a rock star or to be a part of a rock star scene.

There was this immediate sort of scene that happened, like somebody threw a match on some gasoline. The second they started, it was standing room only, turning away people at the door. By showing up, they had endorsed whatever was about to happen, knowing that it wasn't going to be a straight kind of show. They would mix in people that were sort of adept at both sides, like Todd Barry, or Janeane Garofalo or Jim Gaffigan. Joan Rivers would show up.

Then, they would allow people like me just come up and do a straight character. I would do on that show this guy named Marty Shonson, and he was this super-awkward person who got very angry when things didn't go well, and they didn't almost from the very beginning. In my memory, there was a standing ovation; I'm sure there probably wasn't.

I'm sure that I'm gilding it a little bit, but the response was so incredible, and I felt for the first time on stage, that I had found a perfect audience for what I was trying to do. It was that first taste of crack cocaine that keeps people coming back for more and ends up dedicating their lives to it after that. The atmosphere there was electric to say the least.

In May 1997, The State came together for a one-off show in Austin, The Big Stinkin' International Improv Festival II.

David Wain: We saw this other sketch group end their sketch with the punch line of a guy about to open up his pants as the lights black out. We figured as the big shots of sketch we need to do better than that, so we did a bit where after an opening dance number, Ken talks to the audience, introducing the show, while the rest of us change into our costumes for the next thing. But we're actually on stage, in full view, and stripping to full nude. It was pretty funny, I thought.

About a year into the Stella shows at Fez, David, Sho and Black started shooting low-budget, almost guerilla-style comedy shorts. It was if the Three Stooges got less violent and more perverted with a touch of Groucho, Chico and Harpo Marx swirled in.

Michael Showalter: My recollection is that those guys didn't want to do the videos at first. I had to drag them basically kicking and screaming to do it. ... What was really cool was how quickly everyone fell into it. "Oh, wow, this is a thing." We knew right away what it was and what the rules of it were and what the game of it was.

The personas really didn't develop until the videos started. ... Then our characters on stage weren't nearly as impish as those guys. On stage we were much more ourselves, and then in the videos we were sort of these forces-of-nature-type characters.

Definitely the subtle differences between the three Stella guys definitely speak to the differences between Mike, David and I in terms of our personas. I think of David's character as definitely sort of the most clownish of the three, kind of the idiot, to an extent.

David Wain: We always wore a suit and tie, and we were thinking, if we do the short, we can dress in a suit and tie, [and] we could say, "Just earlier today, we were on the way here, and this happened," and we were still in a suit and tie. That was the only reason we were wearing the suits in those shorts. We would go out to usually Mike [Showalter's] parents' house in Princeton and shoot for a few hours, something stupid that one of us had written the day before. People really liked them.

Michael Ian Black: They were born on stage, but they reflected what was true off-stage, too, the primary dynamic being David being the stooge a little bit. Sho and I would gang up on him. That's probably the most distinct dynamic.

Michael Showalter: [David's] the put-upon one, but he's also the one who is the sex maniac. All of the really outrageous stuff usually falls on David's character, and then Mike, I think of sort of the leader, to the extent that there is one. He's sort of the alpha male of the three, and then my character is sort of the normal one. In some strange way he's the normal one, but of course, he's not normal at all.

The videos were getting shown on the old-fashioned screen you pull out, and then you get a projector, and you'd project it onto the screen. It's crazy because it wasn't that long ago that we were doing it.

Aside from co-stars like Paul Rudd and Santa Claus, the Stella shorts nearly all had cameos from a giant dildo.

Michael Ian Black: Once you buy the dildo, you have to make it pay for itself.

Michael Showalter: It was all very funny to us. It was all very ridiculous. I can't speak for David and Mike, but I felt like what we were doing with Stella was just very funny and it was just sort of a world that had its own rules. The rule was the stupider the better. We were definitely trying to push it as far as we could into being as outrageous and offensive, as bawdy as possible and sort of as vile as possible, sexual.

David Wain: It just became a thing of, how far can we push it and how much of our unrestrained, infantile impulses can we act out on? I couldn't really begin to break it down but [a] dildo came out a lot over the years. We got replacements and different sizes and kept it in a box and brought it out again.

Paul Rudd: I loved that in the Stella shorts it was just always there. It was a little bit like finding Nina in the Al Hirschfeld drawings. The black dildo is the Nina of Stella shorts, much like Jim Stansel is now the Nina of every single [Wain project].

David Wain: Jim Stansel was, I believe, the manager of KOAX, a radio station that my father invested in, in Dallas, Texas. We had an old Super 8 movie where Jim Stansel is in a hot air balloon as a promotion for opening the new radio station studio. My dad, on the movie, is saying, "That guy! In the balloon! That's Jim Stansel!" We used to watch our home movies over and over again (on Super 8 projector, pre-VCR) and I just got the name "Jim Stansel" stuck in my head. That's the whole deal.

Michael Showalter: [Stella] was a new kind of comedy sketch where you and your friends could take a camera and go shoot a video, and you played yourself or you played some version of yourself and that morphed into the comedy that then happened. I'm not saying we started it, but we were definitely making comedy videos before anyone else was.

David Wain: It's just from our real personalities and our real relationships, the way that Mike and Mike made fun of me on stage and the different ways that we made fun of each other. We're truly hounding on each other's real-life insecurities and proclivities and just heightening them. In the shorts, it just went even further.

Zak Orth: There was no script for those videos that I was allowed to see. They'd just be like, "OK, now you say this," and I would say that, and then they would be like, "All right, now say it this way," and I would do that. So much of those Stella shorts were in the editing because they were shot so slapdash. I think they took shape in how they were cut together, the timing and all that.

Michael Ian Black: I think [the shorts] probably helped define the tone of the evening a little bit for the other performers. The night was filled with a real gamut of styles, and we were always trying to find new voices and new ideas, but I think the fact that we were hosting it in such a nontraditional way with these nontraditional videos opened up for other performers what would be possible and what you could do on stage. Incidentally, they had the same effect on us; it wasn't one-sided. There was crazy shit going on there every week, which was fantastic.

It was a pretty great lineup, and we would take chances with people, and sometimes they would be terrible and never get invited back, and sometimes they'd be great and never be invited back.

While much of the material on stage and even in the shorts was improvised, after doing a weekly Stella show for several years, the trio realized there was a lot of solid material there and that they could hit the road together, leaving behind the variety-show concept.

Michael Showalter: [We] turned Stella into almost like the Blue Man Group or something. [It] was a really full-scripted, hour-long, theatrical show.

David Wain: We went on the road, and those shows got so tight. I wish we'd gone a bit more, but we'd go two, three weeks with shows, and we were running guns a'blazing. Just how you do stand-up, we knew exactly what things got laughs. We were able to cut out everything that was ever soft or improve it, punch it up. We knew every facial expression, every pause, everything — much of which was definitely designed to look like we were just saying it off the top of our heads. In addition to that, every night new stuff just came out of our mouths.

We did little rock clubs all over or sometimes larger theaters, depending on the market. We did a handful of colleges but never too many of those.

Black, David and Sho in Comedy Central's "Stella"

Michael Ian Black: We were all really surprised that we could go anywhere in the country and people knew that brand. People knew Stella from the videos that had gone online, and this was pre-YouTube. There was no easy way to share and promote this stuff, but people knew it. We saw the opportunity to do a television series, and we understood that we had stumbled onto something.

Michael Showalter: That's really what led to the TV show. We [were] our stage personas and our video personas melded together, and I think that is what became "Stella" the TV show. I think the mindset was to try to do the videos as half-hours, potentially. We didn't think much more than that. It was just taking the same kind of premise that we were doing in the web videos and expanding them to a full half-hour.

David Wain: We did a special on Comedy Central where we did our live show, but when we did the actual "Stella" series on Comedy

Central, there was this conscious effort to define the characters more. ... We sort of did that, but we also embraced the fact that these guys almost by design don't have a huge dimension.

Michael Ian Black: We weren't consciously trying to mimic anybody or pay homage to anybody. We were really trying to just make ourselves laugh.

I didn't want to stay in those same dildo-infested waters. I wanted to try to tell larger stories. What "Stella" became on television was exactly what we pitched to them. The three of us thought it was all really funny and innovative and exactly in line with what we'd been doing. We all thought, "Well, this is gonna be a big hit," and we could not have been more wrong.

"Stella" ran for one ten-episode season on Comedy Central during the summer of 2005.

Michael Ian Black: That kind of just really surreal, absurd, way out-of-the-box tone, it's just not for everybody or even for most people or even for a large minority. It's for a very small number of people of whom I happen to be a part. The most common complaint about it is that it's dumb or that it doesn't make sense, and they're right, it is dumb, and it doesn't make sense, and, to us, that's what made it so funny. We were being as smart about our own stupidity as we possibly could be, but I think a lot of viewers just looked at it as stupid and nothing else.

Stella gets resurrected, when the boys have time. The variety show gets revived every couple of years at San Francisco Sketchfest.

David Wain: Whenever somebody forces us to do a show — we're both busy and lazy — we tend to do no preparation, and then everything we do is either truly winging it or just naturally slipping into old bits that come to mind as we go. ... We all have a fondness for repeating certain things over and over again anyway.

Michael Ian Black: We enjoy performing together. We're good at it, and we continue to talk about doing more Stella projects, but it's like with "Wet Hot," nobody wants it because it bombed. So there's no real opportunity to do anything more with it, at least in television. We talk about touring, but I don't know that the audience is still there for it. It's been so long since it was on television. I just don't know that anybody would care.

Stella's most recent show in 2014 saw special guest comedians, Todd Glass and Andy Kindler, abandon their traditional stand-up and go wild on stage.

Michael Ian Black: I hope that that's sort of what that brand allows people to do in that setting is really let go of their normal material and try new things, and if they fall on their face, that's fine. That's part of it. Certainly we have fallen on our faces many, many, many times doing Stella, but it opens the door to something spectacular happening, and generally the audience is so supportive and enthusiastic and excited to be there that they can be very forgiving. It's generally a very warm night.

Author's note: In 2003, I got a taste of the Stella personas when I interviewed the trio over the phone to preview a performance on November 8, at University of Missouri Columbia. Michael Showalter's "brother," Wedge, made his first and only appearance with the group.

David Wain: When we were doing interviews with Stella, the tone of the interview was somehow set within the first two seconds every time. Sometimes we would just answer questions normally or, more often than that, we would just not answer any questions or, depending on the situation, we just might relentlessly make fun of the person for no reason and not even let them get one question out. I sometimes got uncomfortable with that.

Nothing from my interview with Stella was used in the article. The transcript follows:

David Wain: Hi. Michael Showalter's older brother, Wedge, is here, Michael Black and myself, David Wain.

Michael Ian Black: Hi.

Wedge Showalter: Hey.

Corey Stulce: How's it going, Wedge?

Wedge Showalter: Pretty good.

Corey Stulce: You guys did a little touring this year with the Stella show. How do you think it went?

Michael Ian Black: It's been great so far. Wedge, what did you think?

Wedge Showalter: It was a blast. It was a nonstop party.

Corey Stulce: Did you go on the road with them, Wedge?

Wedge Showalter: I'm there, like, all-purpose crew guy.

Corey Stulce: Kind of like a roadie?

Wedge Showalter: Yeah.

Michael Ian Black: Not like a roadie; definitely not like a roadie.

Wedge Showalter: I'm their toilet to, like, take craps on.

Michael Ian Black: Wedge, come on. He's got a little bit of an attitude about it.

Wedge Showalter: I'm like a human toilet bowl for these divas to take doo-doos on.

Michael Ian Black: Hey, come on, man. We did it for Showalter because Wedge hasn't been doing so well. Wedge worked at the DMV until last month. He lost that job; he needed something to do. So we took him on the road.

Wedge Showalter: I have a Ph.D. in mathematics from Yale.

Michael Ian Black: He's brilliant; there's no way of getting around it.

Wedge Showalter: I invented an equation.

David Wain: He always gets fired from his job, but we can't tell you why.

Corey Stulce: It sounds like a "Good Will Hunting" kind of thing.

Michael Ian Black: A lot like that actually.

David Wain: More like "A Beautiful Mind" kind of thing.

Corey Stulce: Good deal.

Michael Ian Black: Quite the paranoia.

Corey Stulce: I've had the opportunity to see some of the shorts available on the web site. Can you explain a little bit about how the live show runs?

David Wain: The live show is different from the shorts. It's just the three of us onstage just fucking doing it.

Michael Ian Black: Or talking and singing and laughing and loving. There's some hand jobs. There's some wax jobs.

Wedge Showalter: Is that OK with you?

Corey Stulce: That's fine. You guys have been working together for quite a few years. Can you explain how you collaborate on the writing process?

(silence)

Michael Ian Black: Uh, I don't know, just write the shit. I've got a typewriter.

David Wain: It's like, how about if I come in and say like, "Mike, what the hell's your problem?' And he's like…"

Michael Ian Black: And I might be like, "That's some of the best shit. Maybe this should be in Stella." We type it up on my Underwood.

David Wain: We show it to Showalter, and he changes the words around, and you've got yourself some comedy.

Corey Stulce: Is Stella named after someone's grandma or something?

David Wain: It's gonna be weird. We named it after your mother.

Corey Stulce: Her name is Karen.

Michael Ian Black: No, it's not.

David Wain: Not in her glory days, before you were born.

Michael Ian Black: We knew one day our paths might cross, and we knew this might get awkward, but she spent some time in Bangkok before you were born, and her name was Stella at that time.

Wedge Showalter: Hey, hey Don!

Michael Ian Black: His name is Corey.

Wedge Showalter: Yeah, I'm not wearing any pants.

Michael Ian Black: Wedge.

David Wain: Wedge, come on.

Wedge Showalter: Hey, hey Dan.

Michael Ian Black: His name is Corey.

Corey Stulce: Yes, Wedge.

Wedge Showalter: I'm only in my underwear.

Corey Stulce: That's very special.

Michael Ian Black: Wedge is in his underwear. They're like boxer briefs.

David Wain: I wish you could see what's going on in this room. Too bad you don't have a staff photographer.

Corey Stulce: One of the other things I thought was interesting about the short films was the music you guys used. For example, the "Saturday" short film with music by Chicago. Do you guys have to get the rights to use the music for those?

Michael Ian Black: Is this a legal question?

David Wain: No comment.

Michael Ian Black: You'd have to talk to our barrister.

Wedge Showalter: Are you related to the Peter Cetera?

Corey Stulce: No relation to Chicago.

David Wain: I notice that you're from Illinois.

Corey Stulce: Very perceptive. We'll just skip past that question. How do you guys travel when you're on the road?

Michael Ian Black: Jet.

Corey Stulce: You don't take a bus or anything like that?

Michael Ian Black: Jet. We've got a Gulf Stream 4 that Motley Crue toured in, and we lease it from Vince Neil.

David Wain: I live in the jet year-round.

Corey Stulce: So it's pretty functional.

Michael Ian Black: Pretty functional, unless you've got to take a dump, because Gulf Streams don't have bathrooms.

David Wain: I find it tough when I just need to go up to Midtown, driving up the street.

Wedge Showalter: Hey, Jeff, Jeff!

Michael Ian Black: His name is Corey.

Wedge Showalter: Are you in the mile high club?

Corey Stulce: No, I'm not.

Michael Ian Black: Wedge, shut up.

Wedge Showalter: Why, are you too prude?

Michael Ian Black: Shut up!

Corey Stulce: I'm not crazy about flying. So I usually try to sleep.

Michael Ian Black: You don't have to answer him, Corey.

David Wain: Don't even listen to Wedge.

Wedge Showalter: You have no dick?

Michael Ian Black: Wedge, we're trying to do an interview. Can you go in the other room?

David Wain: I really wish Michael could have been here.

Michael Ian Black: Yeah, where's your brother?

Wedge Showalter: He's out.

Corey Stulce: You guys have some pictures on the website. I notice in the pictures from the early days, you look happy, smiling. The pictures from the 2003 tour, you look very solemn. Is there a reason for that?

David Wain: Because when you're older, you're that much closer to death.

Corey Stulce: You guys are still relatively young, though.

Michael Ian Black: Not me.

Corey Stulce: Can I ask how old you are, Michael?

Michael Ian Black: Yeah.

Corey Stulce: Can you answer?

Michael Ian Black: I didn't say I was gonna answer you, just that you could ask.

Corey Stulce: You guys are coming to Missouri this year. Earlier this year we had another threesome that came to town: REO Speedwagon, Styx and Journey. How would say that compares?

Michael Ian Black: REO Speedwagon is the three-man group?

Corey Stulce: No, no, no, three different bands.

Michael Ian Black: Oh, who did you have?

Corey Stulce: REO Speedwagon, Styx and Journey.

Michael Ian Black: That's a sweet line up, dude.

Corey Stulce: Can you relate each member of Stella to one of the groups?

Michael Ian Black: There's only one member of any of those groups that I can name: Steve Perry.

Corey Stulce: Steve Perry is no longer with Journey.

David Wain: They have new singer who sounds just like Steve Perry, right?

Michael Ian Black: What's his name?

Corey Stulce: His name is also Steve.

Michael Ian Black: Steve Perry?

David Wain: What about Kevin from REO Speedwagon?

Michael Ian Black: I don't know who he is.

Wedge Showalter: I like that one from Styx!

Michael Ian Black: Shut up!

Wedge Showalter: In the dick area. I have a big dick in my pants.

David Wain: No, it's a potato.

Wedge Showalter: SHUT THE FUCK UP!

David Wain: It looks like a toothpick, FYI. I touched it.

Wedge Showalter: No, it looks like a hockey stick.

Corey Stulce: Michael, are you still with us?

Michael Ian Black: I'm here, yeah.

Corey Stulce: Now, David Wain and Showalter have their own websites. Why don't you have one?

Michael Ian Black: I had one, but it got overloaded, the server. I don't know. Do you want to build me one?

Corey Stulce: I could give it a shot.

David Wain: Would it be like, Michael Ian Black dot com or something?

Michael Ian Black: That's very funny. I prefer to be more enigmatic than that. I don't like to make myself available to the public.

Wedge Showalter: But he's on Friendster.

Michael Ian Black: Yeah, I'm on Friendster.

Corey Stulce: How many connections do you have on there?

Michael Ian Black: Twelve.

Wedge Showalter: The entire starting defense of the St. Louis Cardinals.

David Wain: You mean your last date?

Wedge Showalter: It's the entire starting defense of the St. Louis Rams.

Corey Stulce: Those are his Friendster friends?

Wedge Showalter: That's eleven of them, and the twelfth one is the punter.

Corey Stulce: Do you guys mind if we talk about "Wet Hot American Summer" for a minute? Michael, I thought your sex scene was very convincing. Do you consider yourself a method actor? How did you prepare for the scene?

Michael Ian Black: What is there to prepare for? I just fucked that dude.

Corey Stulce: Just kind of a let-the-cameras-roll kind of thing?

David Wain: It was simulated when we shot it, but the preparation was that they fucked all week.

Michael Ian Black: I fucked the fucking dude from "Alias" (Bradley Cooper).

Corey Stulce: Who got to keep the talking can?

David Wain: Oh, Rog Benson. That's a good question.

Corey Stulce: Was that Wedge?

Michael Ian Black: That was David. Wedge is taking a dump.

Corey Stulce: The movie has become a cult hit. How does a movie become a cult hit?

David Wain: It becomes a cult hit by failing when it first gets released.

Corey Stulce: So, you were hoping to reach a larger audience.

David Wain: I was very excited that nobody went to see it when it came out, and when the grosses came in and we lost all the money on the movie, we celebrated for months.

Michael Ian Black: We're still celebrating.

Michael Showalter: I celebrated so much that I had to stop drinking alcohol.

Michael Ian Black: Michael Showalter just walked in the room. Hi, Mike.

David Wain: Hi, Mike.

Michael Showalter: Oh, hey.

Michael Ian Black: Can you tell your brother to calm down? He's been screaming during the interview.

David Wain: Mike and Wedge are always arguing, but, yes, we're very happy that it's a cult classic.

Corey Stulce: Do you guys still get recognized for The State?

David Wain: Yes.

Corey Stulce: I read there were plans for a DVD release. Have you heard any more about that?

Michael Ian Black: Never gonna happen.

David Wain: It's coming out in the spring quarter of 2015.

Michael Ian Black: What's the real deal?

David Wain: The real deal is they are actively trying to do it, but there are arguments back and forth every day in the bureaucracy between the distributor and MTV.

Corey Stulce: As far as the members being involved, would everyone participate in it?

David Wain: Absolutely. We're waiting for them to let us. We don't own that.

Corey Stulce: If they gave you carte blanche as to what would be on the DVDs, what would you like?

Michael Ian Black: The Kids in the Hall stuff is really funny. I'd put that on there. Some of the Python shit's great. Early "SNL" I'd put on there. Some of that "Mary Hartman, Mary Hartman" stuff is really groundbreaking, I thought.

Corey Stulce: That might be a problem.

Michael Ian Black: Put "Sports Night" on there.

Corey Stulce: Did you say "Sports Center" or "Sports Night?"

Michael Ian Black: "Sports Night."

David Wain: If I had my choice, I'd put the whole thing on there, as it was.

Corey Stulce: Would you like to do commentary or some stuff people haven't seen yet?

David Wain: There's a lot of stuff people haven't seen and a lot of unaired sketches. We could do commentary. There's tons of material in and around the show that people have never seen.

Corey Stulce: You guys filmed a Stella special for Comedy Central. This will give people a taste as to what a live Stella show is like?

Wedge Showalter: You want to know what it tastes like?

Corey Stulce: What?

Wedge Showalter: It starts with the letter P.

Sho, Black and David

Corey Stulce: OK.

David Wain: Probably pomegranate.

Corey Stulce: Should I guess?

Wedge Showalter: Just leave it at that.

Michael Ian Black: Maybe a pickle.

Wedge Showalter: First letter is P, and the last letter is Y. Just leave it at that.

Corey Stulce: I was talking to Tom Lennon a couple months ago about "Reno 911!" and he said he actually had a copy of The State album that was never released, but it got lost. Do you guys have one?

Michael Ian Black: I don't have one.

Michael Showalter: David has one.

David Wain: I think I do, but I'm not sure where it is.

Corey Stulce: Would you like to see bootlegs out there, or have you heard of any chance of Warner Brothers releasing it?

David Wain: They're very excited about it. They just haven't quite gotten a release date yet. They're very, very excited about it. It's just six years late.

Corey Stulce: That was recorded back in the mid-'90s?

David Wain: '97, '96 maybe?

Corey Stulce: You guys had a "State by State" book that is not in print anymore. Have there been talks about putting the story of The State out in book form?

Michael Ian Black: I don't see that being a bestseller.

David Wain: What do you think, Corey?

Corey: I would have some interest.

Wedge Showalter: Why don't you write it?

Michael Ian Black: Wedge, shut up. Were you journalism major?

Corey Stulce: I was.

Michael Ian Black: What happened? You fail?

Corey Stulce: No, I graduated.

Michael Ian Black: Oh, you work for a newspaper newspaper. I thought we were talking to a college newspaper.

Corey Stulce: No.

Michael Ian Black: What newspaper is this?

Corey Stulce: This is *The Telegraph*, in Alton, Illinois.

Michael Ian Black: Oh, this is the big one.

Corey Stulce: Yeah, so a lot of the language will probably have to be cut.

Michael Ian Black: You can't print English?

Corey Stulce: Sometimes. I'm a little lost right now. Sorry.

Michael Ian Black: Don't be, you're in Illinois.

Corey Stulce: It's just a little hard to hear.

Michael Ian Black: I'll talk closer to the microphone. Is this better?

Corey Stulce: Perfect. OK, let me gather my thoughts for a second.

(pause)

David Wain: We really threw you for a loop there, didn't we?

Corey Stulce: A bit.

Michael Ian Black: Thank god Woodward and Bernstein didn't have this problem.

Corey Stulce: (laughs) Yeah.

David Wain: I'll never crack Watergate.

Michael Ian Black: He understood that when I said Woodward and Bernstein.

Corey Stulce: I tend to stick to the entertainment side of things.

David Wain: You hear of Rona Barrett?

Corey Stulce: I'm sorry?

Michael Ian Black: Rona Barrett, he asked.

David Wain: The greatest entertainment journalist who ever lived.

Corey Stulce: That might give me something to aspire to.

Michael Ian Black: Yeah, she had a nice rack, too.

Corey Stulce: OK, so you guys are coming to the University of Missouri.

David Wain: We're very excited to come out there. We're gonna be in the Jesse Auditorium.

Michael Ian Black: Our first trip to the U of M.

Corey Stulce: How did this show come together?

Michael Ian Black: We're doing knock-off dates, because we're all kind of busy during the week. So on Saturdays sometimes we go out and do shows.

David Wain: We were sitting around thinking, where should we do a show? The University of Missouri-Columbia.

Corey Stulce: Very cool. They have some cool shows there sometimes.

Michael Ian Black: No shit.

David Wain: Are you gonna be there?

Corey Stulce: I would like to, yeah.

Michael Ian Black: What, are you angling for a free ticket?

David Wain: We don't have any tickets, OK, dude?

Michael Ian Black: There are a lot of people in Missouri, and everybody keeps calling. "Can you get us in?" Dude, we can't service everybody. After the show we might be able to service you, if you know what I'm talking about.

Corey Stulce: I'm willing to do pretty much what it takes to get in.

Michael Ian Black: Say no more.

Corey Stulce: I'm not making Rona Barrett kind of money.

Michael Ian Black: You could be by the end of the night. Play your cards right, kid.

Corey Stulce: I think I have enough material here to...

David Wain: Get yourself fired?

Corey Stulce: I know you guys are busy, so I'll let you go.

David Wain: If you have any other actual questions, drop me an email.

Corey Stulce: David, Michael and Michael, thank you.

Michael Ian Black, Michael Showalter, Wedge Showalter and David Wain: Bye, Corey.

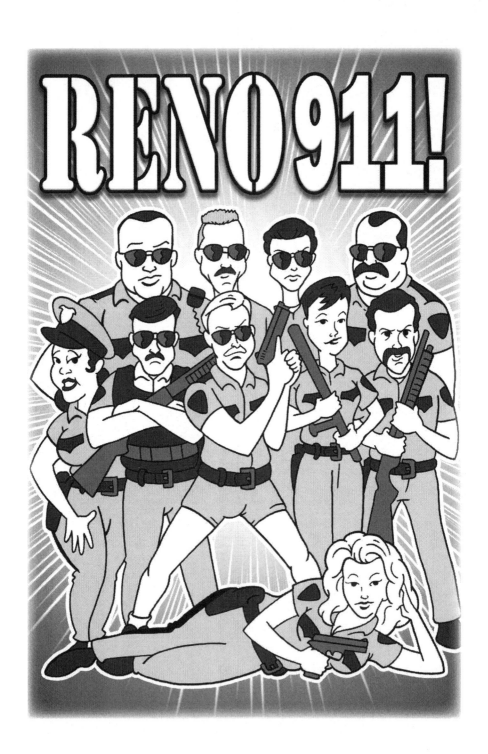

CHAPTER 25

"Reno 911!"

"The State never came together from waiting for permission or asking (for) someone's help. It came from us saying, 'Fuck it; let's go do this."

Thomas Lennon

After "Viva Variety" wrapped on Comedy Central, Michael Black, Tom, Kerri and Ben developed a sitcom pilot called "Hey Neighbor" for Fox that was ahead of its time yet still felt very '90s. In it, they played multiple characters in a wacky neighborhood.

Robert Ben Garant: It's so weird because now there are twenty shows like that where one or two guys play everybody, but at the time it was really foreign. ... Everybody said, "Wow, this is great. There is no way we'll ever put this on Fox."

The pilot didn't get picked up, but there were still opportunities at the fledgling network. Michael Ian Black got married to Martha Hagen, whom he actually met at MTV during The State's run. Because he was already over L.A., Black moved his family to New York and soon after landed the role of Phil Stubbs on "Ed" at NBC.

Meanwhile Ben, Kerri and Tom agreed to create — yup — another sketch comedy show.

Robert Ben Garant: We wrote tons and tons of sketches. They were really, really great.

Thomas Lennon: Beth McCarthy-Miller was directing it. Beth is one of the biggest directors in TV. We wrote really funny stuff. Ben had this brilliant sketch of clerks at a record store who were checking out people's albums. They would look at the records and go, "Ugh. Ew," and it turned into a musical number of these hipster record store clerks just going "Ugh. Ew. Eh." It was just this really cool, almost Blue Man Group-level sketch that was straight-up genius.

Robert Ben Garant: We cast the "Reno" cast to be in it, and that was everybody in "Reno" except for Wendy [McLendon-Covey]. [Before her] was this girl named Amy Brassette, [a] really, really funny girl from

Louisiana. [In his audition], Carlos did an impression of Woody Allen.

Carlos Alazraqui (Deputy James Garcia): [I also] played a guy selling this thing called the Shammy, and it was quite like a napkin, and he went on about it, "It looks like a napkin, but that's where you're wrong!" And I ended with Tony Montana at a children's birthday party, which I came up with on [sketch-comedy show] "Make Me Laugh."... Having a Woody Allen, Jewish character in the middle, a Latino character and a British character is like, "Oh, OK, this guy's got some range." I guess it worked.

Cedric Yarbrough (Deputy S. Jones): I'd only been out to Los Angeles a couple of months before I ran into these weird, white people that had the same kind of sensibility and strange personality and weird sense of humor that I did — and they got my stuff right away.

Robert Ben Garant: The auditions were, "Bring in two characters and maybe an impression if you have one." We didn't audition for actors; we auditioned for sketch comedians. Niecy [Nash] came in with, I believe, a slave girl.

Thomas Lennon: We wrote a sketch for her where it's "Antiques Roadshow" and somebody has brought in a slave. It was an amazing sketch.

Robert Ben Garant: Cedric Yarbrough put a Reese's Peanut Butter Cup on his head.

Cedric Yarbrough: One of the impressions [I did at the audition] was Aaron Neville. I would put a Baby Gap vest on — Aaron Neville wears very tight clothes — I would grab some peanut butter and a Reese's peanut butter cup. I put the peanut butter, crunchy, preferably, on this peanut butter cup and put it on my head and then proceeded to be Aaron Neville. It was a compilation of "Aaron Neville sings your favorite hits. Once Aaron Neville sings a song, it is irreplaceably his," that kind of thing. I would do the voiceover work as well as Aaron Neville. They were like, "Yeah, he's an idiot; he's like us."

I remember it being a lot of really funny sketches. They were risky. I remember the title, "Ugly Americans."

Thomas Lennon: I feel that we were almost at the very top of our sketch-writing game.

Kerri Kenney-Silver: They bought all the scripts and approved them. Sets were being built, and wardrobe's being built, and you're ready to go. ... It was really funny when we were at the table read, and when you're at the table read, you're days away from shooting. ... At the table read, we realized there was no enthusiasm. Tom said, "We're getting the feeling you guys aren't as into this as you were."

Robert Ben Garant: After the table read, the head of Fox said to us, "Look, I don't think we can do a sketch show right now. You guys are just way too old. There's no hook."

Thomas Lennon: I was twenty-eight years old and told that we're probably too old to do a sketch show on Fox, which really blew my mind.

Robert Ben Garant: He basically told us there's really no reason to film this thing because it's never going to be on the air. If I remember correctly, our budget was seven hundred thousand dollars, and we already spent half of it because we built sets; we had a sound stage; we hired Beth McCarthy.

John Landgraf, who at the time was at Jersey Films and now he's the head of FX, was our producer, and we said to him, "Does it make any sense to do something totally different, to make up a brand-new show and turn it in because at least it would have a shot? We know that this sketch show has no shot." John Landgraf talked Fox into it. We had no idea what we were gonna do, but we knew we had to have it turned in a month from conception, to script to everything.

Thomas Lennon: The State never came together from waiting for permission or asking [for] someone's help. It came from us saying, "Fuck it; let's go do this," which we'd always done. The original show was supposed to be a Saturday night sketch show on Fox so I had an instantaneous idea, "What if we did a funny version of 'Cops' that would come on after 'Cops?'"

Kerri Kenney-Silver: Tom and Ben called me and said, "We have this crazy idea. We don't have any money left because it's all been spent on creating the sketch show, but what if we just rented a bunch of cop costumes? We don't have time to write a show. We've never done improv, and the improv we did in college we were terrible at. What if we just wing it with this last four dollars and we do a spoof of 'Cops'? It's on their network."

Robert Ben Garant: We carded up twenty scenarios that we thought would be interesting, "Cops" parody stuff. We played everybody. We played the perps.

Cedric Yarbrough: It was Tom and Ben and Kerri saying, "Everybody, we're gonna do this now. Let's switch gears. Come up with ideas and come up with your characters." And away we go. It was a little bit scary. ... I have to give credit to Tom, Ben and Kerri. They seemed to know what they were doing; so no one really panicked. Everyone was like, "Yep, let's go." I feel like that kind of attitude was definitely what carried through the whole show.

[In the pilot], Kerri's [character] was different ... this odd thing with a puppet. We didn't have the brilliant Wendy McLendon-Covey yet, but the overall relationships — Dangle hitting on me, Wiegel hitting on Dangle, the Garcia and Jones relationship — we found that right away. Jones/Garcia, being cops first, that part of it was "make sure we look the part"; we honor the part. Then you'll find out that they're just not all there. Wiegel can do whatever the fuck she's doing because at least we have this part of it that kind of resembles what a cop show would look like. Dangle having short shorts. That is pretty ridiculous. It could be very sketchy and very ridiculous, but as long as we have this thing here that kind of seems real, it can live.

Robert Ben Garant: We shot it, and by the time it was done editing, most of the crazy cockamamie stuff [with perps] had been cut out, and we focused on the cops. If you look at that pilot, it's exactly "Reno 911!" The theory of "Let's do a 'Cops' parody" we had in advance, but all of the characters and the tone and style really happened in four days of shooting it in Carson [City, Nevada].

Thomas Lennon: The weird thing was it was very close to getting on the schedule at Fox or so I'm told from internal meetings that we heard about. Most of the younger staffers had put it on the dream fall lineup. We made all of the young people's boards, but none of the higher up executives', older people's boards, and we were definitely told the show was too gay for Fox.

Robert Ben Garant: There was a scene where Tom and I kiss, where Dangle pulls over a personal trainer, and they flirt for a long time in this weird, sort of agro-way, and then they kiss and make out. Fox told us there's no version of the kiss that's gonna make it onto the air. They were not gonna show that. We cut it down. Originally, it was forty seconds of kissing; so we cut it down to seven seconds of kissing, and they said, "No, we're not gonna do that." We just refused. We left it in and thought, "Did we really want to do this show? Dangle's a gay character. That's not even a bold joke."

Ben, Kerri and Tom got a call from their management to see if they could keep their schedules open to do advance publicity for the upcoming Fox season. So they thought "Reno 911!" was a go, but Fox passed, which was probably for the best because a watered-down "Reno 911!" wouldn't have lasted for six seasons nor would it have been the show the trio wanted to make.

Fast-forward three years. Ben and Tom had drinks with Jim Sharp, who was back at Comedy Central after "The Magic Hour" with Magic Johnson was canceled. He was looking for new shows, and the guys sent him the "Reno 911!" pilot. Typically, networks do not sell their pilots to other networks because it would be embarrassing for someone else to get a hit from a turned-down show, but the team was able to re-create and re-tape the pilot to sell it to Comedy Central.

Thomas Lennon: We basically turned in the same homework twice.

Robert Ben Garant: Intentionally, in the pilot, Junior does not talk, not a single line. He didn't talk much the first few episodes. Doing the press of the show, I wanted him to be like Elwood Blues, and I thought that would work. It worked for the pilot, that he just stands there and you have no idea what he's thinking, but he gives a look to the camera every once in a while. I wanted him to be that guy. We started doing the press before we really started shooting the show, and I realized this doesn't make any sense. It felt really like a cop-out to have to explain to reporters, "Junior doesn't talk." So I just started talking during the press stuff, and then I found the voice. It's not really that much of a stretch — he's me basically. I think every character is a slightly bizarro version of themselves. I think that's why the improv happened so quickly. I don't think anybody's doing anything crazy out of character. Tom is sort of Dangle, and I'm very much like Junior. If you were to be making fun of yourself at a party, that was our "Reno 911!" characters, basically. Junior is me making fun of me, and I think that's probably true of everybody.

So Kerri is a horrible racist in real life?

Robert Ben Garant: I didn't say that.

Thomas Lennon: Everyone took on the archetype that they felt they should be playing. I played just the gayer version of myself, and Niecy is playing a more ghetto version of herself. Everyone's playing an unchecked version of their id. I happen to be straight, but that's really the only difference. There's a lot of unbelievably persnickety things about me. I know a ton about musicals. I look good with a mustache.

Everyone really stepped in very, very quickly, and this was certainly the most fun thing we ever created because beginning to end. With almost no plan whatsoever, we created an entire world in a couple of days or a week.

Niecy Nash (Deputy Raineesha Williams): [My character] is a culmination of all the women that helped raise me up and every woman I've ever met at the DMV. ... I'm just proud of her — period, her baby head, big booty, all of it.

The improv dabbling The State attempted years earlier was not good, as has been said by all members, but without much thought, Ben, Kerri and Tom created one of the most seminal improvised shows of all time. Most of what's said in "Reno" was not written in traditional, scripted form. Sure, there were setups, but the cast, including the many guest stars, were given the freedom to take the scene wherever they wanted to go.

Thomas Lennon: We knew a ton about television, more than anyone our age could possibly know because we'd done so many shows and so many failures by that point. ... While we didn't know how to improvise, we certainly knew good shows succeed when they have a couple things: one, characters that you can relate to and you love [and], two, characters that are archetypes so that people can look at them and say, "Oh, that's me. That's my friend." The other biggest one is unrequited love relationships, and even if you simply had two of those, you can make something that will work for a long time.

Kerri Kenney-Silver: We suddenly realized, "Hey, we can do improv, and we're pretty good at it." Now, we all use improv.

The first thing that comes to mind is not something that came out of my mouth but something that went into my mouth. We were doing an improv where Tom put invitations to his murder mystery dinner party into all of our lockers. When I opened mine, my instinct as Trudy was to start eating it.

When talking about this book, many people didn't

immediately recognize "The State," but mention "Reno 911!" and every single person grew a smile.

Mary Birdsong (Geisha/Deputy Cherisha Kimball): People come up to me that are fans of "Reno," like fourteen-year-old boys that have never left their videogame console and an architect who went to Harvard, who is a total snob and drinks sherry, and he loves "Reno 911!" I've always loved that [it] has this highbrow/lowbrow appeal.

Thomas Lennon: The two people who love the show more than anyone in the world are chronic marijuana users and law enforcement. Those are our two best demographics.

The Lt. Dangle Halloween costume continues to be a hot item years after "Reno" went off the air. In fact, Tom will post a photo on social media of posing with someone dressed as Dangle from time to time. Those short shorts just might end up in the Smithsonian someday.

Thomas Lennon: My character, Jim Dangle, sees himself exactly like Steve McQueen in "Bullitt," except that he wears hot pants. I wanted to play a gay character but not an effete gay character. I wanted to play a character who's both openly gay and out but whose gayness isn't just a punch line, and come in and say, "I just picked out window treatments." I didn't want to be that guy. In his head, he's a total tough guy, whether it comes off like that or not.

Cedric Yarbrough: Jones' relationship with Dangle was complicated. Jones wanted to keep his job, and Dangle wanted some black dick — that was the relationship. There's an episode where Jones helps Dangle move, and it's revealed that Dangle hasn't called anyone else from the office to help. Then it's revealed that Dangle only lives one trailer away from his first trailer. Tom goes, "What's gonna happen is you're gonna end up fucking Dangle, and we won't see it, but that's what's gonna happen." I'm like, "All right, let's go. OK, my mother's gonna really enjoy this episode."

I had a great relationship with every character, whether it's

Clemmie and our sometimes on and off thing, or the on and off things that Raineesha Williams and Jones would do. You know, maybe one drunken night Wiegel and Jones might've made out, and it was just too weird for Jones. He just didn't continue. It was just such a fun thing to do exploring the ridiculousness of the cop life but also the relationships in between everyone else on the force.

Carlos Alazraqui: I really wanted to play a dick, and I really wanted to play a Barney Fife type ... with some other racist character, Bufford Pusser from "Walking Tall." When we got on set, one of the first things they did was ask twenty questions and that really shaped the character.

[They] put Cedric and me in a car, and they turned the camera on, and Usher is playing on the radio, and he turns it up, and I was like, "We're going to have to listen to this jungle music?" and then it was on. This guy was born. He was a racist, and he was gonna abuse this black cop. So everything happened organically. I didn't know where Garcia was going. I just thought, he's a law-and-order guy, not too frivolous, and he likes his Chevy Aveos, likes to keep it simple. And everything else followed, and we all kind of fell into our characters rather quickly.

Robert Ben Garant: Carlos is not like Garcia at all. Carlos is a California liberal Latino. He's so not this right-wing Republican, racist guy that Garcia is. When he started doing this character, he's basically making fun of cops, making fun of the show "Cops," but it created such a great, weird dynamic. Carlos and Cedric really liked each other right off the bat. They were really both super-excited. They knew it was a great opportunity. They became drinking buddies immediately and really hit it off. It's these two characters that hate each other theoretically, but the actors really love each other. It made this really neat chemistry. Carlos and Dangle, his character hated Dangle, but Dangle is his boss. So it created these cool, neat inter-relationships that really worked. It was really very much by accident. It was by chance that all that stuff came together.

There were a lot of bumps in getting to know each other with Niecy at first, just because Niecy was so into doing her thing, which is such a specific thing. She likes being right up at the camera and talking. We had real bumps with that because we wanted it to be much more action, and we talked it out with her, and it ended up being great.

[Her character] TeTe, she pitched us, and we had no idea what she was talking about, but we just let her do it. She pitched it to us so many times we're just like, "All right, let's roll on it." It's easier to shoot it than to talk about it. So, yep, she wanted the boobs that had to hang down and flop around and the weird hair, and we shot like five of them. Same with Wendy and the water heater lady, she just pitched us that. She's like, "What if I'm walking down the street in my underwear with a water heater," and we're like, "OK, you obviously understand what that means. Rather than try to explain it, let's just shoot it."

Kerri Kenney-Silver went from wearing fabulous, one-of-a-kind couture frocks on "Viva Variety" to donning a frumpy, unflattering police uniform on "Reno."

Thomas Lennon: It's hard to get a pretty girl to play not pretty as well as Kerri does. She plays Woman with Horrible Scoliosis really well.

Kerri Kenney-Silver: Somebody said to me, "I love your character because she's so misunderstood, and she means well, but it all comes out wrong." I hadn't thought of it before, but my reaction was, "No, I don't think she does mean well. I think she's kind of dumb, and I don't think she means well." I don't know where she came from. I love her so much. Certainly that sort of mousy character is in my wheelhouse. That's the kind of character that I've had success with on network television, which is a sort of mousy, Midwestern kind of woman.

I drew on that in a panic when we had to improvise something all of a sudden. It seems like a funny person to put in a position of power and protection for others. I have lots of references for that kind of woman in my world. I love fish-out-of-water characters. I think we all have [those] in our family who speak before they think, that have sort of a combination of old-fashioned view of the world and inappropriate outspokenness. I love those uncomfortable moments of somebody just saying something that they think everyone's going to agree with, and the whole room stops and looks over like, "What in the hell are you talking about?"

Ben, Tom and Kerri's director cohort from "The State" had been jet-setting the globe shooting big-budget commercials, and while the money was swell for his pocketbook, the work was taking its toll on his soul.

Michael Patrick Jann: I came up with the Pets-dot-com sock puppet thing. I cast Mike Black in it. The very first version of that, I think, was good and funny and interesting. The advertising agency decided, "We thought of that," and took it away and turned it into something else.

The character wasn't the sock puppet. The character was the guy holding the sock puppet who was a dude who lived in his basement. If you watch the first one, it's very clear that he's stoned. People who interact with him aren't looking at the puppet; they are looking at the guy holding the puppet. It is a very clear difference. ... That's why when he walks to the door, he knocks literally with his fist, even though his got puppet on it because it's not a puppet. That's why it's funny.

When they took it away, there was controversy with it being too much like Triumph [the Insult Comic Dog]. It became like that, but it wasn't like that originally. The first version of the commercial was super-successful, however they gauge those things. Right before we were shooting it, the creative director of the agency says, "I don't like the character. What if it's not a sock puppet; what about a talking pencil?" I'm not even joking. This super-hipster dude from San Francisco is saying this to me. This is my life. "Why am I doing this?"

Ben, Tom and Mike Jann had drinks at The Red Lion, a little German bar in Los Angeles, and Mike was offered the directing gig on "Reno."

Thomas Lennon: He stepped in very easily. Mike is a really good laugher. When Mike Jann laughs, he laughs really hard and with his entire body, and that's one of the nice things about being directed by Mike. Ben and I probably have the closest sensibility to Mike in the group and probably always have, but the three of us crack each other up a great deal.

Michael Patrick Jann: It really opened up my creative mind again in a lot of ways. One, it's so great to work with people who are super-talented. I'm capable of working with these people and making them better and them making me better, and having that kind of exchange, which was like being in The State.

Cedric said "Reno" gave Ben, Kerri and Tom an opportunity to explore more diverse humor because they were no longer just writing for "what Ben would say, 'honkies.'" Aside from a racially diverse cast, they now had a wider variety of female characters — played by real women — to showcase.

Cedric Yarbrough: Their core group of audience members were and are white kids, white folks. In the '90s, I didn't really watch "The State." I was watching "In Living Color." I was aware of "The State," but I didn't really know about it because there was no one on that show that looked like me or felt like me. So I didn't watch the show. "Viva Variety" I didn't really watch a whole lot. I knew it was funny, but I was still watching other things that I thought looked a little bit more like myself or at least were, I felt, more like-minded.

["Reno"] just upped everyone else's game. Now, Tom, and Ben and Kerri could write something about race that they wouldn't necessarily have done in the past. I remember us talking about — it never made it to air, and I don't know if it was something we even shot; it might've been something we were just talking about — if Jesus is black or not. Some temperatures were getting up there like, "Is Jesus white?" "No, Jesus isn't white; Jesus is black. He was born here. Of course, he's got brown skin, and The Bible says his hair was like lamb's wool." And us actually talking about stuff like that.

The relationship between me and Garcia, that's stuff that we could talk about or now we could have a discussion on CPT time. "What's CPT?" Those kinds of fun, weird, sometimes off-putting conversations, but you can now have that with a diverse group. I felt like that was also a really cool thing about "Reno" and something that not only white guys can talk about but now black kids can talk about or Hispanic kids can talk about that. Now, they come up to me and say, "I was such a fan of your show. I loved 'Reno 911!' I loved some of the racial stuff, undertones that you guys would deal with and make light of and have fun with it."

Because it was first and foremost a spoof of "Cops," there were bullets fired, car chases, physical altercations and explosions. While the cast said it wasn't a dangerous set, everyone got their share of bumps and bruises. Mike Jann was used to big budgets and the stature of stunt coordinators that would be on a Michael Bay film. That wasn't the case with "Reno," though.

Michael Patrick Jann: This BMX is going to fall off the side of the building. If I was going to do a commercial, the guy would be rigged to wires, and we'd remove them digitally. For this show, I'm not joking, let's put a bunch of cardboard boxes on the ground in case he falls.

Thomas Lennon: Every time we could do something, we would try to do it ourselves. There was a bridge-jumper scene, and Travis bets that he can jump and make it into the river where this guy's going to jump and survive. Ben jumped, and he hit the metal bracing that was holding up the soft thing he was going to land on, and he could hear his ankle crack.

I would get hurt on "Reno" all the time. When I would take showers at the end of the day, you know how sometimes you don't know you have a cut until you get soap in them? I was unaware. I was just walking around on "Reno" with cuts all up and down my body all the time from wrestling with Toby Huss or Natasha Leggero.

Toby Huss (Big Mike): All that wrasslin' with the fellas and monkeying around — whew! — no bruises but plenty of erections, that's for sure!

Thomas Lennon: There was an episode where Kerri is walking around a craft store and she fires a double-barrel shotgun at a shoplifter in pantyhose, and we didn't have anybody, so that was me. When she shot the blanks at me, I jumped backward, and I hit the back of my skull on a shelf bracket, and I actually took a tiny chip out of my head. I can still feel the dent where it happened. About a millimeter over and I think it would have gone straight through the soft part of the brain stem, but luckily it hit the hard skull part.

Ben, Kerri and Tom were always looking for playful and creative comics and actors to come in for guest spots. They even let them devise their own characteristics and storylines. It was the only opportunity at the time to be on a hit TV show yet act like you're performing at an Upright Citizens Brigade show. "Reno 911!" featured recurring parts for players newer to the screen like Nick Swardson, Keegan-Michael Key, Natasha Leggero, Jim Rash, Zach Galifianakis and Patton Oswalt. Key appeared several times as Theoretical Criminal — always trying to talk around some twisted tale — and loved jumping into the mix with the troupe of improv masters.

Robert Ben Garant: We met [Keegan], and he came in and did that fast-talking guy. "Hypothetically, if I was to tell you I had a head in my trunk, and I'm not saying I do, speaking hypothetically...." He just came in with that character, and we're like, "Oh, my God, this guy's a fucking genius." The people that we met and got to work with on that show was just a wonderful experience.

Keegan-Michael Key (co-creator of sketch comedy show "Key and Peele"): It was liberating in a different way than "Mad TV" was. I also think the guys were very good and very astute when it came to leaning into what the comedic engine of the character you were playing was. The more you leaned into the character, it seemed sometimes the more plot would arrive so you could get loose stories if you wanted them, and that happened occasionally. I think that for the most part it's just that sense of liberation that you're allowed to go in any direction you want. I think it's probably very fun for the editors. After the time-consuming activity of culling through everything, the editor can still say, "Oh, well this could go here. You know what, let's make this runner be a completely different thing than we thought it was going to be initially."

Tom and Ben are also — in a very positive way — very sneaky. They're very sneaky in that they know where they want to go, but they never let you know that. So it feels free, and it feels like everyone is just having a good time, but they are still, in a manner of speaking, sculpting the performances.

Nick Swardson was the most frequent guest star as the roller skating, is-he-or-isn't-he? hustler, Terry.

Nick Swardson: It's funny, people are like, "You play the same gay guy." No, I don't really. The guy on "Reno 911!" is cartoony and obviously retarded, and I always say that guy's straight on the show. Terry has a girlfriend. It's really goofy. The guy in "[I Now Pronounce You] Chuck and Larry," he wasn't effeminate, even though I was running around in a butterfly costume. The scenes got cut out, but I was playing a real, normal guy. In "Art School Confidential," it was another specific guy. I think they're all different and have their own nuances. I don't just generalize a group of people. Even Terry is a committed character.

Robert Ben Garant: Nick said, "What if I'm on skates?" and we're like, "Great." We had no idea what he was going to do, and he came in with [the character] Terry.

A favorite of multiple cast members was legendary musician Kenny Rogers, who guested as himself on an episode where Wiegel and Garcia act as his security guards. Rogers also popped up under the sheets with Dangle.

Thomas Lennon: He's a real good sport. You can't faze him I found out. It was real, real easy lying around in a bed with him. He's the kind of dude who can go out and knock 'em dead with "The Gambler" and

Kerri Kenney-Silver and Nick Swardson on the "Reno 911!" set

"Coward of the County," then you can go spoon with him, and either way, you feel like he's only talking to you.

Carlos Alazraqui: He was a fan of the show. ... I had [co-producer] David Lincoln give me all the "Gambler" movies, and I crash-viewed them. I wrote a plan on a legal pad. In the car, [I spouted] all the facts that I'd memorized, and [Kenny] was right there with it. He knew everything I was talking about from every movie. "Hey, in 'Gambler Two,' when Brady Hawks decides he's going to escape and get to the funeral..." "Yes, yes, very funny; that's how he got away." He knew everything.

He said, "Let's pull over, and I'm going to pretend to get out of the car." He was making shit up. We're kind of reverential to Kenny Rogers. He's a cool guy, and then he surprises all of us, "Here, here's your fucking book," and we're like, "Whoa, Kenny Rogers dropped the F-bomb!" The ending of that was brilliant, where I get Kerri Kenney, who's dressed like Colonial Sanders, not Kenny Rogers, and I'm sort of attracted to her, and we're both just like, "What the fuck just happened?" That was one of the best endings ever.

A.D. Miles (guest starred on four episodes of "Reno"): [On] one of the episodes of "Reno" I did, I was a guy who had been robbed at a convenience store. It might just be on the DVD, but there was one take that we did [that] was eighteen minutes long. It was almost an entire episode because it just kept going, and they had me strapped to a gurney, and the parking lot in front of the convenience store was on a hill, and they kept getting into an argument, and the gurney would start to slide and get going pretty fast before they'd run down and grab it and push it back and kind of keep the scene going. ... It was so fun, so crazy.

State alum like David, Ken and Michael Black made appearances, too.

Michael Ian Black: I played a pedophile, and I played Cancer Kid, but it was unclear how old he was. He had cancer and was dying but was also racist and misogynistic and foul, which was based on an idea that we talked about in the "Viva" offices when we were bored.

Cedric Yarbrough: You go back, and you say, "Wow, there goes Keegan-Michael Key. There goes Jordan Peele, and there goes Phil LaMarr, and there goes Gary Anthony Williams and Jonah Hill and Zack Galifianakis. We were just really lucky that people got the tone of the show and then were ready to play. After that first season, people really got what the show was, and they were calling their agents and managers and saying, "I gotta get on that show." Natasha Leggero, Chelsea Handler also was on the show. These funny, smart women were amazing on the show, and speaking on funny, smart women, I thought our cast was, pound for pound, the best cast. Everyone was so good and so smart, and Kerri, Wendy, Niecy and Mary Birdsong were just so, so quick, so smart and the fastest, smartest women in Hollywood. I'm just so glad they actually let me actually play with them.

Carlos Alazraqui: Kyle Dunnigan, he was supposed be a one-off character. He was supposed to be this guy who just dropped his ice cream cone, and that was it. "And then I have to go home to my cats." And Wendy was sharp enough to listen and go, "Wiegel likes cats. Hey, Wiegel, come on over here," and then that turned into, "Oh, my God, I'd wish you'd go out and date." That one-off character for Kyle turned out to be series-recurring, all because Wendy was sharp enough to listen.

Robert Ben Garant: Big Mike the Crackhead, Toby Huss, didn't tell us anything. He said, "What if I'm in a wife beater and have a packet of Kool cigarettes under the wife beater?" and we're like, "OK." We didn't know what he was gonna do or anything, and we gave him that wardrobe and pulled up to him at the trailer, and he just started doing Big Mike.

Toby Huss: Big Mike was a pile of oily rags looking for a trashcan fire. He's more like the mayor of his block — a corrupt, chemically challenged mayor who for some reason doesn't have a problem with Nazis but does have a problem with his wife — unrepentant but charming in his crystal-methed, violent and drunkenly ham-fisted way. He likes boats and guns and getting high — just like everyone else. He's no different than you and me, just less misunderstood.

Cedric Yarbrough: Traditionally, our first day would always start with Big Mike, Toby Huss. We would always shoot him first. I think it was a good-luck thing. Hopefully, we would have a good season if we started with Toby Huss. We would have Jones and Garcia stopping Big Mike for a given thing, or then we would have Clemmie and Williams stopping Big Mike for a certain thing. Then we would sprinkle those particular scenes within the season.

Toby Huss: They were jerks. Most of them have what, a third-, fourth-grade education? I think Cedric went to some sort of refrigeration repair tech college. He was by far the smartest. So they're really not good with words and make-em-ups. I remember some guest actors, including myself, making some pretty remarkable stories and "story games" and getting a lot of staring in response. Really bug-eyed staring. And scratching. Ben was a drooler.

Thomas Lennon: There's times where you can see us going and the times that we laughed, we laughed really, really hard. The mustaches have really helped. Wearing sunglasses and a mustache really helped quite a bit, but I remember the times that someone made me laugh on "Reno" are among the hardest times I've ever laughed in my entire life; so there's some really amazing stuff. It's also the length of things. We once let Patton Oswalt talk for twenty-five straight minutes in a scene and never interrupted him ever, and I think you can see on occasion that I'm about to start laughing. I think I smoke two full Merit 100 cigarettes while he talks.

Michael Patrick Jann: If something was really funny, you couldn't help yourself really. There were definitely times when I was practically falling out of my chair. ... I'm a pretty decent audience. I'm not that easy to make laugh, but if you get me, you got me. I have a lifelong professional tolerance for comedy, but great comedy is great comedy.

Guest star, Mary Birdsong, impressed Ben and Tom so much when she played a raging geisha masseuse that she ended up getting cast full-time when Kerri Kenney-Silver was pregnant during the third season.

Mary Birdsong: I almost feel guilty saying so, but I think it was my favorite episode I did of "Reno."

Birdsong was also in the Tisch School at NYU when The State attended.

Robert Ben Garant: We loved her. We'd known her for a long time. She was in "Viva Variety" once, and then she did "Reno" as the undercover geisha, which she pitched us. We thought, "Oh, my God, that's so weird." We just did it, and we know she's a rock-solid improviser, and we knew we needed another straight cop. We need a cop that was just gonna do their job really well because I did and Garcia did, but nobody else really did.

Wiegel, the wheels come off the second she steps out of the car. We needed another cop that would actually cuff people and throw them in the car, which only half of us did.

Mary Birdsong: I knew they were really tight, especially Ben and Tom. I always liken it to twins who have a secret language. They're like a married couple mixed with identical twins, finishing each other's sentences and all that.

A straight-up parody of "Cops" with fake mustaches and wacky domestic dispute dustups could only last so long. It was the bizarre interpersonal relationships between the gaggle of Reno deputies and lieutenant — plus recurring oddballs — that helped keep the show fresh.

Carlos Alazraqui: I really liked the way [Michael Patrick Jann] paid attention to characters and stories.

Michael Patrick Jann: Nobody writes jokes better than Tom and Ben. I can help write jokes. I have funny ideas. One thing I'm really good at is formulating emotional relationships and behavior that's comedic. That was a puzzle piece, and I was able to provide that for the show. That was part of putting people into The State mind, giving people a rationale. Tom and Ben do it naturally. For the other ninety-nine percent of us, we need to have a reason to go be hilarious, a rationale, a basis. If you're trying to be hilarious, it usually doesn't work out. But if what you're trying to do is take a woman out on a date and don't have any money, that encompasses a set of behaviors you can play honestly and will be hilarious.

While Dangle's short shorts could come off after
the cameras stopped rolling, Ben had to keep the
ridiculous redneck two-tiered haircut at all times.

Robert Ben Garant: I had to go to the Kentucky Derby in that
thing. I was in this great, nice suit and meeting all these rich people
and had that fucking haircut. It was not the demographic. It was early
in the show; so nobody had any idea that it was on purpose, the fucking
mustache and the haircut. It was really, really, really bad. People either
thought I was gay or thought I was a cop, depending on where I was. Me
and Tom were in Miami scouting for the "Reno" movie, and we walked
into a club, and some dude just walked up to us high as a kite on cocaine
and said, "Yo, mustaches," and just left. Tom and I quote that all the
time. "Wow, he has no idea that we're on TV or anything; he was just so
psyched that we had mustaches."

The "Cops" spoof was a hit for Comedy Central,
but the team realized that Twentieth Century
Fox still held the rights to any possible movie.
"Reno 911!: Miami" became a co-venture between
the network and the studio.

Mary Birdsong: I think there was a lot of pressure on the guys,
the triumvirate. Maybe they were just totally chill inside. That was a big
step for them, especially Ben directing.

Robert Ben Garant: When we turned in dailies the first week,
Emma Watts, the head of Fox, called us on the phone and said, "We're
watching the dailies, and it looks like we just gave two fourteen-year-
old boys a hundred million dollars." It was all car chases and explosions
and naked girls, all this crazy stuff, but yeah, it was great. The budget of
the movie was $9.3 million, and we shot for twenty days, twelve [in Los
Angeles] and eight in Miami.

The Rock drove himself to set. He worked for scale and just did it. We
pitched him the idea, and he said, "I love it. It's great." He just came and
did it, and he was no maintenance at all.

The State reunites during the filming of "Reno 911!: Miami."

Carlos Alazraqui: We didn't really spend as much time introducing each character to the new audience that hadn't seen the series. It's hard when you try to stretch it out, but we did great. There's a lot of great gags. Toby Huss was great. It was a blast to make, and for the budget that we spent on it, it did great.

Robert Ben Garant: I go back and think, "Should we have done something different?" The trailer for it tested higher than any Fox comedy trailer did that year. When it came out, I think it only made twenty-one million dollars. Rotten Tomatoes hated it. I don't know what we could've done differently. It needed to be what it was. I can't imagine it not being not a documentary for the budget. It is what it is, but it's so weird, the vitriol that came out for the movie.

It's so funny, things that I do that I'm super-proud of get hated, and things that I do that I hate get slightly less hated. It's very odd to me that people hated that movie so much because we did a press tour, thirty cities, and in every city we would screen it, come in at the end in character and do a Q&A. I saw it thirty times with audiences, and it fucking destroyed. It killed. So when the reviews came out and everybody hated it, "Jesus Christ, what do I gotta do?"

Kerri Kenney-Silver: Unfortunately, "Borat" came out right before we did with unheard-of success. Everyone at Fox is expecting two hits in a row, and our movie at that moment was considered a major failure, but if you look back, we made our money back the first weekend, which would be considered a success but not in relation to "Borat."

Mary Birdsong: To this day, when I think of some of the greatest acting I've ever seen, I remember Toby Huss when he played the German hotel manager. I was just blown away. He could've done a whole movie as that character. I was really impressed. He wasn't just funny. He had amazing acting chops — twisted and sick and weird as hell but really grounded. He knows that this guy exists somewhere, and that's really disturbing.

Toby Huss: First of all, Birdsong is nuts. (There's another book for you to write.) Yeah, an entire movie of [me] would be great, if the movie was seven minutes long and there was a five-minute car chase. The idea came from the wardrobe, which Tom and Ben let me choose. Seemed like a dirty, German, smoking, sexy puppy-man would work well in Miami.

Though not all on screen at the same time, "Reno 911!: Miami" featured cameos by all the other members of The State.

Todd Holoubek: They got each of us to do little roles. ... That just made everybody comfortable enough to be able to get together again. I think everybody was like, "OK, there are no hard feelings either over Todd leaving or what happened with 'Viva Variety.'" Everyone else was getting their careers going, and so nothing really mattered anymore. That was actually the first reunion. We weren't all on the stage at the same time, but most of us were on set at the same time. And then we all met at a bar. Everything was really cool and went back to our day-to-day lives.

For the sixth and final season of "Reno 911!" the characters of Garcia, Clemmie and Kimball were gone, and new faces Joe Lo Truglio and Ian Roberts of Upright Citizens Brigade were added. Carlos said he found out he wouldn't be returning to "Reno" via email.

Carlos Alazraqui: I know it's not flattering, but if you want the truth, that's the truth. I'm not gonna sugarcoat it.

Thomas Lennon: It wasn't for no reason. It was like when you're in a band and people can get difficult sometimes, and we felt very much, with Wendy and Carlos, like we had done a lot to get them out there in the public eye. At the time, we weren't creatively really seeing eye to eye at all.

I'd like to preface this with, a million percent, it was a mistake to replace the cast. I don't think it was a good idea. I know it was a mistake to replace the cast, but you have to realize in that kind of relationship where you're improvising with somebody every single day and doing tons of scenes, you've got to trust them, and they've got to trust you. Not with Mary, because she was definitely in it and working really hard, but Carlos and Wendy weren't as in it at the time. We'd get asked things like, "Well, when can we audition for other pilots and shows and stuff?" We'd be like, "You know what, fuck it, man. We're killing ourselves to make this thing good. It's turned into a hit. Let's all appreciate how great this is before we have one foot out the door."

Kerri, Ben and I, speaking for the three of us, we felt like the people that got replaced, at least Wendy and Carlos, their hearts weren't as in it as ours were, and that felt in a small way almost like a betrayal. How could you take this for granted, this amazing thing that we've created? It was a rash, bad decision that was made, and I regret it, and I'm still friends with Carlos.

Carlos Alazraqui: I don't think it was done correctly, but I get it. That's the way it has to go sometimes. For a while, it hurt. You get bitter, and you get angry, and at some point you have to let it go, and I'm much healthier because of it. I think I'm more mature now. I understand there were some ways that I could have improved our chemistry together, too.

Mary Birdsong: I was surprised, but on the other hand, I knew all our contracts were up. I wasn't even sure if the show is coming back. ... That was a double whammy. "Oh, wait, the show is coming back! Oh wait, I'm not coming back, and Carlos isn't, and, wait, Wendy isn't. Are they moving us to Hawaii or something? Is this going to be a Dick York/Dick Sargent 'Bewitched' situation? Is Joe Lo Truglio playing me?" Actually, I think that would've been brilliant in hindsight if they tried to pass Joe off as Kimball and given him French braids. I know he'd be game.

Joe Lo Truglio: I was very nervous about it, to be honest. I obviously trusted [Ben, Kerri and Tom] implicitly and was so happy when they asked that, I jumped at that chance, but I didn't want to disappoint. A lot of that was just my own insecurity. These were friends I knew for so long, and I knew how they worked, and I knew that this show that had been going five years was such a different animal. The machine was running so smoothly, and they had a way of working that went so well that I didn't want to trip it up. I was also joining the cast with arguably one of the most talented improv people, Ian Roberts from UCB. It was scary, but I also knew that I was going to have to up my game, which was exciting, and really be put to task, which was exciting, and working with the best, which was exciting. So it was a gigantic challenge for me, but to Tom, and Kerri and Ben, they didn't even blink.

Ian Roberts: They accuse me of turning it down. "Yeah, we offered you a role on the show, and you turned it down," but what happened was I'm very loyal to my writing partner, Jay Martel, and if I go up and do a big acting role, I leave him unable to work. He's not making money while I'm off making money. Peter Principato is their manager and my manager, and [he] said, "Hey, what do you think of 'Reno?' Are you a fan?" I said, "Sure, it's real funny." "They are thinking of offering you a role as a regular on the show." I said, "I don't think I can do that to Jay." I didn't understand how quickly they filmed. ... Peter explained, "Look, it's twenty-two days of shooting." So then I was more happy to do it. I was excited to do it, but then they'd kid me. Tom and Ben will say, "You turned us down, you asshole," but, yeah, that's how I got approached for it, through my manager.

Cedric Yarbrough: It was scary and also a little bit painful because I did a lot of stuff with Carlos. We built up this thing, and we'd been doing it for five seasons and a film; so having Joe and Ian was scary for me, even though I'd worked with [them before] and I love those guys. Those guys are brilliant. You see what they're doing right now; they're amazing, but when you switch up a show like that, it's difficult. Not to compare us to the show "Friends," but if you take out Chandler and bring someone else in, it definitely changes the rhythm of the group. To have Wendy, Carlos and Mary gone, it was definitely a blow for me. You have to try to get adjusted to it.

Ian Roberts: I was allowed to create a lot, actually. They asked me, "So what do you want to do?" I had just a few things. I said, "One, I want to have heart attacks that I hide from everyone." At the time, I was two hundred sixty five pounds, and I was so unhealthy and just bloated, and I guess that's the way I felt about myself. "I'm gonna die;" so that was one bit. I got to have one heart attack in the season, and they rolled up in the car and asked me how I'm doing, and I play it off, "I'm OK. I'm good." The other thing was I wanted to cry and berate myself; so we did this scene where I was in a bathroom stall going, "You're so weak. You're so weak. How come nobody likes me?" I was just in there hating myself, and then I came out, and they're like, "You OK?" and I'm like, "Yeah, I'm fine," and I asked if they were OK.

Joe Lo Truglio: I wanted to have a mustache, that kind of Fu Manchu mustache or handlebar mustache.

Ian Roberts: Nobody has just mustaches anymore, especially big, hang-over-your-lips mustaches. My wife and I went to buy a pumpkin for Halloween, and the guy — I got this vibe he thinks I'm a cop — he goes, "Hey, why don't you take a bag of gourds? It's on me, for the family." I think that's because he thinks I'm a cop like, "Here's a little something extra for you because you're a cop," because really only cops and firemen have those weird, big mustaches.

Joe Lo Truglio: I just jumped into it, and we found things as we went along. It was really great to see the three of them grow as writers and actors or producers in a way that was different than The State. You realize that when the numbers are smaller, you have a more specific type of comedy. One of the things I love about Tom, Ben and Kerri is that they love physical, slapstick stuff, gags. It ended up being very easy to do these scenes because they suffered the conflicts in such a way that the game was very clear. OK, he has the hiccups, and there's a ping-pong ball stuck in her vagina, and how can we get it out? Whatever it was, you were able to play the game very well. Once I realized that everything that you needed was there, it became very easy.

Thomas Lennon: No one will admit this, but if you look at the season six episodes, they're really, really good. Probably people were too angry to really watch them open-mindedly.

Cedric Yarbrough: I don't know if the audience ever really took to this new crew though most of us were there. I don't know if the audience felt the same with the show, and after that season, we were done.

Even though the show ended in 2009, Tom keeps those short shorts handy. The cast of "Reno 911!" has performed live at San Francisco Sketchfest, assembled for police fundraisers and even helped get a sheriff elected. Cedric and Carlos cameoed in character on Comedy Central's game show "@midnight," where Tom and Ben are executive producers. (Despite that the Garcia character was killed off and his ashes shot from a cannon in season six, he's been revived for subsequent appearances.)

Cedric Yarbrough: I adore each and every one of those guys, and I would love to do another "Reno" if it were to pop up and be able to work with all of our schedules. I love that that cast now is working so damn much. Everyone's got their own thing going on. ... I think being able to bring all of our fun guest stars back would be so much fun. You see "Wet Hot American Summer" now and what they've been able to do on Netflix, and having such a powerhouse cast is pretty cool and pretty wonderful. I'm hoping that we'll be able to do that some time.

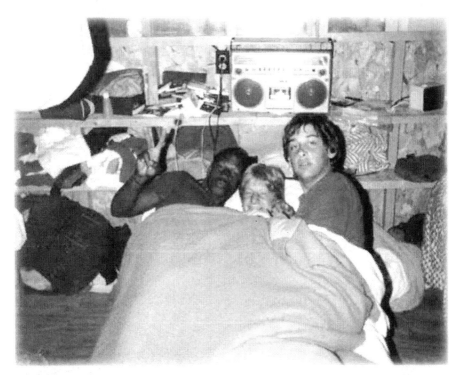

David Wain, right, gets cozy at Camp Modin in summer 1984.

CHAPTER 26

"Wet Hot American Summer"

"My first actual kiss was not at camp, but everything else was. Fill in the blank. Everything else was at camp."

David Wain

Michael Showalter's and David Wain's love letter to summer camp took blood, sweat and years to build its legion of devoted, quoting fans. "Wet Hot American Summer" found its voice through midnight screenings and word of mouth from comedy geeks and hipsters. It became a litmus test for friends and sex partners. "I'm not sleeping with that chick on the first date if she can't quote 'Wet Hot.'"

It achieved a unique status among cult flicks when a prequel series was released on Netflix in summer 2015. The series not only reunited the entire cast but also added new heavy hitters like Jon Hamm and Kristen Wiig. And it all started with two, young lads who loved living in the woods during school breaks.

David Wain: My first actual kiss was not at camp, but everything else was. Fill in the blank. Everything else was at camp.

Michael Showalter: I started going to sleepaway camp in fourth grade, and I started going to day camp in first grade. I'd been going to camp ever since first grade, basically. ... I finally did an eight-week thing when I found a camp that I liked. My summers growing up were all about going to camp. That's just what summer was to me, go to camp and then maybe do a family vacation, but the big thing was sleepaway camp. I went to a bunch of them that I didn't like before I found one that I did like.

David Wain: I went to sleepaway camp first when I was eight or nine years old for three weeks at Camp Wise in Ohio. It was in the summers of '78 and '79. Everyone was talking about Skylab. Skylab could fall, and I wondered what would happen if it fell at our camp. Then I went to a camp in Maine the next year, when I was ten, the summer of 1980, called Camp Modin. Halfway through the first summer, my parents came to visit, and I begged them to take me home because I was

Michael Showalter as Coop

homesick — not that I didn't like it, but I just really had enough, and I just wanted to go home so bad. My parents got all their courage up and said, "No," and forced me to stay, and they left. I will always be grateful to them for that because it's really the subsequent years at camp [that] truly defined my life and also, unexpectedly, my career.

The summer of '81, which is when "Wet Hot" takes place, I actually didn't go to camp. I went to magic camp, and I went to tennis camp. I visited [Camp Modin] because all my other friends were still there. Then I went again '82 to '85 as a camper and '86 [as a] counselor. Basically, the kind of bonding you do with other people at camp is on a different level, or it was for me, than anywhere else because you're living with each other 24/7, and you're having adventures as a young person away from your parents for the first time. Our camp was very easy going. [That's] a polite way to say it — just totally disorganized and not much going on. It was a lot of hanging out and having a blast with some friends. I still consider my camp friends like true family to this day. Those times were truly defining, spiritual, wonderful experiences of bonding and learning about myself.

Michael Showalter: The people, the vibe. The camp that I eventually went to that I really liked is very similar to the camp in "Wet Hot." It's just [a] ragtag operation but sort of goofy and charming and fun. The other ones that I went to were a little bit more structured. ... I was asked to be a counselor but decided not to do that.

David Wain: There was a rule that you could go to the movies from camp anytime you wanted, as long as you walked to the theater, which was twenty-three miles away. We did it once a summer. We'd get up, and the whole group would walk down the highway for twenty-two miles from where we were in Canaan, Maine, to Waterville, Maine, where the theater was. There was also an incredible ice cream place called Rumold's that had batting cages and ice cream. They had a thing called the Icky Orgy, where if you could finish it, you got a button that said, "I ate at the Orgy."

By the time you got to the movie theater, you didn't care what was playing, which, by the way, was "Young Doctors in Love."

Michael Showalter: I played a lot of ping pong. I played tennis, and I did a lot of the theater stuff, the talent show and the musical. I was very social. I liked the dances. I was a big arts and crafts kid.

David Wain: The big thing that every camper did was sneak over to the girls' side in the middle of the night. ... It was OK but definitely technically against the rules. There were some nights where they were like, "No, really, really don't go. Don't do that." You had to sneak past the director's house and go onto the highway, and across the highway and then back down the girls' side of the road. It was very adventurous at night, pitch black. I think we were all basically good kids at heart; so we never got into too much trouble.

The director of the camp was this idiosyncratic, Israeli counter-terrorist trainer named David Adler, and he was very into the movie "Rambo." When that movie came out, he would try to take kids as often as possible to see it and indoctrinate them into having a Rambo attitude. We used it as a verb. "OK, guys, let's Rambo this together." I could make a whole book about summer camp because I've thought about it so much over the last twenty years.

Michael Showalter: There was an entire cabin of kids who, the entire summer, did other things than everybody else. All they did was go on these adventures; so you'd see them on Tuesday, and then they'd be gone for five days because they'd be rafting, or they were hiking, or they were camping, or they were climbing a mountain. Then they'd show up again, and they'd be there for twenty-four hours, and then they'd be gone again. The counselors of those kids were called the Adventure Counselors. Victor and Neil [in "Wet Hot"] were very much fashioned after those guys for me. There was an Andy in my camp. All those characters, there was someone like that at my camp, for sure. In terms of like directly basing someone off of it, the ones that most stick out to me are J.J. and Victor.

David Wain: My main camp experience that made it into the movie was that I drove a van of kids up to Mount Katahdin for an overnight trip, and instead of staying overnight with them and the other counselor, I bolted back to camp in the van in order to see this girl that I had met and wanted to make out with. I smashed the van in the road in the middle of the night and was trapped. After that, the camp made a policy that junior counselors were no longer allowed to drive vans, which is a smart policy since I had probably gotten my license two days before.

I just didn't want to stop coming. I had no desire to be a counselor, and, in fact, part of what inspired me in "Wet Hot American Summer" is exactly what it was like, me being a counselor. In some ways how it's portrayed in the movie and the TV show where the counselors are basically doing what the campers do, which is run around, trying to get some girl to make out with them, have fun with your friends, and hang out and talk, whatever, that so defined my life at camp. I was sixteen years old when I was a counselor. As it happened, I was assigned to a bunch of fifteen-year-olds; so they were basically my age. They were my peers. In fact, one of my campers went on to take over and purchase and run the camp [and] still does to this day. He's turned it into a modern summer camp. You can't have a camp like we had that was so blasé anymore.

Showalter and Wain were already performing
together at Stella shows in New York City when
they started to pen the story for "Wet Hot."

David Wain: We were writing this other movie, which was a little
more complicated. It was like a "Say Anything" high school thing. We
were like, "This is gonna take a lot of time. While we're still working
on this, what's something that we can just write and shoot right now?"
Our friend, Sam Seder, had made this great movie called "Who's the
Caboose?"

This was long before Larry David or anything. He had a thirty-page
outline and shot the movie from the outline and basically had funny
people come in and improvise all the scenes. I was so inspired by that.
It was so funny, and Jon Benjamin and Sarah Silverman are the main
people in it with a bunch of other people that are really incredible. We
were like, "Let's do that." "You know what it has to be? Camp," and it
just seemed like, "Yeah, of course, camp. Has to be the next thing. That's
great. We can shoot wherever, outside. Just write an outline."

Zak Orth as J.J., Joe Lo Truglio as Neil and A.D. Miles as Gary

Michael Showalter: We both definitely had very formative and memorable camp experiences. We were like, "Let's do 'Meatballs.'" I'd seen that movie and was really blown away by how authentic and funny it was and how cool it was. For me, there was a lot of wanting to try to do something like that.

David Wain: I believe it was '97, and we were like, "This summer, we'll go outside with whatever camera we can afford and just shoot a bunch of our friends, improvising off an outline." That's how it started, and basically the more we started writing it out and the more that nobody wanted to give us money, the more it turned into a traditional screenplay.

We worked on it on and off, but a lot on; so three years while we were trying to raise the money. ... We were having readings, and we were trying to get financing, and we were sending it everywhere at that time.

Paul Rudd (Andy): They told me about "Wet Hot American Summer" the night of meeting them at [their play] "Sex, Wieners and Boobs." ... They had that script for a long time. David said, "Can I send you this script?" I think the only thing anybody had ever seen me in up to that point was "Clueless." I said, "Yeah, absolutely." I immediately read it and thought, "This is the funniest thing I've ever read. Oh, my God, I'd love to do it." Then it got made a couple years later.

Zak Orth (J.J.): I would say a good ninety-five percent of what we shot was what was on the page, and then maybe every now and then somebody would throw something in, or they'd catch some little bit of magic that was ad-libbed or improvised, but it was written, and David held it down. He did an amazing job.

David Wain: We knew Janeane before Stella, which is how we got her on Stella. We had met her through The State at various parties in New York. Janeane was definitely our celebrity friend; so we tailored that part for her in the movie and asked her to be attached to it as our first step at trying to get it made. I guess Stella was definitely an element of how we got to meet and got to know other people in the community.

Janeane Garofalo as Beth

Janeane Garofalo (Beth): At the time, I was working a lot in film so it seemed like it would be helpful to have somebody that was in films [to] agree to do it. It was just one of those things because I was having some success in the film world. "Look, we have a film actor in it."

In March 2000, David and Michael started scouting for camp locations and found what they were looking for at Camp Towanda in Honesdale, Pennsylvania.

David Wain: It was covered in snow. It was a bit terrifying as we were set to start shooting in May.

Way outside of Hollywood, one hundred fifty members of cast and crew descended on the camp and moved into the bunks.

Mitch Reiter (director of Camp Towanda): They came in late-April and stayed until mid-June. That is my crunch time for getting camp ready. ... We have a couple hundred campers and staff coming in.

I'm sitting at my desk when I hear on the walkie-talkie that they're trying to get this fire going, and it's pouring rain. They were deep in the woods. I put on the poncho and drove out. I said to David, "Let me help you start the fire." He said, "Mitch, it's raining." "David, I'm a camp director. I can start a fire." A couple of minutes later, there was a fire, and they were so happy. I saved the day. Of course, what I didn't tell them is I put one of those starter bricks up my sleeve and slipped it into the fire. It would start during rain or snow.

Janeane Garofalo: We lived at camp, which I loved as a kid who had gone to summer camp and loved it. It was a thrill being back at summer camp with that particular group of people. It really was one of the best times I've ever had doing anything. It was just bliss. It was as good as when you are lucky enough to go to summer camp and it goes well, 'cause summer camp can be as shit as any school experience, too.

But sometimes you get real lucky. That's why you don't want to leave at the end of the summer and then you spend the whole school year looking forward to camp again. It was the same thing. It was a great group of people having a great time at camp, literally, at camp, in bunks, and eating in the cafeteria and all of it. It was just a great, great experience, I think, for everyone.

Mark White (production designer): I read the script. I loved it so much. I couldn't believe how much I loved it. Just roaring with laughter. I kept telling myself, "You have to get this job." I got to the point [in the script] where Nurse Nancy says, "It's for my pussy," and I said, "OK, that's it, I have to get this job."

A.D. Miles (Gary): Even though I'd done a few things before that, [it was] ground zero for my career and probably a lot of people's careers that were in that movie.

Paul Rudd: It's that thing that everyone always says, you're at camp. That's exactly what it was like. Everyone was, I think, a fan of everybody else. Everyone got along really well. Everyone watched everybody do their scenes because we were stranded. We're out in the middle of nowhere, couldn't go anywhere. Whoever wasn't shooting would go into town, which is like thirty minutes away, and buy the beer, and then we'd have a party every night. It was

Paul Rudd as Andy

incredible. I think the whole experience was major for everyone involved.

Michael Ian Black as McKinley and Bradley Cooper as Ben

Michael Ian Black (McKinley): My initial impression was that I didn't fully get it but that I trusted it would be hilarious. On the page, some of it is like, "Wait, what? What? What's going on?" But I also knew that they knew what they were doing. I knew that they knew that it was funny, and I was right.

I didn't know if they would ask me to be in it. I was trying to be very gentle with the subject and support them in any way that I could both to atone [for "Viva Variety"] and to get my fat, grubby face into that movie.

Joe Lo Truglio (Neil): We couldn't believe we were able to make a movie with our friends. It was like getting away with something and at any moment they were gonna shut us down. Not that that was ever a real threat, but in my head it was, "Can you believe this? This is nuts that we're able to do this." There was a lot of rambunctious celebration because of that.

Ken Marino (Victor): Showalter called and said they're doing "Wet Hot" and they had a small part for me. The part of Victor wasn't mine originally. I was like, "OK," and they're like, "Do you want to read for it?" and I was like, "What? Do I want to read for 'Wet Hot'?" and they're like, "Yeah," and I'm like, "No, I don't want to read for 'Wet Hot.' Either offer me the part or don't."

I got offended by that. I was like, "What are you talking about?" and then they said, "All right, don't worry about it."

Chris Meloni (Gene): It was so much fun, and it reminded me of The Little Rascals. "Hey, Darla, Spanky, let's put on a show."

Mark White: Skylab was pretty tough. I didn't know how that was going to work out with no money. It was all built from Home Depot.

Zak Orth, A.D. Miles and Michael Showalter

Whatever we could think of we screwed together.

I love Nurse Nancy's infirmary. That was fun for us. We went crazy with the details. There were bloody Band-Aids and old cotton swabs. We were more than happy to stick them in. I love the boys' bunks. When we dressed the bunks, we decided who each kid was. This is the fat kid. This is the mama's boy. This is the guy who plays the accordion. We made a little story for each one.

The sets that we built, which were few, were the radio station, the equipment shack where Michael Black and Bradley fuck and the heroin den. Those were the three builds that we did.

At Camp Towanda, April showers brought May downpours that brought June puddles.

David Wain: One of the most vivid memories I have happened almost every morning. All of us were living at the infirmary, but my little room opened up in the back to the outside, and every morning, my alarm would go off at 6 a.m. for the shoot, and I would open the door, and right before I would basically say a little prayer like, "It can't still be raining. It can't be," and I would open up the door, and it was like sheeting down so hard. "OK, here we go. Here's another day." We'd just trudge through the rain, and I wore these ratty, black, leather dress shoes because I felt like if I gave in and bought boots that I was giving into the rain, admitting that it was gonna keep going. "I don't need to buy boots because it's not going to rain anymore." I think it was twenty-five out of twenty-nine days.

Michael Ian Black: From a weather perspective, it was terrible. It was monsoon season.

Janeane Garofalo: Because "Wet Hot" the movie was their first big movie and it was raining all the time, they didn't have the luxury of saying, "Now, let's do this variation, this variation." It was like, "We gotta go because the real camp starts in two weeks."

David Wain: Many scenes were supposed to be outdoors and moved indoors. Other scenes were just shot under a cover to make it seem like it was out of doors, but we were totally under a big tarp. Other scenes we had to shoot way faster when there was a tiny break in the rain, and a lot of it we just shot in the rain. It didn't show up on the film because if you don't light for it, you don't often see the rain. I remember very well, for example, the scene when Katie and Andy are outside the cafeteria and he says, "You're crowding me. Fuck you, dyke," that one was in an absolute monsoon. We just covered up that one little space against the wall of the cafeteria where they were, but the actual sound in the dailies was just not even. There's no chance we could use it because it was covered in rain; so we had to replace all the voices in that.

Mark White: I was building the can-of-vegetables puppet in this damp, breezy room. You never felt like you were inside. They were bunks; the wind and the rain blew right through them. Your fingers are freezing.

Marguerite Moreau (Katie): Oh, my God, it was so fucking cold. It was like you didn't get undressed from your three layers of clothing, and somewhere underneath your layers was your costume, unless you were shooting, and you just slept in that outfit. You drank

Marguerite Moreau as Katie

into the night, took a nap, either by choice or because you gave up, and then you would roll into the mess hall in the morning and just strip down for your scene, whenever that was.

Chris Meloni: I just remember these beds. They were just springs. "Here's your mattress." It was a half-inch-thick, plastic mattress on top of these springs. And you brought your own sleeping bag for the top, and after day one the sleeping bag was filled with mud.

David Wain: There were so many crazy rain-related things we had to do. We completely tore up that camp. We shot it in May and June, right before they were going to open it up for the kids, and the camp director was absolutely furious with us.

Mitch Reiter: All these years later, there are a couple spots I've never been able to recover — just destroyed.

Janeane Garofalo: Michael and David were stressed beyond belief and yet never took it out on any of the humans they were working with, which is a very good trait. There are some directors who are really well cut out for it, and they are them. They enjoy it. They are kind to people even when they are beyond stressed. I would never want to direct anything. Good God, it's one of the most stressful things. You witness people who handle it brilliantly and who do not, and those people that do not, I don't understand why they're doing it.

Chris Meloni: In the middle of all this stress, people tend to close down, and yet [David is] always able to take in whatever thought anyone may have, whether it's Showalter or an actor, and he's able to just engage it unemotionally. Quite a feat.

Michael Ian Black: What worked about "Wet Hot" is, as collaborative as it is, it's also very much their vision. It's very much driven by those two guys. It's hard to achieve something that big if it's a shared vision of eleven. It's just too hard. There's too many voices to satisfy. I think it can only work the way it worked.

Things get weird in the movie when Rudd's character, Andy, throws a drowned kid out of a moving van to hide the evidence that he wasn't doing his job.

Paul Rudd: I remember when it came out and people thought, "Oh, it's a satire of a summer camp movie." I've always thought that really misses the mark. It isn't a satire of a summer camp movie. The one thing that David and Michael have always done is kind of have fun with tropes that we've all gotten used to, more so than just satirizing genres. I don't think that is interesting to them at all, and it's not something that they've ever really done. ... It was really more of an absurdist kind of thing where we're mocking just movie tropes and then adding in so many things that are just bizarre but funny to us.

Michael Showalter: I think that was just our comic sensibility and the kind of jokes that we told and the comedy of the movies that I grew up loving, to a somewhat lesser extent, but still had those kinds of jokes in them, whether it was "Airplane" or Steve Martin movies, "The Man With Two Brains" and "The Jerk" and what have you. Those movies had that absurd quality to them, where jokes like that actually weren't so weird or out of the ordinary.

If you go look at those movies and you look at the story lines and what happens in them, they're ridiculous. The mastermind villain in "The Man with Two Brains" is actually Merv Griffin, and that was normal. So we were just going where it seemed natural to go.

Marguerite Moreau: I read the barbecue-on-the-face scene, and it ended with some amazing thing that didn't make it into the first film but was still so funny on the page. You just pan over at the end of the scene, and there's Tim Robbins and Morgan Freeman carving chess pieces on the set of "Shawshank Redemption." I don't think it translated to film as effectively, but even reading that, I became so passionate, and when I went in for the audition the next day, they said, "No, no, no, I think we want you to read for Katie instead."

I was so excited by the fact that I had no idea and I had to figure out what was this girl's fucking thing. It just made sense of when you were sixteen, and you're trying to play both sides of the fence. I remember torturing this kid in junior high by being like, "Well, we can go together, but we're not going out," because I wasn't totally sure that we should be going out forever. I related to the moronic flip-flopping of Katie. She has no idea. Hormones are going crazy, and it was really fun to play that in my early twenties.

Janeane Garofalo: [David and Michael] know what they want, but they are totally open if you've got an idea. If they don't like the idea, they won't use it, but it really is helpful to the actor to build your confidence when they at least pretend to like it. Some directors are quite cruel. If you try something, they will say something that is terribly embarrassing to you and that can really shut you down. ... That can be a real bummer. [David and Michael] don't do that.

While the set was drenched with rain during the day, at night it was soaked in booze.

David Wain: It was totally insane. There was a quite a bit of drinking and hooking up and drugs and just everyone having a great time. Everyone's living together. No one's getting paid. Everyone is far away from home. Many of us working on our very first professional shoot of any kind. A lot of really funny, great people. A real recipe for having a blast.

Janeane Garofalo: Alcohol, alcohol, alcohol, alcohol, alcohol and I say that with no pride because I was the biggest drunk of all. I, shortly thereafter, quit drinking. I quit drinking in 2001, and unfortunately I should have quit before "Wet Hot," but, boy, that was fun. I must've fallen down and hit my head eight thousand times, and how I didn't crack my skull open, I have no idea. On those hard, wooden bunk floors. I was always falling because it was raining every day. There's nothing but mud and slippery floors and me drunk. And people worrying, did I crack my head open?

I'm sure Michael and David, who were too nice to say it, were terrified that I wouldn't be able to shoot. I always knew my lines, and I was punctual. It was one of those things where I was just having the best time, and I never knew when to stop. I was always, "No, let's keep going, let's keep going. Who cares if the sun's coming up? Doesn't matter, let's just keep going," and that, unfortunately, probably gave Michael and David another headache, but they were too nice to say anything about it. I was able to shoot, and I never had terrible hangovers, oddly. I think I was always still drunk as we started in the morning, but it was so enjoyable. Sometimes when you're in such a good mood, it carries you through everything. It is true what they say, mind over matter. I was so happy that I don't recall having my usual horrible hangovers with the head of cement and vomit involved. I don't think I threw up once, which is really saying something for me at that time. Again, I don't say it with pride.

Mark White: We were all drunk, but half of it was just to warm up. That part should've made it miserable, but it didn't. It's the most fun I've ever had at a job.

Mitch Reiter: We had a lot of fun with the cast and the crew. If they had worked for me, I would've fired them all. I probably would have fired me, too.

Michael Ian Black: It was different for me for a few reasons: one, my wife was newly pregnant. I was dealing with that, and I didn't drink, and most of the social scene at night was just about getting totally fucked up. I could participate to a point, but it wasn't the kind of fraternalia that it was for other people.

I was living there in the nurse's quarters. Who didn't? David Hyde Pierce didn't, wisely. I think part of him may regret that a little bit, but he was a forty-year-old guy with a lot of money. I think he felt like, "I don't need to live in the nurse's quarters."

Ken Marino: It was a completely different experience because in "Wet Hot" the movie, we were all kind of stuck in the same place because of the rain and because of the reality of the location and the budget; we were all just staying at the camp in the nurse's quarters and in the bunks. That's what bonded us. I met A.D. Miles the first day. A.D., Amy [Poehler] and myself were the first few people in the bunks. ... I just made lifelong friends. It was just one of those magical, magical kind of times.

Zak Orth: I've never, ever before or since had an experience like that where we're all living in close quarters together and shooting. ... If you had a day off, you went to the set anyway because what the hell else were you going to do?

Joe Lo Truglio: I remember me, A.D. Miles, and Ken Marino and maybe [Bradley] Cooper, after we ate at one of the restaurants there, we're outside, and one of us stepped on a loose rock, and as they stepped on it, farted. Then, miraculously, everyone there did the same thing, had one stored up and was ready to make a spontaneous real fart gag come to life. I was impressed by the gastronomical discipline that everyone had there.

A.D. Miles: I couldn't say anything more to describe it than that documentary ["Hurricane of Fun"] did, which for me, was one of the weirdest things ever. It's so unusual that you would have a picture-perfect time capsule of such an important part of your life. I kind of describe it as like, if you ever go back to your old elementary school, when you walk in the smell hits you and it's kind of like a sensory thing, it brings back the whole vibe of that time in your life, and it's crazy how it can be so visceral. That's how it felt like watching that documentary; suddenly I was just like there again, and I could smell the stinky bunks and cigarette butts and Bushmills, I think, was the liquid of choice at the time.

Janeane Garofalo: There's not one weak link in that chain. You couldn't put together a better guest list for people to be with in the rain and a case of Jack Daniels in a cabin. Honestly, there really is not one person you could say, "Bummer." It was a joyous occasion, I think, for all involved.

Marguerite Moreau: I was definitely seven to ten years younger than everybody else; so my eyes were as big as saucers. ... I think I did the best I could, but it was also the first time I'd ever seen friends work together.

I had started acting when I was twelve so I was always the only kid on set, and it was always adults, professionals, producers, directors, writers. Everybody was an adult except for me.

This was the first time I had worked on a set where everyone was way closer to my age, and they were all friends, and I was like, "Oh, my God, this is the only way to work. This is heaven." The fact that the material was so fantastic was a bonus.

Beer was a great bonder.

Janeane Garofalo: "Isn't this great? We're all friends, and we all like each other." Most of us knew each other, and that's amazing, to be in a movie where I already know everybody. The only ones I didn't know were Chris Meloni who became a friend immediately and Marguerite Moreau, I think. Oh, Elizabeth Banks. Now, did anybody know [Bradley] Cooper, [Amy] Poehler, [Elizabeth] Banks, [Paul] Rudd would go on to be superstars? ...

Who would ever think that that many people from a movie would go on to achieve what fifty-five percent of the SAG [Screen Actors Guild] actor union achieves? It would be unusual enough if one of them went on to the type of stardom that that group has experienced.

So, that is, in and of itself, highly unusual that that many people would go on to be as successful as they are for a sustained amount of time. It's a business that you can be in and out in two seconds.

Joe Lo Truglio: [Paul Rudd's] scene picking up the plate is one of the classic film comedy bits ever. It's just so good. I don't think I was there when he shot it, but I remember hearing about it even then.

Paul Rudd: Well, that's nice to hear. ... I think in the script it said I was kind of annoyed bussing my tray, but I don't remember. It's been so long since I read that script, but I knew that I was gonna bus my tray.

Chris Meloni: They'd be like, "OK, we have a dance routine here, a montage," and I'd go, "OK, so what's the dance?" and they'd go, "We don't know." As I remember it, I choreographed the dance scene. I suggested

a homage to "Kung Fu" where he snatches the M&M from my hand, "... and that's when you will be ready, my son."

Michael Ian Black: I don't really have a performance in "Wet Hot American Summer." I'm literally just hitting marks and saying the words that they gave me. I have no backstory. I really have no characteristics other than I have sex with Bradley Cooper. That's literally the entirety of my character. So I brought nothing to it.

Chris Meloni as Gene

Marguerite Moreau: You're pulling for the professor to get tenure or Beth to get the professor — why do you care? But you do, and I think that's a really fine line, but I think that's a special place that makes people love movies. That's what I love. I want to get my heartstrings tugged, and when I'm really into it, all of the sudden, have it turn and somebody slips on a banana, and I'm almost falling over in my seat.

While "Jane" by Jefferson Starship opens the film, "Wet Hot" is packed with retro sound stylings courtesy of co-composers, Craig Wedren and Teddy Shapiro, longtime State collaborators.

Craig Wedren: Around 1998, Shudder to Think started shifting from making records and touring to film scoring. We did our friend Jesse Parrish's first film and some stuff with the "Velvet Goldmine," and we scored Lisa Cholodenko's first movie, "High Art." When David and Michael started making "Wet Hot," first they hired Teddy [Shapiro] to do it because they knew they wanted to do a more traditional score. I was still unproven in that arena at that point, so I was like, "I can do it. I can do it," and they were like, "We totally want you to do it, but we want

Teddy to be the point-person composer."

He comes from a more traditional conservatory background. I come from more of a pop and punk background, and there's so much crossover.

Theodore Shapiro (co-composer): We're close enough friends that we're able to come in and mess with what the other one is doing in a good way. On "Wet Hot," there'd be a lot of occasions on which I would write something, and then he would come in and go, "Let's get rid of that, and what about this riff?" or "Hey, what about this counter line?" and it's a very nice, good and productive collaborative relationship. He obviously comes from a different background and just thinks differently, and I have to say, after working with him on "Wet Hot," I would definitely start to internalize some of the things that I would anticipate that he would suggest and sometimes add them before he got a chance to tell me to add that.

Craig Wedren: Teddy and I just started hanging out every day, scoring this movie together, and it just turned out to be a really beautiful, highly complementary, collaborative team because our skill sets were so compatible without too much overlap. We wound up writing "Higher and Higher" and a few of the other songs for it.

Theodore Shapiro: We've joked over the years that no matter how many other things we do, we're always going to feel like "Higher and Higher" is our most famous accomplishment for our entire careers.

Craig Wedren: What meager dreams we have!

"Higher and Higher," the pop anthem of the flick, was released on seven-inch vinyl in 2015.

Chris Meloni: I have a rock and roll friend, and he's got all these platinum records on his fucking wall. I want that on my wall.

A.D. Miles: When the movie wrapped, I went up to — I think it was probably Janeane or Zak Orth or a couple of the people who I know had done movies before, and it was the first time I'd ever been in a movie; so I was just like, "Is this unusual? Is this what all the movie sets are like?" and they were like, "Absolutely not, this is one hundred percent lightning in a bottle. This experience was very unique so you should treasure it always." I knew going forward that that was a pretty amazing and unique experience.

Marguerite Moreau: I took a ton of people to see it in Los Angeles, and a lot of them didn't even know The State. We were a huge crew in the one theater in Westwood that doesn't even exist anymore, and there was a fire, and we all had to leave the theater. When we were outside, there was an earthquake. Trying to get people to see this movie was impossible when it came out. So it just seemed like this fun, special thing that we made, and the fact that people connected with it on their own and it became their special thing, that was really unique in and of itself.

Distributed by USA Films on July 21, 2001, "Wet Hot American Summer" initially only made $295,000 in a limited run in theaters.

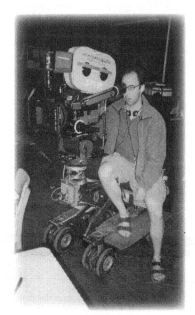

David Wain

David Wain: There was definitely a small but very devoted following from moment one. They essentially wanted to keep it alive, and I was on the same page and really wanted to do whatever I could to help because I believed in the movie and I thought it was great, and if there's a chance it could be seen more or for longer, I support that and will work with that.

Janeane Garofalo: Michael and David have worked tirelessly over the years to keep that thing out there until they paid everybody who lent them money to do it with interest. That was very, very important to them. Seriously, they felt a real moral obligation to everyone who helped them and the people who believed in them to make sure that they made good, honored their transactions with them. A lot of people don't do that. They also believed in it so much that they just kept having surprise showings of it, midnight showings of it, contests of "Dress up as your favorite person," all kinds of stuff until it just grew and grew and grew and grew until Netflix realized it makes sense to do this. It could have just disappeared sort of quietly, and they refused to let that happen. I'm quite thankful that they worked so hard. I'm really grateful to them.

Paul Rudd: It was tremendous. It was such a fun experience for all of us and moving for all of us. I think the shooting of the movie holds such a special place for all of us personally, and over the years people would come up to all of us and just say, "Hey, 'Wet Hot American Summer.'" I think we were aware that "Oh, there are people out there that have a real affection for the movie."

The movie didn't make international stars out of Bradley Cooper, Amy Poehler, Paul Rudd and Elizabeth Banks, but it certainly helped their hipster comedy cred, and it did cause a lot of other cast members to get that, "Hey, aren't you ... ?" thing in airports and restaurants.

David Wain and Amy Poehler

A.D. Miles: I've got friends like Zack Galifianakis that I moved to New York with, who is now one of the biggest comedy movie stars in the world, and Bradley Cooper, who I'm still good friends with from "Wet Hot" and who is probably the biggest movie star in the world. I'll have dinner with those guys, and it's just an incapacitating level of fame as far as trying to enjoy yourself. Maybe twice a month, somebody will come up to me on the subway or the street and say, "Hey, I'm a big fan. I love what you do," which is just the perfect thing to hear on your way to work or when you're out the in the world. It's like, "Oh, this is amazing; thank you so much," but in no way is it intrusive or anything. So "Wet Hot" is something where it has a special place in the hearts of the fans that, when they see someone from the movie, they probably at that point have watched it twenty-five or thirty times; so they really feel like they know you. So it's exciting to see that people still love it so much.

The lines of dialogue that fans repeat ad nauseam could fill another chapter. If Chris Meloni had a dime for every time he heard someone say to him, "dick cream" ...

Chris Meloni: I'd be a wealthy, wealthy man. ... That became the litmus test of, were they really a fan or were they an "SVU" fan? As soon as they went, "Dude, 'Wet Hot American Summer,'" I went, "Oh, OK, I know who you are."

Mitch Reiter: As time passed and it became a college cult favorite, here is my opening line at [Camp Towanda] staff orientation. I say, "By a show of hands, how many of you picked our camp because of 'Wet Hot?'" I'll say about eighty percent of the new people raise their hands. I go, "Bad decision." Everyone laughs. "While we might look like that camp, we don't act like Camp Firewood." Everyone gets a good chuckle out of it — for bragging rights for our staff, and our alumni, they think it's cool.

Rumors swirled for years that "Wet Hot" would have a sequel or become a musical, and David and Showalter were asked about it in nearly every interview they did. A live reading/reenactment with much of the original cast took place at San Francisco Sketchfest in 2012, and in 2013, it was announced that Netflix would air a prequel to the movie as a limited series.

Joe Lo Truglio: The first movie was so precious, and I was worried that [the show] just wouldn't be as good as the first one and that people would be disappointed. Whenever you do a sequel or prequel, you're like, "Man, I just don't want to mess it up and have people say, 'You didn't really need to do that.'"

I had no doubt that David and Mike would write a super-funny script, and they did, but more it was, will it all come together and have that same intangible thing that the first one had that really raised it up? I think it did. There was a moment in this new one, Ken and I did a scene where we're doing a crank call, and I just remember feeling like, "This is funny." I could feel like this is a really fun thing to do, and that was a relief.

Zak Orth: I knew that it was such a transformative experience for everybody that did it, and I knew that, once I knew that everybody was on board to do it, I knew it would be different, because with people's schedules and stuff like that and we weren't going to be living together or anything, but it was the same thing. When I had a day off, I went to set because the people that I love were there.

Ken Marino: Everybody clearly is in different places and can only give so much time. David, the wizard that he is, and Showalter, the wizard that he is, they figured out a way to shoot everybody within the restrictions of everybody's schedule.

A.D. Miles: There were all these different ideas about what it was going to be, and by the time it actually really seemed like it was happening, I'd heard it kind of come and go so many times that I was like, "All right, well, let me know when you start shooting or whatever." I think the emergence of Netflix as an outlet for this kind of stuff is what the game-changer was, and they were able to put the capital into it and give these guys the free rein to let them do what they needed to do to make it authentic to the original. We've done a bunch of these things, like "The Ten," which was a giant ensemble cast and just all the hardships of "Wet Hot" with the nonstop rain. David is this unbelievable force when it comes to crazy variables, unrealistic time schedules, just insane logistics. He not only never waivers in his pressing forward to get it done, but the general overtone of "This is fun. This is silly. We're having a great time," never, never waivers.

Joe Lo Truglio and A.D. Miles on the set of the Netflix series "Wet Hot American Summer: First Day of Camp" in January 2015

I can't honestly put my finger on a single time when David ever seemed frustrated or overwhelmed. If it was an overwhelming situation where we're trying to shoot a campfire scene in pouring down rain, it was more of just a shrug and a laugh and a smile and, "Well, then that's what this is gonna be." When you started looking at the board of the scenes that they wanted to shoot for the series and the schedule for people like Amy Poehler and Bradley and Paul Rudd ... I thought, "It looks impossible, but I have no reason to think it won't come together because it just seems to always come together."

Janeane Garofalo: Nobody is going to say "no" to Michael and David. They're the two nicest guys in the world. I mean that would be terribly ungrateful. Plus, it was really enjoyable. It's not like I've had the career or the sustained success that those guys did; so to me it's like, "Hey, I'm in an A-list vehicle." I'm in a project with big movie stars. I have not been that lucky probably since 2001. To me, it's like, "God, I feel like a real actor again." I'm in a thing that didn't cost five dollars to make that no one will ever see, which is basically what I've been doing for the last twelve years, making Indie films that no one will ever see and failed pilots here and there and some episodic TV shows. That's not me being bitter. I'm saying I got lucky for a brief period of time in the '90s. I'm grateful for it.

I would never be in it if I hadn't been in the first one, and I don't say that sarcastically. I'm being sincere. I am not at a level that would've made it into the Netflix "Wet Hot." I'm not being douche-baggy about it. I'm saying that's the reality. The level of talent they have in the series and the people they brought in that weren't in the first one but are in this mythical first day of camp, that is the A-list that I am nowhere near, and Michael and David would not have given a slot that big to me. They just wouldn't when they have access to what they have access to. There's no way I'd be in this if they weren't obligated to because I was in the first one. They would never admit that's true, but it is true.

[There's] lots of green screen because they didn't have access to everybody at the same time because some of the people were in New York, and some of the people are working nonstop for the next seventy thousand years. Bradley Cooper, Amy Poehler, Paul Rudd, Elizabeth Banks, you only have them for minutes at a time. Not only are they hyper-busy, they have kids and stuff, and they are frequently on different parts of the planet.

Marguerite Moreau: It was super-exciting, but at the same time it was jump on and ride with the best of them. It was just so fun, and everybody is so nice, and nobody's changed. Everybody still brought that great enthusiasm for what they're doing, and that is the most heartwarming thing. ... I asked Elizabeth Banks, "You've gotten to work with so many amazing directors on some really awesome projects, what has been your favorite?" And she said, "My favorite is this." I was like, "Really?" and she said, "Yeah, this is the most fun stuff that I get to do." That says a lot when you have so many amazing experiences and have gotten to travel the world and are like, "Of course I'm coming back to do

'Wet Hot.' Fuck yeah." That's the spirit that I think that whole group of The State embodies.

Chris Meloni: They called me and said, "Hey, we'd love for you to drop by the office so we can discuss your character's arc." I was like, "All right, what do you have to say about Gene's arc?" when they explained to me what it was, I was like, "Oh, my God, OK." I really shouldn't have expected anything less. I was really beyond happy.

One of the things I'm very proud of and also I'm very thankful to the guys was, they sent me the scripts and I read them, and I spoke with [David]. "You know, I think that the fight scene is a little underwritten. I don't mean to be disrespectful, but I just thought that you build Gene up into this Rambo-esque nutcase." I jotted down some notes for him, and to their credit they got a fight choreographer who choreographed the shit out of it, and they shot the hell out of it. It was just fantastic. They took the suggestions in the spirit of "Let's just make it better," and I think they obviously saw the advantages of it. They focused their resources and time to shoot it correctly and to really make it what I thought was just so much fun.

Paul Rudd: I would have liked to have done it for a longer time with more people, but it was a lot of fun. Part of me was a little bit nervous just because you think, "Oh, God, why are we doing this? Why are we revisiting something that people really love?" but when I read [the scripts], I was like, "Oh, my God, these are really, really funny." Again, that's David and Show. They really cracked this, and it's that rare thing.

Cans of vegetables aka Mitch as created by production designer, Mark White

Michael Ian Black: I will say that, in the TV show, fifteen years later, I was more confident in doing nothing. I was more confident in my ability to stand on the mark and say lines and trust that that was what I was supposed to do as opposed to put on a hunchback or fall down or something else. In that respect, I was a little more seasoned.

Mitch Reiter: Me being Mitch that was turned into a can of vegetables, I guess that was their tribute to me.

Joe got to play opposite his wife, Beth Dover, who has popped up in State-related projects like "Children's Hospital" and "Burning Love."

Joe Lo Truglio: I've known how incredibly talented Beth is for eleven years, and now I just get giddy watching everyone finally arrive at the party and be like, "Hey, man, this is all right. She puts out some good sex and knows how to put out some good music, you know." Beth and I have always clicked when we've worked together as actors so I was thrilled and really, really, really happy that David and Michael offered her that role and had as much confidence as I did in her.

Craig Wedren: With every project, David and I seem to up the ante in terms of ambition where it comes to our collaboration. "Wet Hot," the TV show, was definitely the biggest thing we've tried to do. It's four hours' worth of score, in all different genres, twenty-five or thirty new pop songs of the era, originals, a whole musical inside of the show.

David and I are very similar because we grew up together in terms of ambitious thinking and always biting off just a teeny bit more than we can chew. Being perfectionists and slobs at the same time is really great for the product and really frustrating for people we work with. It's sort of highly ambitious and detail-oriented and sometimes sort of careening and chaotic, but it usually comes out really well.

It's really this ongoing, very, very beautiful collaboration. There's so much respect and love there, and even though we certainly both get frustrated with each other's habits or idiosyncrasies, what we make together is just very special. There's really no other director with whom I have enjoyed that level of no-words-necessary, psychic partnership. We have the same tastes. We come from the same place. We grew up eating the same food, drinking the same water and listening to the same music; so when he says, "Green," I know exactly what kind of drum fill and chord that is.

Zak Orth: I learned the lesson that "it doesn't necessarily matter what or where you do what you do, it's who you do it with," and if you can get a group of people that you just have fun with doing stuff, then that's everything. Working with David and Michael and everybody that did "Sex (aka Wieners and Boobs)" and everybody that did the Stella shorts, everybody that did "Wet Hot," we were all so happy to be there that it really taught me that it's who you work with more than anything else.

Mitch Reiter: It's been fun. The old coal shed were Bradley lost his virginity, I guess, is still there. It was falling down then, and now it's really falling down. We've propped it up. We had it on eBay for twenty-five hundred dollars. We did not get a bite for it. It's a giant beehive right now.

We do get phone calls every now and then from "Wet Hot" groupies that would like a tour of camp. We've toyed with the idea of maybe having some kind of fun off-season thing. Maybe that's something that David Wain might want to do, have a reunion there sometime. We're open to it.

The cast of "Sex (aka Wieners and Boobs)"

CHAPTER 27

And Then This Happens

"We sat down and wrote this play about as fast as we could type, which I remember was similar to the feeling that we had when we were staying up and writing The State's Christmas show."

David Wain

Beginning with Stella, the members of The State realized their insular instincts would only take them so far. By befriending and collaborating with other funny people, they began rooting a Comedy Family Tree that would eventually become a lush forest.

But first, let's talk sex, wieners and boobs.

Maria Striar, a friend of Michael Showalter's from Brown University, co-founded a theater company called Clubbed Thumb in New York City. A week before one of their summer 1998 plays was to be staged, it was canceled, leaving the theater dark. Clubbed Thumb offered the slot to Showalter, thinking he or his Stella cohorts might be able to cobble together a quick comedy/variety show.

David Wain: Me, and Joe and Michael said, "No. Fuck it, let's write a play." We sat down and wrote this play about as fast as we could type, which I remember was similar to the feeling that we had when we were staying up and writing The State's Christmas show, my first State show.

Joe Lo Truglio: The more legendary thing about the play is the name. A few days after Maria made that official call, she called Showalter back and said, "We need to put an ad in the paper and there's a deadline." We didn't really have the play quite yet. We just had a title that people would want to see, "Sex (aka Wieners and Boobs.)" Any of the three of us would go see a play like that. Once we got the ad out there, we just had to decide what the story was.

We first thought of a story arc, a simple one, a very common one, one that we could branch off: "High Noon," a new sheriff in town story. That's really all we had.

From there, we gathered some ideas from State stuff that we never used. There's also some stuff that we used from Stella. ... We had this time crunch [so we took] all these funny ideas, funny characters and scenarios and kind of threw them into this spine of "High Noon."

Eventually we began to flesh them out in a more narrative way. We used improv games that the guys used in Stella a couple times, and once we had that basic outline that's when we started going to our cast.

We went to Todd Holoubek and a few other friends of ours. We know we wanted some music throughout the whole play, and Peter Salett was doing a lot of music at the time. Our friend, Shari Albert, really funny from NYU, then Nina Hellman, who was also a good friend of ours and in many respects, an honorary State member. Once we had those folks, we started to play to their strengths and write some material that we knew they would be able to do well. We worked on some dance choreography because we figured the more we throw at the wall, something would stick.

We had these characters. We had some improv games. Let's get some music. We'll get a couple songs in here. How about some really dumb dancing? We'll get a strobe light in. Strobe lights are always good. We started to just pepper the show with gadgetry and smoke and mirrors around what we hoped would be a very funny arc.

Michael Showalter: That took on a whole life of its own.

Zak Orth: One night, we were at a party, and Showalter was like, "Do you want to be in a play?" and I was like, "Yeah, sure, that sounds great. When?" and he said, "Tomorrow." So, we rehearsed for a couple of days and then we put on "Sex (aka Wieners and Boobs)."

Todd Holoubek: I had more fun on that than I had in a long time. It was one of those things that everybody, even to this day is like, "Wow, let's do that again!" but it will never recapture that initial glory.

There was a lot of freedom. Everything you wanted to do, the answer was, "Yes," which was interesting because all of the sudden you had to make your own decision. You couldn't just throw out a bullshit idea and hope somebody else supports it. The answer you knew was yes. So we were like, "Do I really want to do that?"

Joe Lo Truglio: The whole energy of the show was the energy eight-year-olds would have if they're in the living room putting on a show for their parents. It was very silly. It was absurd at points, but it

Sho, Joe and David wrote the play "Sex (aka Wieners and Boobs)"
in just a few days.

was fun. We just wanted to have that energy that we slapped it together. We played to that strength because it was really the only choice we had. It ended up working very well for the show.

David Wain: It was the first time I ever worked with Zak Orth, and I think it's when I first met Paul Rudd.

Paul Rudd: As soon as [Zak and I] finished shooting ["Romeo and Juliet"], we came back to New York, and he said, "You wanna go see this play that my friends wrote? ... It's the guys from The State." I said, "I know those guys. Those guys are funny."

I thought it was hilarious. One of the things I thought was so great was in the middle of this ridiculous play, they just break into a scene from "Glengarry Glen Ross," and it goes on for a while. It was really dramatic, and it had nothing to do with anything. "Oh, this is so my kind of play."

Nina Hellman: We did it at SF Sketchfest a few years ago! We did a revival. It was great.

Joe Lo Truglio: What was great about that production, besides the original cast for the most part, was that because we didn't really have time to rehearse it, we were limited to two run-throughs, and then we had to do it. We ended up using three teleprompters at the base of the stage, which gave it an element of "SNL." We remembered a lot of what we did, but every now and then we'd have to glance at the teleprompters, which added to the whole "doing a show in your family's living room at eight years old" feel. It was very sloppy but fun energy.

Nina Hellman: We did it again in January; then we did it in L.A. one time, and then a year later we did it again. It was just like this thing that never ended, but those were really, really, good, fun times. We were such a tight, tight group. We went to the beach together all day, and then we would do the show, and then we would hang out all night.

Joe, David and Michael get notified by the publishing company whenever someone pays for the rights to perform "Sex (aka Wieners and Boobs)," so they've attended other productions.

Joe Lo Truglio: The three of us are still excited that people are still doing the play. It's quite amazing for a play that was literally written in two or three days, [and] thirteen years later it's still being produced.

Michael Showalter: Another thing that's cool about seeing it performed is seeing other people trying on the sense of humor, almost like a pair of pants. They're trying on the comedy and are like, "Oh, wow, this is funny the way it feels to do these jokes." It's like having somebody trying your food. "Tastes pretty good, doesn't it?"

I'm making at least one hundred fifty dollars a year off of it.

Together, the produced screenplays of Robert Ben Garant and Thomas Lennon have grossed more than

$1 billion, including the mega popular "Night at the Museum" trilogy as well as the Lindsay Lohan opus "Herbie: Fully Loaded."

"Ben Garant and Tom Lennon wrote that hilarious book, 'Writing for Fun and Profit.' They are absolutely right about every single thing they say in that," Janeane Garofalo said. "You either make your peace with it and take the money or don't do it. Because it's incredibly emotionally taxing to be stressed like that, and have your creativity censored and have the product suck sometimes. All you did was try and make it good but your name is on it."

Over fifteen years, Ben and Tom have written roughly forty screenplays together, and eleven of them have been produced. Mike Jann was partially responsible for the pair's writing partnership.

Thomas Lennon: Mike Jann had been hired to adapt and direct this book called "You Are Going to Prison." It was written by a guy named Jim Hogshire who had been in prison three times. It was just a manual on how to deal with being in prison. It was for a company called Beacon Pictures, and Scott Lew was the executive on it. Mike brought us in. He's like, "Look, I write a little bit, but two of my best friends and two of the most prolific writers of The State are really great, and I want to bring them in on this project to write with me." We owe a lot to Mike because Mike brought us into that one hundred percent. But then an interesting thing happened, which is we'd talked about it a little bit and started working on it a tiny bit, and Mike went away to make "Drop Dead Gorgeous."

Mike Jann ended up using Tom's voice as the cameraman in the mockumentary "Drop Dead Gorgeous," a little film with a growing cult of fans.

Michael Patrick Jann: It's a funny thing, in the same way that the devoted following of The State is younger than The State, I think so is the following for that movie. The first time I went into meet with the people at New Line [Cinema], as it existed then, to talk to them about that movie, they're twenty-six years old, I said, "This is a movie for very unhappy thirteen-year-old girls who think Hollywood is bullshit." That was my lead. It's shocking that they gave me the movie to direct because that was literally my thought from the beginning, and that was the movie I set out to make, for a group of people who were like, "I fucking hate you people."

Joshua Grannell aka Peaches Christ: In the old days, a cult movie found its audience on the midnight movie circuit, like "Pink Flamingos" or "Eraserhead." But in the last twenty, thirty years, with home video and cable television, a lot of these cults are built in people's living rooms. I think "Drop Dead Gorgeous" is the perfect example of that. And the reason I wanted to do a drag tribute to the film is that it's so wonderfully transgressive, unapologetically offensive and extreme. It's good camp. There are tons of "campy" movies, but only a few are actually good and wicked the way that "Drop Dead Gorgeous" is. I love this movie.

Meanwhile, Tom and Ben were learning the really hard way how to write a movie.

Robert Ben Garant: [Tom and I] had the exact same sense of humor. It was natural for us to start writing together. We'd never written a screenplay before, and we didn't write an outline at all. We just sat down and started writing it. "Page one, OK...." We did it the exact wrong way to do it. "OK, I guess we should meet our main character first, right?" "Yeah."

We would get to certain points in the script, like where our main character is arrested, and we just sat looking at each other. We had no idea. "Now what happens?" "Well, Jesus, he would really lose his shit, wouldn't he?" "Well, yeah." We didn't think ahead at all so it was very intimidating. I remember being really intimidated by the idea of having to write something that was one hundred pages. I thought that was going to be impossible. It was really hard to try to sit down and just go through it day by day. ... We trudged our way through it, page by page, and it was really not fun and really hard.

One of the reasons Tom and I wrote a screenwriting book is because [other books] don't really talk about outlining either. Most of them talk about how to come up with your story, but they don't really talk about what's the best way to sit down and write the damn thing.

Their first screenplay collaboration, "Let's Go to Prison," wasn't the first of their movies released. "Taxi" with Jimmy Fallon was a big hit. "The Pacifier" with Vin Diesel and "Herbie" all came out before "Prison," giving the pair some cachet in Hollywood.

Thomas Lennon: We never sit in a room and just pound our heads against a wall. We never stand at a computer together. When we need to talk about things, we meet socially in a bar. We'll do that for several hours, but we'll never meet in a conference room. We'll never meet at my desk. We sit in a bar as if we're ex-pats in Paris in the '30s, and we'll have a glass of wine and talk about stuff.

We don't do any of the drudgery of writing together because we've done it so well for so long that I think we've figured out a lot of the pitfalls of how to not grow to hate your writing partner. Writing partners, it's as hard as a marriage, except with more money at stake. There's a lot to be figured out about it, and we don't ever fight. All of our disagreements happen in the work, where if he writes something and I think I have something better, I'll change it, and I'll put in what I have that I think is better. But we don't discuss it. ... The only trick about that is you have to be very altruistic, and you have to recognize if the other person's work is better, leave it. You have to put your ego aside sometimes.

Robert Ben Garant: I think there's some areas where I go a little broader and some areas where he goes a little broader, but we have very similar senses of humor. We both work our ass off. We both really write a lot and ... neither one of us never fights for something because we wrote it. Neither of us ever pulled the, "Trust me, this will work" card. ... We're just, "This is a joke, and if you don't think it's funny, then we're 50/50, and we can either argue about it, or we can write another joke."

We're both willing to throw stuff away, and neither of us are precious about our material.

Thomas Lennon: He's one of the most dedicated, hardworking people I've ever met. I trust him implicitly. ... We've pitched more than anyone you've ever met, and there's something to be said about that because a lot of a pitch is like doing a two-person improv and someone having your back, someone that you feel very comfortable like on a trapeze with who you know is going to catch you. That is a very valuable thing. If we dive into a bit, you know that the other guy has your back and is going to play along, and we never question the other one.

He's the only person I've ever met in my entire life who has the identical work ethic to me, which is a lot of what it's about. The other part of the partnership is I'm usually trying to keep up with him, which makes me better. ... I think both of us also genuinely see that there is a big picture that we are part of, and us being unified is way, way more valuable than us being divided.

Ben and Tom experimented with the world of independent film with "Hell Baby," a horror-comedy that they co-wrote, directed and performed as ass-kicking Italian exorcists. It's a criminally-underseen effort starring Rob Corddry, Riki Lindhome and Keegan-Michael Key. Tom and Ben wrote the wacky neighbor role for Key.

Keegan Michael-Key: I don't think that's something that I knew, but that's very flattering; that's nice to hear. We had an amazing time and once again, another experience where it was a lot of improv. We had so much fun.

Rob Corddry: I think [Tom and Ben] have the same philosophy that I have. We have a script, and we're very happy with it, but we also have cast some of the best improvisers working today, so it'd be silly not to let them use their talents. On "Hell Baby," Rob Huebel and Paul Scheer, as the cops, made me laugh the hardest. It was hardest not to break during their scenes because they were always different and just hilarious. I would love to see an uncut version of that first interrogation scene in the house. It was so funny. It was one of the funniest days I've ever had on set.

Riki Lindhome: I tested for a show that Tom and Ben were doing against Natasha Leggero, who got the part. Tom called me afterward, and he was like, "I'm going to write something for you, I promise," and I was like, "Cool." Then two years later, "Hey, do you want to do this thing?" and I took a night to think about it because it's a pretty intense part, and then I called him up, and I was like, "Yep." So that was my first real time working with them.

I remember the day it came out on iTunes, it wasn't even featured.

Thomas Lennon: I thought it was a really funny, interesting, tiny movie that we made with some friends for two million bucks, and it literally never came out at all. It came out on five actual screens, one of which was in Lubbock, Texas, I'm told. It was crazy-odd. I remember being at Sundance. We'd show the movie. It would get great reactions, huge laughs beginning to end, and then I would go back to the condo we were staying in and would look it up, and I'd read the meanest, shittiest review of anything we'd ever done that same night. ... "Fuck this, while giant studios are breaking our heart, indies are breaking our heart, too. So fuck it. I'm going to back to L.A., and I'm going to get a fucking cushy TV job if I can." About six days later, I got an offer for "Sean Saves the World," and I took it.

Robert Ben Garant: "Hell Baby" is mostly Tom. We did something different. We both decided to write an entire draft. Tom wrote the first draft of "Hell Baby" and then gave it to me and I tweaked it. Then I wrote a movie called "Action Number One" that is still sort of in development.

Tom and I were both a little bit like baffled and beat up by the fact that critics hated it so much. Critics really killed it because critics started attacking it before it had distribution. ... In the old days, when they worked for newspapers, they weren't writing for themselves, but they were writing for the people in their town of Orlando, Florida. They couldn't just be snobs and hate everything. They had to tell you "What

I liked about 'Pacifier' and what I didn't like about 'Pacifier,'" and now it's just a bunch of bitter people who are really, really critical about stuff that's not smarty-pants.

Returning the favor, Lindhome and Natasha Leggero cast Tom in the pilot for "Another Period," a "Downton Abbey" spoof for Comedy Central. Initially, Joe played Riki's husband, but once the pilot was picked up, he was already on Fox's "Brooklyn Nine-Nine," so David obliged and joined the cast.

Riki Lindhome: Tom is just amazing in everything. He's the only person I've ever met that can improvise in 1902 slang, off the top of his head. He just makes up words, and they just sound like they're phrases. He's just goes, "Wet Christmas, it's a scandal!" and you're like, "Is Wet Christmas a thing?" and he's like, "No." Or he goes, "Scott's Froghat," and you're like, "That sounds like it's a thing," and it's not.

Michael Ian Black on my show is just so amazing. We wrote that for him from the beginning. We knew as far as pitch goes, it was a weird show to sell. ... We were like, "Who could play this?" and in a second we thought of Michael. We wrote it in his voice, and crossed our fingers and hoped he would and felt very lucky when he did.

I basically want every cast member from The State to be on "Another Period." That would be my dream come true. ... When I saw "The State" I was like, "That's what I want to do." That's what made me go into comedy. I remember [the sketch with] the tacos in the mail, and in the end the guy disappears, and the mailbox starts moving. I was like, "Oh, you can do anything. I want to live in that world. You can just do whatever you want if it makes you laugh. I want to do that." It was always in the back of my mind and to get to work with those guys. Now it's a little surreal.

Michael Ian Black: Nothing makes me happier than feeling a part of a kind of larger comedic community and feeling like other people think I belong within it. It's something that, as The State, we didn't have. We didn't know anybody else when we were The State. All we knew were ourselves, and it's taken this many years to feel like, "Oh, yeah, there's this whole other world out there of really funny, awesome people, and they like us," and that's a great feeling.

When it came time to direct his second feature, David collaborated on the script with Ken Marino. "The Ten" takes on "Thou shall not kill" and the other nine Commandments.

Ken Marino: David had an idea of doing ten sketches loosely based on the Ten Commandments as maybe a State movie. That was never embraced, or there was no movement on that within the group. This was kind of around the dark times of The State. We were at Kerri's wedding, and we're like, "Hey, let's write something together." Because he lived on the East Coast and I lived on the West Coast, we said, "Let's just lock ourselves in a room for seven days and work twelve hours a day and come out with a first draft." The first attempt at that was sort of a baby step, which is it became a sketch movie as opposed to a linear story.

David Wain: It was a fun way to bang something out. I think it gave the script some of its whimsical feel.

Ken Marino: "The Ten" was an experiment. We're like — and I'm not saying this was a great idea — "Let's not go through anybody. Let's filter this through me and you, and let's try to make this movie without changing it, without anybody giving notes." That's what we did, and it is a pure swing at doing an omnibus movie that is simply filtered through Dave's and my head.

David Wain: We did write it thinking, "Let's write something we think is funny and not worry about what an audience or a financier might think of it." We were often surprised when we were shooting it that anyone had put any money behind it.

I just wanted to make a movie that I would want to rent when I was in college, where I can get a little stoned and watch "Kentucky Fried

Movie" or "Amazon Women on the Moon." Let's do our version of that. The problem with doing that is the movie has no heart. It's simply jokes, and I think when you do something like "Children's Hospital," which is fifteen minutes long, that's fine. But when you do a ninety-minute movie, you need something else to hang it on other than just absurdity and jokes. Otherwise, people start to get a little annoyed. In fact, we address it at that end of the movie. There's a big song and dance number at the end where we talk about what's this movie about and we're like, "It's all about love" because it wasn't about anything. We're like, "Let's give it heart just by saying it's all about love."

When we were writing it, we were like, "What is this movie about? It's about nothing. Fuck you." Those were the original lyrics, and I was like, "We can't, after asking somebody to watch a movie for ninety minutes, then say to them, 'Fuck you,'" so we 180'd on that and said it was all about love and kind of winked about the fact that we're trying to make it about something when it obviously wasn't.

While writing "The Ten" between coasts, Ken also wrote "Diggers," a blue-collar dramedy about Long Island clammers in the '70s. Paul Rudd costarred in the film before taking on the role of narrator in "The Ten."

Paul Rudd: Ken's one of my best friends. He's really talented, really funny, loves a good bit and is a really passionate guy. When it comes to whatever it is he's working on, whether he's writing it, or directing it or acting in it, he puts everything that he is into it. He's another guy that will just crush me; he's so funny.

Ken Marino: Rudd, he's sort of Waino's muse. I think Rudd is super-funny, crazy-talented and just like a great guy. When I wrote my first script, which was, without question, fueled by the same competitive drive that happened in The State, the reason I wrote a script in the first place was other members of The State were writing scripts, and I was like, "Well, if they can do it, I can do it." I wrote "Diggers," which I set out to be a big, broad comedy and turned out to be this slice-of-life little dramedy. I went to Paul, and I remember him reading it and being like, "Absolutely,

I'll do it" and being really wonderful about it. Paul is a special guy.

"The Ten" is almost a State reunion.

Ken Marino: We tried to get everybody in there, even just for a photo in the final vignette about the guys naked listening to Roberta Flack. There's just a photo of Michael Jann. So we wanted everybody to be represented in some way because Mike couldn't make it out.

Q&A with David on "The Ten"

As a kid, what was the first thing you remember about the Ten Commandments?

David: I guess I saw them in temple as a kid. I thought, "I don't understand those Roman numerals. Somebody is gonna have to explain them to me." I still don't understand them. I know the V is like five; that's all I know.

What did you think when you discovered what the ten represent?

David: I figured that's a good idea. Ten's a good number. Ten rules to follow. Some of them are a little amorphous. "Honor your father and mother." How do you know if you're actually doing that? You get some wiggle room.

Was it originally done as a goof, or was it always going to be a serious motion picture?

David: I don't think it is a serious motion picture.

It was hard to catch and write as I was watching the movie. Can you pronounce the fast food chains mentioned in there?

David: McDownalds. Bwerger King. Woundys.

Woundys?

David: Mmhmm.

Have you considered yourself a coveter?

David: I've coveted. I've more probably coveted my neighbor's wife more than thy goods.

Did you rank what you thought were the more serious commandments?

David: No, we didn't think about it like that. We didn't really pay much attention to the proper order. In fact, in the rap song at the end we have a line that says, "Is that really their actual order?"

Are you a fan of production numbers in films?

David: I'm actually not, especially in comedies. We've seen them before. It's not the freshest way to end a movie. To be honest, with a movie with ten stories like this, you had to do something that made you very aware that it was over. I feel like that was the best way to do it. We tried to give it that live-show look.

Pre-production on "Role Models" with Paul Rudd and Seann William Scott was already underway when a new director was needed. David came aboard only a couple weeks before filming.

David Wain: It was terrifying. I had just made "The Ten," but it was never even intended to be super-successful. I got this call from Paul saying, "The director has dropped out. Do you want me to give them your name?

Paul had already done a draft of it, and I still felt like "Wow, it's just so far away from the kind of tone ... I don't know if I would know how to do this." When you sign on to make a movie as a director, you're talking about living and breathing that thing 24/7 for eighteen months or

Frequent collaborators, Paul Rudd and David Wain

more. It's a big commitment. I was really scared about it. On the other hand, this is an opportunity to get in and make a studio movie, which I don't know how many of those are going to come around.

I had already planned on going on this rafting trip with my friend where I wouldn't have my phone for days so that was kind of perfect timing to completely unhook and think about this. "It's good money. It's a good opportunity, but I don't know...." But when I got back, they were like, "OK, you're going to do it. Let's start tomorrow at...." It wasn't really asking me whether I would take the job was part of anyone's vocabulary. I jumped in literally the next day and just hit the ground running.

I remember calling my wife, girlfriend at the time, saying, "I don't know what I'm going to do. Can I quit? I'm miserable." By the end of the six weeks, we had gotten to a script we were pretty happy with, and we had gotten the team sort of gelled back together, we were kind of ready to do it, and the shoot itself actually went pretty well.

Paul Rudd: I feel a real partnership with [David] that has certainly grown over the years. ... One of David's gifts is really being cool under pressure. The mood of a set is always determined by the director. Even with "Wet Hot American Summer," where this is his first movie and it rained every single day except for three, and instead of freaking out, he was laughing and going, "OK." He was very calm and said, "We'll work around it; we'll figure it out." He was unflappable in his demeanor. He was doing all of his work but creating this vibe of a party. I've worked with him on other things where I know stuff is happening behind the scenes or from a studio level, and he never seems to get his feathers ruffled; he never loses his patience. He's always making some kind of joke, and it makes for a really pleasurable working experience.

Paul has also starred in David's other feature films "Wanderlust" and "They Came Together." Surprisingly, Paul didn't guest-star on the Adult Swim TV show David co-created with Rob Corddry, "Children's Hospital," which ended on April 22, 2016, after seven seasons.

David Wain: There was a writers' strike, and Corddry had this idea for a web series. ... I liked Rob because I'd worked with him on "The Ten" and thought he was great, but his pitch, honestly, it was not exciting to me. His pitch was one line, "It takes place in a children's hospital, and it's fun." My first impression was, "What exactly is funny about a children's hospital?" It's one of the least funny areas imaginable.

Rob Corddry: My daughter hurt herself. I was bringing her to Children's Hospital here in L.A., Sitting in the waiting room, it struck me as the least funny place I'd ever been in my whole life. I thought, "Well, it'd be kind of funny to have a 'Grey's Anatomy'-type show where beautiful people just have sex in the workplace but the workplace is dedicated to healing children.

David Wain: On the strength of loving Rob, I basically said, "I'm happy to help out. I'll come work on it with you." I helped work on the script. ... Lo and behold, they made a deal, and it got picked up, and it turned into an actual series on Adult Swim. Then I started really being more full time helping around the show, writing, directing, producing and, quickly I started to really appreciate how much fun it is.

Rob Corddry: Ken and Lake Bell were the first two I'd cast. We were even toying around with Ken playing both he and Rob Huebel's role. He would just have a mustache for one of them. I think I came to my senses and said, "Why don't we get Rob Huebel?"

For our first season, it was a five-minute web series. ... It didn't seem like the kind of comedy that we/you would want to watch for over fifteen minutes, let alone write. We've done two double episodes now, and they're fun and challenging in their own way, but it's really just confirmation that there's no reason to do it any longer than fifteen minutes.

David Wain: It's an eleven-minute show and having that sandbox to play in and those lines to color in, it's so much fun. We try to write these epic scripts with multiple subplots and a lot going on and often the same number of scenes and the same number of production elements as would be in an hour-long show, but we just squeeze, squeeze, squeeze.

I wrote the one that shows an entire year over one episode, and there's another one that I wrote about a country weekend, which has a bunch of different plots going on. To me, how much can you squeeze into eleven minutes is a lot of fun. Once you get to the edit, you have to continue to snip it down, down, down, down, down, more than you ever thought you could. The worst thing in comedy is when you outstay your welcome. So I like eleven minutes.

Rob Corddry: It's all been pretty surreal with all the guest stars. We have a lot of people that we've admired for years, like Marla Gibbs is on this season. Ernie Hudson was on a couple of years ago. That was pretty cool, the black Ghostbuster. We had Barry Bostwick on this year and Shirley Jones. We ended up cutting the whole bit, but Marsha Brady (Maureen McCormick) was on, and I'd come into the makeup room just to say "Hi." I'm totally flashing back to my grade school crush, flirting with Marsha Brady.

David Wain: Last season I got to be in bed with Cheryl Tiegs. That was pretty awesome.

Michael Showalter's second directorial feature — after 2005's "The Baxter" — was released on March 11, 2016. "Hello, My Name is Doris" is a rom-com starring national treasure, Sally Field.

Michael Showalter: I've been a fan of hers forever; so it was really intimidating to work with her but also like a hugely exhilarating and this amazing learning experience for me. I had a blast working with her; I felt like we really had a pretty close relationship on the project. Her character is front and center in every scene in the movie and has a lot of, goes through a lot of stuff emotionally as a character, and so we really worked together the way an actor and a director sometimes do.

Showalter has gravitated to more behind-the-scenes roles lately, producing and writing TV shows and movies. He's not opposed to appearing in front of the camera, but his passions currently lie behind the scenes.

Michael Showalter: I'm about to direct this movie which is written by Kumail Nanjiani and his wife, Emily Gordon. It's a true story about their relationship, and it's a kind of pretty amazing true story. It's being produced by Judd Apatow, which is exciting to work with him and his group of people. Our other producer is Barry Mendel who has worked with Judd a lot but who has also produced a bunch of Wes Anderson movies. It's just been a really interesting and cool experience so far.

I've always enjoyed historical movies. I would love to do a period comedy, like a Jane Austen kind of movie, something that's set in the 19th century or the 18th century. ... I like the dramedy genre in general. I like a mix of serious and comedic. I've done so much silly comedy, although I hope to be doing "Wet Hot" forever.

Kevin Allison performs at Festival Supreme in October 2014.

CHAPTER 28

Risky Business

"I realize that I get to be
funny now, and I get to be
serious and emotional in the
job that I'm doing. The most
rewarding thing is that people
write back that the show has
changed their lives."

Kevin Allison

For someone who tells stories for a living, it took Kevin Allison a long time to find his voice. It was hidden beneath layers of Midwestern, traditional values; Catholicism; shame — and Frankenstein's creature.

Not that Kevin didn't let his freak flag fly. He was always the first to streak a party, but that was after enough beer and shots to at least present the illusion that it was the liquor doing the pants-dropping. Internally, there was that hint of guilt — and perhaps his mother's voice — sneaking through.

"Nonconformist" was a dirty word, according to Kevin's mom, but it fit Kevin like a snug pair of assless chaps.

"My becoming a comedian when I was a little kid, the class clown, was a way of dealing with the fact that I knew something very weird was inside me," Kevin said.

For more than a decade after "The State" went off the air, Kevin struggled to find the right outlet for his "silly, perverted, oddball self." While his former cohorts were building a cadre of comedians to work with via Stella, Kevin was struggling to squeeze his square peg into Hollywood's round hole.

He waited tables to pay the bills and struggled with bitterness and resentment at the business and his past stage partners. Beginning in 1996, Kevin began penning one-man shows packed with kooky characters, such as a guy who's convinced he's Charles Manson, a tragicomic take on Frankenstein's monster and a plastered Peter O'Toole type.

"He was a Shakespearian actor who was supposed to be doing a scene from 'Hamlet,' but he was clearly just so fucking drunk, so alcoholically beside himself, that he couldn't make it through the scene," Kevin said.

Fed up and broke, Kevin left performing arts at the turn of the century to work as an editor for various publications. For five years, he didn't set foot in front of an audience. An invitation from the website, Mediabistro, to teach a sketch comedy class got Kevin to put aside built-up stage fright and social anxiety. The class was packed with State fans who remembered him fondly.

"For the first time ever, I was standing in front of an audience where I could be totally absurdist, goofy and ridiculous one moment and then be completely heartfelt and completely emotionally vulnerable and raw the next," Kevin said.

Being Kevin in front of a class was one hurdle, but doing the same in front of a paying crowd is another. He used regained confidence to try yet another one-man show filled with veiled versions of himself, called "F*** Up."

"I felt like it was really ballsy of me to be putting a show like that together, admitting, 'Yes, I kind of fell off the face of the Earth. Yes, I'm trying to get back on this horse. Let's have a little reckoning of what happened to...'"

"F*** Up" was performed at San Francisco Sketchfest in 2008 for a handful of people, including Michael Ian Black. Kevin was mortified to face his friend after the show, especially after some technical hiccups caused him to scream his lines, literally begging to be heard.

"It was classic Kevin Allison insanity: a bunch of really extreme characters, doing really extreme things, and it was entertaining," Black said. "Knowing Kevin and knowing the real insanity that is his life, it seemed to me that it would be a much richer vein if he started telling his own stories, true stories."

Kevin asked, "'What did you think of the show?' and Black said, "I feel like the audience just wanted you to drop the act and start speaking from your heart as yourself."

"What I literally said to him was, 'Oh, God. Fuck. I feel like me, real, raw Kevin Allison, is too many weird things that don't add up in a way that a Hollywood agent or a Hollywood executive would understand, or think that the country would understand. For example, I'm too gay and raunchy but at the same time too friendly and polite and a Catholic boy from Ohio. I'm too in-your-face, wildly absurdist, but at the same time I'm also very serious and intellectual and psychological sometimes," Kevin said.

"I just feel like trying to be myself on stage would shoot me in the foot. It just feels too risky.'"

Michael said, "That's the word. If it feels risky, then you're probably onto something actually. If it feels risky, you're probably opening up a bit, and I bet an audience would start opening up to you."

Kevin was thirty-nine.

Kevin Allison: I've spent most of my life starving. I've spent most of my life without health insurance, without any savings, etc. I might go on like this until the day I die. I might as well say, "Fuck it," and pursue being balls-out as a performer and being as true to myself as I can. I was finally ready to hear Michael's words, "Just say, 'Fuck it,' and get up on stage and be yourself." At this point, what have I got to lose?

Michael Ian Black: That's an uncomfortable conversation to have with somebody right after you've seen him perform, but I felt like he needed to hear it. His character work was fine and funny, but there was no depth to it, and his own life is so rich that I just felt like he should take a chance and start looking at that stuff.

Kevin Allison: I went back to New York City, and I called Margot Leitman because I knew she [and Giulia Rozzi] had this show called "Stripped Stories," where people told true stories about their sex lives. I thought, "Wouldn't it be really risky if I told a story about the first time I tried prostituting myself, my first attempt at working as a hustler, right before The State was picked up for series by MTV?" The day of the show, I called Margot, and I said, "I don't think I can do this. This feels too graphic, and it's too icky; it's too vulnerable. I just feel like it's too risky." She said, "Oh, my God, that's great news!"

Margot Leitman: I understood that everybody's life was going to go on after they told the story. In fact, some people's lives would even get better. We had couples that had met at the show, and two guests fell in the love at the show after they each had really raw performances. Kevin was maybe about the third person in a row that panicked a day or two before the show and said, "I don't want to do this." It was something I kept hearing about his fear of being himself, and he just couldn't, and I got on the phone with him and was like, "You just have to dive into this fear and see what happens."

Kevin Allison: I was like, "All right, all right, you've convinced me." So I got up on stage that night, and I told this story about attempting to prostitute myself when I was twenty-two years old, and to my surprise, it was like night and day. I thought everyone in that audience was going to be like, "Ugh, he's too annoyingly gay and yet kind of emotional and yet too absurdist at times and too this, too that, too the other."
My own mother's voice in my head: "You run up the stairs too much like a girl. You use too much facial expression. You use too much of the

range of your voice, etc." She used to tell me that kind of stuff all the time; so that's what I thought was going to come back at me, and frankly, that's probably what I thought that the executives back at MTV and everyone else always thought of me.

When I told this story that night, I was amazed because for the first time I was actually looking into the eyes of individual audience members. It wasn't like where I was reciting someone's lines. I was literally conversing with the audience, and I noticed that some people were giving me really positive feedback. Then I noticed that I had to try to win some other people over. I just started to feel this electrical connection to the audience. "Oh, wow, they're really listening. They really know that I'm going out on a limb here." They were laughing and following me, and I could just feel the listening in the room had an energy that was totally different than when I was up there reciting lines as Frankenstein's monster or a Jewish comedian from the '20s.

Margot Leitman: I believe it was the first time he told a story onstage, and he was himself, and he was wonderful. He was awesome. He killed. And everyone loved him. And his life the next day was not cut short by doing that.

Kevin Allison: After the show, people weren't just coming up to me and saying, "That was funny," but saying things like, "Well, I've never prostituted myself, but that emotion you expressed totally reminded me of something that happened between me and my mother when I was in the seventh grade."

What happens when you share true stories on stage is people often won't be able to relate to the specifics of what you went through, but because you hit on such an honest examination of some of your emotional reactions to things, it strikes a chord with people. It's a little bit different from fiction, and I really felt like, "Whoa, I have hit on something here, and Mike is right; I have endless stories about ridiculous shit I've done."

The word "risk" was used by both Michael Black and Margot Leitman. So Kevin decided he was going to create a show called "Risk!" where people's true stories would run the gamut from hysterical to heartbreaking to horrifying. Yes, there was already "This American Life," but like the stories themselves, the show would be uncensored — perfect for a podcast.

Kevin Allison: I knew from those twelve years of going nowhere with my career that if you give me the opportunity to be either too lazy or too scared to follow through with something, I will take that opportunity. But I figured, if I created a podcast, then every week people would be writing to me saying, "Wait, where the hell is the episode?" Indeed, to this day, we're still late a day or two sometimes, and believe me, there are a lot of responses from people, "Where the fuck is it?"

I knew that this would be good for me to start exploring being myself on stage, but I didn't yet realize how it would also turn me into a little bit of a therapist and a coach. I'll say something like, "Hey, Toronto, we're coming into town. Who's got a story?" and a fan will write back, "Well, I was molested from the time I was five 'til the time I was eight." I'll know that I'm going to have to spend some serious time on the phone or on email helping that person walk through it.

I realize that I get to be funny now, and I get to be serious and emotional in the job that I'm doing. The most rewarding thing is that people write back that the show has changed their lives. A young woman wrote to us the other day, "I know I wasn't supposed to be listening to 'Risk!' when I was fourteen years old because I know it's not for kids, but I'm seventeen now, and I was sexually assaulted. I was raped six months ago, and I knew after it happened that I had to go get help. I knew where I had to go get help. I knew I had to alert the police. ... I knew all this stuff, and I had the wherewithal to do it because I learned what adult life is actually like from listening to 'Risk!' all those years."

We had a man write to us that his son was lost to heroin, only nineteen years old. He said, "I couldn't break through to him. I couldn't relate to him. He wouldn't listen to anything I was saying, and then one day, I was like, 'I want you to listen to this episode of this podcast with me.'" He played the episode called "Under the Influence," which is all drug stories, and typical of any "Risk!" episode, there is one really funny one, there's one scary one, and there's one that's tear-jerking. He said it was after he listened to that episode with his son that he finally had a breakthrough with his son and said, "My son is now off of heroin, and I feel like that episode of 'Risk!' was what helped the gateway to getting there."

Anyone could create a podcast, but turning said podcast into a viable business where you can do it full time and not starve is not so easy. "Risk!" was growing a following, but it was still just monthly and needed a better presence on the web and someone to organize the logistics of live shows. Enter Kevin's eventual producer/best friend JC Cassis, a New York City-based musician.

JC Cassis: I watched "The State" since I was a little girl. I loved it, and I'd just never forgotten all the crazy sketches and all the funny lines and characters.

I started looking into podcasts and saw "Risk!" hosted by Kevin Allison ... and I was like, "This is amazing. I'm so glad that Kevin is doing something and is still as funny and ridiculous as ever." Then I started following him on Twitter and Facebook and ... I wrote him a Facebook message. "I'm so glad to see that things are going well for you and that you've found a partner. How great! I love the work on 'The State,' and I just started listening to 'Risk!' and it's so great, and I hope you're well." Then I saw a Tweet from him a little while later saying, "Seeking an assistant, email me if you're interested." I thought, "It's never going to happen, but I'm looking for a day job that I don't hate, and it would be really fun to work for Kevin Allison; so I'll at least try."

Kevin hired her more or less as an intern because there was no budget to pay JC. At least it wouldn't be a day job she wouldn't hate. So JC plugged ahead and worked to make "Risk!" a successful venture.

JC Cassis: How do we organize this company in a way that makes sense? How do we set systems in place of, this is how this person gets paid. This is why they get paid, when they get paid, how much, from where. How do we optimize everything we're doing so that it doesn't ooze money and we only lose money on things are that investments, and we make as much money as we can on things that we can make money on? It came from this total scramble of meeting in coffee shops and trying to figure everything out to now; we're a fully-fledged company with multiple income streams and multiple branches. There's the storytelling school. There's the online storytelling instruction. There's corporate workshops. There's the podcast. There's advertising for the podcast. There's the live shows for the podcast.

What's really cool and what has become more and more important to me over time is the fact that we're totally best friends. There's nothing we can't share with each other. There's nothing we haven't shared with each other, and we really, really understand each other — even though sometimes we completely don't.

Kevin will always make fun of me about the way I say "Wed-nes-day," with three syllables, and I don't understand why he just can't function like a normal human being in the world. Other than those trivial misunderstandings, we really, deeply understand each other in terms of just every other aspect of our lives: professional aspirations, personal relationships, just everything.

He's somebody that I can talk to about absolutely any thought or feeling that I'm having, even if it's something that I know I couldn't tell other people without them condemning me.

He'll be like, "Oh, yeah, that's reasonable. You just have to handle it like this — but I feel the exact same way."

Artist Rene Martinez created the Risk! logo.

"Risk!" has attracted a who's who of comedians because they're able to drop any air of persona and unleash a long, deep, funny but sometimes sad tale. Hearing the likes of insult comic, Lisa Lampanelli, get real on "Risk!" is a trip. The live show bounces from New York and L.A., hitting hip stops like Portland and Seattle and even occasionally going international. On the "Risk!" site, you can hear Margaret Cho, Dana Gould, Dan Savage, Bobcat Goldthwait, Trevor Noah, Janeane Garofalo, and, of course, other members of The State. (Ben Garant even told a different version of the Teenage Mutant Ninja Turtles story in this book at a live show.)

Robert Ben Garant: Some people still try to be funny, but I think a lot of people are just telling a story that they've never told before. People really challenge themselves to truly do it, and that really takes a risk, telling interesting stories.

Michael Ian Black: I was happy to support it, of course. I've only done a couple, mostly as a function of time and laziness on my own part, not any lack of desire to participate. He doesn't need me. He's turned it into a pretty phenomenal project all on his own, and he deserves enormous credit and kudos for that.

[He] really carved out his own space with it because when it started, it easily could've been [a] "This American Life" copycat, but he has figured out his own niche for it. I think really [he] distinguished himself from that and from "The Moth" and became one of the premiere places to tell stories in the country.

Joe Lo Truglio: I had a great experience working with Kevin and was just thrilled that he had found something that he locked into so well. This goes back to the Koo-Koo Koach™ in the Bahamas, where this perfect meeting of his great writing talent and his performance talent finally came through in such a singular voice.

Kevin was always a risky guy. Kevin always liked to be working on the edge both in his real life and his professional life. So "risk" couldn't have been a better word for his show and the push-the-envelope nature of Kevin as a person.

When he was helping me structure my story and giving me pointers, Kevin helped me set up my microphone and GarageBand, which kind of blew my mind. Kevin, the most absent-minded; Kevin couldn't drive a car; Kevin wasn't able to do some of the simplest mechanical things. He might trip on an escalator, but here he was, over the phone, explaining to me how to record and edit and send these mp3 documents. On a purely technical level, I was floored and couldn't believe it, and then on an artistic level, just a mastery of storytelling and setting up and reviewing pieces of information in a certain way. "Yeah, man, you're there. I can't do what you're doing," and I was really excited about that.

Kevin Allison: There are some members of The State, I don't know if I'll ever be able to convince them to do the damn show.

Joshua Grannell aka drag superstar Peaches Christ: I've been a storyteller on the "Risk!" show twice, and both times I ran my story by Kevin who helped me refine it and offered suggestions. He's a really great audience for storytellers and is able to help you figure out what's working and what's not. Because of working with Kevin and being on "Risk!" I actually created a local storytelling show in SF that I've been producing called "OutLoud."

Kevin Allison: I look back on the twelve years between the breakup of The State and the beginning of "Risk!" as my years of being in the belly of the whale, being lost out in the wilderness. At the time, I was so scared and so filled with resentment and so unsure of what do to with myself that I had a lot of bitterness about a lot of things.

Now, I look back, and I'm actually kind of thankful for having had such a rough time during those years because I feel like it kind of helped me see that I like to be doing a slightly different kind of work than a lot of my peers. I like to be able to be as silly and childish and absurdist as I want in my performances of this or that, but I also really, really need an outlet for speaking much more seriously and emotionally and spiritually as well.

"RIP, Billy Joel," say Ken, Todd, Kevin, Tom, Joe, Ben and Kerri.

CHAPTER 29

Supreme Reunion

"Quite frankly, the fact that
none of us are dead yet is
crazy, and to be able to see
all eleven of us in the
same room is special,
and I'll never not recognize
the value of that."

Ken Marino

Author's note: In late 2008, my family moved to the Bay Area, where I discovered — a bit too late — the best comedy festival on the globe, San Francisco Sketchfest. In January 2009, The State was going to have its first full reunion with all eleven members on stage together since MTV, and, of course, it sold out before I even heard of the festival.

I waited patiently outside the venue for hours, hoping for a standing-room-only or last-second seat to open. I chatted with Kevin when he walked up. And my eyes said, "Sneak me in," but it was dark outside. It didn't happen.

That missed opportunity gave me pause. Why hadn't someone written a book about this unique gaggle of characters? I decided that night that I could be the guy and research began. The first thing I did was transcribe the hours of commentary tracks on The State DVDs to get some backstory on the creation of the MTV show.

Then I approached each member separately to gauge interest. Eventually, after some smooth-talking, The State was convinced I could proceed, and in January 2013, I began interviewing them all.

A year and a half later, The State members let me know that they would once again be reuniting for Jack Black's Festival Supreme in Los Angeles on October 25, 2014. Finally, it was my chance to be a fly on the wall and watch The State assemble a show.

Rehearsals took place at the UCB Theatre, apropos as The State and UCB continue to share an affinity. The State members typically communicate via email chains that start in one direction and veer off in another. For example, in one chain I started when sending new chapters to the members, it spiraled off as Michael Jann welcomed a new daughter to the world.

"They go on and the subject line has nothing to do with what's going on," Todd told me. "Because they go on for like a month and they don't end. You wake up, and there's thirty emails just from The State about a chicken leg or something. It's always entertaining to read; it's much better than the news. That's how we stay in touch; it's kind of like we're all in the same room."

An email chain bounced around as State members shared their dream set list, and favorites began to emerge, not surprisingly including tried and true group numbers like "Hormones," which at this point was more than a quarter-century old.

Despite the Festival Supreme line-up including Jack Black and Kyle Gass' Tenacious D, Zach Galifianakis, Cheech and Chong, Fred Armisen and Nick Kroll, buzz was building about The State getting back together.

"I just went to go see a movie at the L.A. Live Regal Cinemas yesterday, and a guy giving me my popcorn, he was probably twenties, was like, 'Hey, I just got tickets to Festival Supreme.' The hype is already beginning. If people at the concession stand at the Regal Cinemas in downtown L.A. are already buying their tickets, we've infiltrated them," Joe said in July 2014.

It's not so easy to get The State all together, especially now that one of the members lives nearly ten-thousand miles away from L.A. Todd decided twenty-five years in New York was enough and wanted to explore the culture, food and people of Korea. What started as a yearlong plan is going on four as of this writing.

Todd Holoubek: A lot of my artist friends said, "Come on out to Korea." It helped that I had a job when I got here. That's always nice. Everything just kind of fell into place. The opportunity presented itself, and I was like, "Yeah, I would love to see what that's all about."

Every two years, I renew a contract to teach so I guess I'm here indefinitely. My schedule is full. If it's not broke, don't fix it. ... When we walked away from MTV, you think, "Well, we could've stayed." We could've. Why walk away from it when what I want to do is happening? The food here is amazing, and I've met such good people, and I seem to keep doing really new and interesting things. I saw a guy play saxophone accompaniment to a deejay the other night.

The State decided to pepper some "greatest hits" with a new "Hi, We're The State" that addressed the demand for their recurring characters to make an appearance.

"Jack Black and Kyle asked, 'Are you going to be bringing back all of those great old characters from the television show? Like Barry and Levon, the pudding guys, or Doug, the rebellious teenager who's always 'outta there,' or even Louie — 'I want to dip my balls in it' — and when they asked that question, we knew there was only one answer, 'No fucking way.' No, we don't want to do that, but then somebody said to us that if we didn't do that, it would be like going to a Billy Joel concert and not hearing 'Piano Man.' 'How would that feel?' It would feel pretty shitty ... and so now we present Billy Joel's 'Piano Man,'" Michael Ian Black said.

During rehearsal, The State practiced harmonies

The State, sans Michael Ian Black, gathers in an L.A. apartment for a run-through of their show before Festival Supreme.

---

before a surly, forty-year-old teen Doug took a solo line: "He says son can you play me a melody, I'm not really sure how it goes, but it's sad and it's sweet and my dad has stinky feet and I'm outta heee-re."

Then the barrage of recurring characters marched on stage, beginning with Louie, followed by "Chicken sandwich, Carl!" and then ... Hans and Franz?

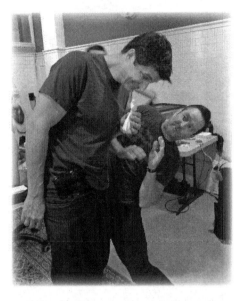

Because The State only has a couple recurring, the joke was they would spout as many other characters' catchphrases as they could while "Piano Man" played on: "We're going to pump (clap) you up!" "Dyn-o-mite." "I pity the fool." "The dingo ate my baby." "The dingo ate my balls." "Hello, Newman." "How you doing? (Joey from 'Friends.')" "Not ̶they call me Mr. Tibbs." ̶o for your country, but ̶o for you." ̶g the sketch: everyone ̶idarity and say, "Billy

̶allow everyone to be ̶f the show.

Top: Ken and Tom rehearse the mob-themed sketch, "Paolo."

Bottom: Sho and Todd do their best Hans and Franz from "SNL."

Kerri Kenney-Silver: That's scary. Then you're in a venue where the sound is questionable, and where are you going to change? It was scary. The stakes were high. Jack is obviously someone we look up to. We didn't want to disappoint, and there were a lot of tickets sold and, we wanted to really do it right. We were not taking it for granted at all. We were very honored to be asked. So it was very stressful. Very stressful.

It was really like the old days, the beginning of college. "I've got a wig. Don't forget to bring those shoes I need to wear." It was nothing like the TV show where we had a band of people. We just had a few people that we ran around like crazy for a few days getting Carvel ice cream cakes and so forth.

Kevin Allison: That was an epic week. It was really, really fun to all be back together again. It was also stressful. You forget that sketch comedy is complicated. There's a lot of details to it: the costumes, the props, memorization of lines, choreography and all that stuff. It was hilarious — a little bit like one of those shows back in college — where a couple days before we find out, "Oh, you're going to have to do it on a stage outside using handheld mics."

Todd Holoubek: That's why I think Festival Supreme seemed really cool. We're like, "What? Heavy metal and then a comedy group? Great!" Strawberry Festival all over again, except there was no strawberry festival.

The MTV show theme song was performed live by its composer, Craig Wedren, whose band also provided the live accompaniment to "The Jew, the Italian and the Red Head Gay" theme and encore "Porcupine Racetrack," which was completely over the top with a gospel choir.

Craig Wedren: It was awesome because I got to relive my very ideal role in The State, which is to be the guy who provides the jams and not have to be the guy who gets into any jams with anybody in The State.

Kerri Kenney-Silver: I'd say the biggest fear of all and the biggest question, right up until we went on stage, was, "Wait, where do we change where the audience can't see us?" In college, we wouldn't have cared. We would have done it on stage. Now, we're a bunch of middle-age people going, "Well, I don't want to be seen in my underwear." It was very, very stressful.

Author's note: I saw Ken Marino in his underwear. He has nothing to be stressed about.

The other chatter during the final rehearsal was the status of Michael Ian Black's flight. He performed the night before the reunion across the country and missed his morning plane.

Kerri Kenney-Silver: I kept using the word terror. That's how I felt. It was the actor's nightmare because honestly I didn't believe Michael was going to make it. Everybody was much calmer than I was, but I kept saying, "What's Plan B? Who's going to take his lines? Shouldn't somebody being learning his lines?"

The final run-through was without music cues and costumes, just a couple props. I was a little worried. "What is this going to look like at 11 p.m., outside, in front of thousands of drunken heavy-metal comedy junkies who just lost their shit during the Eagles of Death Metal concert?"

Kerri Kenney-Silver: I'm always just so concerned with the written, with the sketch and which wig I'm going to wear for this, and I forget that ninety percent of what's about to happen is that the audience is going to be involved. And that's a good thing, because you can't count on it in comedy because they may not be there for you because you may not be doing your job. Or they may not be able to hear you or whatever. So it's always a pleasant surprise when they show up for you, and they're reacting in the way that you dreamed that they would. I'd say that happened a million fold at that show.

Just like on the TV show twenty years earlier, the "Red Head Gay" refrain exploded into a "Godspell"-esque showstopper, with The State united in front of a crowd for the first time in five years. Suddenly, they were NYU kids again, glowing, verve exploding from their fingertips

Top: "Hi, We're The State" at Festival Supreme. Center: Joe, Jann and David provide sound effects for "Porno Theater," while Ken smiles. Bottom: A real gospel choir joins The State onstage for the "Porcupine Racetrack" finale.

... until they ended the tune with an extended, faux, breath-catching bit. "Good night, Los Angeles," David yelled, before the theme song kicked in.

Immediately, the classic sketches drew raucous appreciation from the throng in front of the stage. "Hormones" had not lost its punch.

Joe Lo Truglio: We were able to add self-awareness to the fact that we were forty and doing this, which I think went over well in the reunion show. I was most proud of that sketch because, for me, the beginnings of The State always had its foundations in theater and visual gags and jokes and premises that can be really elevated by the visual nature of the choreography and the blocking. That was really special to do because it was, in essence, like the epitome of a stage sketch, and here we were doing it again twenty years later.

Despite no run-throughs with a full cast or full energy, the normally over-rehearsed State blew through a forty-minute set with ease. The energy bounced back and forth from on stage to the jacked audience until the encore. It was a marvelous night at the "Porcupine Racetrack," as the eleven members nailed their solo bits with a surgeon's precision, climaxing with Tom gliding on stage in a full porcupine costume.

As the crowd's cheers overtook the band, surely The State had to be thinking, "We should do this every night."

Joe Lo Truglio: Being on stage while it was going on, yeah, there were a couple of moments of, "Wow!" flashing back and seeing a bunch of eighteen-year-olds. Suddenly, it was like a weird "Jacob's Ladder" moment where there was a flash of us at eighteen doing this skit, and then we're back in the present, and we're forty. It was not as scary as "Jacob's Ladder" but certainly as refreshing and jolting.

Tom's custom porcupine costume was made for Festival Supreme.

It was almost as if the crowd was excited about just seeing these eleven humans together in one place again rather than any technical display of the show.

Craig Wedren: There was a very specific point where we, the band, were off to the side, and they were all working through some sketch, and no one member of The State could see everybody else's faces because they were too close to each other. The vantage point that I had, I could see everybody's expression, and I was like, "If I could make one piece of art and die, it would be to take portraits of every single one of these faces right this very second." Honestly, it just said everything about everything about their relationship. It was just exasperation, and it seemed like it took everybody's deepest reserves, will, tolerance and community to see it through it.

Todd Holoubek: I didn't wear my glasses for the first half of that show. I didn't realize that many people were there. It was full, all the way to the other stage. I paused for a second.

Backstage, after the show, the members of The State held court as their comedy contemporaries tipped the hat in their direction. "Weird Al"

Former MTV veejay, Jesse Camp, left, is a State mega fan.

Yankovic nodded his head in approval. Garfunkel and Oates aka Riki Lindhome and Kate Micucci congratulated their pals. Former MTV veejay, Jesse Camp, gushed that, "The State was my Led Zeppelin" and glommed onto Michael Black, not wanting the moment to end. P!nk, who happens to be Kerri's best girlfriend, was there to support her chum. "She loves The State. So she wanted to come and see it live," Kerri said.

Chatter of "You guys should do another TV show ... or Netflix" was met with smiles and nods, but by Sunday morning, Todd was on a plane to Korea, and the other members were ready to get back to their day jobs.

Kerri Kenney-Silver: "Why don't we just do this at colleges?

Why don't we..." and then inevitably everyone gets back to their work and their call time and their schedule for whatever they're doing, and deadlines for writing something and their kids' lives and it dissipates. It will flare back up again when there's another opportunity. Someday, we'll do it, but it has to organically be the right time. The fact that all eleven of us made it on to that stage that night is a miracle unto itself.

Ken Marino: The State, they're my brothers and my sister and to be with them and to spend time with them is always special thing. ... Quite frankly, the fact that none of us are dead yet is crazy, and to be able to see all eleven of us in the same room is special, and I'll never not recognize the value of that.

We have a huge chest of stuff that we've never done, which to me, that would be the fun thing to put together, just a bunch of the sketches that never got made, because I know that there's some crazy, funny things.

Michael Ian Black: One of the things that I think everybody feels, I know I do, is that when every one of us does well, it furnishes the larger legacy of The State. I think that's important to all of us. I think we all feel like there's this hometown that we come from, and we're all interested in the hometown getting its share of the glory.

Credits

Editing: Kate Esquivel and Michael R. Montgomery
Cover design: Amy Rachlin
Color cover photo: Seth Olenick
Black and white photo: Amy Rachlin
Page design: Jason Lewton and Corey Stulce

Photography

Howard Bernstein: Pages 503, 506, 508, 509, 510, 513, 519, 522
From Wendy Johnson: Page 28
Amy Rice: Pages 511, 521
Mark Rogers: Author photo
Jana Rosenblatt: Pages 244 (Doug), 260 (Ben in drag), 296 ("The Pope's-a-Visit"), 303 ("The Jew, the Italian and the Red Head Gay"), 304 ("Monkeys Do It II"), 305 ("Where's the Mousey?"), 306 (Tammy Wilkins), 307 ("The Bearded Men of Space Station 11"), 309 ("Freaks") ("The Funeral"), 313 ("Porcupine Racetrack"), 317 ("Race"), 319 ("Slinkys"), 320 ("Tenement"), 332 ("Bacon"), 366 (CBS special), 385 ("Manzelles"), 414 (Johnny Blue Jeans), 433 ("Viva Variety")
Corey Stulce: Pages 237, 525, 550, 562, 567-568, 571, 573, 574
Mark White: Page 527
Additional photos from The State archives

Illustrations

Joe Anders: Pages 108 (Teenage Mutant Ninja Hurdles), 247 (Louie), 251 ("Tape People"), 255 ("$240 Worth of Pudding"), 266 ("Service with a Smile"), 278 ("BMX Motortrome" 1995), 312 ("Porcupine Racetrack"), 323 ("Taco Man"), 325 ("Sal & Frankie"), 327 ("Cutlery Barn"), 470 ("Reno 911!") Editor's note: On page 278, the illustration mirrors the typed sketch's spelling.
Glen Hanson: Back cover
Joe Lo Truglio: Pages 60, 71, 116, 147, 181
Rene Martinez: Page 559
Michael Showalter: Pages 68, 94

Author's acknowledgements

Thank you first and foremost to The State for trusting me to tell your story.

Kendall Austin Stulce: I truly appreciate your patience with this long project. Without you, this book would not have happened. I love you, sweetie.

Kate Esquivel: You kept me sane, on track, and you did so much more that I will take credit for.

Joe Anders: Thank you for always agreeing to put pen to paper for me. Your illustrations make me smile every time I see them.

Michael R. Montgomery: Your honest feedback was so encouraging. Thank you for dusting off the red pen and taking it to the pages.

Seth Olenick: I love your eye. You captured the essence of The State in your photos, and I'm so proud to include one on the cover.

Amy Rachlin: Thank you for giving balance and a sense of fun to the front cover — and for taking a great photo of eleven funny kids way back when.

Jana Rosenblatt: You dug through your archives and came back with some amazing photos of The State members at their best. Your images make the MTV pages sing!

Glen Hanson: Your illustration for the back cover could be the basis for a State cartoon. You captured them wonderfully.

Jason Lewton: So glad I remembered that you were awesome at page design! I really appreciate the long hours and the amazing results.

Susan Taylor: You never bored (or appeared that way) of hearing about my updates, and your encouragement was a big push to get to the finish line. Thank you, my dear friend.

Thank you: Carlos Alazraqui, Jon Bendis, Mary Birdsong, JC Cassis, Rob Corddry, George Demas, James Dixon, Janeane Garofalo, Bradley

Glenn, Joshua Grannell, Bill Hader, Nina Hellman, Doug Herzog, Toby Huss, Eli Janney, Wendy Johnson, Beowulf Jones, Eileen Katz, Larry Kenney, Keegan-Michael Key, Margot Leitman, Tim Lennon, Riki Lindhome, David Lipsky, Tim Lohmann, Chris Meloni, A.D. Miles, Marguerite Moreau, Niecy Nash, Zak Orth, Mitch Reiter, Ian Roberts, Paul Rudd, Shani Russell, Andy Samberg, Teddy Shapiro, Jim Sharp, Steven Starr, Mike Still, Joe Stulce, Nick Swardson, David Thayer, Matt Veenstra, Marianne Ways, Ken Webb, Craig Wedren, Mark White, Mo Willems, "Weird Al" Yankovic, and Cedric Yarbrough

Index

From left, Black, Todd, Ken, Vladimir Lenin, Kerri, Joe, Sho, The Joker, Ken Webb, U2's Larry Mullen Jr., and Ben kept NYU silly in the late '80s.

About the author

Author Corey Stulce wasn't hired to pen the history of The State but was inspired to start writing this book after hearing Thomas Lennon say this at San Francisco Sketchfest in 2012:

"The secret to all of every industry: just start doing it, and they won't notice that they never told you to. If you want to be a hand model, just start doing it. Somehow people forget that they never gave you permission."

Corey has interviewed and written about comedy legends from Mel Brooks to George Carlin and Phyllis Diller as well as contemporary humorists such as Judd Apatow, Paul Feig, Kate McKinnon and David Sedaris.

His first book, "Laugh Lines: Conversations with Comedians," was released in 2011. Corey spent a decade as a magazine/newspaper Features and Entertainment editor in the St. Louis metro area, and his writing has appeared on NBC, in newspapers and magazines all over the country, as well as dozens of entertainment websites.

For more information visit:

Coreystulce.com
Twitter: @coreyshame
Facebook.com/coreystulce

Corey Stulce photo by Mark Rogers

Made in the USA
Lexington, KY
17 August 2016